GLORIETA

QUINN KAYSER-COCHRAN

WESTLAND BOOKS

For Carrie, Keira, and Cullen

"I pray to heaven we have a war... the sooner the better."
—John Baylor, Texas legislator
and Indian agent, in correspondence, 1856

PROLOGUE

This story is based on true events.

In July 1861, during the first year of the American Civil War, firebrand Indian fighter John R. Baylor led a small party of Texans north into New Mexico Territory. Near the town of Mesilla, they routed a larger but poorly led Federal force based at Ft. Fillmore. Following this lopsided victory, Baylor declared himself governor of the Confederate Territory of Arizona—an empire encompassing nearly everything between Texas and California.

With a Confederate foothold in the Southwest thus established, former U.S. Army officer Henry Hopkins Sibley made his way to Richmond, Virginia, met with Confederate president Jefferson Davis, and laid out plans for a full-fledged invasion of the North American West. First, Sibley proposed to raise a brigade in Texas, march up the Rio Grande, and capture Santa Fe. From there he would attack Colorado Territory and seize its mines. If successful, Sibley explained, the entire Southwest—even northern Mexico—would eventually fall to the South. The Confederacy would have ample gold and silver for its treasury, and Pacific ports would enable the South to bypass the Union's Atlantic blockade. Surely, these developments would hasten diplomatic recognition by Europe's great powers and encourage them to provide badly needed assistance. Davis had been told—likely by the man himself—that Sibley, a West Point graduate and career soldier, well knew the region, and further, that his plan held the potential for huge gains at little risk to the Confederacy. On these exigencies, Davis commissioned Sibley a brigadier general and bid him return to Texas with orders to guide the brigade "according to circumstance and your own good judgment."

In late October 1861, the newly christened Army of New Mexico stepped off from San Antonio, Texas, with nearly four-thousand men and fifteen artillery pieces. Five hundred miles later, on December 17, they reached Franklin, Texas. After waiting for unusually severe winter weather to break, Sibley's brigade crossed into southern New Mexico on January 3, 1862.

In war-rooms and parlors back East, hardly anyone paid any attention to these or any other events west of the Mississippi River. Few outside the West were ever aware of the brutal conflict that erupted along the Frontier, or that for several months in 1862, an enormous swath of the continent—and perhaps, had fate ordained, even the fate of a nation—hung in the balance.

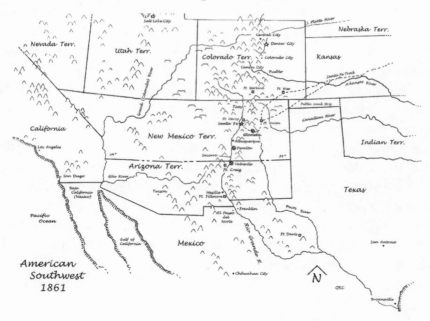

PART ONE

TOUCHED BY FIRE

Glorieta Pass, New Mexico Territory, March 28, 1862

Crawling slowly along the arroyo's sandy floor, Jacob's progress was slow. Though protruding roots tore his sleeves and scratched his face, the young captain was grateful for the furrow's protection, certain that battalions of engineers with picks and shovels couldn't have built a better concealment. Only inches above his head, bullets and shell fragments practically filled the air, yet none had come especially close; within the arroyo, he and his fellows were safe.

Moving fitfully, Jacob tried hard not to jostle his men, hunched over rifle breeches or busy tamping loads into their muskets. He shook hands or exchanged nods with friends and to all and sundry relayed the orders that had come down from headquarters. Some boys had screwed their eyes shut and their prayerful hands trembled; others looked wild-eyed and furious, their whole bodies tensed like springs. He could not guess how he looked to them. By the time he reached the trunk of an enormous pine tree, toppled across the gulch like a bridge, he was drenched in sweat and caked with dust. He dropped to his stomach, closed his eyes, and tried to fix the hillside's features in his mind: some seventy yards away, he'd seen blue-coated figures crouched behind a low stone wall, but just how many he couldn't tell; twenty yards farther was a dense screen of trees and a second stone wall. *Lord, there may be hundreds up there and we will be exposed every step of the way.*

Jacob opened his eyes and rolled onto his back. The air was heavy with the smell of burning sagebrush; overhead, streamers of smoke raced east beneath a restless sky. *That's pretty*, he thought, though this notion was as weightless as its subject and he shook his head to clear

1

it. *Sixty, seventy yards to cover—then we'll regroup and do it again.* At least he hoped he would have that chance—*Dear Lord, please let me live, but if this is the end, please take me quickly. Please. Amen.* He wondered whether these miserably tense moments were his and his friends' last or perhaps a prelude to immortality. Might victory here somehow tip the entire war in their favor? He claimed no special ability to discern Divine Will, but did not think this outcome impossible. When he tried to picture Adria, he quickly stopped, afraid that conjuring her memory in such a wretched setting might somehow degrade it. *Stop.* Touching the brim of his hat for luck, he pushed these camp-thoughts aside—*Concentrate.* Those blue-coated figures waiting across the meadow were all that mattered. Soon he and his fellows would leave the safety of the arroyo; soon he would have to lead them. Pebbles and dirt spilled onto his shoulder and he brushed them away. *Please, don't bury us yet.* He believed he was ready. He hoped so—had to be. His heart was beating so fast that his whole body ached. *God, forgive us for what we are about to do,* he prayed. *Forgive me for the things I have already done.*

Somewhere to his left someone whistled. *Was that Adair?* He looked up and saw that it was. *God, save me.* Jacob pulled his hat down tight and whistled back. *Time.*

Brownsville, Texas, June 1, 1861

Early the previous summer, Jacob Stark had stood in a shade of a pentroof on the barn's north side. *Damn this heat,* he remembered thinking. *A hundred degrees, certainly.* Then he had whistled to his friends and they had been quick to drop their shovels and join him.

༄

Elijah Fisher sat heavily on an upturned crate. "What, you're done?"

"No," Jacob scoffed. "Doc brought water is all—told me to call y'all in for some. Said he couldn't stand the thought of dead wastrels littering his property."

Briggs Hardy threw his spade on the ground in disgust. "Don't recall as Doc bought us at auction—son-of-a-bitch is gonna kill us, workin' us this way! Damn it, why can't we wait until the sun goes down? Wouldn't put *him* out none and surely *we'd* suffer less."

"Doc didn't take this heat into account," Fisher seconded.

Jacob wiped sweat from his brow. "He just wants it done—I want to be done, too. Bucky asked me to work later tonight, so this is the only time I got." Fisher and Hardy took long drinks from the jug. For a long while, the boys said nothing and listened to the buzz of giant cicadas in the salt scrub. In the distance, one heifer lowed and several others answered. Then for a moment, the insects and cattle all fell silent, and Fisher swore he could hear the surf breaking at Boca Chica, three miles east. Jacob poured water over his head but didn't feel any better for it. *Too humid. Briggs is right—this is all bullshit.* His skin was dark brown from working in the sun, and he was tired. Beyond tired. His eyes grew heavy, and he let his head drop.

Hardy glanced at Fisher, who nodded for him to proceed. "Hey, Jake, haven't seen you much of late. How you been?"

Half asleep, Jacob startled at the sound, though he did not open his eyes. "What?"

"Look worn, son," Fisher said.

"Hell, I *am* worn," Jacob answered, and despite being drowsy, his voice was edged.

"Yeah, well—"This time Fisher looked to Hardy for confirmation before continuing. "Thought you should know that I saw her yesterday."

"Saw who?"

"Sarah. At Morgenstern's, pard—boarding the Kingsville stage."

Jacob chose not to respond. High overhead a lone seagull screeched and wheeled away.

"Tipped my hat," Fisher continued, "but she looked away—didn't say nothin'. Looks likes she's healed up pretty good, though."

"That's...good."Jacob opened his eyes."Good for her."He supposed that made it sound like he didn't care, but he *did*. Cared immensely, but there was no way to go back and fix things, and no point in wondering whether or not he could've done anything differently—that much he already knew. He looked out over the south pastures, where cattle were moving single-file toward the northern troughs. He stood and reached for his shovel, but his hands were slippery with sweat and it clattered to the ground. He reached down, picked it up again, and leaned it against the trunk of a fan palm.

"She'll be fine," Hardy offered.

"Maybe." Jacob scratched a mosquito bite on his elbow and yawned. "But what about us? When are we gonna tell Doc?"

"Already did," Fisher said. "Last night."

"Ah," Jacob grunted as he pondered this news. "Explains his lack of amity just now."

"Shit," Hardy fumed, "he can't expect us to stay! Stay here and dig ditches while our friends go and fight? There's nothin' here, no reason to stay!"

Jacob agreed but did not actually say so.

A few moments later, Fisher cleared his throat. "Doc's gettin' old, though. Hard on him, running this place without us."

"It'll be harder if we stay," Hardy countered.

"Yeah," Jacob nodded, "Bucky says they're gonna pass a conscription law soon, so either we go now—with our fellows—or wait around until we're shipped off to Virginia."

"Don't give a damn about Virginia," Fisher said.

"Then what are we waiting for?" Hardy removed his tattered boots and poured out small piles of sand and soil. "Doc's gotta understand! He will, won't he, Jake?"

Jacob shrugged. "Don't matter either way. Saw big Charlie Spence at the Mercado last week—remember him? Said he knows twenty others ready to form a company—George Orth, David Lamb, and the like. Sounds like he's serious."

"Me, too," Fisher said. "Texas forever and damn anyone who disagrees."

"Boys, this is *it*—we are Confederates now!" Hardy whooped, struck the blade of his shovel with his boot, and had to duck as the handle swung past his head. "We official? Jake, you're in, right? You good?"

Jacob squeezed his hands together. He was neither good nor well, but figured that the only way he might ever get back to himself was to leave Brownsville and never look back—too little of his time there had been happy. "Yes," he said at last, "I'm in." Spinning the shovel's handle in his hands, the blade scratched a figure eight into the sandy soil. "Besides, Fish here has broken the heart of every girl within a hundred miles, so we may as well strike for parts unknown."

It had been so long since Jacob cracked a joke that at first Hardy missed the gleam in his friend's eye. On its face, this statement was absurd: despite handsome features, Fisher was a nervous thing and hilariously awkward around women.

When at last Fisher laughed, Hardy finally realized why Jacob's tone was unfamiliar. "Pshaw, Fish, don't take his stuff," he said. "Hell, none of us can talk their way inside a petticoat the way you can."

Fisher sighed. "Luckily for y'all, that's true."

This time Jacob laughed, too. Reluctantly, Hardy and Fisher took up their shovels and stepped back into the blazing sunshine. For a few seconds more, Jacob lingered in the shade. Seeing Hardy grinning like a fool, he guessed that his best friend was imagining himself in uniform, performing great deeds. When he employed the same tactic upon an imaginary version of himself, however, the resulting image did not likewise lift his spirits.

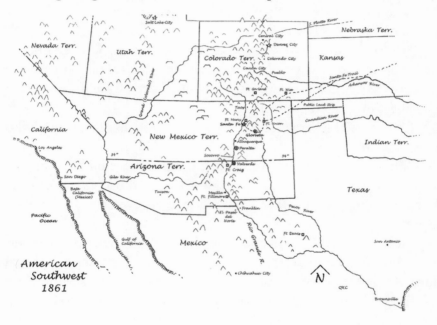

1-WESTERN US MAP

Lo que no se puede remediar, hay que aguantar
(WHAT CANNOT BE REMEDIED MUST BE ENDURED)

Santa Fe, New Mexico Territory, November 17, 1861

Adria Magdelena Carrizo settled onto a bench and watched the moon rise behind a cherry tree's leafless branches. Harvest moon, bright and full. She sighed. Several times a year her father held parties to curry favor with his business associates and the city's social elites—two groups for which she did not necessarily care. Though many guests had already departed, enough remained that the sounds of conversation and laughter still carried outside through the open windows. Adria found these events boring; rather, she loved the outdoors and its sweet, earthy smells: lathered horses, sage, and *piñon*—its piney scent quite heavy that evening. Wood-smoke, too, for it reminded her of wet spring Sundays when her mother, Irinea, was still alive and they had stood near the kitchen fire making *biscochitos:* flour, salt, saleratus, lard, sugar, anise seeds, brandy, cinnamon. Manuela, the head cook, had walked on eggshells during these intrusions, for the other *doñas* she had worked for rarely ventured into kitchens except to accuse the servants of incompetence or theft—although nothing had ever happened. Those quiet hours had all been peaceful: the matron of the house had baked sweets while her adoring little girl clung to her skirts, helping in a child's unhelpful way.

Now almost seventeen, Adria was a lively and intelligent young woman who had grown to resent the rigid circumscription of her world. With her mother gone, it was reasonable to expect that she would look after the welfare of her father's many employees in the same way that the other *patrones'* wives did, but he controlled the family's finances so jealously that she was unable to effect any social or charitable acts. All that remained for her to do was to sew, play cards, and endure perfunctory visits with her peers—distractions for which her patience had worn thin. As a younger girl—and with her mother's approval—she had enjoyed freedoms that astonished her acquaintances: swimming in the frigid *rio*, gathering pine nuts in the surrounding hills, riding horseback all across their *rancho*. Since her mother's death, however, these and other liberties had vanished, leaving Adria more housebound than the servants, and filled to distraction with unformed yearning.

"Ria?" a woman's voice called from behind.

Adria chose not to reply—not out of wickedness but merely for something to *do*—something unscheduled, unexpected. Except that having routinized rebellion, these little fits of obstinacy *were* expected. She didn't mean to anger anyone, but sometimes she just couldn't help herself. She longed for something—anything—new. She kept her eyes fixed on the moon, nearly ascended into the clouds, but still bright enough to throw shadows beneath the trees that bordered the shallow river.

"Girl," the woman called again, "do you hear me?"

Wistfully, she recalled other things about her mother: how she'd loved a particular portrait of Adria at age five, believing that it captured the numinous light in her little girl's eyes, and how she'd insisted that it be hung in the *sala* where the greatest number of guests might see it; her voice and how she loved to sing quietly as she sewed; and how, despite her husband's trenchant disapproval, she'd deposed her mother-in-law's *santos* from their *nichos* throughout the house, replacing them with images of Saint Ferdinand III of Castille—patron saint of prisoners and parents.

"Ria, it's getting cold," said her old *chaperona*, drawing closer. "You'll catch your death."

"Benéfica," Adria whispered, "do you feel it?" With a rustling of blue taffeta, she rose from the bench and approached a set of French doors that opened onto the patio.

"The chill?" The woman pulled a richly embroidered silk shawl over the girl's shoulders. "*Sí, niña*—in my bones, I feel it."

"No." Adria pulled the garment tight while the old woman helped smooth her long, dark hair. She turned her wide eyes back to watch the last of the moon's bright arc disappear into the pewtery gloom. "Not that. A sound, a smell on the wind—I cannot say, exactly. Something huge—terrible, perhaps, but I believe it will be different than anything that has come before." *Different*, she thought, *from the way things are now.*

Adria stared into the darkness while the *chaperona* studied her profile. Though they spent much of each day together, it startled Benéfica to realize how much Adria had grown to resemble her mother. *Sounds like her, certainly, in both timbre and the words she chooses, and anyone can see that she chafes, as her mother did, against limited expectations.* But going against tradition had intensified—not remediated—Irinea's restlessness and Benéfica worried that soon Adria would find the same insurmountable obstacles in her own path. For though the world might change, it would not, could not do so overnight, no matter how badly bright young women wished it might.

At least not until now. Whispered rumors that soon a Confederate army would overrun New Mexico were everywhere—Adria had heard these, certainly. Perhaps this was the cause of her restlessness. Surely, that was all. Sensing that they had been away too long, Benéfica placed a hand on the young woman's shoulder and guided her indoors. "*Carrida*, nothing good arrives on the cold wind. Now, hurry, please—the guests are all waiting and your father's in an ill humor."

Fort Marcy, Santa Fe, New Mexico Territory,
December 4, 1861

Standing before a silvered dressing mirror, Edward Canby paused to look at his hands. Fingers stiff with cold, he noted a faded scar across the knuckles of his left hand. *Twelve years old—splitting cordwood in Kentucky,* he thought. His long face was rather gaunt, save that upon reaching his mid-forties his nose had widened and his jawline softened. A thatch of dark hair partially covered his prominent ears, and his considerable height made it necessary for him to stoop to see his full his reflection in the glass.

"Look ancient, don't I? Haggard."

"Handsome, Col. Canby," his wife, Louisa, corrected. "You look *handsome.*"

Small and thin, Louisa had delicate features and a slender nose. Despite her habit of worrying about after almost everyone she knew, her dark hair was free of silver and she had retained a smooth, fair complexion far longer than many of her peers. However, like most everyone in Santa Fe at that time, she looked pinched, haunted by fear and exhaustion.

"Certainly feel old," he said.

"Well, if you're old, then so am I and that is nothing I want to hear."

Louisa handed Edward a brass-mounted scabbard belt. A West Point graduate, he fastened the heavy brass buckle with its eagle insignia and tugged reflexively on the belt until the scabbard fell parallel with the left seam of his light blue trousers. She brushed a pine needle from the dark blue dress coat's sleeve and pulled at the standing collar until it straightened. "Now, Father Martínez—*he's* old."

Edward smiled in agreement and fastened the last of his uniform's gilt buttons.

From behind, she slipped her arms around his torso and pressed a cheek against his woolen coat, inhaling its faint scent of dust, gunpowder, and sagebrush. "There—much better."

"Thank you."

Although Col. Canby was the U.S. Army's highest-ranking officer between Missouri and California, he had furnished his quarters at Fort Marcy with only a few pieces of simple pine furniture. Blue winter light spilled down whitewashed adobe walls and threw cool shadows across a wide-plank floor. Sounds carried in from the freight yard: hoofbeats, fretful shouts, and wagon wheels that cursed for want of grease.

Louisa shut her eyes and held tighter. "You'll be careful?"

"Of course." The colonel tugged at the gold braid on his shoulder scales until the coat lay properly. When he tried to turn, however, he found Louisa's arms locked tightly around his torso, her face hard against his spine. Her body shook softly, and he realized that she was crying. "Louisa, please—I'll protect myself as best I can." It always upset him to see her upset, but *this!* Again, he tried to turn, gently, but she held him so that all he could see was his own tired reflection and the ridiculous pomp of his uniform. Ribbons and braid, indeed, when the only ornaments that mattered to him were the thin arms wrapped around his waist.

"Not you, too, Edward!" Louisa wept. "I cannot lose you, too!"

"Darling—"

"This wretched shape," she whispered. "How has it come to this?"

"Dearest, please—" he said, but she did not stop.

"God save you—you are my day and night. If anything happened, I couldn't go on!"

He studied her delicate, white-knuckled hands. "I'll be fine," he insisted, but she did not believe him.

You do not know that, she thought. She leaned into him until he supported nearly her full weight.

He stared into the mirror as black crows of doubt took flight. *Only twenty five hundred troops,* he thought, *scattered across the territory, and most of our Southern-born officers have resigned. Ordinance, quartermaster, and commissary stores are cached in lightly defended depots or with Indian agents of questionable loyalty, and now the enemy is on our doorstep. Indians have redoubled their attacks on the outlying settlements and for months Washington has failed to send funds sufficient even to pay the regulars, nevermind recruit new volunteers— the situation worsens with each passing hour...*

"How many are there?"

Her voice startled him and he answered carelessly. "Texans? Four thousand, perhaps—we aren't sure. They're on the Rio Grande now, but there may be some on the Pecos as well."

"What will you do?"

"The Second Dragoons have abandoned Hatch's Ranch and returned to Fort Union—thankfully Bill Chapman has just completed our new fieldworks."

"So you'll go there?"

"Union? No, Gurd and I will hasten down to Fort Craig—"

"South?"

"—to reconnoiter," he continued. "Native scouts tend to exaggerate numbers, so I want to speak with Kit Carson or someone else I can trust." He hated to burden her with raw intelligence but he was too weary to censor himself. "Mesilla's fallen—Doña Ana, too. A lynch mob in Piños Altos has murdered the town marshal and nailed a rebel rag to the flagpole there. Washington has its own troubles and cannot help. I don't..." Sensing his task's full weight, his voice trailed off. He turned his head and stared through the small window at a tiny square of the infinite blue above—one great, unblemished dome, untroubled by the ocean of pain and confusion below. *How must we appear to God?* he wondered. *How small?* No cruelty, no folly hidden from that unblinking eye. Brother against brother, a divided house descended into madness. Disgusted, he shook his head. *Beetles scuttling across a dirty plate, fighting over scraps of food.*

A solitary fly buzzed loudly against the pane and wrenched him back into the cold room, but to Louisa, who still clutched at his frame, his voice sounded small and distant: "I do not question the need of this but it is nothing for which I am prepared." Words caught in his throat. "These men—these men are *friends!* My God, I am...this is not..."

Louisa released her cinch, let her hands drop to the hem of the colonel's coat, and tugged until the garment lay smoothly over his oiled leather belt. Understanding his need for support, she dabbed her eyes with a kerchief and quickly composed herself. "I trust you, Edward, whatever comes—already we've withstood worse. I was being selfish—I'm sorry." Dust motes traveled in and out of the light.

"My angel, you don't—"

"Now and forever," she said. She wiped her eyes again, stepped between her husband and the mirror, and adjusted the buttons and braid. "You are my beloved, now and forever." She smiled bravely, so he put his hands on her shoulders.

"Now and forever."

Her trembling lip and watery eyes broke Edward's heart. He took her in his arms and held her tightly—as tightly as he dared without causing her more pain. For a long time neither of them spoke. The fly in the window continued to buzz while outside the wagons rolled past, filled to overflowing with the instruments of war.

Texan Encampment, Town of Doña Ana, New Mexico Territory, January 4, 1862

All that autumn the weather had been unusually hot; even the onset of winter had brought little relief. For almost two months, they'd held a course, west-northwest, across the vast emptiness of western Texas. No rain, no birdsong—only heat, dust, and a pitiless blue sky. Of their total, nearly fifteen hundred rode as cavalry, though nearly twice that number walked. Barely a third of them wore uniforms; most were dressed in work clothes or butternut-dyed homespun, but every one of them stank of woodsmoke, sweat, and dust.

The column had bivouacked at Fort Davis. From there, individual regiments proceeded at three-day intervals so that the waters of the small *aguajes* and springs upon which their lives depended could recharge. Their supply train snaked for miles: wagons, buckboards, batteries of small brass howitzers. Iron-rimmed wheels pulverized the soil; hooves tramped out a discordant drum roll. Dust-caked skinners followed, driving herds of lowing cattle and draft animals through the dry chaparral wastes. Mile after mile, the sound of clinking harnesses, shouted commands, and low voices—individual notes in a monstrous symphony—were subsumed by the endless *thrum-thrum-thrum* of hob-nailed boots.

After evening roll, with his company bedded down for the night, Jacob Stark had time to think: *They aren't like us: our needs opposed, customs dissimilar, faiths irreconcilable—their prayers are lies raised to a false god. Now blood is flowing and just as well. All this age we have lived side by side as strangers, gorging ourselves on hate and for our sins we must reckon.* A sentry neared, quiet as a ghost, until a nickering horse alerted Jacob to his presence. He pretended to sleep until this phantom vanished, and then held his journal up to the moonlight and squinted at old entries:

28 Oct., 1861—Seventeen mi. over scrubland and by that I mean the infantry covered seventeen miles; likely we rode 40, back and forth, protecting the column's flanks, carrying messages, guiding stragglers. Light clouds, windy, warm.

10 Nov., 1861—Fifteen mi. Clouds, winds, dust. The land here is flat and nearly featureless, except at White's Spring where grows a solitary cottonwood, and from this tree our scouts strung up two Indian bucks—the most solemn sight I have ever seen. I know that I should not care about such things, and yet it lingers in my thoughts. So much of the violence surrounding me is perfectly senseless—I am sick and tired of it, yet see no way to make it stop. Perhaps no one can. In camp, we hobbled and watered our horses before turning them out to graze. Now to bed. Dad Green enforces a strict schedule: roll call at 4 a.m., retreat at sundown and another check at 8 p.m.

17 Nov., 1861—Early start; cold coffee. Nineteen mi. over flatlands bristling with maguey, cheatgrass, and ocotillo. Barren mountains on the horizon. Pitched my old shoes in hopes that these new ones wear better. Our first real cold spell: dark gray skies but neither snow nor rain. Rec'd news of Southern victories in Missouri and Arkansas, which does confirm that were are in God's favor. May this always be so, for soon enough we will have our own fight.

21 Dec., 1861—Encamp'd all day. Very cold now. Sunlight through broken clouds. Dried cattails poking above the ice in a shallow crick nearby. Wash'd shirt and socks in a boiling tub. Can hear our horses cropping grass. Light duties to-night, so I will write more. Quite a debate at mess: Briggs and D. Milton near to fought over religion and I had to separate them before things turned ugly. Milton sees God's hand in every outcome; reckons that only through J. Christ does one attain any happiness in this life or the next, and that believers ascend to Heaven whilst others are forever consigned to Hell. Briggs, conversely, cannot conceive of God as having any concern for the affairs of

man; indeed, if He creat'd the universe, subsequent events disprove any continued interest. Neither vantage squares with me, but I cannot declare wi. firm conviction where lies my faith—it is there still, but in dreadful shape. As a child, I was told that God makes no distinction between the Commandments, but this strikes me as arbitrary and illogical. I have violated all Ten, yet my conscience does not similarly account; surely, some trespasses have passed beyond memory, while others I cannot forget no matter how I try. Perhaps the good Lord has endowed me wi. a soldier's heart in order to spare me those pangs that afflict virtuous men in times of war. On watch now. Clear skies, our fires slumber, and the stars have emerged.

25 Dec., 1861—Christmas—God rest ye merry. Bitter cold, snowing hard. No duties. Capt. Shropshire sent his nigger 'round wi. enough tobacco and brandy for several companies to share. All appreciate his decency and thoughtfulness.

He took out a pencil and began to write:

4 Jan., 1862—Happy Nw. Yr. Infantry started early this a.m.; caught up to them at ten miles. Yesterday crossed into N. Mexico Territory. Truck farms and small vineyards on the valley floor; Mexican boys burning weeds along the ditch banks, gaping as we ride past. East the Organ Mtns rise like a whipsaw humped up on its back and somewhere up there is the pass over which Baylor ran the Yankees to death in the heat of July last. Cold these past several days, tho. Light, scudding snow that doesn't stick; skies cleared o' noon. Camp'd now. Terrible wind and I am always cold. Despite our fatigue, tho, we are in good spirits for with every step we—

He looked away from the paper and glanced over his shoulder. Some commotion was erupting: men were shouting as they fanned out from the white canvas headquarters tents, moving like ripples on a pond. An unseen current jolted the camp from its torpor: voices hoarsened and movements became rushed. He tossed the journal into his rucksack, muttered a vague prayer, and stood. Then with one arm, he grabbed his saddle—propped up to dry beside the fire—and with his other a canteen, musket, and cartridge box. Heart pounding, he ran to wake the others.

"Boys, if you only knew it, I am the worst enemy you have."
— Henry Hopkins Sibley, taunting his former U.S.
Army comrades as he departed
New Mexico for Texas, June 1861

Village of Lucero, New Mexico Territory, January 5, 1862

With a small, three-pull telescope, Texan Maj. Frederick Metzger traced the road to its end. Atop a low *banco* one hundred yards from the river stood a cluster of buildings: two houses, two barns, various sheds and coops, and what looked like a storehouse built of basalt block, all set without apparent regard for order. An adobe wall encircled one corral, while pole fences defined others. Nothing but a ranch—clearly so, despite others' speculation that the spread was somehow connected to old Fort Thorn.

Nothing but a ranch, yet whoever was inside had brought the Confederate's progress to a crashing halt. Eight hours earlier, five Texan scouts had been ambushed there and the two survivors had raced back to Doña Ana with reports of an uprising by hundreds of armed New Mexicans. Then, under cover of darkness, someone had nailed the Stars-and-Stripes to a cottonwood pole in the yard, and for both these acts Metzger resolved to punish those responsible.

On the hilltop to his right, two howitzers boomed and the coins in his pocket jangled. Explosions and billows of dust followed as one of the storehouse's rock walls collapsed. Falling rubble pocked the adjacent fields; gray smoke coiled above burning timbers.

"Soften 'em up!" someone whooped in the field below. "Soften 'em up! Sons-a-bitches, we'll be there soon!" Others began calling for those inside to come out and surrender.

Once his ears stopped ringing, Metzger could hear muskets barking down in the canyon, spalling rock and splintering wood. He set the brass scope on the ground and picked up a map he'd made of the hillside below, one hundred rods by ten. Dotted with greasewood, this parched slope rolled gently toward a series of short, steep embankments at the river's edge. He curled his lip in disgust. *Alles ist hier tot und Grau*, he thought: everything is dead and gray. Leaden clouds looked ready to spill but the water they held was predestined for somewhere far away. *Alles getötet*: all dead. Snow-covered mountains dominated the far horizon, but here beside the river, everything that should have been alive was instead brown and withered. Drowned in deep gray shadow, even the river looked flat, greasy—dead. *Alles*.

Metzger— or "Fritz," as his fellow officers knew him—drank water from a tin canteen. His height and build were average. His complexion was ruddy, his eyes were hazel, and his thinning hair was reddish-brown. Born twenty-six years prior in the German state of Saxony, his appearance was so youthful that he had sought to compensate by growing a beard; ironically, it came in gray. This feature, coupled with his serious disposition, led most to presume that he was much older than he actually was.

Again, Metzger took up the map and noted the positions of various Texan companies. Protected within a network of dry irrigation ditches, these men had done little since midnight except listen as Mexicans splashed away under cover of darkness, and to their own artillery crews setting up on the hillside above. Detached from the Fourth, Fifth, and Seventh Texas Regiments, few betrayed any anxiety—indeed, most were busy talking and paused only occasionally to snipe at anyone foolish enough to show in the buildings' windows. Others Texans played cards or smoked—a few had even fallen asleep. Having served as a military engineer before coming to America, Metzger scowled. To his mind, most of the Texans were too lackadaisical—too many freebooters and scoundrels for a professional army. He fumbled absently with the lead, acorn-shaped identification tag that he kept on a leather thong around his neck. Another howitzer boomed, and sporadic fusillades from inside main house followed. Completely unscathed, the Texans laughed and hoisted their caps on ramrods above their concealments.

"Good morning, Major," he heard someone shout.

Startled, Metzger turned and saw Tom Green and his staff officers dismounting on the far side of a greasewood thicket. "Sir!" he called and immediately tried to follow with a detailed account of the situation.

The colonel told the major to wait, however, and began to fish around inside a leather tobacco pouch. Tall and broad-shouldered, Green had risen to fame during the Texas Revolution and he was revered throughout the brigade. Nearly fifty, the youthfulness of his face was undercut by deep bags beneath his pale blue eyes and a slight sagging at the corners of his mouth, but his voice remained steady and his manner was direct. "Now then, Major—," he paused to spit, "—where do we stand?"

Metzger handed Green his map. "They move not, Colonel: no skirmishers, *sporadisches musketry aber sie übergeben nicht*—"

Heavy smoke drifted across the hillside and the colonel coughed. "Come again?" He waved his adjutant forward.

"They surrender not."

Green scanned the map and passed it to his adjutant.

Metzger pointed across the hillside. "Captain Bradford *fing am Tagesanbruch*—"

"Daybreak?" Green understood some German—many Texans did, owing to those immigrants' prevalence in the counties around San Antonio.

"*Ja.*"

The colonel glanced at his pocket watch. "Ten minutes, roughly."

"*Ja.* That building has collapsed, *und* those two sheds are now burning. Their men are in those buildings concentrated."

Green studied the scene for a moment before pointing to a half-dozen bodies lying in the open field. "We lose anyone?"

"*Nein, aber zwei Männer haben geringe Wunden gestützt.* Neither is serious—both should recover."

"Praise the Lord." Green chewed his lip. "Any sense why these ones are dug in this way? Like ticks—"

"*Sie scheinen nicht, zu wissen, was sie tun.*"

Some pronouncements the colonel could not translate. "Try that in English?"

"They have no leader." Dust filled Metzger's eyes, and he rubbed his face with a handkerchief.

Green eyed the battered buildings. "One of 'em had best come out and lower that flag," he said, his voice trailing off."

"Major Metzger?" Green's adjutant, Joe Sayers, cut in, "here: I made a rough copy." He handed the original map back to the colonel.

Metzger pointed confidently at the main house. "*Ja*, Colonel, it is only a matter of time..." The major's voice trailed off as unexpected movement behind one of the buildings caught his eye. Realizing what was happening, his face went pale. "*Ach, nein! Schauen Sie oben*—oh, look, *look! Schnell!*"

Turning as he stood, the colonel saw dozens of ragged men emerging from a hole in the wall of the rock storehouse. Like ants fleeing a disturbed hill, they ran to and fro before tossing their weapons aside and bolting headlong for the leafless brush that hemmed the river.

"They run!" Metzger shouted, his voice growing frantic. "*Stop them! Shoot, shoot! Nein, nein—stay where you are!*"

Dozens of Texans jumped up and gave chase even as their officers shouted them back; others fired aimlessly and accomplished nothing except for nearly killing their fellow Texans.

"Aw, son of a *bitch!*" Green roared, "*Don't let 'em get away!*" But it was no use–there was no way to trap the deserters and it wasn't until several tense minutes after the last New Mexican hit the river that order was restored. Deeply embarrassed, Metzger fumed in silence while Green watched the last man thrash his way through a willow brake and out into the icy river beyond. Several of the runners submerged and did not reappear. At last, the colonel spat and jabbed a finger at the station. "I counted twenty five or twenty-six. How many are left, then?"

"Dreizig."

"You certain?"

Metzger could barely hear him over the wind. "Thirty, *ja.*"

Green took the glass from Metzger and for a full minute scanned the buildings. "Hell with 'em," he said at last. "I want the ones that stayed." He pointed to his adjutant. "Joe, go tell Bradford to double-load, depress his barrels, and aim for that forward wall—"

"Neither bolts nor cannister we have," Metzger interrupted. "Grape only."

"You send for wagons?"

"Ja—none came."

"Damn it, Major, don't take no for an answer." Green gestured to Sayers. "Stands of grape, then, just as sunlight hits those windows— blind 'em, see?" He set one hand on Metzger's shoulder and with the other gestured at points on the hillside. "Fritz, send companies from here, here, and here—in that order. Now, hurry! Sunup will be here in less than five minutes."

The rising sun pierced the clouds, littering the desert floor with patches of light.

Sayers departed for the artillery pit while Metzger wrote out Green's orders for the infantry. Finished, he sent two young messengers downhill bearing scraps of paper. The men in the ditches began to stir. Muskets were reloaded, bayonets fixed in their sockets, gear stowed. Orders were relayed along the lines, followed by the sounds of clinking metal, clicking hammers and prayer.

At the artillery pit—merely a patch of level ground cleared of rocks and brush—Sayers and the gunnery chief spoke briefly. When they had concluded, the artillerist turned and barked out commands. His crews worked feverishly until the guns were ready: mates swabbed the barrels, cut fuses, and loaded rounds. Sayers plugged his ears with his fingers.

On the canyon's lip, Metzger watched as Green knelt to study the battlefield again. "Why here?" the colonel muttered.

"Kit Carson is among them," Metzger offered. "Ragsdale saw this man—"

"No." Green waved dismissively. "Not him—nothing but chili farmers down there." He stood and brushed the dust from his wool trouser-fronts. "Nothing but a low, Yank-funded rabble, and this all-fired stubbornness is gonna get 'em killed." He turned and walked briskly back to his horse.

Metzger lifted his scope again and this time he thought that the Texans inside the ditches looked ready. He saw Sayers and Lt. Bradford near the howitzers—indeed, Bradford was looking back at him through a field glass of his own. On Metzger's orders, an aide took a small white flag with a red square at its center and waved a quick, precise pattern to the artillery chief. Sunlight began to spill over the valley's rim. Bracing himself against the wind, a standard-bearer stood and unfurled the Confederates' flag: a huge red banner with a single white star. Men pressed against the ditches' walls and sighted on the station below.

❧

The breeze stopped and a stillness settled over the field, so complete that even from his high perch Metzger could hear confused voices inside the buildings. For an instant he felt sorry for these *peones:* as Green had said, probably no more than poor tenant-farmers pressed into "service" by their de-facto owners; induced, perhaps, by the promise of ten new dollars, the forgiveness of an old debt, or a kid goat—all to face a superior enemy in a war that couldn't have meant less to them had it taken place in far-off Siam.

Then a gust of wind made him shield his eyes. Turning, he saw the Stars and Stripes on the ranch's flagpole snap taut, and any empathy he had evaporated. They were Yankees—every one. *They deserve this*, he thought.

Two years before, a petty spat with a low government official had turned violent, forcing Metzger to flee from New Hampshire into Canada, and forcing him to abandon everything he owned—money, books, and scholarly papers. He and his wife were separated for almost nineteen months. Accordingly, he swore never to trust the United States, the Union, or Yankees again—even those who had never once ventured more than fifty miles from the banks of the Rio Grande.

Almost sick with bitterness, he narrowed his eyes and signaled the artillerist.

Denver City, Colorado Territory, January 5, 1861

The letter, from a former parishioner at the Wyandotte Indian Mission in Kansas, confirmed the news that his older brother, Lewis, had been killed in battle in Missouri. A big clash, evidently: 16,000 combatants, half on each side, a few miles south of Springfield.

Seated at his desk, John Chivington let this news sink in. Papers spread before him included a third draft of the sermon he'd been writing for an upcoming service; small invoices addressed to the Rocky Mountain District of the Methodist Episcopal Church; a day-old copy of the *Rocky Mountain News*. His wife and young son laughed at some private joke in the next room.

Thinking that he should relay this news to his mother, Chivington opened an inkwell and stared at a blank sheet of paper, but nothing appropriate came to mind. Neither rage nor sorrow—nothing. *Just as well*, he thought. Lewis had sided with the Confederacy—with slavery—and the Lord had rendered the only possible verdict. *Weighed in the balance and found wanting*—where was the sense in mourning?

He glanced out the window where, despite a stiff wind, the spindly little trees he had planted the previous spring refused to shed their last yellow leaves. A wood-seller's wagon turned onto the street in front of their home. For the next several minutes, Chivington stared blankly at the wind-whipped trees, thinking vaguely about an event from his Ohio childhood and about the recent troubles in Missouri and Kansas—troubles he had witnessed first-hand.

From the other room, the sound of his boy's laughter brought him back into himself, and he rose from the desk with the letter and envelope in-hand. He crossed the room to a woodstove, opened the grate, and threw the papers inside.

Then he went out a side-door and hailed the wood-seller.

Village of Lucero, New Mexico Territory, January 5, 1862

The howitzers discharged in unison. Even ninety feet away, their hard, metallic thunderclaps shook Metzger's body and made his ears rings. *"Der Anfang des Endes,"* he whispered, perversely enthralled.

Hearing the air split, the Texans at the base of the hill pressed themselves into the dirt seconds before the shells exploded. Flash and report were indistinguishable; clouds of dirt and dust flew high into the air and then settled over the fields. From the highest trenches, the Confederates began to yell—low-pitched at first, though this wailing quickly grew louder and then passed beyond recognition. Later, Metzger would write to his wife that this sound had worked its way beneath his skin and raised the hairs on the back of his neck. Last of all—and curiously subdued—came the sharp crackling of muskets and other small arms.

Jacob Stark's company boiled up from their trench and sprinted across the field. The Mexicans behind the first adobe wall were all dead or dying, so the Texans ignored them and continued toward the main house. Charlie Spence kicked in the front door and fired a shotgun blindly into the void. Returned fire splintered the doorframe around him and forced him to duck behind the wall. Stepping forward, Jacob sighted on a man who was struggling to reload and fired. From inside the building, it looked as though opaque beams of sunlight were about the only things still holding up the sagging roof, and the smell of black powder and cold sweat was nauseating. Backed against the walls, shadowy forms cried out to each other in Spanish and in a blur of motion, one of these lunged at Jacob. A knifepoint skipped across the Texan's left shoulder blade, tore his gray wool coat and gashed him twice—down through the skin and muscle. Twisting to escape the pain, Jacob spun, jammed a revolver against his attacker's temple, and fired. Turning sharply, he fired twice more at a gathering in the far corner before falling to the ground. Stumbling through a side door, another rawboned Mexican boy fired a small derringer point-blank into a Texan's gut. When next he turned to aim at Jacob, Briggs Hardy struck the weapon with the back of his hand so that it discharged into the wall and powdered plaster filled the air. Other Texans bayoneted this Mexican in his side and left him gasping and writhing on the ground. Reaching down, Hardy grabbed the two wounded Texans by their collars and dragged them backward into the cold sunlight. From the side-yard, another soldier lobbed a turpentine bomb through an empty window and flames quickly engulfed the building. Coughing hoarsely, the last defenders staggered outside; those who cooperated were thrown onto the icy dirt and any who ran were shot. Struck twice in the back, one young sheepherder made it all the way down to the river and splashed nearly forty yards from shore before he slipped under its surface. Finally, a knot of gaunt, gray-haired defenders emerged from another shed, waving a filthy white rag.

With that, it was over. The whole skirmish lasted less than two minutes, and those Texans yet to reach the bottom of the hill before it ended had to be kept from venting their adrenaline on the prisoners. As the main house burned, its southern wall began to lean. Within minutes, it collapsed and threw great swarms of sparks into the pale yellow sky.

While other Cameron Guards bound the captives' wrists, Hardy helped Jacob over to one of the few undamaged sections of adobe wall. Even with this prop behind his back, the pain in his shoulder left Jacob nearly unable to breathe. He thought he might pass out.

Tired but elated, Hardy panted heavily. "That was somethin', wasn't it? Came through just like we said we would." Despite seeing Jacob's blood-soaked jacket, he could barely contain himself: "Bloodied, sure, but you're alive! Alive, man—*alive!* Beautiful! Saw you shoot that first son-of-a-bitch. Sure did, but I never saw the other one 'til he stung you, Jake. Sorry, pard—good thing he didn't connect no better than he did."

Jacob nodded, but even that small motion caused an unbearable flare of pain in his back. His legs buckled and he slid down the wall, leaving a bloody smear in his wake.

Lunging forward, Hardy caught his friend in time to keep him from toppling face-first into the dirt. "Someone!" he shouted, "get the surgeon down here! Fish! Charlie! Run, get the surgeon!"

∽

As Green and other senior officers descended the road, the surgeon and his assistants rushed to treat Jacob Stark, Dan Milton, and a third soldier—the only Texans seriously wounded. Once Green reached the valley floor, Green had to halt his horse as hordes of cheering men pressed around him. "Damned proud of you!" the colonel boomed, shaking every hand he could reach. "Fine work here— just exactly what we need!"

"Three cheers for the colonel!" someone called.

Green lifted his gray slouch hat as the soldiers cheered again and again. He leaned toward Metzger and pitched his voice low: "Want to commend Captain Stark personally. How is he?"

Metzger said that he did not know so Green turned away, walked his horse beyond the press, and then spurred it northward. Faster and faster, he rode across the field. The wind stung his eyes until tears flowed across his cheeks and the Texans' pickets gaped in amazement as he thundered past. His heart swelling with satisfaction, within that moment he sincerely believed that Almighty God had ordained their eventual success. Near the river, where muddy water slapped at rounded stones, Green reined to a halt. The sun ducked back inside the clouds and icy wind roared down the valley, tossing the leafless willows in its wake. Looking back, he watched as his troops raced to loot the ranch before it was consumed by fire. *Will every Mexican farmhand hold out unto death?* he wondered. *Good Lord, at what price will we take Santa Fe?* Watching his men toil beneath a pall of black smoke in a dead field far from their homes, an acute meanness stung his conscience: *This wretched wasteland—nothing*

27

here is worth even a drop of their blood. To the west, Green watched as blocks of ice in the river spun this way and that, influenced by currents, sandbars, and flotsam. He felt similarly directionless. His beloved Republic had been absorbed by the Confederacy, and while he shared his fellow Southerners' visceral dislike for Union, he thought of himself primarily as a Texan—only the meaning of that word had changed. With the Republic's demise, much of what he believed—the cornerstone on which he'd set his existence—had crumbled. Nothing fixed, no circumstance sound; the Republic was dead and with it the ideals that given it life:

—That nations, as well as individuals, were amenable for their acts to the public opinion of mankind...

—That all men had the right to secure their lives, liberty and property...

—And that when a government failed to protect these rights, then all men were obligated to overthrow that government.

And having surrendered these ideals, had God withdrawn His favor? *Are we no longer worthy? Forgive us our carelessness, O Lord.*

Even before Secession, Green had doubted that the United States would last: its constituents' concerns were too varied and its federal bonds too weak. Indeed, why should Texans comply with laws drafted for the sole benefit of Massachusetts's mill-interests? No luck and no thanks. And slavery? *Damned abolitionists.* A convenient hook for Yankee hats—nothing more. As far as he was concerned, Abe Lincoln had won a rigged, meaningless election and by force of arms meant to preserve those infernal laws and venal systems that protected Northern industrialists; he was a tyrant at odd with the Lord's plan, unfit to lead a citizenry that was free by the grace of God. Now an unholy leviathan was scourging Texas and the South. *Indeed, Satan himself bests us.* He had been to the North; seen its monstrous factories and teeming cities; seen how life there meant nothing, and he strained to conceive how the Confederacy might prevail against such evil. He prayed that God would recognize and bless the Confederacy's superior principles and fidelity to Him, for it seemed that these were about their only assets. Better people with a superb fighting spirit—*Except that we are so few.*

And in due course—enthralled by Henry Sibley's grand vision of a Confederate West—they had crossed this fearsome desert to prove their strength and ability to operate beyond the limits of Federal power in the West—except that having arrived, there was nothing here worthy of conquest. *Emptiness as far as the eye can see!* Of course, Santa Fe was a storied trade center but the rest of New Mexico Territory was empty. *My God, there is nothing here! Nothing! What in God's name are we doing?* He shook his head to clear it. *Stop— these misgivings must stop.* No, California was the real prize—indeed, some in the column wondered why they had not moved directly on Los Angeles. Santa Fe, Denver, and Salt Lake City were of little circumstance except as watering holes on the way to California. With its Pacific ports, gold mines, and fertile soils, slavery and Southern ways could be implemented there on a grand scale.

Green cracked a wan smile. *Lord, help me keep these doubts well hidden.* Things had to work out—*had to.* But how could their underfed, ill-equipped army—however noble its enterprise or worthy its spirit—complete this herculean task? *And General Sibley! He is unfit—no!* he thought, *I mustn't ever think that.* No good ever comes from thoughts like that—better to keep on the sunny side. He sighed. *My word, Tom, you are a muddle.* Perhaps everything would turn out well; perhaps the assumptions on which their campaign was based weren't altogether specious; perhaps the inadequacies—in personnel, money, and matériel—that had galled him as they had embarked would somehow resolve. "As you will," he whispered. Indeed, beyond Divine Providence, nothing else mattered. He bent his head in prayer: *Thank you, Lord, for sending your Son to ransom my soul. Bless this splendid army, and give me the courage to lead these men.*

Opening his eyes, he pressed his horse's flanks with his bootheels and started back.

Village of Lucero, New Mexico Territory, January 5, 1862

———————

Green waited beside the road as lines of prisoners were marched past. Major Metzger wheeled his animal counter to Green's and saluted. *"Getan,* Colonel. Few good weapons they had, very little gunpowder—"

"Then what drove 'em so?" Green murmured.

"—und ihre Aufladungen—their boots—rubbish."

Green exhaled. "Look, Fritz, this is nothing personal but some of the staff has complained that you use too much German. Most times I understand you but the others do not—English from here on out, okay?"

"Ja, okay."

"Good. Leave 'em their boots—burn everything else."

"Yes, Sir. Captain Stark *ist hier."* Metzger gestured across the corral. *"Stark!"*

୬

Moving slowly, Jacob crossed the road to stand before the colonel. A sling supported his left arm and shoulder, both field-dressed beneath large, bloody bandages.

Metzger nodded approvingly. "Captain Stark led his company into the main building *und* himself killed three."

Green studied the boy and judged him to be about nineteen years old (indeed, Jacob did not know his own birthday; twenty is the answer he would have given had the colonel asked). Layers of dust and soot had neither diminished the brightness of Stark's eyes nor concealed the earnestness of his expression, though the pain in his shoulder had drained much of the color from his face. Dark,

30

shaggy hair covered the tops of his ears and close-cropped whiskers sprouted from his chin. Apart from his injuries, he looked as solid as a church—physically, anyway, though there was something in his bearing, something almost feral that led Green to surmise that the boy was no gentleman.

Indeed, Jacob's pedigree was checkered. The last of six children born to hardscrabble parents, they had given him up for adoption not long into his sixth year. Though neighbors in the town of Washington, Arkansas, had quickly taken him in, they were peculiar fundamentalists whose rigidity instilled an attitude of permanent rebellion in the boy. Even his stepfather, who took perverse pride in the beatings he administered when Jacob read books other than the Bible, could not break him. In 1856, when the family moved to eastern Texas, he'd taken advantage of the disorder and run away—on his thirteenth birthday, in fact. Thereafter he had done what he could: tanned hides in Charleston, Louisiana; then to Galveston and Lavaca in Texas, where sold newspapers and learned carpentry. Like most footloose boys his age, he drank, fought, and gambled almost constantly. For some time his home was a canvas sheet strung up between two trees, and it was there he'd met Briggs Hardy—a young, hotheaded drifter very much like himself. Then, just before he turned eighteen, two things had happened: he landed steady work typesetting for a newspaper in Brownsville, Texas, and met his future wife, Sarah Linscomb. Looking back, he could not honestly say that he and Sarah were in love, but she was patient with him and—despite her chronic loneliness—her companionship was comfortable. Within three months, they were married and ten months later, in 1860, a little girl, Jenny, was born. For the first time in his life, Jacob was truly happy; for once, he could picture himself settled. There hadn't been enough hours in the day to spend with his daughter, yet even she with her beautiful little hands and bright eyes could not stabilize him. Maybe nothing could. He began to spend more and more nights away from home, prowling for old troubles, and for these sins his family had suffered. Indeed, even more than his upbringing, if there was anything that accounted for the wild look in Jacob's eye, it was the knowledge that his thoughtlessness had resulted in his daughter's violent death and the complete destruction of his marriage. Even his decision to fight could be considered a selfish act: while others complained about Yankee tyranny and the specter of Northern dominance, Jacob had signed on because he could find no other outlet for the anger that was driving him mad.

Green leaned down from his saddle to shake his hand. "Not badly hurt, I hope?"

Jacob shrugged with his right shoulder. "Just a stick, Sir."

"Painful?"

"No, Sir," he lied.

"Good. Go see the quartermaster about a new jacket."

"Yessir."

"Fine work, Captain—very capable. You see their leader?"

"Reckon it was red breeches there." Jacob pointed to a body laid out among others. "No breakfast forever."

"Certainly not." Green laughed quietly. "Suppose that's Kit Carson?"

Astonished by the idea, Jacob tilted his head for a better view of the corpse. "Couldn't say, Sir—Carson's aspect is unknown to me."

Green grinned and shook his head. "Forget it—that's a joke between Metzger and me."

"Yessir."

"Your company's horses are up top?"

"Yessir."

"And you can ride in your condition?"

"Yessir."

"Very well." He handed Jake a brief note. "Go find General Sibley's ambulance—probably five, six miles back on the *camino*. Tell him we have cleared the road and that the Army of New Mexico may proceed. Want him to hear it from an officer and a participant."

"Yessir." Jacob saluted and went to where the rest of his company stood waiting.

Metzger winced as Green spit out his enormous wad of tobacco; an index finger followed to remove stray shreds from against his gums. Green looked up, caught Metzger's eye and winked. "Wife'd kill me if she knew."

Metzger shrugged. "Everyone has a vice."

"Yeah, what's yours?"

The captain shook sand out of his hair and scratched his head. "Contempt for humanity."

"That's a good one," Green laughed.

"Someday something will ensnare me. 'The gods are just, und of our pleasant vices make instruments to plague us.'"

"Shakespeare?"

"King Lear."

"Seemed right but I haven't read it since college." Green spat out a few tardy threads of tobacco and gestured toward the high road. "Detail a company to march those natives back to Doña Ana—let Baylor decide what to do with 'em."

"*Ja*, Colonel."

Green's eyes followed Jacob, whom others were helping up the road. "You're from Brownsville, right? You know much about him—Stark, I mean?"

"Personally, no. He is a good soldier, very reliable...but," he paused, "he...I do not know how to explain."

"Try." Green patted his saddle in search of the water bag he kept tied there.

"There is talk..." Metzger glanced uphill but could no longer see Jacob.

"Don't hold back."

Metzger exhaled. "You know of Juan Cortina, *ja?* Of our recent troubles in the border counties?"

"Mexican bandits shot up Brownsville, sure."

"*Ja*, well, Stark led one of the counter-raids, *und* things I have heard from others who were there."

"Things?"

"Rumors."

Seeing that dozens of enlisted men were within earshot, Green's would not speculate as to what this meant. "So much noise drifts up from the border, it's hard to sort fact from fiction. Are these 'rumors' widespread?"

"*Ja*," Metzger admitted, "but he is respected nonetheless. His company is efficient," he hastened to add. "There have been no troubles." Lost in thought, Green remained silent. A buckboard loaded with moth-eaten blankets rolled past. "Colonel, Sir, I am sorry those men from the ranch escaped," Metzger said. "That was my fault alone, *und* I—"

"No." Colonel Green watched crews re-limbering the howitzers for transport. "We did what we came here to do. Look, Fritz, know what told me that Kit Carson wasn't down there?"

"No, Sir."

"Ragsdale counted near two hundred men here last night, but there were fewer'n sixty this morning, and that number kept falling— that told me that no one was leading them. Even without leadership, they fought well—I can only imagine how they will improve once led. I don't want anyone—you, me, or the men—to think otherwise."

"Yes, Colonel."

"Respect an enemy unto his defeat." Another company went past and started up the road. "Our leadership is—hell, maybe I shouldn't have sent Stark after the general," Green said. "Old dad's probably well under water by now but...no. Beyond my control." He squinted north into the wind. "We have so more to accomplish—this is only the start."

"Yes, Sir." Metzger saluted.

Green paused for a long moment, so long that the major expected him to say more. Instead, Green looked confused, as though he'd forgotten what he meant to say or else how to say it. For several moments, he blinked helplessly at Metzger, who in turn tried to conceal his astonishment. At last, the colonel put his head down and without a word spurred his horse north, upriver, toward the column's front.

For a long while, Metzger stared after him, unsure what had happened or whether it meant anything. He hoped that it did not, but for some time after he could not shake the fear that it might.

Central City, Colorado Territory, January 7, 1862

Ragged men filled Eureka Street to overflowing. From Washington Hall's second-story balcony, territorial dignitaries Jerome Chaffee and Henry Teller made short, fiery speeches and charged the atmosphere with expectation. Electric-blue clouds of breath hung in the air, pierced by spills of sunlight between the false-fronted buildings. Save for muted sounds—a woman's cough; the squeak of boots on cold, dry snow; a horse's jangling harness—the crowd was reverentially quiet. His speech concluded, Teller turned and without fanfare introduced the territorial governor, William Gilpin.

Bundled against the cold, Gilpin stepped forward and leaned against the rail with both hands. "Ladies ..." he began but the dry air made him cough and he paused to spit into a handkerchief. "Ladies and gentlemen," he resumed, "I stand before you reluctantly, for the news I bring is troubling—most troubling!" He paused for breath and took a sip of water.

Applause—and a few jeers—rose from the crowd.

"Like you," Gilpin continued, "I pray that President Lincoln and the U.S. Army will preserve the Union—preserve a government sanctioned by God Himself! And though we are very far from the old states, now that contest is of imminent concern right here. Ladies and gentlemen, just yesterday I received word that a rebel army, some forty-five hundred strong, has entered New Mexico Territory! At this very moment, these traitors are marching up the Rio Grande *meaning to attack and seize Colorado!*"

The crowd erupted. Men howled and stamped hobnailed boots on soot-stained sidewalks. Stares drew shoves and punches followed.

When two men brandished knives, a squad of blue-jacketed soldiers had to rush forward to separate them.

"We cannot stand by!" Gilpin bellowed. "The battle against treason is a perpetual death struggle—"

"*You lie!*" barked a tall miner from Georgia. "Flannel-mouthed sum'bitch—Southern men will burn every town in this godless nation!" A chorus of boos began but the man would not stop: "Won't have a marse, no *sir!* No one owns *me!*"

"How these fice dogs bark!" Gilpin mocked but the most rabid of the pro-Unionists weren't so readily discouraged. Several lunged at the heckler, clutched at his duckcloth coat, and knocked his hat into the mud. With punches and kicks, his friends fought to pull him back. The crowd parted, rocks and bottles sailed over the breach, and the window of a dry goods store crashed inward. Quickly, soldiers formed a new cordon with their muskets, leaning hard against a seething wall of bodies. The governor waved his arms and tried to regain the crowd's attention. "Ignore him! He'll get his! Ignore him. Friends, Col. Slough—commander of the First Colorado Regiment—will appeal for volunteers now. Please, let him speak!"

The mob did not settle but those who turned toward the balcony saw John Potts Slough—a thirty-three year old lawyer, tall and sturdy, with a neat, square beard and piercing eyes. What they could not see was that Slough had little interest in organizing the territory's defenses except as a means to further his political career. Disgusted by frontier society—or, to his mind, the lack thereof—Slough cared little for his fellow citizens and was perfectly happy to thunder away from a perch far above the street: "For years, the people of the Southern states have spread secessionist poison, and like fools we've done little to stop them. Tolerated *treason!* To what end, friends? Have we profited? *No!* Secesh interests want you to believe that belligerence and anarchy shall obtain—that their little revolt is no cause for alarm. By God, they want us to sue for peace!" He swept the crowd with a stern glare. "So shall we? Our forefathers' sacrificed precious blood to build this nation. Shall we discard this birthright on the duskheap of inconvenient ideas? No, damn it, we must *fight!* We *must* stamp out this rebellion! We *must* carry the fire south! There is no other way! Are you with me?"

"*Yes!*" the audience shouted.

"Then heed my appeal! Since July last, we of the First Colorado Volunteer Regiment have been preparing for this crisis but friends, without your help, we cannot stem the tide. Patriots, your country needs you! Colorado needs you! *Heed my appeal!*"

Pro-Unionists—a majority on the street (and throughout Colorado Territory, generally)—cheered so that the secessionists' protests were overcome. Standing as fifty against more than seven hundred, these would-be Confederates found themselves backed into a tight, bristling knot.

Nearly as wild as the crowd below, Slough leaned across the rail. "This nation *must* endure. *Long live the Republic!* Protect your homes! Your *families!* These wretches—"

The tall Georgian heaved a half-empty bottle at the balcony, and though it missed Slough's head by inches, the window behind him shattered. "*Liar!*" the Southerner bellowed, so fiercely that the veins in his neck bulged and spittle flew from the corners of his mouth. "Won't ever bow to Lincoln! Like *hell!* You whoresons want a fight? Well, come and take it!"

Again, the mob surged forward, only this time soldiers could not—or would not—stop them. Desperately the Southerners fought back but sheer numbers were against them and after less than a minute, they retreated in haste down A Street.

As the brawl moved away, order slowly returned to the street. Again, Gilpin pounded on the rail. "This is what we face! Friends, if their treachery does not move you, then God save us all!" Cries and whistles echoed off the false-fronts. "Stop them—*stop them!* Or have I misjudged your spine? Will you accept subjugation?"

"No!" the crowd barked.

"Treason? Will you allow them to destroy the Union, to plunder Colorado, to use her riches to prop up the rebellion?"

"No!"

"Then *fight!* Get your bristles up and *fight!*"

Again, the crowd roared and the sound was truly frightening. Windows rattled in their frames and horses stamped nervously in their hitches. Miners, millhands, teamsters, shopmen, and woodcutters all shook hands and clapped each other on the back: the native-born alongside Swedes, Cornishmen, Irishmen, Englishmen, and Germans—all schisms briefly healed, all factions united.

"Come on, step up." Slough elbowed the governor aside. "Agents are on the street—yes, those men there! Enlist today as individuals or companies! God bless these United States! Unity, friends—*unity or death!*"

Within seconds, the enlistment clerks were mobbed. Calls went out for more paper and each scribe wrote as fast as the nearest volunteer could bark out his name, age, and occupation.

୫

As the mob roared, down the block the owner of a small saloon glanced through the wavy plate glass of his front window. "Jaysus," he muttered, lamenting both the commotion outside and the pitifully small crowd of customers. Despite a blazing cast-iron stove near the front door, the room was still cold, and his young curate was nearly exhausted from continuous runs to a woodpile in the alley. His few patrons were drinking heavily, which was a comfort, but the hordes of ruddy-cheeked men raging up and down the avenue were not. "This clatty nonsense—how will I make wages?"

Business in that subfusc little village *was* bad—had been for months, but only on that day due to the ruckus outside. Far greater problems lay in the forty rugged miles between Central City and Denver City, nevermind that Denver was eight hundred miles from St. Louis—and all over very poor roads. Only abundant gold offset the exorbitant cost of freighting in supplies, and lately gold was no longer abundant. Already much of the district's easy wealth—placer gold, washed free from the soil with simple hand tools—was gone. Lately even the district's rich hardrock outfits had encountered difficulty. As miners probed deeper underground, they found ore riddled with recalcitrant sulphur compounds, and known recovery methods had stopped working. Charlatans and fly-by-nights descended with multifarious "extraction processes," all of them hokum and fruitful only in extracting money from the desperate and unwary. Even good, well-capitalized mines were hemorrhaging money; unemployment was soaring and despairing pioneers were departing in droves.

Much of this was lost on the barkeep, though. The composition of ores concerned him only insofar as mines employed miners, whose pay then ended up in his till. Barking like dogs, the crowd outside was something else. Perhaps some would come inside after the rally and buy drinks, or, if they disliked what they had heard, break every window along Eureka Street. He scowled and spat on the floor again. "Wretched," he said to no one in particular. "Tearin' itself apart. Mark my words: before this is over, we will all of us be up to our necks." But the regulars paid him so little heed that only the arrival of a wiry wallop of a man saved him from mumbling to himself.

"Tom, old friend," the boy said, "Has Jimmy-boy been here this morning? We were supposed to meet here a half-hour ago—"

"Jaysus, if it ain't Peter MacInnes." The barkeep motioned him around the bar and pointed to the back door. "Come on, boyo, quickly." When he turned back, he was dismayed to see that boy had not moved from his stance near the bar. "Come on!" he swore through clenched teeth, "ye can't stay here—have ye not heard?"

"Heard what?"

"Hurry up, scuddler." Dust motes swirled in the cold, stale air as the barkeep continued toward the door. "About James—the sheriff nearly took him. Tried to cut him from the herd and bundle him away but he ducked in here, same as ye—have ye not seen him?"

"No," Peter said, his eyes flashing. A sudden change came over the boy's features: his eyes narrowed and his jaw tightened so that he seemed to age ten years. "Where is he now?"

"Jaysus, Pete, I told ye—"

"No, Tommy, ye did *not!* Where is James?"

"Don't know," the counterman admitted. He pushed on the door, which let a blast of freezing cold air inside. "Said if I sees ye, I must tell ye that ye cannot return t'yer diggings, but to meet on the road above Benjamin Dry, and wi' naught but daylight. Said ye mustn't be seen—catch on that?—and that he'd tell the others. Sorry, Pete, but that's all I have."

Though Peter tried hard to remain composed, his features soured and his hands, knotted into fists, began to shake. For months, he and his companions had tried to make a go of mining and failed—and now this.

One of the barkeep's employees ducked between them and stepped outside for another armload of firewood. The sunlight on snow was almost blinding, especially since their eyes had adjusted to the bar's dim interior.

The barkeep, an immigrant himself and at heart a rather decent fellow, leaned against the doorframe and lowered his voice. "Pete, most *everyone* finds trouble up here—"

"Ye don't know the half," Peter said. "This has followed us here."

"Even so, maybe I can help. I know good people—"

"No," Peter said, suddenly eyeing the huge man with faint suspicion. "Ye've been good to us, Tommy, but this trouble is ours alone. So long, friend." Then, before the barkeep could say anything more, the young man stepped through the door and started down the alley, halting for a look at each corner as he went.

For several minutes, the barkeep stared after MacInnes, neither alarmed nor even particularly curious about the young man's hasty departure. Wasn't the first time a customer had come into his bar, asked strange questions, and then disappeared; likely wouldn't be the last, either. Some things were better left alone—or deliberately forgotten, a skill the barkeep had honed to perfection. Central City was a long way from anything that resembling proper civilization, and sometimes knowing too much was unhealthy. Then the fellows playing cards at one of the tables called for more drinks, so the barkeep stepped back inside and returned to work, within minutes forgetting that he'd ever seen or spoken with anyone named James Hay or Peter MacInnes.

Central City, Colorado Territory, January 7, 1862

The governor shook a well-wisher's hand and climbed into the coach. Lost in thought, he drummed his fingers without stopping. Seated opposite, Col. Slough chewed on his cuticles as the tapping drove him mad; unable to stand it any longer, he shifted in his seat so that his knees struck Gilpin's. Though this small violence jolted the governor from his fog (and stilled his fingers), he took no notice of the colonel's half-hearted apology. "We'll have our number before sunset, John—four full companies, minimum."

From his seat outside, their driver raged at his mules to start forward. As the coach swayed heavily on its leather suspension straps, it felt for the entire world as though it might shake apart at the next pothole; within fifty feet, Slough felt nauseous. He swallowed hard as he read from a paper, "Sam Tappan's report lists one hundred from Boulder County and about as many from Breckenridge, Parkville, Georgetown, and Empire combined. Seventy-five, eighty from Oro City and environs, plus a hundred more from Tarryall and Fairplay together. Five hundred here today. Another five hundred-odd between Denver and Golden—two hundred from Cañon City and the Spanish counties down south."

Gilpin picked his teeth carefully with a small pocketknife and tallied the numbers in this head. "Around sixteen hundred, yes? That'll do. Can't be more than eight or nine hundred rebs altogether."

"So few?" Slough said.

"Those big numbers were for the public's edification." The governor stared at his knuckles. "I've heard that the graybacks believe that they can live off the land and gather enlistments in New Mexico

41

Territory as they go, but my God! There is no one down there! Priests and dirt farmers, only." Gilpin reached out the window, through the roll-up curtain, and banged on the front boot.

A bodyguard leaned down from his seat next to the driver. "Yes, Governor?"

"When you see Forbes, have the driver stop so that we may talk."

"Yes, Governor."

Gilpin withdrew into the coach and tried to get comfortable on the hard wooden seat.

Their progress was slow, hindered by the hundreds of men milling about. Some were returning to work, others to their lodgings—far more meant to drink heavily to celebrate their enlistment. Many stopped and stared as the coach rolled slowly past. *Idiots.* Slough lifted a curtain and glanced out the window at the wall of faces—unwashed, unkempt, revolting. *Idiots, I will set you straight.*

Unmindful of the vehicle's approach, two drunks came to blows and staggered into the roadway. One of the lead mules flinched and the driver had to pull up hard to keep from crashing. Dozens of onlookers—the governor's bodyguard included—shouted at these brawlers until one of them drew a pistol from his belt and fired. The bullet sailed harmlessly but Gilpin still flinched.

"God*dammit,*" Slough growled. He drew a revolver and pulled the curtains aside for a better view. Although he had once been thrown out of the Ohio Legislature for assaulting a fellow lawmaker, this time he kept his temper in check.

Gilpin slid from his seat until his shoulder blades rested on the cushions. "What is it?" Slough watched as bystanders seized the drunks, disarmed the one with the gun, and pummeled both. When the driver bawled again, the vehicle surged past the ruckus and then there was nothing to see except the same unwashed swarm as before. "Colonel," Gilpin demanded, "what's going on?"

Shotgun still balanced across his knees, the bodyguard leaned back and nodded to Slough: "All clear."

The colonel re-holstered his weapon. Again—though the word *idiot* dominated his thoughts—he forced a genial laugh. "Nothing to worry about." He grabbed Gilpin's elbow and helped him up into his seat, cheered a little knowing that at least *he* hadn't dived for cover. "Nothing at all."

☙

The governor's aide was waiting beside the road at the mouth of Packard Gulch. Sensing that he was momentarily unwelcome, Slough lit a cigar and stared out the opposite window. Gilpin reached beneath the curtain to receive a folded note. Palming this paper, he read it, tore it into tiny pieces, and swallowed them. Then he took a small bag of gold coins from his jacket and discreetly slipped it into the aide's hand.

Gilpin leaned toward the aide and spoke quietly: "Sheriff Keheler can release that cracker loudmouth after dark—fellow's apt to be lynched in broad daylight. But go to his cell and remind him that if there's loose talk or if I ever see him again, I'll have him chopped up and thrown into the deepest hole I can find."

The aide nodded solemnly. "I'll be clear, Governor."

"Do."

The aide stepped away and slipped back into the crowd.

Gilpin settled back to ponder the past few months' events: Charley Harris and his secessionist friends hoisting a rebel flag on Larimer Street; self-styled raiders staging hit-and-run attacks on teamsters near Pueblo—thank goodness the very worst Southern sympathizers had left to fight for their home states. Even still, the flow of goods and emigrants to Colorado had slowed to a trickle, and Indian attacks—*good God, the Indians!*—certainly had not let up. Their interdiction of commerce's rightful flow across the prairies would have to be punished—and soon—yet even this was not his chief concern. While the prospect of rebels on the territory's southern doorstep was alarming, perhaps it would finally galvanize Washington to address the cold realities that *he'd* been facing for months. Without ready goods and consumers, Colorado would wither on the vine and all his plans for farms, cities, and railroads would be for naught—or worse, might not be realized until *he* could carve out the share to which he was justly entitled. Slough might not be the right man to face the Texans, but he was organized and ambitious, and if he could raise and deliver a regiment of Coloradans to Fort Union in New Mexico, then at least the territory's resources would be available to more-skilled leadership. Gilpin gazed with satisfaction at crowds of men flocking uphill to enlist. When he leaned forward to clap Slough on the knee, the colonel jumped. "Things are finally underway."

Slough smiled politely and scanned the crowd, but the word *idiot* had lodged in his mind and vitiated his thoughts. His eyes leapt from face to face: *bet that one with his fly open is a pervert—idiot; there's one can't even lace his boots—idiot. Jesus Particular Christ, is everyone here deficient?* Feeling a little ill, he tapped ash from his cigar and faced the governor. "Anything else I should know?"

"I'll have copies of Edward Canby's dispatches delivered to you," Gilpin said, genuinely surprised at Slough's betrayed tone. "My New Mexican counterpart, Henry Connelly, says the two thousand Texans between Franklin—"

"Hold on! A minute ago you told me there were eight or nine hundred!"

"Well, perhaps—"

"Give me an honest account, Governor," Slough snapped. "Seeing as I'm headed that way, I'd surely like to know."

"Calm down, John. No one is quite sure. Intelligence from down there rarely *is*, if you take my meaning. Can't be *more* than two thousand—that I know—and whatever their number, disease and skirmishing will halve it before they reach Santa Fe. I soldiered down there as a younger man—did you know that?—and believe me, New Mexicans *hate* the Texans. After Lamar and Snively's raids, Walker's folly—Lord, honestly, you couldn't find a kind word or a cup of warm piss for a thirsty Texan."

Slough said nothing and leaned forward to tap more ash out the window.

Gilpin tried to placate the temperamental colonel. "Think, John—think of the freedom. Need weapons? Issue a sight draft and I will endorse it. Supplies? Buy whatever is available or seize what you must. Take these men wherever and use them however you want. Trust me, the Texans' appetite for conflict will diminish long before you meet, and then you can administer the fatal stroke. Once statehood is achieved, you'll be able to write your ticket to Congress—but only if we work *together.*"

"We are attached to the Department of Kansas," Slough said, "not even authorized to enter New Mexico. Surely the Federals will not permit a freelance."

"I'll work on that, but remember that the district's commanding officer is isolated *well* south of Albuquerque—I think you'll have fair latitude."

Slough glanced at the tiny, fast-moving clouds that peppered the sky. The Governor's logic had appeal. For weeks, he'd thought along the same lines but somehow the pieces still hadn't quite fit and the nebulousness of it all made his guts ache. What he felt wasn't anger or apprehension, but *fear.* Something was wrong but for the life of him, he couldn't tell *what.* He flicked the nub of his cigar out the window, half-hoping it would land on a miner's hat and catch (though it bounced harmlessly into the mud). Staring into the distance, he saw smoke rising from a chimney. "Maybe this will all blow over."

Taken aback, Gilpin scrutinized Slough and wondered if he had made a mistake in appointing an opaque and hotheaded civilian to lead the force entrusted with his territory's salvation. *Hell, with my future. Steady now, Bill—this game is dealt. Play out the hand before you make any changes.* He waved to a well-wisher in the crowd and reached back outside to tap on the side panel. "Let's *go!*" He turned and tried to catch Slough's eye but the big man's thoughts were clearly elsewhere. "Fine work today. Of course, now we'll have to find a means to pay for all this, but that can wait until we return to Denver."

"Good." *Idiot.* Slough exhaled as he caught a receding glimpse of Washington Hall. "I'd like to never see this place again."

Governor Gilpin stared at him and frowned slightly. *Yes, play out this hand but for pity's sake hedge your bets.*

Between Central City and Denver, Colorado Territory, January 9, 1862

At four a.m., three wagons carrying twenty-five men—miners, teamsters, tradesmen and one teacher—departed unnoticed Central City and went the Mount Vernon route down to Denver. These were the last volunteers brought into the First Colorado before it set off for New Mexico.

&

It was almost noon when the boys awoke, stiff and sore from their long ride. They jumped down from the wagons into shin-deep snow. The sky was a dazzling blue and they had to shield their eyes from the glare.

A processing clerk took their names before another a blue-coated soldier directed them toward a row of stick-built barracks. Each man was issued one set of long-johns; two pairs of blue, woolen pants; a black leather belt; two cotton shirts; a blue, woolen jacket; a six-by-four woolen blanket; a forage cap; two pairs of woolen socks; one pair of good leather boots; and a tin plate, cup, and spoon. They stepped outside and each was handed a muzzle loading .58-caliber Springfield rifled musket, a seventeen-inch socket bayonet, an empty cartridge box, and a tin canteen. One man in ten received a tin soup pot, skillet, and coffee pot. Then another soldier arrived and shouted at them to form lines.

&

At mess that night—thin beef broth with root vegetables, hard rye bread, and coffee—James Hay nodded discretely across the table to

Peter MacInnes. "Any chance he'll give up now and go home?" he whispered. "Have we got away?"

"No." Peter dipped the corner of his bread into the broth, let it soak for several seconds, and crammed the resulting doughball into his mouth. "Conroy came a long way to find us, boyo—this burl has bought us a little time is all."

"Only?"

"Yeah." Peter wiped soggy crumbs from his beard. "We might've faced him down, but with the sheriff and who knows what else after—it's a miracle we got away, damn-but."

"Jaysus."

"Like as not, boyo, he will never stop hunting."

Hay's eyes flashed as uncomfortable memories replayed themselves in his head. "It was his fault—brought it on himself, he did."

"Bloody apt he did," Peter said. He dumped a half-cup of weak coffee onto the dirt floor. "Do it again if I had to."

"Oh, see?" Hay added, trying to strike a hopeful tone, "maybe in time he'll give up and scapper back to the old states."

"Maybe," Peter answered. "But even if he don't, at least this time I will be armed."

"All of us—see, boyo? There's the spirit."

"Don't get your hopes up." Peter rose and collected his utensils. "We aren't away yet—not nearly."

Hacienda Carrizo, Santa Fe, New Mexico Territory, January 12, 1862

Don Enrique Anton Carrizo picked at his food in silence. All evening his guests had devoured the latest gossip, but he did not share their appetite. He sighed heavily. Seated around his table, segregated by gender, were family—his younger brother and sister-in-law, who ranched east of the mountains in El Cerrito; and his older spinster-sister, Teresa, who'd tucked a long-stemmed clay pipe into her hair as an ornament—and several socially eminent guests. Near the long table's waist were his daughter, Adria Carrizo, her intended fiancée, Basilio Ortiz, and his younger brother, Felix.

The don watched Basilio mop his sweaty face with a napkin. *My God, he is ugly—one of Goya's idiots in the flesh. Chin's so weak there's naught between the nuez de Adán and his upper lip.*

Still, *feo o no*, Basilio had a head for numbers and his parents, Ramon and Beatriz, were rich—likely the second-wealthiest family in the entire territory. The don would have preferred Felix for a match with his daughter, except that supplanting a firstborn son like Basilio would have violated social norms. Indeed, on the sole occasion the don had even hinted at this, the boys' parents had made it perfectly clear that they would never depart from tradition. Adria, he knew, cared little for either boy, but in time, he expected that she would appreciate the wealth and security conferred by such a union. Or not. Either way, that very evening he meant to announce her and Basilio's engagement. Indeed, with Texans having already overrun Mesilla, he felt pressure to finalize the transaction before everything was ruined. *Strange—all nature knows the Confederates are coming, yet no one will say anything. Just as well.*

Personally, Don Carrizo saw the invasion as an opportunity: obscured by the Texans' dust, he could settle *many* lingering scores. Certainly much was at risk, but seated at his well-set table, unconsciously tapping his fork against the side of his plate, he felt his confidence growing. Favor, he believed, lay close by, shining in the darkness like a cold, hard diamond.

⁓

Servants brought champagne and desserts: French chocolates, candied fruits and nuts, and more. Just when the don began to relax, Spruce Baird, the territory's former attorney general, leaned forward and cleared his throat. "Y'all, I've heard things here with which I do *not* agree. So that it's clear where I stand, I want to propose a toast to the Confederate States of America. Glasses up!"

The other guests' reactions ranged from gritted teeth and clenched fists to hearty laughter and scattered applause. Don Carrizo tried to speak, but Louisa Canby was even quicker: "Judge Baird, that's treason!"

Baird fixed Louisa with a cold eye. "General Sibley's coming, Ma'am, and nothing—certainly not your husband's little tin-plate army—gonna slow him down."

Louisa rested her spoon upon a plate. "Unlike *your* friends, sir, my husband has chosen to honor his commission!"

"Not for long, he won't."

Don Carrizo held up a hand toward Judge Baird. "Sir, I will not have guests bickering like this in my home—not tonight, not ever. Please, everyone, calm yourselves while Serafin refills our glasses." A servant came forward from his station along the wall and poured more wine.

"Hold on!" Baird objected. "For too long it's been this way! Can't a man speak his mind? I *said* I want to toast the Confederacy and I *mean*—"

"Spruce!" Rafael Armijo rested a hand on the judge's forearm. "Not now."

"Now!" Baird shook off the restraint and glared around the room. "Guns on the table!" He gestured at the territory's former surveyor

49

general. "Bill Pelham's with me, Ward Copely there—the Armijo brothers."

Chairs scraped across the floor as guests pushed away from the table. Don Carrizo opened his mouth to speak, but again Louisa Canby was quicker and turned to face Manuel Armijo: *"Señor,* for shame! Are you not the captain of a militia? Have you not sworn to protect the United States government?" Manuel looked thoroughly uncomfortable and mumbled something about 'obligations' and 'interests' but did not exactly answer.

"Credit him with common sense," Baird said and took another drink.

"You there!" Basilio Ortiz rose from his chair and confronted Baird. "Apologize at once!" Though he trembled, Basilio stood his ground. He had worn his military uniform that evening in a provocative show of allegiance; craving Adria's approval, he saw instead that she was staring down at her plate.

Even as other guests began to murmur, Don Carrizo fought an impulse to roll his eyes.

The judge seethed: "What, you gonna run me down, boy?"

Bishop John Lamy quietly tried to clear the air. "Judge Baird, honestly. We are guests, invited here to break bread. Your words—"

"Forgive me, your Holiness," Don Carrizo hissed, "but he is no longer welcome. Get out, Baird! *Now!*"

"Indeed," Basilio added.

"Boy," Baird snarled, "just who do you think *you* are? You're a paper soldier—without that costume, you're *nothing!*"

Basilio's face reddened. All evening he'd felt perfectly unimportant, but the cold disdain in Baird's voice made his temper flare. "Sir, where is your dignity? Your respect for the law?"

"Ain't *my* laws," Baird hooted.

"Wrong, sir!" Unaccustomed to speaking out, the shy, bookish Basilio took stock of the situation and faltered: "The...the Constitution cannot be ignored—cannot be discarded like... what, like *newspaper!* What gives you people the idea—"

"'You people'? Of all the..." More amused than irritated, Baird drained half his glass and continued: "Listen, boy: when I finish a paper—when it's no longer relevant—I burn it. Abraham Lincoln is the vilest fraud ever committed against a free people and Washington is hopelessly corrupt—don't tell me I don't need new papers."

Beside Adria, who had slumped even lower in her chair, Felix Ortiz—Basilio's younger brother—ignored his mother's pleading look and stood. Only nineteen, he was taller and far sturdier than his older brother was, and he was shaking with impetuous rage. *"Enough!"* he shouted.

"Well, well—" Baird began, but Felix waved him off.

"You're *drunk!*" Felix said. "Who are you to speak this way?" He pushed in his chair and started around the table.

"Watch that, *chileño,*" Baird said. "On my honor—"

"Güero, you have no honor!" Felix reached the end of the table and faced Judge Baird. "Forever talking about it, yet the word means nothing to you—*nothing!*"

Baird stepped sideways and hurled his glass, striking Felix below his right eye. Wine splashed across the tablecloth as bright droplets of blood fell onto the floor. Lifting a hand to his face, Felix stood motionless even as Don Carrizo began to bray for his servants. Other guests struggled to separate Baird and Don Carrizo's brother, who'd jumped up and struck a fighting posture.

"Cowards!" Baird taunted, even as he was hustled toward the door. "Nothin' but cockalorum!"

Don Carrizo grabbed a heavy silver candlestick and brandished it like a club. *"Get out, now!* Martín, get in here! Tircio, bring me my pistols!"

Scowling at Louisa, Baird clutched at the doorframe. "Sibley's Brigade *will* effect Southern principles here—we cannot be stopped. Tell your husband he'd better run!" Louisa Canby covered her mouth with a napkin.

Eyes burning, his cupped hand welling with blood, Felix glared at Baird. "Watch your back, *güero.*"

"You watch *yours*," Baird hissed as Pelham and others pushed him along a hallway and out into the night.

In the stillness that followed, the hall clock's movements were like the blows of a blacksmith's hammer. Carrizo sat down hard, drained off the last of his wine, and motioned for a refill. Again, he drank it in seconds. Felix's parents went to his side, while Basilio stared morosely at Adria's profile. Someone summoned a doctor.

"Don Carrizo," Manuel Armijo shifted uncomfortably in his chair, "I should go."

"Don Armijo, you've done nothing wrong."

Louisa Canby coughed politely but did not elaborate, and the other guests whispered nervously. Two servants accompanied Felix from the room while others cleared away the broken glass and stained linens.

Regaining his composure, the don smiled. "Ladies and gentlemen, let no more of this evening be stolen—may fellowship and fair conversation restore that which was taken. Everyone, please finish your desserts. Please." No one did. The don rose from his chair and motioned to a servant for another refill. *You jackass, Baird, you have ruined my evening!* "Pray, friends," he said quietly, "forgive me for inviting such a brute."

"Not your fault," someone said.

"He's a beast," Ramon Ortiz agreed. "There's nothing you could have done."

"Still, I hope you will forgive my poor judgment and stay—we mustn't let tonight end this way, and I have some important news that I'd like to share. What say we settle our nerves before returning to the *sala*, no? Ladies, my sister-in-law will entertain in the parlor—gentlemen, let's retire to the billiards room."

⁓

On the far side of an awkward half-hour, the remaining guests returned to the hacienda's largest room. Carrizo himself stood against a wall with Basilio on his right and his daughter seated on his left. "Ladies and gentlemen," he began, "thank you for coming tonight—and for staying. Your presence honors us—to have so many dear friends is a blessing. Thank you, everyone, thank you!"

Despite their subdued feelings, the guests clapped politely.

"As many of you know," the don continued, "this coming spring, Adria turns seventeen. With each passing year, more and more she favors my dear Irinea, God rest her soul." Many around the room blessed themselves at the mention of Adria's mother, deceased more than a decade.

Feeling ill, Adria gulped and fought to keep from crying. Though she and the don never spoke about money, she'd overheard enough to know that the family's finances were unsound, heard that her father had mortgaged his businesses and borrowed heavily to purchase land up and down the Rio Grande valley, and that with the Confederacy poised to overrun the territory, creditors were calling in loans nearly as fast as new ones could be secured. Indeed, she guessed that she was bring paired off with Basilio Ortiz more for economic reasons than social reasons ones and the prospect appalled her: saying no meant incurring her father's wrath, yet saying yes to a hapless, colorless— chinless—*terrón* was nearly as painful to imagine. She did not love him; she could not *imagine* loving him. His confrontation of Baird notwithstanding, in her mind he would forever be the peaked, awkward boy she'd known since childhood. She rose unsteadily from her chair and placed one hand on the backrest for balance.

"Adria—," Don Carrizo smiled, "—be seated."

Conditioned by years of obedience, she sat and let her hands drop into the ruffles of her blue silk dress. She saw Louisa Canby looking at her with kind eyes, and this embarrassed her so deeply that she quickly looked away. She felt as if she were drowning. *Control yourself.*

Servants began carrying trays of champagne through the crowd. The don took a glass and raised it. "A toast!" He turned to his right. "Now, if Basilio Ortiz—"

Even though her legs still shook, this time Adria rose and walked away. Even as her father called once, twice, neither did she stop nor hesitate until she was well beyond the guests' startled whispers.

Carrizo motioned sharply for Benéfica. "Lock her door and do not let her leave." The old woman departed, and the *hacendado* turned to face his astonished guests. "I am so very sorry," he said and bowed to the Ortizes. "The unpleasantness earlier was more than my daughter could bear—please forgive her."

"Of course, Don Carrizo." Ramon Ortiz smiled, though the don knew that he was far from happy. "With all that's happened tonight, small wonder she's upset."

"*Gracias,* Don Ortiz." Again, Carrizo raised his glass but having nothing to toast, instead he bid his guests farewell. "Friends, thank you for coming tonight. *Gracias,* one and all."

Stunned by the party's abrupt conclusion, the guests looked at one another in bewilderment before starting toward the exit.

Returned with a large plaster across his face, Felix Ortiz said nothing and elbowed his way past his older brother. While Basilio escorted his mother toward the door, Ramon Ortiz lingered for a moment, his thoughts a turbid mess. *What to do? What now?* Adria Carrizo was a beautiful girl, certainly, but it was less clear whether she was fit to be their son's wife or a mother to his children. *So young and headstrong—she may be too much for my gentle son to manage.* While her sudden exit had been improvident, the whole evening had been most peculiar, and so he resolved to watch and wait. Rather more troubling, as there was no solution in sight, was Felix's reckless behavior. Brash acts were his hallmark and Ramon was so tired of his second son's conduct that he no longer bothered to conceal his preference for the boy's older brother. Even so, at that moment, *none* of these things were his biggest worry: for although such feats weren't normally attempted in winter, with Texans surging up the Rio Grande, only that afternoon he'd ordered his *caballeros* to begin moving his immense beef-herds away from the Rio Grande east to pastures along the Pecos River. It would cost a fortune, of course, but Mother Mary! Otherwise, those gray-coated locusts would strip him clean—*they'll take everything!* Glowering at the thought, he started after his wife.

In another corridor nearby, Don Carrizo reached out to steady himself on an ornate, gilded chair. *What a disaster!* And so much hung in the balance—*everything, really.* While some unhappiness on Adria's part understandable, he could not permit her to make him look like a fool. Emotions were luxuries; this was business. Perhaps she was too young to grasp the full breadth of his problems, but vowed to make her understand the necessity of an alliance with the Ortizes. Circumstance had limited their options—hers as well as his—and this was something she would simply have to accept. *My own daughter—by God, no one can deny me!* It was late, however, and he needed to say good-bye to a few remaining guests. He glanced in a mirror, made certain his clothes and hair were tidy, and nodded to his own reflection. Then he spotted one of Adria's hair combs on the table and scowled. *Acting like that when I have given you everything—everything! Enough. Come daylight, hija, there will be hell to pay.*

Confederate Encampment, Old Fort Thorn, New Mexico Territory, January 17, 1862

Sunrise at the shore and the sea, sky, and sand were all yellow. Palm trees and sea oats rustling in the breeze. Jacob stood beside his wife and looked out over the water while their daughter played. He turned, waded into the tall grass alone, and emerged on a street crowded with oxcarts and fishmongers. Matamoros. Foolhardy, given the climate in those days, but so what? No one had bested him yet.

Racial tensions had been high ever since Juan Cortina's men had taken bloody revenge on Brownsville's white residents for abuses—real and perceived—committed against the area's Mexican residents. Arson, shootings, and stabbings had been commonplace that summer, but because Jacob was young and this unrest had not affected him directly, he'd thought himself invincible and gone about routines as usual.

His employer had sent him across the border with a saddle in need of repair, because everyone knew that the best saddlewrights lived on the Mexican side of the river. Problem was, as far as Jacob believed, no one in Mexico was ever in any hurry, and so he'd waited for hours just to get an estimate of the work's cost. *Jesus, these people!* Of course, he'd been drinking some and so he began to look for trouble, as was his habit at that time. Inside a storeroom, he'd noticed an odd leather sack tucked carefully behind a box and was surprised at its weight. *Silver—my word, there is almost two-hundred dollars in here!* He'd retrieved the saddle—still broken and leaning against a sawhorse—and stepped out onto the streets of Matamoros. He'd near to made the plank-bridge when the saddler's oldest son caught up and tried to stop him. That time he'd fought his way clear, but it wasn't more than a few days before the son—emboldened by Juan Cortina's raids—went to find where Jacob lived. Too drunk that night to resist, he had lain in a ditch and watched as they broke the windows and lobbed torches inside. Unable to save their daughter, Sarah had emerged, inconsolable, her hands and arms horribly burned. The heat drove Jacob to his knees and he could do nothing except watch as gray ash floated down like dirty snow.

～

Heart pounding, joints stiff and sore from sleeping cold, Jacob startled awake. The stitched-up cut on his shoulder throbbed. Disoriented, it took him several moments to recognize where he was. Others began to stir; out in the scrub a cricket chirped. Disjointed thoughts drifted in and out of his head. *Please, God, take away this pain.* He rose from his bedroll and went about his business. Months earlier, he would lie abed and catalogue his regrets—the things he had done or had failed to do—but not that morning: there were duties to perform and a schedule to keep. He collected his gear and urged the others to hurry and do the same. He doused their fire with a bucket of dirty water. *This eternal grief.*

Later, after ten miles and a stop for weak coffee, Jacob remembered his dream. *The one perfect thing in my life—the only thing—and she is dead because of me. Forgive me, Angel.* He pulled the brim of his gray forage cap all the way down to his eyebrows and spit in the dust. As far as he could see, there was nothing ahead but miles and miles of empty desert.

He shouted for the others to re-form ranks.

PART TWO

❧

A SKY SO FOUL

Confederate Encampment along the Journada del Muerto, New Mexico Territory

———————

6 Jan., 1862—Three kills at Atarque Station: Mexicans all—counterfeit Yankees. Odd: I feel nothing much—no vengeance, satisfaction, guilt. A little of each and others still, but nothing particular. Nothing redemptive—merely a job, like raking leaves. Thought I'd be fretful, before and after, but wasn't. Spirits lifted knowing that I am still alive, but now that we are back on the trail I feel spent. Shoulder hurts badly tonight. The First Asst. Surgeon prescribes whiskey, which I give to Briggs—I am done with liquor. The pain is cleansing and my troubles are small: Dan Milton, wounded in the skirmish on Jan. 4, died of his wounds and as his captain, I hold myself somewhat to blame. No doubt he is with Jesus, just as he believed. We left First Lt. Simmons and others (smallpox, consumption, &c.) to rest and heal in Rincon, a ragged, one-horse town squatting at the foot of a dark red cinder hill. Our speed must increase if we are to have any hope of achieving our goals.

10 Jan., 1862—Ten mi. of dry, sandy track, but we had to raise and lower the wagons over too many washouts to count. Skies the color of a bruise, but no snow. Col. Green called me aside after supper and we spoke briefly—friendly talk. He is considerable of a man and done much: lawyer, legislator, soldier. I had nothing nearly so interesting to say, of course, but he was polite about that. Inquired in a roundabout way about doings in Matamoros but didn't push and I did not volunteer overmuch. Don't even want to think about that, nonetheless talk about it.

15 Jan., 1862—Ten mi. again. Made our diggings beside a dry creek bed, but overnight a storm dumped so much sleet and rain that it flooded violently, washed away three wagons, and drown'd several mules. Every-body safe, though. Come daylight all that water sank right down into the sand, leaving us as cold and dry as ever.

20 Jan., 1862—<u>Much</u> colder and the rain has turned into snow. Stayed in camp all day. Carpenters rebuilt two damaged wagons, but we had to abandon several others that were beyond repair. Cleaned weapons, smoked and slept all afternoon. My horse has thrown a shoe. Three members of F Co. are missing—deserted, presumably.

21 Jan., 1862— Indians drove off fifty head of our cattle just after midnight. Two companies from the Seventh gave chase, but achieved nothing. Barely eight mi. to-day—very muddy. Dead animals at regular intervals beside the trail. Cold supper, as our mess cook could not fight the rain and snow. Wretched country.

Está viniendo
(IT IS COMING)

Santa Fe, New Mexico Territory,
January 24, 1862

Don Carrizo sat slumped behind his ornate desk, smoking. He stared morosely at the papers spread before him—bills and demands for payment, mostly—aware that the safe behind him contained but nine hundred dollars cash money. Even the inkpot on his desk was dry.

There was a knock at the door and Nestor, his ancient servant, leaned inside. "Felix Ortiz—shall I show him in?"

The *hacendado* gave a curt wave and the younger of the two Ortiz boys strode into the room. Dust fell from his riding coat and his boots thudded on the tile floor. "Nestor!" the don barked.

"*Sí?*"

"His coat."

The servant took the offending garment from Ortiz and backed outside.

Don Carrizo stubbed out his cigarillo and studied Felix: depthless black eyes (the right one of which was purple, swollen, and underlined by two inches of stitchery) and a faint moustache made him look older than he was, but it was an angry set to his jaw that added ten full years. Most presumed the boy was in his late twenties instead of eighteen. He was considerably taller than his older brother, Basilio, with stronger features and a much sturdier frame, and long ago, the don had judged him the more useful.

The don gestured toward a heavy upholstered chair and Felix sat while he took a key from the top desk drawer and opened the Day & Newell Parautoptic safe—a massive, cast-iron thing that had cost him princely sums to freight in from St. Louis. "I want you to go through Peralta to Rancho La Rinconada."

"*¿Abajo de Los Lunas?*"

"You know this place?" Carrizo studied his own knuckles, covered with scratches.

"Papi and I stopped there some years ago."

Carrizo looked pleased. "One of the old grants. Its *hacendado,* Don Luis, is ill and has no heirs. He agreed to sell me his share but his wretched cousin, Jorge, will not cooperate."

"Jorge Luis? The pederast?"

Carrizo raised an eyebrow. "Where did you hear that?"

"I was told to avoid him while we were there—was I misinformed?"

"No... No."

Felix sneered. "Papi says old Jorge is a heretic, too."

"There you are misinformed: the reason he wants the property for himself is so that he may give it to the Church and steal his way into heaven. A perfect waste, of course, when I have an anxious buyer in Missouri. Felix, why does everyone try and cheat me out of what is mine?"

"Don Carrizo, I do not know..." the boy faltered.

"Don't answer." The don exhaled. "No one does. But it is harder to sell a thing if first one does not have it—not impossible, but harder, certainly. This is why I am sending you south."

Felix exhaled heavily through his nostrils. "What would you have me do?"

"*¿Están sus hombres listos?*"

"*Sí.* A week from Sunday, Sílo will take two companies to Fort Craig, but I will remain *Rio Arriba* with the third company as a home guard."

"Then you have time. Select men you trust, but fewer than ten," Carrizo said, noting the pistol tucked into the young man's belt. "Tell them Pino or Canby has ordered you out on a reconnaissance—"

Felix sucked against his teeth. "How will I make them believe that?"

"They don't have to, *hijo*—you're an Ortiz." The don counted out fifty dollars and swept it into a leather sack, which he tossed across the desk. *"Por tí."* Then the don counted out more gold dollars and bagged these separately. *"Por los otros.* Now, listen carefully." The don laid out a simple plan. In truth, any of his hirelings could have done the job, but he saw these assignments as a means of binding the boy to his will, and very soon, there would be a great deal more that needed doing. "As I said," Carrizo concluded, "Don Luis is without heirs, so we must do this before his will is re-written and Jorge inherits everything. You will receive five percent of the final sale to do with as you wish."

"Peralta's three days' ride," Felix complained.

"And two thousand dollars is near to Governor Connolly's annual salary."

"Lo siento, Don Carrizo." Chastened, Felix stood and bowed. "Forgive me."

"Basilio may be the first son, Felix, but you are the better man. Remember, *hijo*, I was second, too. In due time you will have everything he's been promised."

"Gracias, Don Carrizo—I won't let you down." Eyes blazing, the young man bowed and went out.

For several minutes after, the don stared through the window and thought of a million small things and nothing particular: letters he needed to write, the weather, and, unaccountably, his deceased wife's smile—though he quickly banished this memory before it overwhelmed him. He sighed and closed the safe. He worried whether he might be placing too much trust in Felix, and then he worried that the Texans might advance too quickly. He grimaced. Throughout the territory, uncertainty covered all things and no one—not even he—could know what things, if any, that God might permit to endure.

Santa Fe, New Mexico Territory, January 25, 1862

Louisa Canby chanced to see Adria Carrizo as their carriages passed on the Camino de Olmos. "Adria, so very good to see you!" Louisa called, and she meant it. "It's only been a week, yet it feels much longer. Are you going into town?"

"No, ma'am—to my cousin, Joséfa's."

At first when Adria directed her driver to stop, he objected (only the day before, the don had decreed that Adria was not permitted to speak with anyone except family), but since Louisa was a familiar face and they were safely away from the main roads, he complied.

Louisa stepped down from her carriage and went over to the girl's runabout. When Adria smiled and leaned down for a hug, her movements were noticeably stiff. Moreover, Louisa saw bruises that the girl had tried to cover with mineral powders. "Señorita," Lousia said, "may we speak in private?"

Again, the driver objected, but Adria said something in Spanish and he promptly helped her alight. As the two women walked a short distance ahead, for several moments neither of them spoke.

At last, Louisa collected her convulsive thoughts. "Adria, are you in danger?"

Deeply ashamed, Adria said that she was not. *You can do nothing*.

Had she known Adria's mind, Louisa would have disagreed strenuously. Many years before, the Canbys had lost their only child, Mary, and since arriving in Santa Fe, they had adopted Adria in their hearts as their own. While the don did not appreciate the Canbys' attentions, because of their social standing, he tolerated them, and the girl visited the couple frequently. "If you need somewhere to go—" Louisa began, but Adria cut her short.

"Mrs. Canby, please—this looks like more than it is."

"I do not—"

"Nothing you can do will help—just the opposite, in fact."

"Adria!"

"*Please,* Mrs. Canby! There is nothing you can do—nothing! You *must* understand!"

"Adria, this is wretchedness and I am *most* unhappy."

"Do you promise?"

"I do *not*—if I see the need, Adria, I will bring all that I can to bear. You are *always* welcome in my home—*always.*"

"Thank you." The girl wiped at the corners of her eyes. "Not yet." She nodded and stopped to wait for her vehicle to catch up.

A minute later, her driver stepped down to help her up into her seat. Louisa noticed that the man would not look her in the eye, which made her even angrier. With kind words and promises to visit each other soon, the women parted. As the girl's carriage rolled away, Louisa waved. She waited until it was out of sight before shedding tears. *This sordid world!* Then she climbed back into her own vehicle and her driver flicked the reins. For the remainder of her errand she ground her teeth together and thought a hundred ways to separate Adria from her father. Even in town, where she ran into several people she knew, her expression remained grim, as befit someone whose loved ones were squarely in harm's way.

Confederate Encampment along the Journada del Muerto, New Mexico Territory

Jacob pushed through sea grass with the barrel of a shotgun. The wind was up. *Hombres* seated around a roaring fire, sharing *un bote*. They raised their hands in surrender but nothing could stop him—not protests from his fellows, not even bloody hands clutching at his legs. The Mexicans begged for mercy but he reloaded and executed them all. Other Texans—even the hardest among them—cast troubled looks and thereafter give him a wide berth. "What has happened to Jacob?" they whispered. Nearby, buildings burned so fiercely that the moon and stars were blotted from the sky.

He continued dreaming, and though his sleep was fitful, he couldn't wrench himself awake. Then came something else—something new...

Mid-morning beneath a flowering tree, his baby girl in his arms. She reached out and ran her tiny fingers over the white blossoms; sunlight filtered down through the leaves. He could smell the sweet blossoms and his baby's hair. "Dearest," he whispered and she laughed and rested a tiny hand on the side of his face.

๑

He awoke, rubbed his eyes, and saw that it was not yet light. Grains of sand were stuck to the side of his face. On the other side of camp a bugle sounded. As others pulled on boots and rolled up blankets, he remembered where he was. Cold wind slapped his face. *Still here.*

Stiff and sore. Cold wind, cold coffee. No luck.

Assemble, fellows—quickly now.

Quickly.

๑

10 Feb., 1862—Ours is one of four companies sent to secure traces east of the mountains while the rest of the brigade follows the river-road. At intervals couriers cross the intervening range to apprise each of the others' progress and four days ago Briggs and I made one such ride over a high, rugged pass. Our main column resembles nothing so much as an inchworm (and not merely for its lack of speed): movement occurs in spurts, and the front cannot seem to advance unless the rear is nearby. Various units and our animal herds are forever raveling and unraveling, requiring greater expenditures of time and energy than the paltry distances covered ought. Apaches pick off the stragglers, man and beast alike. That said, I would rather that our unit was among those that are following the river. At least the Rio Grande gathers life to its banks—ducks, teals, egrets, beaver, &c.—while we transect a landscape of desolation. This is the worst place imaginable: severe mtns. above a loathsome desert plain, the pink soil of which supports only greasewood, prickly-pear cactus, and a type of grass that our livestock cannot eat. Four men from Kirksey's E company, Seventh Rgt., have deserted. The wound on my shoulder is beginning to heal.

11 Feb., 1862—Off before dawn and camped by 3 o' the afternoon. Set pickets, as we are nearer Fort Craig and have seen Yankee scouts. Haas is gravely ill and may not live out the night. To-day we ate the last of the corn we took from a farmer's *granja* back in Doña Ana and though we do what we can to supplement rations, my weight is off considerable.

12 Feb., 1862—Can now say that I have been in a bona-fide blizzard. At least we were encamped: the Fourth & Seventh marched all night to join us here; now none of these frostbitten arrivals will venture more than 10 feet from their fires. Buried E.R. Haas this a.m. on a snowy hillside overlooking a plain of boulders: a lonely place to wait out Judgment. Small skirmish near the river. Lt. Col. Scurry's men exchanged shots with a force of New Mexican volunteers and our scouts captured 21 of them. We are unimpressed wi. these greasers' stuff, as they break and run after a volley or two. They appear anxious merely to get away and so we can only conclude

that they are not the Yankee's natural allies. After supper the Gen., Col. Green, &c., awarded promotions. With poor Simmons still in Rincon wi. the pox, Briggs Hardy is our new First Lieutenant, acting, and on the second ballot, the boys elected Eli Fisher our First Sgt.

13 Feb., 1862—Col. Green recalled us over the mountains wi. orders to lead a foraging party at Paraje farms to-morrow. Will take the Guards plus a detachment of Phillips' Brigands. These fellows call themselves the 'Santa Fe Gamblers,' which grates on my nerves. Blowhards, every one. We have had nothing but trouble wi. them since Mesilla, where three of their number beat and killed a Jew merchant who refused to sell them brandy.

Village of Paraje Fra Cristobal, New Mexico Territory, February 14, 1862

From the start, the Texans' raid was a disaster. With Jacob's company on a bad trail, Junior Walsh and his squad of Brigands took advantage of their absence and assaulted nearly everyone they met. By the time the Cameron Guards backtracked and reached the village, two buildings were on fire and panic was in the air.

Jacob grabbed Junior's arm and spun him around. "Hey—"

Junior brushed off the restraint. "Where'd he go? That boy took it!"

Seeing no boy, Jacob tried to catch his breath. "Took *what*— what do you mean?"

While Jacob's men forcibly restrained other Brigands from torching a third structure, Junior ran to a wall, leaned over it and pointed. "There he goes—little bastard's got a map!"

Seeing a figure in the shadows, Eli Fisher gave chase but almost immediately tripped over another small body lying in the weeds. "Lord Jesus," he muttered before shouting to the others.

From a hillside above town, a musket cracked and one of the Brigands wailed in anguish.

"Get down!" Jacob shouted, "Fish—go 'round the barn! Briggs, find that shooter!" Another bullet buried itself in the adobe wall behind him. Village residents—mostly women and children—ran everywhere, screaming and clutching their belongings. Briggs Hardy nearly collided with a woman and her infant, but as he reached out to steady her, she screamed, swatted his hand, and ducked inside a doorway. Some in Jacob's company dove for cover; others fired in the direction of the last muzzle flash. "Go!" Jacob ran across the open plaza, pulling his men by their collars. "Shit, *go!* Get out of the light!"

Flames lapped at the large barn's sides and the mules inside screamed. Hardy unbarred a door and a torrent of panicked animals broke free, forcing soldiers to leap out of the way lest they be trampled. Taking advantage of this confusion, the lieutenant grabbed a dozen men and scrambled counter to the herd, into the nearest field, and emerged at the edge of a barren peach orchard. Crawling some fifty yards, they found themselves behind a pair of figures lying in the tall grass at the edge of a dry ditch. Hardy waved three others forward. At the sound of rustling chaff one of the figures turned, though not fast enough, and a Texan clubbed him from behind. The other shadow rose and tried to run before it was tackled and pinned down, too. There was an anguished cry in Spanish and the two soldiers began to shout.

"Jake!" Hardy called, "We got 'em!"

᥿

A few minutes later, Jacob dusted off. "Fish, check every house, every building—no more surprises." Fisher departed.

Bloodied and bruised, an old Mexican man and a boy of about thirteen were marched (or, in the case of the old man, dragged, as the Texans had broken one of his legs) onto the plaza and made to lie face-down next to the well.

"That's the one!" Junior spat. He and the Brigands—even men from Jacob's company—began to call for the pair's execution.

Charlie Spence pointed as the wounded Brigand, delirious with pain, was lifted into a wagon. "Cap'n, look what they did!"

"Can't let it stand!" George Orth seconded.

"Quiet," Jacob ordered. "They're gonna talk first." With a deafening roar, half of the burned-out barn collapsed. Flurries of sparks washed over the Texans and some even had to beat and swat at the embers that caught in their clothes.

᥿

Eli Fisher's detail returned with two bodies and laid them out on the plaza. Both were young, no more than eleven or twelve, and shot point-blank in the back—one's coat even had flash burns on it. As soon as the old man saw them, he began to weep.

Jacob ground his molars in frustration. "Lord, we came here for *hay*! Who the hell started shooting?"

Fisher pointed at one of the bodies. "There's the one I tripped over."

"Someone speak up," Jacob demanded and the plaza went quiet. He searched the Brigands' faces. "Come on, now!"

Several moments later, José Garza stepped forward. "Junior shot 'em, Sir."

೧০

All four Brigands gave conflicting accounts (the fifth, whose left elbow had been smashed by a musket ball, was in such pain that Jacob discounted his ravings as worthless; four hours later a surgeon would amputate his arm below the shoulder). It took near ten minutes for Jacob to learn either that the old man and his boys had approached with hands raised or that they had attacked without provocation. Every Brigand called for the old fellow's prompt dispatch, yet none struck Jacob as especially trustworthy. His unease grew with every word they said.

"Don't think we can just execute the ol' compadre," Eli whispered.

"Maybe we can."

"Jesus, Jake, don't take up that burden—let Dad Green or Baylor decide."

Jacob pondered their situation. "Can't wait until then."

In large measure, the Brigands represented the territory's worst element: rustlers, thieves and barroom brawlers who saw the Confederate invasion as a chance to raise hell without fear of the consequences. Junior Walsh, for one, was an ugly brute who had robbed and murdered a teamster in Mesilla (for which crime a Mexican laborer had been falsely accused, tried, and executed). As well, many of the others were violence-prone and capable of senseless cruelty, which made followers like Garza equally dangerous.

From the things he'd heard them say, Jacob recognized their type (and not a little of himself), and with every contradiction his frustration increased. "Stop!" he said at last. "This is going nowhere. Briggs, haul the amigo to his feet—call him to account."

"He's gonna lie!" Junior bawled.

"Quiet."

"That's what *pelados* do! Won't get no answers—"

"Speak again," Jacob snapped, "and you'll wish you hadn't! Eli, come with me—I need your Spanish." Hardy cleared the square so that Jacob and Eli Fisher could question the captives without interruption. Across the plaza, another building collapsed and swarms of embers scurried before the wind about like frightened mice.

❧

Following a brief conversation, Fisher relayed that the old man was *alcalde*, or mayor, of a village across the river, visiting family; that when they returned from their family's sheep-camp they had been surprised by Anglo soldiers; and that in the course of being searched, it'd been discovered that one of the boys was carrying a map of the Texans' encampment.

"Ask him why they shot at our men."

"No, no—*todo es mentira,*" the old man wheezed.

"What's that?"

"Said that ain't true."

"Who, then?"

"Los otros."

"Others, sure. Whose boys are these?" Jacob eyed the shivering teenager.

Eli relayed the question. "*Nietos*—his grandsons."

Jacob winced. "The Brigands say his boys mapped our diggings. Does he still have the map?"

Eli put this question to the old man and paraphrased his lengthy reply: "Says a Yankee sympathizer from a town upriver paid the boys to sketch our camp. Once he found out he told the boy to destroy it, but this was right before Junior and the others ambushed 'em."

"Search their clothes." Neither was carrying anything; the dead boys' pockets were empty as well. "Where's the map?"

"Says the big Anglo took it. That would be Junior, certainly."

"Certainly would." Jacob said. "Junior, get your ass over here!"

Even before he was halfway across the plaza, Junior began to yell. "What'd he say? He's *lying*, goddammit!"

"Junior, shut up. Y'all don't even know what he said."

"Can't trust 'em, Sir. Until you've lived with 'em, you can't know what they're like."

"Lived with 'em for years, Junior. Now, where's that map? *Compadre* says you took it from him and so did your buddies."

"Don't have it."

Jacob and Eli exchanged looks. "Come again?"

"Lost it in the confusion, I guess. I don't know, honest."

"A minute ago you said the boy took it." Jacob beckoned to one of his soldiers. "Charlie, watch Junior."

"What for?" Junior bristled.

"Garza—"

"Garza's *lying!*"

"Junior, so help me," Jacob threatened.

"Jesus—they're fuckin' *pelados*, Cap'n! Ain't worth nothin' to us!"

"Who controls the food 'round here, stupid? General Sibley ordered us to leave 'em alone." Jacob pulled Fisher aside for a conference. "What do you make of this?"

"A plumb mess, Jake." Eli scratched the back of his hand. "Don't know what to tell you."

At that moment, Hardy arrived carrying an old flintlock musket. "Found this in the grass by the *'cequia*. There was a man's jacket, too, and a water-bag and the weeds are all mashed down like someone was layin' there—think we missed some others."

Eli questioned the old man who conceded that the whole village had turned out when the Brigands arrived, believing that they were bandits or Indian raiders.

Jacob kicked at a tuft of grass. "Then we can't say for certain that *amigo* or his littles shot at us."

"Pretty clear they didn't," Hardy countered. "Their weapons are still loaded—this one's been fired."

Eli glanced over his shoulder. "What's with Junior, then?"

Jacob gritted his teeth. "Damn it, I hate this." He went to where the Mexicans lay, cut the ties from the don and his surviving grandson's wrists, and motioned for them to sit up. Jacob squatted on his heels and looked into the man's eyes. Though his face was tear-streaked and dirty, he returned the Texan's stare. In silence, the two men studied each other until Jacob reached out and took the old man's wrist, drawing his hand forward and rotating it so that the Mexican's palm faced up. The old man winced, but with his free hand Jacob reached into a small bag slung from his belt, retrieved four gold coins and placed them in the old man's hand. The man stared blankly at the money, bewildered. "Fish, ask him his name."

"Sena," was the answer.

"Tell Don Sena that I'm deeply sorry for his grandsons' deaths— tell him I'd give him more but that's all I got."

"Honest?"

"Exactly that. Tell him this is my fault—I should've controlled these fellows; tell him I'm sorry." Eli looked unhappy but knelt and relayed the information as Jacob walked toward the plaza's center.

❧

Half of Jacob's company started for camp while Eli Fisher led the others on a second sweep around the village's northern limits.

"Briggs!" Jacob called, "bring 'em over." The lieutenant marched three Brigands forward, pausing to kick at a stray dog that nipped his boot. "Hand your muskets to the sergeant."

"What's this?" Junior huffed but the others complied.

"Knives, pistols—anythin' else," Spence said. Then he paused. "Wait, where's Garza?"

Junior glared at another Brigand, who glanced nervously toward the burning barn. "He run home," the boy said.

"Say again?" Jacob stared, incredulous.

"Junior said he was gonna kill him, so he ran. José's family lives up north, *Rio Arriba*, so like as not that's where he'll go."

"The provost can deal with him later," Jacob said. "Y'all move out."

"Yeah?" Junior scoffed. "You gonna let the greasers off?"

"Shut up," Jacob said.

"What'd I do?"

"Disobeyed orders, set fire to property, murdered children—wanna add to the list?"

"You're takin' a Mexican's word over a white man's?"

"His made sense."

"Won't suit the boys, Cap'n—gold ribbon on your sleeve don't give you the right to put on airs." Jacob stepped forward and stood squarely in front of the Brigand. At almost six-foot, five-inches tall, Junior towered over Jacob, yet Junior took a step backward. "Won't suit 'em," Junior complained. "Shot two white men and you let him go—you let him *go!*"

"That's enough!" Jacob clenched his teeth but Junior wouldn't stop.

"You did the same thing to them Mexicans in Brownsville, you hypocrite. Ain't no different the way I see it—"

"You shut your mouth!" Jacob drew his revolver, jammed the barrel under Junior's chin, and pressed so that the Brigand had to backpedal to keep from choking. His teeth clattered together as his back struck the wall.

"Yeah, we heard about you," Junior wheezed. Breath hissed from his nostrils and his lips parted to reveal stained, ragged teeth. "Gonna shoot me, too?"

Jacob cocked the hammer, pressed harder, and lifted Junior's chin. Sick with fury, Jacob's pulse pounded in his head. He could see veins bulging in the Brigand's neck. After an age, he lowered his weapon. Junior moved away and felt gingerly along his throat. Jacob motioned with the revolver. "Go."

The sullen Brigands shuffled away and stood in line against a weather-beaten coyote fence.

"Don't mind him," Hardy told Jacob.

"He's right, though."

"No, he *ain't,*" Spence insisted.

"We'll march 'em back." Hardy said. "Think you'd best wait until Fish comes 'round."

༄

Waiting in the dark for Eli's patrol to return, Jacob watched flames reflecting off the river's glassy surface. Behind him, the last of the huge barn's walls collapsed and the fire rapidly lost its intensity. *Son-of-a-bitch is right,* he thought.

By dawn, a mound of smoldering ash was all that remained of the barn. Despite its want, the structure was never rebuilt.

Fort Craig, New Mexico Territory, February 16, 1862

Fort Craig stood on flat terrain immediately west of the Rio Grande, 150 miles north of the Mexican border. Northern vistas were dominated by the streaked sides of Mesa Contadero—a volcanic plug on the valley's floor that forced the river into a C-shaped diversion around its base. Leafless willows and cottonwoods lined the brown river; nearer to the fort, nothing grew except cholla and greasewood. It was a miserable place for miserable events and the weather that morning fit the setting: despite the cold sunshine, an arctic wind howled across the plain and covered everything with alkali grit. The fort itself— fifteen acres of low stone and adobe buildings—was nestled into a wide, shallow basin and hard to see from a distance. A steep-faced earthen wall with sixteen-foot waysides and a wide, steep-sided ditch at its foot surrounded it. This angled architecture provided protection from low-caliber artillery and allowed Federal defenders to cover every approach with massed muskets. Gun emplacements bristled with artillery pieces; additional "Quaker guns" made from lengths of painted cottonwood gave the illusion of even greater strength.

Approaching in the pre-dawn darkness the Texans had first believed the fort abandoned. Colonel Canby kept his entire Federal force hidden inside and the Rebels halted their casual advance only after a U.S. flag was raised above the battlements. The Federals assumed an all-out assault was imminent but Col. Green was afraid that the fort's defenses would devastate any approach across open ground. After several hours of nervous posturing, neither side could draw the other out, so their officers went forward to parley.

e◦

On stony flats south of the fort, battle flags and white banners flut-tered wildly, stiffened by a cold wind. Colonel Tom Green packed his jaw with chewing tobacco and he spat carefully to keep from spat-tering his gray wool coat. Beside him rode Maj. Samuel Lockridge, Maj. Frederick Metzger, and two privates—one bearing a white flag, the other the Texans' red banner with a single white star.

"Anyone know what Canby looks like?" Green shouted as they cantered north. None did but all took it on faith that he was among the approaching Federal delegation, also bearing white flags and battle pennants.

"Vexilla regis prodeunt inferni," said Metzger, recalling a line from Dante, though none of the others heard.

Near a shallow gully, Green signaled for the others to halt while he rode ahead. From the north, a single blue-clad cavalry officer did likewise. Despite the morning's adrenalized tension, Green felt very well, confident that either by negotiation or force Fort Craig would be in Confederate hands by nightfall. His Union counterpart even noticed the grin on his face as he neared.

Green studied his opponent's insignia, puzzled. "Edward Canby?"

"Captain David Brotherton, Fifth Infantry, U.S. Army. Mister, your actions here are unlawful—"

"Stop," Green said, "go get Canby."

"Colonel Canby will not meet with you. You and yours must remove downriver and quit this territory immediately." Green's face grew so red that Brotherton had to bite his lip to keep from laughing. "Taking up arms against the United States government is an act of treason, but you may depart in peace—"

"I will *not* forget this lack or respect," Green seethed.

"Nor will this nation forgive yours. Ownership of this fort isn't up for negotiation."

"Our terms—"

"Mister, we reject your terms—all of 'em."

"You're gonna regret that." Green's voice took on a decided edge. "Run, tell Canby that we *will* take this place and that we will show no mercy once we do!"

Brotherton didn't immediately reply, but seeing the Texan unhinged—seeing their antagonists just as vexed and weary as they were—made him feel better. Over previous weeks, the captain's imagination had inflated the Texans' abilities to a point that the Federal's odds of survival, let alone success, seemed impossible. In their exchange, however, he had glimpsed the truth: the Texans were not invincible, but mortal men subject to the same vagaries that beset every human endeavor. Recognizing that the rebels had come to negotiate because they doubted their chances of taking Fort Craig by force, he nearly laughed with relief. "The colonel's position is firm," Brotherton said.

Regretting having lost his temper, Green lowered his voice to compensate. "Mister, I'll drop shells in there 'til our barrels melt. See how resolute his stand once those walls crumble."

"We both know you haven't the means."

"Watch your tone." Green spit out a stream of tobacco juice, barely missing the captain.

"Walls here are six feet of adobe mud and basalt block. Our spies tell us that you've nothing but a few twelve-pound smoothbores— take a whole week and all your Dupont just to punch a hole in the stables."

"Listen, boy, we'll deliver all *you* can handle!"

"Can't deliver anything over twelve pounds." Tugging on the reins, Brotherton edged his animal away from the Texan's.

"Insult me again, I will kill you," Green said, resting a hand on his sidearm.

Brotherton readied to draw but kept his voice level: "Every piece inside the fort is pre-sighted to five hundred yards—rifled twenty-fours, twelves, sixes—you wouldn't make it ten yards." Though the Texan bored his eyes into the captain's, Brotherton merely nodded and tugged on his horse's reins. "Pardon me while I go inform the colonel of your decision to leave."

"In two hours I will *level* this place!" Green shouted, fighting a sore temptation to draw his revolver. "And once I'm through I'm gonna hang you from that cottonwood—let the magpies peck out your eyes!"

Brotherton, however, merely tipped his hat and spurred his horse back toward the fort. Green fumed as he watched the Yankee ride north. Unprepared to have his bluff called, he was tormented by a single thought: *Lord, now what?*

෴

Green's staff circled in behind him as the Union officer rode away. They noted the tight set of his jaw and rode in silence for several minutes before any dared to speak. Major Metzger tried first: "Did they agree—"

"No." Green stared straight ahead and guided his horse over the crest of a low ridge. "They did not." He spat out his chaw and wiped a glove on his saddle blanket.

Major Lockridge tried next: "Will we lay in for a siege, Sir? My crews have pieces set in those low hills to the west."

Green slowed his horse to a walk. He looked at the magnificent battle line before him: the Texans' dress was motley, but their banners snapped in the wind and sunlight glinted on polished steel. "Fort's too strong."

As senior artillery officer, Lockridge had been studying how to get ordinance into the fort. "Colonel, we can inflict enough damage that an assault should carry—blast all kinds of holes in those walls."

"No." Green stretched his neck, trying to crack a few vertebrae and relieve the tension that had built up at the base of his skull. "We haven't the time or supplies—we'll find another way."

"Sir—" Lockridge persisted, but already the colonel's mind was elsewhere.

Indeed, Green was so absorbed looking at the fort and its damned flag that he nearly walked his horse into Jacob Stark's. "Good Lord, be careful! I didn't see you there, son!"

Jacob was carrying a dispatch from Gen. Sibley, who lay sleeping in his ambulance, too drunk to command. "Yessir, sorry. Brought you a note from the general's adjutant." After the botched raid at Paraje, Green had generally shunned Jacob; mindful of his abilities, however, that morning he'd relented and let the boy off with a stern reprimand.

Green spat out a loitering thread of tobacco. "You switch sides, Stark?"

"Sir?"

"There's a smart of blue on your back."

Jacob looked at his blue wool broadcloth-jacket with gold ribbon on the sleeves. "Took it off a dead Yankee, Sir. My gray coat's finished and the quartermaster couldn't find me another."

"You and others, too—no matter. Now, pardon me, son." Green turned to Lockridge and Metzger. "Gentlemen, I must speak with Riley and Bill Scurry before we proceed. And the General," he hastened to add. "Jacob, how is he now?"

"Still in his ambulance, Sir."

Green took the paper and scanned its contents before tucking it into his vest pocket. "No great hurry, then. If the Yankees will not fight then they can rot inside that damned fort—reinforcements can blast 'em out later. Lockridge, Metzger, follow me. Stark, go find Col. Sutton and Maj. Pyron—tell 'em they are requested at a junta."

Confederate Encampment near Valverde Ford, New Mexico Territory

17 Feb. 1862—Ystrday noon rec'd orders to withdraw south and cross the river. Disappntmnt pervades, as we are ducking a fight that we are all confident of winning. Late in the afternoon Teel's artillery came down from the hills and suddenly all the cavalry in Yankeedom charged out of Ft. Craig. Our crews unlimbered their guns in a ravine and began whooping and waving them in, looking to murder them wi. canister just as soon as they topped a rise, but at the last minute, the bluecoats reined in and that was all. Maj. Metzger confirms that we will bypass the fort entirely and re-cross the river at Val Verde Ford. Canby can either come out and fight us there or stand pat as we take Albikirkie, Santa Fe, and Colorado. Either way, it is clear his forces are no impediment.

20 Feb. 1862—Camped opposite Fort Craig; scouts say Canby glasses us from the porch of his quarters. Travelled through *bosque* most of the day: many paths meander beneath soaring cottonwood galleries and the going is easy. Elsewhere, tho, we must hack through a witch's broom of dry branches, impassable to animals and those walking upright, and miserable for those who dare to crawl. Poor footing for the livestock, too. Trees all have high-water marks on them, making me very glad we are not here during the spring flood. Pedregal mesas form the eastern bank—lavic stairsteps leading up and away from the river. Frazer's Arizona Rangers hacked a new road onto one such terrace, through a tangle of mesquite brush, and we had to help push and pull each wagon through terrible deep sand. Made camp within sight of the fort. Yankee skirmishers came fwd,

but these were only Mexicans and they broke and fled across the river once our howitzers open'd up—otherwise no action to-day. Dad Green and I spoke again about the debacle in Paraje. Natives now say that we are murderers and thieves, and our ability to trade for resupply has been grievously injured. Green said the Brigands have been nothing but trouble since we left Mesilla and that he should not have allowed Phillips to insist on their participation. Junior Walsh is in irons and what fate awaits him, I do not know; the others were assigned extra duties but otherwise not punished. Thought I might be demoted but wasn't. Lucky. Am resolved to permit no further distractions.

21 Feb. 1862—Jolted awake early this a.m. by an explosion and call to arms. Scouts report that Union raiders forded the river around two a.m. and lashed explosives onto the backs of two mules, wi. a view to stampeding our beef and depriving us of food. Pickets saw the fuses sputtering and said that the mules turned instead and followed the Yanks back to the river, near to killing them. Went to sleep laughing but woke to find that First Regiment's tenders had let half our mules wander down to the river where a Yankee patrol herded them inside their fort. The loss of these animals may severely cripple our speed. Following a quick inventory, we've decided to abandon several wagons-full of tents, blankets, and personal effects.

P.S. After breakfast, we are marching around the Black Mesa to Val Verde Ford. Maj. Pyron reports the road ahead is clear. Either Canby fights us there or we will continue north and cut his supply lines. Despite the cold, excitement is high and morale is excellent. Already I hear companies singing The Texas Ranger and Dixie. Here it is—

Camp Weld, near Denver, Colorado Territory, February 22, 1862

Major John Chivington's mood was black. Governor Gilpin had offered him a chaplain's post in the First Colorado Volunteers but the reverend had refused and instead, despite a lack of military training, insisted on a fighting command. Gilpin responded by appointing Chivington a major. Tasked with the day-to-day administration of the First Colorado, for months he'd struggled to house, equip, and provision the regiment, all without adequate funding from the territorial government. The governor had concocted a scheme to present businesses with warrants and drafts against the U.S. Treasury but many merchants, rightly suspicious of their legality, refused to honor these instruments. This left Chivington with no option except outright seizure.

Most, including one sutler presented with scrip in lieu of cash for tack and saddles, had objected strenuously: "Friend," he complained, "what am I to do with this?"

"How's that?" Chivington replied coldly.

"This paper is worthless!"

"Not if I say otherwise, *friend.*"

"I am unwilling—"

"Look, you may take that paper as an evidence or not but either way we *will* have those goods."

The sutler glanced at the soldiers milling about his store, casually helping themselves to his wares, and realized that the sooner these undisciplined lice left the premises, the sooner his losses would cease. "Very well. Do you know when these might be redeemed?"

"I do not—why don't you write the governor and inquire?"

∽

Tired of these mundanities, Maj. Chivington began to agitate for deployment, believing that Slough was content to remain in Denver indefinitely. He wrote to Maj. Gen. David Hunter, commander of the Union Army Department of Kansas, stating as much and was promptly reprimanded for subverting the chain of command. Embittered, Chivington turned a blind eye to his bored troops' worst predations against nearby towns and farms. Fights between soldiers and citizens—even with the county sheriff (one fight ended with a Firster putting a deputy in a chokehold)—became daily events that consumed more and more of his energies. Weighted down by these frustrations, Chivington conceived of every new difficulty as a Divine test of his resolve.

୭

The major was a large man, standing almost six-foot-five and weighing nearly three hundred pounds. That day he was heavily bundled against the bitter cold with a union suit, two wool shirts, pants, and a light jacket beneath a heavy blue duckcloth coat. He wore extra-heavy mittens and had the ear flaps of his fur-lined hat pulled almost to his shoulders. Completing this tableau, his thick beard and moustache were heavily speckled with frost. "Jesus, show mercy." He patted his horse's shaggy neck and tapped his heels. *"Git!"*

The horse waded through deep snow toward a field where Peter MacInnes, newly commissioned as his company's First Lieutenant, was attempting to lead his fellow miners on a march. "Left side, *close up!*" the boy shouted. "Come away! Together, fellows! *Come on—*"

"Stop!" Chivington bellowed, "where is your captain? Who's leading?"

Peter looked up and saluted. "We're understrength, Sir—it's me 'til one's assigned."

"Who are you?"

"First Lieutenant MacInnes, Sir—Pinebark Independent Company, First Colorado Volunteers."

"Well, for pity's sake, Meekness, *lead!*"

"Aye, Sir." Peter faced his charges and shouted without venom or conviction at Matt Maher, who was out of line and had shouldered his musket incorrectly: "Ye tory! Tighten this rout!"

Chivington watched for a few moments longer before his temper boiled over. "No, stop, *stop!* Stay right where you are. What's the matter with you sloppy Irish turds?" He dismounted and brushed past the flustered MacInnes until he stood opposite Maher. "You, Private, do you know Lieutenant Meekness?"

"Sir?"

"You knew each other before you enlisted?"

"Pete MacInnes, Sir? Aye—well afore."

"Thought so." Chivington scratched his beard and glared at Peter.

"Sir—" Peter tried but the major cut him short.

"Be *quiet!* Boys, this is not Central City, Boston, or Ireland! I don't care how you knew each other previously because you are soldiers now—nothing more. Not friends, cousins, neighbors—*soldiers! My* soldiers! Meekness is *my* soldier, too, though he is failing you! He still believes that you are drinking buddies out for a walk and that soon you will return to the whorehouses up in the mountains. Well, lace up your boots, boys, because you are about to face men who mean to put bayonets between your ribs! If you fail to learn what you must, then you will *die!* Meekness should be teaching you discipline, order, precision, yet all I see are sloppy lines and this—*this* one fully three feet out of step, with his musket held incorrectly! Lord, have mercy! Because Meekness has failed you, needs be that I must step in and teach you myself!" Peter's face went bright red. Chivington was famous in Denver for his fiery sermons, audible for blocks around his church, and he began to scream with Old Testament fervor. *"See this?"* He confronted Matt Maher and waved his right hand. *"This,* dunderhead, is *right!* Over here, on the other side of my body, is *left!* Do you understand the difference?"

Maher, who was not an idiot, nevertheless grew flustered. "Right, S-S-Sir, and left," he stammered, getting it exactly backward.

"No!" Chivington punched Matt hard in the stomach and knocked him sprawling in the snow. Unseen by the major, Mike Maher stepped forward to protect his brother, though others quickly and quietly restrained him. *"That* was merely five fingers," the major bellowed, "mortal flesh! Imagine how Tredegar steel will feel as it

reaves this life from you! How in your last seconds you will hate Miss Meekness for her failure to reinforce the simple difference between *right* and *left!* Lambs, you are not soldiers unless you can follow a command! Anything an officer orders—anything!—you must do it off the reel, *together!* You are no longer individuals! Advance alone and you will *die! Am I clear?*" The boys responded feebly, transfixed by Matt Maher's struggle to inhale. "Damn your eyes, answer me! *Do you understand?*"

"Yes, Sir!" they shouted, none wanting to become a caution themselves.

"Again!"

"*Yes, Sir!*" they shouted, and this time the sound could be heard a mile away.

"Meekness, will you lead my soldiers?"

"Yes, *Sir!*"

"Better! Volunteers, walk ten paces south and reform lines." As the others shuffled away, he leaned down and spoke quietly to Maher, who was gasping for breath: "Chin up, lamb—chest out and you'll get more air. Don't hold this against the lieutenant—I know he's giving his all but I want as many of you as possible to make it back alive—understand?" Maher tried to speak but could only manage to nod. "That's it," Chivington said. "Now, they're going to march to field's end and return. Rest here and fall in once they do."

"Yes, Sir," Maher rasped.

Chivington rose to his full height, walked over to his horse and climbed into the saddle. He wheeled around until he stood at the formation's head. He removed his hat and revealed a balding pate fringed by unruly hair, his sweaty scalp steaming in the freezing air. "Boys, I hope that now we understand one another." His dark eyes flashed. "The Bible tells us that 'he who ignores discipline despises himself but whoever heeds correction gains understanding.' Now, march correctly or we will come to another understanding! Lieutenant, stay this course as many times as you think necessary but that number is your call. Now move, move, *move!*"

Peter called out steps and the ranks moved forward, not yet perfect but better, certainly. As they passed the major, none dared to make eye contact. From his saddle, Chivington watched them march, satisfied that he'd made his point. *If by my efforts we succeed, then surely the Lord will bless my designs, for without safeguard from the pestilence of sin, no seedling can reach full flower.* He glanced over his shoulder at ribbons of smoke rising from the chimneys and stovepipes in Denver, some two miles northeast. *Indeed every corner of this territory cries out for salvation. My Lord, my God, use me as You will, for I am equal to the task.*

∾

Simultaneously on the other side of the field, other units drilled or gathered around their mess fires to down stolen eggs, ham, cheese, apples, and canned oysters—anything to break the monotony of their bread-and-beef rations. Colonel Slough and A Company's captain, Edward Wynkoop, rested in their saddles and watched Maj. Chivington tear into Peter MacInnes's company. Slough cupped his hands against the breeze and lit a cigar. "Want one?" he offered Wynkoop.

"No, thanks—trying to quit."

"I quit trying."

Slough tossed the match into a snowdrift and blew out a plume of smoke, which curled around his head and dispersed on the wind. The First Colorado's move from the old Buffalo House to Camp Weld had been extremely popular with Denverites, as a precipitous drop in criminal activity had followed. Slough had stayed busy with his law practice and rarely visited the camp; every time he did, its culture and customs were a confusing affront to his sensibilities.

Wynkoop gazed intently across the field. He, too, rarely visited Denver, preoccupied with gathering enlistees and supplies from the territory's more distant settlements. "Those the Irish kids from Central City?"

Slough nodded. "Independent company—arrived on the ninth. They're hard enough—almost feral—but they're sloppy and of course they're months behind the others in everything. Formation, drill, tactics—everything. Hate to say this about boys headed into battle, but they'll have to learn by doing."

Wynkoop cringed as Chivington punched Matt Maher. "Provided the reverend don't kill 'em first."

"Amen." Slough exhaled another plume of smoke.

"Any change in schedule?"

Slough studied the cigar's burning end and tapped a nub of gray ash into the wind. "Colonel Canby sent instructions to proceed to Fort Wise as soon as possible and wait. Depending on developments, from there we'll continue either to Fort Union or Fort Garland."

"What's your gut say?"

"Fort Union, unless the rebels split their column and march on Taos as well. Then who knows."

"And if they strike the Pecos?"

"Fort Union still—it's the keystone."

In the distance, Chivington screamed at the Pinebark Independents to begin marching: "Now move, move, *move!*" Muffled by the deep snow, his voice still came booming across the field.

"Four-to-one our Fighting Parson gets shot by his own troops." Slough exhaled another cloud of dense blue smoke.

"Unkind of you to say but probably true."

"He fights without conscience and he'll keep those micks in line—that much I like." Slough stared intently at the giant preacher and pursed his lips. He hated being absent so much and thought that he'd missed his best opportunity to shape the brigade into a worthy fighting force. He knew they viewed him as an interloper; whenever he reprimanded a troop he was met with hostility and open defiance. Chivington, conversely, could do no wrong. *For God's sake, he just punched a man and for this, no doubt they will praise him with high hosannas!* Worry clouded Slough's mind. He needed to bring Chivington swiftly to heel—and swiftly. He determined then to inquire among the other officers and assess just how pervasive the major's influence had become. *Ambitious conniver.*

Realizing that Wynkoop was still staring at him, he made a sweeping gesture toward the stables, where teamsters were loading wagons with huge quantities of matériel. "There will be fewer troubles once we're on the trail. Go inform the yardmaster that I want to leave at first light."

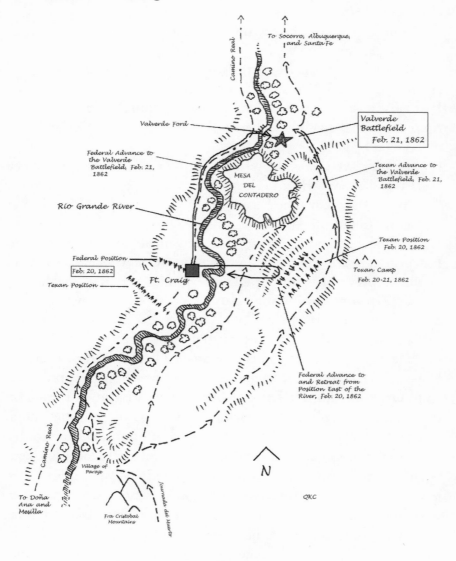

2-VALVERDE MAP

Valverde Ford, New Mexico Territory,
February 22, 1862—morning

Weeks before Col. Slough, Maj. Chivington and the First Colorado Regiment reached New Mexico Territory, volunteers from other parts of Colorado Territory had bolstered Federal defenses south of Albuquerque. Early in February 1862, Capt. Theodore Dodd, for one, led volunteers down from Cañon City and the farm-villages of south-central Colorado Territory. Hastily thrown into service, these raw troops first manned Fort Craig's walls as the Texans demonstrated against it and then, three days later, found themselves deployed in a convex arc at Valverde ford.

Dodd's seventy-one man force held the extreme Union left and for some time the fighting there had been slack. His men lay on their backs against a long sand dune, eating and catnapping in the cold sunshine. Halfway through an apple that had been his only meal since four o'clock that morning, Dodd knelt to look out over a field of short sedge-grass. Told to watch for companies of Texan cavalry that were reportedly nearby, he had thus far seen nothing.

Farther south, the battle had raged since nine a.m., when the Texans' forward units blundered into Union companies that already occupied the river's eastern bank. Intense early action had resulted in the Confederates' infantry and artillery slowly being pushed away from the river, into the shadow of Mesa Contadero—Black Mesa, the Texans called it—and by early afternoon it appeared that Union forces were in control of the entire field.

Downriver, a pair of Union twenty-fours was shelling Texans on the marshy eastern side of an abandoned river channel. Every few minutes these cannon sent fused case-shot into the trees; fifteen to twenty feet above the ground these missiles exploded and mowed down anything unlucky enough to be caught standing. Captain Dodd had just watched one of these rounds when in the corner of his eye he noticed something odd. He stopped chewing and tried to see into the *bosque's* enveloping gloom. His eyes widened. "Jesus Christ, Son of Mary!"

Startled from a surprisingly deep sleep, Private Luis Mandonado, a young farrier from the town of San Luis, blinked. *"Capitán, qué es?"*

Dodd shouted for his company to snap-to and re-trained his small field glass on the woods. "I'll be damned," he said and tossed the half-eaten apple over his shoulder.

"Capitán?"

"Luis, what decade is this?"

Still groggy, Mandonado raised an eyebrow. "Sir?"

"Lancers!" Dodd rested the glass on his knee, pulled two six-shooters from his waistband, and made sure each was loaded. "Not since Oldham at Balaklava! If I lived twice, still this would be the damnedest thing I'd see."

As he peered over the dune's lip, Mandonado saw four lines of horsemen. Each carried a twelve-foot lance topped with a long steel blade; below each point was a long, red swallowtail-pennant. *"Hijole,"* he muttered. Curiosity satisfied, he slid back down the dune to re-check the load he'd tamped into his musket.

Dodd stood. "Coloradans, here they come!" he shouted. "First line, wait for my command! Second line, wait one-two-three seconds after the first volley—then pick your targets!"

∽

Across the field, Texan Capt. Willis Lang saw a single company of Union infantry behind the low dunes that paralleled the river. From their gray uniforms, he assumed they were Mexican volunteers like those the Texans had blasted back across the river the day before—this was encouraging. Comprised of recent German immigrants, Lang's company was one of Gen. Sibley's favorites, and he had sent them north to buckle this outlier and re-establish the Confederates' right flank. Confident of driving these Yankees into the river, confident that this action would hasten the entire battle's end, Lang could hardly contain his excitement: *"Männer! Machen Sie* Texas *stolz! Sie wissen was zu tun! Für den Ruhm von* Texas, *Vorwärts!"*

No other persuasion was necessary and no reproach for the result applied, for as much as these men were obeying Lang's order, so, too, were their actions a product of the sectional hatred that had festered since the nation's founding. Ten across and four deep they began to gallop across the meadow; cold sunlight flared on the guidons and the crimson pennants streamed like fire. Their horses' hooves churned up sand and grass and some had tears of joy in their eyes. A hundred yards out they lowered their lances and began a German-inflected Rebel yell.

༄

Dodd stood, raised his revolver, and shouted once more: "Coloradans, steady! *Steady!* Men, they are Texans! Give 'em hell—*Fire!"*

A broad sheet of flame spurted from the dune crest. Dodd's men volleyed with buck-and-ball from near point-blank range, slaughtering Lang's cavalry. Nearly every horse and rider in the company was killed or wounded. The repulse was so brutal, so thorough that Dodd's first ranks were reaching for their second weapons or beginning to reload before they realized that scarcely any targets remained.

With shouts of *"¡Muera el Tejanos!"* Dodd's Coloradans surged over the dune's crest. In the meadow, a few dazed Texans disentangled themselves from bloody heaps of men and horses and broke for the trees. Few escaped: one Coloradan discovered a wounded horseman crawling through the weeds, ran a bayonet through the back of his neck, and shot away the top of his skull. Others were similarly dispatched. Within hours, Lang's first lieutenant, Demetrius Bass, would die on a surgeon's table, his shattered arm futilely amputated; and Lang himself endured another nine days in such wretched agony that at last he stole another man's pistol and committed suicide. Among Dodd's Coloradans, only three received wounds.

"*¿Cómo ves?*" Mandonado blinked at the jumbled bodies. For the rest of his short, troubled life, Luis's dreams would be haunted by the sounds of men's screams and bayonets tearing into flesh.

"Fought with antiques." Dodd kicked aside a broken lance and shook his head. Then he heard riotous, prolonged shouting and turned west to face the river. "Jesus Himself, what now?"

∾

With Col. Canby at its head, a party of Union officers began crossing the upper ford. Thought the colonel rode straight and tall, true to form he wore an expression that bordered on sorrow. "Well done, Captain," he said quietly.

Other officers were not nearly so reserved. "Yes, indeed!" one exulted and slapped his knee. "Bully for you, Captain!"

"Splendid work!" another gloated, "top-shelf."

"Thank you, Sirs, thanks!" Dodd replied, unable to keep track of who was speaking.

Canby's adjutant, Gurden Chapin, glanced at Dodd's men, still sweeping the field. "I see you were supported by artillery, yes?"

"No, Sir." Dodd hesitated, confused. "We are here by ourselves."

Chapin pointed to Mandonado's weapon. "Meant that man's musket—we don't see those much anymore."

Like most volunteers, Dodd's Coloradans had furnished their own weapons and these included a wide variety of rifles, muskets, and shotguns. Mandonado had somehow come to possess a .69-cal. Springfield rifled musket—a monstrous weapon that fired huge wads of lead at relatively low speeds, and inflicted appalling damage on its targets.

Chapin regarded him with amusement until finally Dodd understood. "Luis certainly had the last word—isn't that right, Private?" Mandonado smiled weakly, embarrassed by the attention.

"Perhaps we'll requisition more for the regulars."

Canby, meanwhile, had been staring at the dozens of bodies strewn across the bloody grass. When a solider fired his musket to put a wounded horse out of its misery, he jumped. "Damn it!" He spat on the ground, but recovered quickly. "Anything happen here before this, Captain?"

"Pot-shots only, Sir," Dodd said and wiped gore from his jacket's brass buttons. "Then these fellows up and charged us with spears."

"Passing strange." Canby pointed across the field. "Reload and move up to those taller dunes, then—any Rebels show, give them a similar welcome. My hat's off to you and your men, Captain—well done."

As the colonel rode away, Dodd and his volunteers cheered.

Guiding his horse between mangled bodies, Canby smiled and waved in return, though his mood remained dark. *My God, let this terrible war end soon.*

≈

On the river's eastern bank, terrific noise and smoke testified to the ferocious struggle that was unfolding there. Canby and his staff angled south toward a tall embankment in search of a better view to Mesa Contadero. Gurden Chapin caught up with the colonel, handed him a dispatch, and gestured toward a snarl of willows, the bare branches of which shook as if tossed by cyclone winds. "Roberts and Duncan are holding," he said.

The colonel took Chapin's paper and read as he fished in his coat pockets for a cigar. Finding one at last, he clamped it in a corner of his mouth and turned sideways in his saddle. "Still have that glass?"

Chapin handed a small telescope to the colonel, who noted the positions of various units' flags. Seeing that the Texans had withdrawn their artillery behind protective cover, away from the withering fire of the Union's heavier guns, he offered the glass to the officer beside him. "What do you see, Kit?"

Christopher "Kit" Carson took the glass and surveyed the field. For a full minute, he watched as blue-coated Federal troops chased Texans across a wicked tangle of logs at the river's high-water mark, well away from its edge. He exhaled and lowered the piece. "On the brink, Colonel—progress everywhere along the line." Then Carson said something in Spanish to J. Francisco Chavez, his second-in-command, and Chavez nodded in agreement. Canby grinned

97

dryly, thinking that this was the most he had heard Carson say in weeks—maybe ever.

Well before the war, Kit Carson had achieved notoriety as a national hero. Born in Missouri, he'd run away at fourteen and joined a westbound wagon train. In 1843, he caught the public's attention as the guide of one of John C. Fremont's epic western transects. Thereafter he'd worked as a fur trapper, soldier, and Army scout; learned seven Indian languages and taken both Indian and Hispanic wives. Despite these deeds, he simply did not possess the flamboyant personality his admirers expected; that caricature—which Carson hated—was the creation of a sensation-hungry press for consumption by a worshipful public. Being illiterate, Carson had never read any of these stories himself, though he was well aware of them and constantly tried to deflect the attention that followed. Taciturn at best, by age forty-one he'd become even more withdrawn, his speech severely measured, and he rarely offered unsolicited opinions.

"Dodd's Coloradans fought well," Canby ventured.

Carson agreed that they had.

"Your natives ready?" Given Carson's reticence, he knew better than to expect details.

"Yes, Sir," Carson said. "This is their land."

At the war's onset, Carson had resigned his post as government agent to the Indians of northern New Mexico and accepted a commission as the First New Mexico Volunteers' commanding officer. Carson's long residence in Taos, his good reputation, and his fluency in Spanish had helped draw hundreds of Hispanic New Mexicans to the Union ranks. But, though their numbers were a welcome boost, most white officers—Canby included—doubted their worth as front-line troops.

Canby studied Carson's profile, but Carson was so focused on the field that the colonel left him alone. Canby pointed to positions along a series of grassy dunes to the right. ""Good. Put two companies there—send the others with Col. Pino to the center."

"Yes, Sir." In Spanish, Carson barked these orders to a young private who saluted and rode west toward the river.

The wind began to push clouds of acrid smoke upriver. Canby motioned to a second messenger. "Duncan needs reinforcement, too. Ingraham will move south to help Hubbell and Mortimer protect Hall's battery. Go." The rider saluted and splashed away across Valverde ford. Canby spun the soggy cigar stub in the corner of his mouth. "Time, gentlemen. Turn that right flank and they will crumble. You're the fulcrum, Kit—I'm counting on you."

"Colonel, my men will not run" Carson said.

"Very well. Gentlemen, let's ride to the center with Kit and then go find Major Duncan."

∾

A huge explosion rocked the *bosque* and threw wood and sand far out into the river. Lost in thought, Canby paid scant attention to the noise. *Where the hell are they?* Again, he took the glass and scanned the woods; back and forth, he swept the *bosque* in search of a sign—anything—that might reveal the Confederates' location. On his fourth pass, the colonel spotted a lone horseman halfway up Mesa Contadero's flank, shouting to someone in the trees below. Canby followed this man's gestures and noticed dust rising above the treetops—dust in sufficient quantities to suggest that something large was on the move. Men, horses, wagons—he couldn't tell, but there was no longer any question that something on the *bosque's* far side was stirring. "Gurd, come here!" he shouted before handing him the glass. "Ten degrees below that big rock—tell me what you see."

The others passed the glass hand-to-hand and all agreed that something big was afoot.

"*There!*" Chapin shouted. "Left of those dead trees—Rebel cavalry! One company, two companies, three—and more formed up behind!"

Canby spurred his horse toward the front and the others followed. "Are they built up anywhere else?"

The others responded with a collective "No."

"Kit?"

"Nothing you haven't already seen, Sir."

R.S.C. Lord, a cavalryman agreed. "Nothing on my reconnoiter, Sir—this must be their main thrust."

Canby pointed to a messenger. "You there: find Wingate—tell him to run full chisel! Then find Duncan and tell him help's on the way!" As the messenger galloped away, he pointed at Carson. "Kit, the center is yours. Come what may, you *must* protect McRae's guns, understand?"

Carson saluted and he and Chavez rode west toward the river to try and find their commands.

Canby watched his soldiers getting ready even as the Texans did likewise. *Infantry—three, four, five. Good.* He couldn't shake the sense that something was amiss but believed that this foreboding was simple nervousness. Desperate for a better view he halted at the top of a dune and stood in his stirrups, but despite this vantage, all that presented was an empty sand plain. McRae's battery, set atop a small eminence, was firing on small detachments of Confederates. *Is that their main force in those woods? If not, where could they have gone? They haven't vanished—this must be it.* "No movement anywhere else?" he shouted again. "Anything? Captain Lord?"

"No, Sir." Lord shook his head. "McRae has about a hundred skirmishers pinned in those sand pits. No other activity, Sir."

Canby unease grew. He was prudent man, cautious and thorough in everything he did, and with all signs suggesting that the Texans' main assault had formed up across from Duncan, he wanted to stack the odds further in the Federals' favor. He called for another messenger. "Find Carson and tell him to stop. Now he must turn right—him and Pino—hard and fast, no time to lose! They must turn south. East bank, right along the waterline!" Canby watched the express depart, unable to shake a sense of disquiet. By then the wind had picked up and sand began to sting the officers' faces.

While the other officers made plans and checked the locations of their units' flags, Canby stared in silence at a silvery willow, its branches dancing wildly. When at last he commenced to chew on the unlit cigar, it promptly unraveled and spilled tobacco leaves across his lap. Disgusted, he spat the whole mangled mess out onto the sand. *Sibley, old card—where have you gone? What trick are you trying to play?* He stood in the saddle again, saw Carson and Pino's troops turning south, and for a brief moment permitted himself to relax.

ᵔᴥᵔ

Holding their rifles aloft, Kit Carson's men were mid-river when four companies of Texan cavalry charged out of the *bosque*. Carson's New Mexicans emerged onto loose sand and volleyed into the Texans's right flank just as double-rounds from Hall's battery detonated in their midst. As with Lang's company of lancers, the Confederates' momentum was completely smashed. Though many of the survivors tried to regroup, chaos prevailed and others galloped back through the *bosque* and beyond. Sensing a rout, Canby's Federals began to chase these unfortunates and in this manner, a huge gap was opened in the center of the Union lines.

Observing from a distance, Canby glanced skyward and saw eagles soaring on columns of warm air rising up from Mesa Contadero. *A fine omen, if I believed in such things.* To the north, McRae's batteries continued their deadly work, emptying the dunes before them. *We held! Thank you, God, we held!* At last, the colonel permitted himself a smile. *Summon our reserve companies to finish off any holdouts and it will all be over.* He guided his horse down the dune face to rejoin the others. Glancing at the sky a second time, however, he realized that circling birds were buzzards, not eagles, and he frowned. He patted his coat pocket in search of another cigar.

Before he'd even reached the dune's base, the colonel spotted a disheveled soldier running directly toward him. "Colonel Canby!" the man shouted, "Colonel Canby—we found 'em! Every Texan on earth is up near the ford—they're set up to jump McRae!"

"Quickly, show me!" Fear curdled Canby's stomach and he forgot all about the cigar.

The young messenger pointed northeast. "Behind those sand hills—we couldn't see 'em back there! There's fifteen hundred if there's five!"

"Gurd, hand me that spyglass—quickly!" Again, Canby stood in his stirrups. Out across a blinding sand plain, edged with cottonwoods and heaps of driftwood, he noticed something. *What is that?* He squinted to see through the shimmering glare until at last he saw them: a great crescent of infantry, more than a thousand strong and a half-mile wide, all along the tops of the easternmost dunes. Already some companies had started across the sand; others were pulling artillery pieces forward, right into the void at the center of his own lines—fewer than four hundred Federals stood in their way. "Dear God," he whispered, "we have no center." He looked at McRae's battery, firing leisurely, and realized that from their position neither the crews nor their supports could see up onto the plain. *Oh, God, I was wrong. Wrong and now we are all of us in mortal danger...* He tossed the glass back to Chapin and grabbed another express by the coattail. "You—ride south! Find Duncan, Carson, Wingate, Mortimer, Hubbell, Deus, Chacón—every officer you see! For God's sake, soldier, tell them to turn north as fast as they can! *All of them! Ride like the wind! Ride!*"

Valverde Ford, February 22, 1862—early afternoon

Jacob Stark's company had dismounted east of the *bosque* and moved forward as skirmishers. Winded from their race across loose sand, they had made it within a hundred yards of a Union battery before its supports began to pepper their advance with random, panicky fire. There beneath the towering cottonwoods, flying lead hissed and snapped—a metalline hail that brought down piles of branches and dead leaves.

"Halt!" Jacob shouted, "Take cover!" and the Cameron Guards dove behind berms of coarse gravel. Sweaty despite the cold, the Texans unbuttoned their jackets and took huge gulps of water from their canteens.

Twigs and chaff were lodged in every crease of Jacob's shirt, woven so thoroughly into his dusty hair that it looked like nothing so much as a bird's nest. He glanced upward and rolled sideways as a ten-foot long branch fell exactly where he had been.

Eli Fisher crawled sideways until he lay within earshot. "Way too hot, Jake—we can't stay here!"

"Have to!" Jacob shouted as the Yankee fire team directly ahead of them began to double-charge their howitzer with canister. "If they try to reinforce from across the river, we *must* block 'em—hold your ground!"

Briggs Hardy rose up on one elbow and took another drink. "Lucky we made it this far."

Fisher raised his head to see over a mound of sand, but a bullet buried itself nearby and sprayed him with wet earth. "Jake!" he shouted, "This is madness!" He paused to wipe grit from his eyes. "We are open on every side!"

"Fish, stay put—*that's an order!*" Jacob pulled himself forward on his elbows and as he lifted his head to look around a stout log, a bullet perforated his left sleeve beneath his armpit.

Wide-eyed with astonishment, Hardy clutched at Jacob's coat and pulled him back. "You hit?"

"I don't ... don't know," Jacob sputtered. He lay on his back and felt gingerly along his side but discovered no wound. "They have our range."

"Hadn't we best fall back?" Hardy scanned the riverside, where muskets were popping like fireflies. "Jake?"

"No!" Jacob bristled, *"No!* Fish—can you see Major Lockridge?"

Fisher twisted his neck for a view of the plain east of the grove and saw rank upon rank of Texans pouring over the dunes. "Yes! Four hundred yards—they're closing fast!"

"Be patient, then! Tell Charlie and the others that way to concentrate on that first pit! Draw those guns over here! Target the crews or their supports on the left!"

"Okay, got it!"

Round after round, the Union batteries continued firing.

"And Fish!" Jacob called again to his sergeant. "They're using canister! Tell everyone to stay low—low as they can and we'll be okay!" A shell exploded fifty yards to their left as Yankee gunners sought their range.

Hardy glanced around a dune slope as he loaded his musket. "Ain't this somethin', Jake? For the glory of Texas."

Jacob finished loading both his revolvers and stowed his kit. Lying in the dirt, he reached out and shook Hardy's hand. "Same as last time, pard—see you at supper."

On the highest dune to their right, a soldier stood and unfurled the Texans' red banner with its single white star. Behind him, an unearthly yell issued from fifteen hundred mouths as the bulk of Sibley's Army rose and charged the Federals' line.

❧

Armed with shotguns, muskets, and long knives, the Texans reached the high dunes nearest to the river and began to climb. Their artillerymen lobbed case shells two hundred yards before them and mowed down rank upon rank of New Mexicans. Other Federals met these attackers halfway down the slopes and fired into the onrushing mass of Texans. Hand-to-hand, men clawed at each other with anything available: pistols, sabers, knives—even sticks and rocks. Bodies began to pile up at the foot of the *banco.*

Eli Fisher fired a Maynard rifle at one blue-jacketed officer and missed. Reloading, he rested his weapon across a cottonwood log and began searching for other targets. Twenty yards to the west, Hardy swore to himself as a stocky, bearded Yankee shot a wounded Texan who lay helpless on the ground. He tried to line up a shot, but smoke and dust enveloped the field and then there was nothing he could do but fume.

At once, it was apparent that the Texans's fierce charge had completely overmatched the Federals. Rank upon rank of blue simply melted away, as though sudden waves had rolled in from the desert and smashed them aside.

సా

Major Basilio Ortiz watched as one smallish band of Texans advanced to within a hundred yards of his position. He removed his cap and ran his fingers through damp strands of hair. On his left, scattered Confederate units had already crossed the main dune field, but these were hundreds of yards away and would have to pass McRae's artillery before they came within range. No, it was the smallish company on his right flank worried him, and he pulled at the ends of his moustache. Basilio's combined units of militiamen and First New Mexico Volunteers were deployed as supports to the right of the Union's guns, and through sheer numbers alone, he was sure they could handle anything the Texans threw at him. *It's time.* Raw as many of his soldiers were, he was determined to see that they fought well and demonstrate to Canby and the other Federals' that their lack of confidence in his people's abilities was unwarranted.

In the back of his mind, he also hoped to impress Adria Carrizo. Hours earlier, as his command forded the river, he'd thought about her and he wished she could see him in his splendid new Federal uniform. *Perhaps she would see me differently—think differently about me.* When he pictured her face, he smiled softly. Soon the fighting would end and he would have another chance to make her see that he deserved her affection. *There is still time.*

Once in the field, however, all extraneous thoughts vanished. Witnessing the enemy's rapid advance had precipitated his mental energies, and when they stopped and took cover, he decided that he was pleased for the opportunity. *Good—we will bring the fight to you, then.* The air began to buzz with hot lead. *"Jejénes,"* he joked nervously with a lieutenant.

"Big ones! *Ellos picadura, también.*"

He glanced at his pocket watch—*The time has come,* he thought. He withdrew his sword from its scabbard and pointed to an isolated copse. "Ready! There in that grove! Aim! *Fire!*" The infantry loosed a tidy little volley upon the field, but as no Texan there was struck, it was only sound and fury signifying nothing.

Seeing nothing but cut up branches and pocked earth, Basilio frowned. *"¡Capitánes!"* he shouted to his officers, *"¡Tejanos en los árboles!* Advance to that *farol's* edge and mass your fire! Two volleys and then we advance with fixed bayonets!" Then, for reasons he could not fathom, virulent confusion swept through the New Mexicans' ranks and all firing practically ceased.

"Major, Sir!" Lt. Mondragon shouted, *"Capitán* Gil's men are still across the *rio*—Ruiz is missing, too! We advance now, we'll have no reserves—no connection to the *artillería.*"

Flustered, Ortiz looked west toward the Rio Grande. "Why is Martin on the other bank?"

"Yo no sé—they wouldn't cross."

"Gomes?"

"He crossed but hasn't been seen since."

Mother Mary, why was I not told? His watery eyes widened. *Why didn't I notice?* A quick count convinced him that numbers were still in his favor, but not to the extent that he'd believed only moments before. A sudden thought preoccupied him: *My brother, Felix, was born to fight—would that he was here.* He looked back at the shimmering brown river, half-expecting to see Ruiz and Gil appear with their men. What had happened? At dawn, they had marched together from the fort, and just hours ago they had stood shoulder-to-shoulder on the river's west bank—their absence made no sense. Hector Ruiz was one of his best friends: there was no way he would run from a crisis. *Maybe he cannot bring his volunteers across; maybe something terrible has happened.*

On his right, he heard shouting as Capt. Bagida's company rose spontaneously from their crawl along an embankment and fired. *"No!"* Basilio bellowed but they were too distant to hear over the crash of musketry. None of their bullets found targets—all sailed harmlessly into the cottonwoods and took down nothing but twigs. Stopping to reload, their own gunsmoke rolled back and blinded them.

"Get down!" Ortiz screamed. *"Tell them to get down!"*

Motionless, exposed from the knees up, Bagida's men made splendid targets and the Texans obliged. Struck multiple times, eight of their number fell. Immediately the others stopped reloading and ran for cover, their cheers turned to bleats of fear and confusion.

"Major, Sir?" Lt. Mondragon begged. *"¿Qué debemos hacer?"*

What can I do? Ortiz felt panic wash through his system. *Bagida's men massacred, Ruiz gone...*"Nothing," he coughed.

"¿Nada?" Mondragon pleaded, glancing toward the grove where the Texans had reloaded and begun to fire into the terrified volunteers' backs.

Basilio shook his head. "I mean that we'll hold this ground. Go, find Bagida! Reassemble his men—cover them as best you can. Have all companies return fire immediately!"

"¡Sí!" Mondragon saluted and went to go find his command. A few muskets began to crackle, once again tearing the cold air apart.

One minute later, Ortiz caught new movement in the corner of his eye and turned. Bagida's men were sprinting for cover in the willows; many had dropped their weapons. Even more ominous, on the dune crest opposite McRae's guns a Texan had risen up and begun to wave a red banner with a lone white star. Around this figure, more men appeared, as suddenly as if they had emerged from the sand beneath their feet. *Up from Hell*, Basilio thought. At intervals along their line were snub-nosed howitzers, all seemingly trained upon his force's precarious position. *"¡Dios Mio!"* he whispered, and despite the whirring bullets, he ran to intercept the last of Bagida's command before it vanished.

Valverde Ford, New Mexico Territory, February 22, 1862—late afternoon

Union forces on the right made a titanic effort to hasten north before the entire army was swept from the field. Canby was himself two hundred yards behind McRae's guns when the Texans charged. As shells detonated overhead and their comrades fell, dozens of native volunteers broke and fled for the river and neither McRae's nor Canby's entreaties could stem the tide. "For God's sake," Canby shouted, "stand and fight! *Save the guns!*" But he could do nothing: so panic-stricken was the irregulars' retreat that they plunged head-long into the reinforcements and simply carried them away.

Basilio Ortiz grabbed a musket and threatened the wild-eyed volunteers that were stampeding toward him. He fired into the air but they came on unabated, knocked him to the ground, and gashed his scalp to the bone. Still on his knees, he turned and whispered *"Alto,"* but by then there was no one left to hear.

"Damn it!" Canby raged. *"Stand your ground!"* A few volunteer units and other regulars rallied and fought back, but already the terrified vanguard was a quarter of the way across the Rio Grande.

಄

Eli Fisher spotted the same Yankee officer he had targeted earlier—Capt. Alexander McRae, who was directing blasts of shot and shell into the onrushing Texans. All day, McRae had fought like a man possessed, taking colossal risks, and leaving himself exposed to enemy fire. The previous evening he'd told his crews that he didn't care whether or not he lived, as his North Carolinian family had—upon learning of his fidelity to the Union—disowned him. Fisher would have ended the captain's sorrows then, but as he made ready to fire, Confederates swarmed the battery and attacked its crew. McRae and Texan Maj. Samuel Lockridge squared off over one of the guns, shouting at one another until others' bullets took them both. "Damn it," Fisher said and lowered his rifle again.

~

Moving from gun to gun, the Texans fired and hacked at anything blue, driving away their Union crews with gusts of lead and steel. In one pit, a splintered crew wheeled their howitzer oblique to its original position, desperate to enfilade the entire battery and possibly disable the captured pieces. As Private Cort Hoaglund pulled his thumbstall off the gun's vent, however, a Texan in a torn white shirt and brandishing a pair of revolvers jumped up onto the caisson. "Back away—back away!"

"Wait!" Hoagland shouted. With one hand, he stabbed at the Texan with a handspike and missed; with the other, he tried to keep his sweat-fogged spectacles in place.

"Fat pig, that's all you got?" The Texan fired and struck Pvt. Hoaglund in his left shoulder.

"*Stop!*" Hoaglund tried to ward off a second shot but discovered that he couldn't lift his arm. Another bullet struck, this time above his left wrist.

"Fat sow," the Texan sneered. "You can't do *shit!* Drop that spark and run, you pig!"

Oblivious to the violence boiling around them, Hoagland glared at his tormentor and as blood began pouring from his arm, the private began to sob. As the only child of dour Wisconsin farmers, Hoagland had enlisted to escape his wretched childhood, but here, resigned as he was to dying, something in the Texan's cruel taunts unleashed a torrent of deeply suppressed humiliations. "*You bastard!*" he seethed, ripping the burning fuse from the gun's back, "You're all going to *hell!*"

Then the Texan fired again, and as Hoaglund fell, he thrust the sputtering fuse into the caisson box, detonating the three hundred and ninety pounds of gunpowder stored inside. The resulting fireball annihilated the nearest half-dozen soldiers, Confederate and Union alike; all within a hundred feet had to gasp for breath as the concussion tore the air from their lungs. The brass howitzer's two hundred and twenty-pound barrel cracked and wicked barbs of smoke blew far out over the river. Nearby willows combusted and within minutes the wind drove this smoky fire east from the riverbank. Unable to flee, several wounded men died in the blaze, trapped beneath a sky that had gone dark as night.

～

Jacob's company brushed the sand from their eyes and ears. The huge explosion atop the dunes to their right had intensified their restlessness, and several wondered aloud whether they were ever going to fight.

"Stop that!" Jacob ordered. "Cameron Guards, *ready!*"

"Your ears ringin', too?" Hardy closed one eye and touched his head.

"Yes," Jacob snapped. "Fish, keep that far end in line! *Aim!*"

Suddenly Union forces under Maj. Benjamin Wingate counterattacked. They fired into the Texans beyond McRae's battery and killed dozens, including a popular colonel, John Sutton. Seizing on the Texans' momentary confusion, Union gunners labored frantically to drag away and reload the few pieces that remained under their control.

"Guards," Jacob shouted, *"Fire!"* Fisher, Spence, and the others unleashed a deafening volley. Wingate was wounded and the reinforcements he was leading crashed into one another as their first ranks stumbled. Yelling wildly, the men of Jacob's company rose and hurled themselves against the Union's disorganized flank.

Sprinting across the sand, Jacob shot the first Yankee he met and directed a second volley against the reeling Federals. Twenty yards to the right, he saw a New Mexican officer calmly loading a revolver even as pitched fighting swirled around him. Jacob noted the Mexican's gray eyes, sharp nose, and weak chin; his hands shook and he seemed dazed, maybe even lost. The two men locked eyes. No one else had paid this fellow any attention: the Mexican appeared so wan and bloodless that Jacob wondered if he was not already dead—some kind of spectating ghost. Taking no chances, quickly Jacob leveled his own revolver and fired. The Mexican staggered, fell backward, and disappeared as the leafless undergrowth swallowed him whole.

❧

With McRae's entire battery captured, the Confederates turned these guns around and used them to shell the retreating Federals. Captain Trevanion Teel brought up his own batteries and hammered the last Federals from their positions east of the river. By this time, even the arrival of Kit Carson's fresh New Mexican reinforcements could not stem the tide. Withdrawing before his entire force was lost, Col. Canby ordered several units to provide cover as a bugler sounded the call for a general Federal retreat to Fort Craig.

❧

Briggs Hardy followed a *brecha* cautiously, pushing aside the dense brush, meaning to find the New Mexican officer that Jacob had shot and take his fine revolver. A sharp, metallic tang polluted the air. Following a well-marked blood-trail, he saw a pair of boot-tips pointed toward the smoke-stained sky. Rounding a snarl of dusty branches, he came face-to-face with Basilio Ortiz, seated in the dirt with his back against a huge log. Blood stained the Mexican's shirtfront. He wore a curious expression, Hardy thought—some admixture of weariness and resignation—but showed neither fear nor alarm at his approach. *I'll be damned.* Ortiz had not attempted to move or fight so Hardy lowered his weapon. "Your revolver," he said and pointed to his own. *"Dónde?"*

"Don't know," Ortiz wheezed, and coughed up blood. "The Yankees would not train us properly."

Hardy said nothing and continued to look for the missing weapon.

"They will blame us anyway."

"The hell you say?" When Hardy stopped and tried to read this inscrutable heap, a strange empathy overtook him. He knelt, took his

112

own canteen, and poured water over the New Mexican's cracked and bleeding lips. "Hold fast—someone'll come."

"No matter." Ortiz exhaled heavily. "Rio Arriba is open, but the way north *es muy difícil.*"

"What's that?" Hardy puzzled at this unsolicited prophecy but the Mexican only coughed and closed his eyes. The Texan retraced his steps out of the thicket. Alone on the field, he laughed and shook his head. "Can't hardly account," he whispered and loped easily toward the river in search of his company.

⁓

From Black Mesa's northern shoulder, Col. Green watched with justifiable satisfaction as the Yankees retreated. His jaw packed with plug tobacco, he wished there was some way he could prolong the moment and its clear outcome, blessed by God—all perfectly well and good. His left leg was wrapped with bloody bandages. At midday, a one-ounce ball had cut a four-inch-long furrow in the top of his thigh, and later shrapnel from a Union shell had carried away a small piece of his calf. The pain had been wicked, though whiskey had made it bearable. He was worried for his troops, of course—he always worried about *them*—but as he watched the setting sun, he also felt a satisfaction that he hadn't known in years—not since San Jacinto during the Texas Revolution. *Lord, today we have labored mightily in your fields and I pray that you will accept the sacrifices we laid down in your name. Thank you, Jesus. Have mercy on the dead—theirs and ours. Grant us victory so that we are forever free to praise your name in the same way as our forefathers.*

Spotting Frederick Metzger on the traprock trail below, he whistled. Despite Metzger's friendly wave, Green found his intrusion mildly annoying. He spat his chew into a jumble of basalt boulders.

"*Herr* Colonel," Metzger called, "how are you?"

"Better."

Encased in dirt, dried sweat, and power residue, Metzger was too tired for anything beyond the dry recitation of facts: "The Yanks have *eine weisse Flagge* raised."

"A white flag!" Green exulted. "Oh, praise the Lord and present 'em with terms!" As Metzger's horse neared the flat where Green was waiting, the colonel looked out across the river. Already watchfires were burning in the fields before the walls of Fort Craig.

"We are shooting those who will not surrender."

"Gonna have that Brotherton smartass shot, too." As they scoured the *bosque* for wounded men, a cold wind carried the searchers' faint shouts upward, and for several minutes both officers listened with rapt attention. The setting sun had turned heavy northern clouds blood red but below these the horizon seethed, black and impenetrable.

Major Metzger tucked his chin against his chest. "Any orders, *Herr* Colonel?"

With great reluctance, Green tore himself away from the majestic view. "Inform all officers of the Fifth we will meet in camp at eight. Bring any further news to my tent and I will take it to the General myself." He glanced north again and noted the deepening gloom. "How do you rate our chances now, Fritz?"

"Better," he said but when he followed the colonel's gaze, he found the churning blackness on the northern horizon unsettling. "But this fear I cannot shake …" he began but lost his train of thought.

"Take heart," Green countered. "Fear can be useful—focuses the mind like nothing else. Don't worry if our plan isn't clear yet—soon enough, we'll do what we were made for."

"To Denver?" A gust of wind rattled the dry brush between rocks and sent a shiver down Metzger's spine. "The Salt Lake City *und* San Francisco?"

"Beyond, if needs be." Green shifted uncomfortably in the saddle. "That which Heaven wills cannot be denied."

Watching as the red sun bled into a purple sky, Metzger did not answer. Ever since the skirmish near Mesilla he'd been haunted by a fear that they would run out of time—a poison stronger than even the colonel's optimistic estimations. But who could honestly say? *Perhaps he is right.* With Canby's defeat, Albuquerque and Santa Fe lay unprotected. *Ja*, with Fort Craig's stores, they could seize both Santa Fe and the capital of Colorado Territory. Soon all of Texas and the Confederacy—perhaps all the peoples of the world—would assign proper significance to their achievements. He straightened his back and sat tall in his saddle. "This is a great day."

"It is, indeed. Now, go tell the others that I will see 'em at eight o' clock."

Metzger saluted and rode down to the river while Green rode east toward the Texans' dry camp. Twice along the way, however, the pain in the colonel's leg had flared so brightly that he'd laid forward on his horse's mane and held on tightly for fear that he might black out.

Near Colorado City, Colorado Territory, February 22, 1862

Even as the Federals' defenses at Valverde were collapsing, the First Colorado Regiment was encountering troubles of its own. A mere three days out of Denver and already Col. Slough's force had nearly torn itself to pieces. The inciting incident, as they often are, was relatively minor: Capt. Charles Kerber and the German immigrants of I Company were resentful, having been denied a third wagon to carry their gear like the other Coloradans. As the regiment broke camp near Colorado City, I Company refused to form lines in preparation for marching south. Slough rode back to investigate and immediately ordered Ed Wynkoop's A Company to disarm Kerber's men—even leveling his own revolver at Kerber. Kerber's men responded with brandished muskets.

"You shoot the captain," someone cried, "we'll put sixty holes through you!"

Seeing no easy alternative, Slough hurriedly scampered away. Chivington quickly ordered another wagon found for Company I, though Tappan, Wynkoop, and others began to worry about their chances under the colonel's temperamental leadership.

PART THREE

❧

THE ROAD NORTH

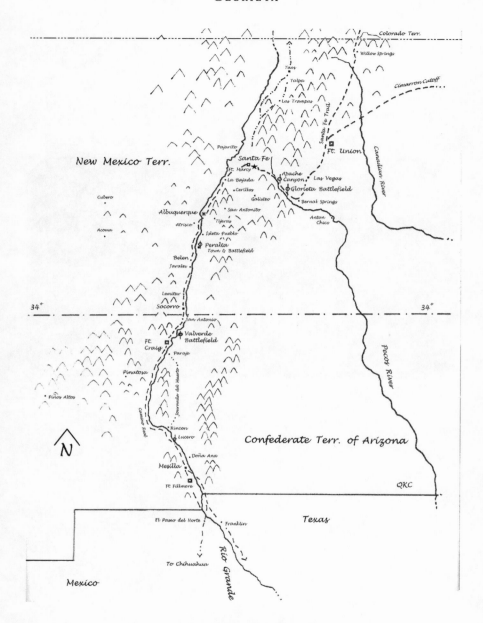

3-NEW MEXICO MAP

Confederate Encampment, Valverde Ford, New Mexico Territory

———

22 Feb., 1862—Dreadful tired and disaffection pervades. No one can say we did not win at Val Verde but Yankee treachery may upend us yet. They fooled Dad Green, we reckon, as the white flag sent out from the fort was not to surrender, as is customary, but to allow each side to gather its dead and wounded. Then under cover of darkness, the Yankees took back one cannon, various small arms and one of our regimental standards, which honor should have forbade—except that these people have no honor, no dignity, and no shame. Lt. Col. Scurry and Denman Shannon have return'd from meeting wi. Canby and report that the fort is well guarded and stocked wi. food, ammo., &c.—frankly, everything we lack. Unclear what Big Brass will have us do: the fort is too strong to capture and we have but five days' provisions. Unless we can hasten north and seize gvt. storehouses at Socorro and Albikirkie, our whole campaign may founder for want of food. Just as bad, so many horses were killed in the battle that Fourth Reg't was asked to turn theirs over to the Fifth so that at least one cavalry regt. may operate at full strength, and to the quartermaster, too, so that his boys can still pull the wagons that we have left. This means hundreds are now infantry instead of cavalry, which slows us considerable. Cannot see the outcome of all this but it cannot be good.

P.S.—We all pray that soon Green will lead us. Like St. Lazarus of the Bottle, Gen. Sibley has emerged from his ambulance and sown confusion. No one likes the man now and many kick that he is not Texan. Daily we struggle to keep scores from deserting. Briggs and

I pooled our funds to buy beef from a drover for our mess. Probably mule, but tasted near enough to beef that none complained.

23 Feb., 1862—Yesterday interred our dead, 20-some from our regiment alone. Total casualties are about 300, plus two-dozen simply unacc'td for. Near midnight, Fisher's cousin, Hal Persons, died of his wounds and we buried him at dawn. Many more wounded, some grievously, including Big Al Mitchell of Company A and Silas Johnson of Company C. All night the surgeons and their assistants chopped and sawed as best they could while the rest of us stuffed our ears wi. rags in the vain pursuit of sleep.

24 Feb., 1862—Camped in the lee of a jacale outside the sm. village of San Antonio. Tall white peaks dominate the wstrn horizon. Ten mi. to-day. No pursuit by the Yankees; they have evidently chosen to stay inside Fort Craig—cowards. Very cold now, wi. dry snow blowing sideways across the road. Very hungry and my feet are perfectly miserable despite now having pair of boots that Eli pulled off a dead Yankee—very superior to those I purchased in San Antonio. Between the boots and my blue jacket, friends slander me as the most "Northern" man in the Army of New Mexico, but I get the joke. Buried Rob Wilbanks after supper. Reminded that every step we take leads us to our graves. Rob was good fellow—among our best, and what of it? Seeing friends suffer terribly, I pray this is the low ebb and that their sacrifices will not have been in vain.

25 Feb., 1862—Warmer to-day. Socorro ahead. Scouts report that Pino, reportedly Kit Carson's right-hand man, will mount a defense there, but the natives continue to desert. Every day since the battle, we capture sullen Mexicans fleeing north from Fort Craig. We make them swear not to fight again and then parole them, as we cannot feed or administer so considerable a number. In truth, we can scarcely provision our own. Yankee details have stripp'd the country bare and what nature alone provides is too poor even to feed the livestock. What folly, to let the Yanks to run before us and remove or burn their stores. We must improve our speed but Dad Green says that Gen. Sibley has a timetable in mind and means to see it kept. The Mexicans here are silent, sullen, and I do believe that they

are counting us. Others leer as we pass or turn and run inside, and none will trade willingly. Flagpoles hereabouts are empty, but like as not under every bed is a neatly folded U.S. banner. Unaccountable arrogance from a defeated and inferior people. Four-man patrol vanished in the hills west of here last night. As they were not the type to desert, some conceive it was Indians or Yankees who took them, but to my mind Mex. bandits are likeliest—these people were born treacherous.

Socorro, New Mexico Territory, February 25, 1862

On Socorro's outskirts, on a narrow street edged with whitewashed adobes, Jacob Stark's Cameron Guards overtook another company as it marched several dozen Mexican captives south.

"Stark, ol' dad," John Shropshire called, "tell me you found something good."

"Morning, Sir. Dry goods and corn—four wagonloads. Y'all?"

The tall, gregarious Shropshire laughed and gestured at his captives. "A whole lot of nothing."

Jacob looked at the Mexican captives. "Let Canby feed 'em."

"Amen."

"Oh, congratulations on your promotion, Major." Jacob reached into his saddlebag, retrieved a bottle of bourbon that his company had liberated from a Yankee-owned store, and handed it to Shropshire.

"My, oh, my! Much obliged, Jake—I'll save you some. Hurry, though—all wrath's ready to move." Shropshire saluted before motioning for Company A to continue south with the prisoners.

Jacob returned the salute, called Eli Fisher forward, and tasked him with delivering their spoils to the quartermaster. Then Jacob and Briggs Hardy went in search of Col. Green.

༄

Despite receiving evil eyes from the locals, the boys lost no time in finding Socorro's central plaza. Square-shaped, it was roughly four hundred feet on each side, and fronted by stout adobe buildings and porticos. At the center of concentric wheel ruts stood an enormous cottonwood, easily one hundred and fifty feet tall and at least ten feet in diameter at its base. Like most New Mexican towns, Socorro's plaza had been designed as a shelter of last resort; in times of crisis, armed residents would pen their livestock on the plaza and barricade the entrances, turning their settlement into a walled fortress. On that day, however, the plaza was wrecked: every store had been looted, the streets were paved with horseshit, and large bloodstains gave proof that for some, the day had ended badly.

On the square, the boys reined their horses aside as a small detachment from Seventh Regiment exited down a narrow lane. Hardy spied Col. Green and his adjutant across the plaza and pointed. The colonel was leaning forward in his saddle, looking ill, and clearly favoring his bandaged left leg. Focused on events beneath the cottonwood, he didn't see the boys until they reined to a halt beside him. "Anything?"

Both saluted, though only Jacob spoke: "Sir, we confiscated the stock from Governor Connelly's store in Lemitar and burnt the building. Two loads of corn from a government warehouse and one full wagonload of hay."

"Our best haul so far. See all the captives?"

"Yessir—heard they surrendered without a shot."

"About right." The colonel raised his right index finger. "McNeill lobbed a single case over town and Pino set down right-smart to conference. Guess he knew better after Valverde."

"They should all be this easy."

"Yes. Oh, and the surgeons found a big cache of medicine, so a hospital's been established for our sick and wounded—we've plenty of both."

Angry shouts and curses drifted across the plaza.

"Sir, what's this?" Hardy asked.

Green pointed to a trio of men standing against a wall. Bound and blindfolded, each man had a noose drawn tightly around his neck. In turn, all three ropes were looped over the cottonwood's huge lower branches. "Arboreal justice. The Brigands again—Junior Walsh stole a major's horse and fled during the battle; that dark-haired one got drunk and stabbed his sergeant; and the third one is a deserter, captured on the river's east bank. The general means to set examples by 'em."

"Were they tried?" Jacob asked.

"As time allowed—Baylor washed his hands right quick."

"Colonel Baylor's here?"

Joe Sayers pointed north. "Signed the warrants and got. Provost has his orders now and I need to take the colonel to see Dr. Jordan."

"Need help, Sir?" Jacob shared a look of concern with Sayers.

"No." Green shook his head. "Thank you, though. Doctor J dosed me with red precipiate this morning, but the fever's returned so it's time for another call. So long, boys." Weaving a little in the saddle, he reined his horse around Hardy's and crossed the plaza; Sayers tipped his cap and followed.

"He'd best recover," Hardy murmured.

"Trouble, otherwise," Jacob concurred but his attention shifted suddenly. "Ever seen a hanging?"

Hardy held up three fingers. "A fellow what molested a gal in Jackson, Mississippi; a sailor in Velasco who killed a bartender; and four niggers in St. Louis." He paused. "Don't know what they did— maybe nothin'. You?"

Jacob shook his head. "Not before now."

⁓

In camp that night, Jacob turned in early and retrieved his journal from the bottom of his ruck. Outside his tent, some mild commotion made his heart race. He waited on edge, half-expecting the provost to come and haul him away. Instead, once the clamor faded, he scratched a hasty, undated entry:

Have done something rash: in Socorro today three men were to be hung for various crimes. The first two went as scheduled (Junior Walsh was one of these, and Lord help me, I did nothing), but I stopped the third. José Garza—another of the Brigands from Paraje—had been captured as a deserter. He was so frightened and the punishment so harsh that I stepped in and stopped it. Cannot say why except that if executions are meant to deter misconduct, here that aim was subverted for want of an audience. With none but guards in attendance, it wasn't but murder. Don't know why I defended Garza; I don't know him, and he's Mexican to boot. Only know that it wasn't *right*. Have defied Baylor and the General's orders. Wasn't my place to interfere, yet I <u>did</u>, and now I am on edge. Unsure what will happen. Reckon that trouble has come and now I cannot sleep.

Jacob closed the canvas-bound notebook, blew out the candle, and rolled onto his back. Hundreds of stars were visible in the slender space between the tent's flaps and he watched until the brightest one wheeled out of view. He listened for footfalls but heard only the wind soughing in bare poplars and a cricket's persistent song. For hours, he stared at that small slice of the heavens, desperately seeking answers that never came.

Rancho La Rinconada, New Mexico Territory, February 28, 1862

Smoke rose above the ridge—rose until wind sheared and hurled it eastward across the river. From the high road, they saw farm buildings, some reduced to ash, while others burned still. Weapons drawn, the Texans dismounted, and despite their efforts to make sense of the devastation, no plan revealed itself. Jacob knelt to steady himself against gale-force winds. He raised a small field glass and squinted through the dust and snow. One mile north, a curious swarm emerged from the river and galloped north across tablelands toward Bernardo.

"Indians?" Hardy shouted. "Jake?"

The main house's roof fell, its viga burnt through, and flames tore into the sky. Overhead, crows cawed and gave a wide berth to the smoke. "Militia," Jacob guessed, studying the marauders' tack and kit. "Gray jackets, but they ain't ours."

"Let's get after 'em!" someone shouted and others, too, began to clamor for reaction. Jacob tried to wave them off.

"Can't let 'em do this, Cap'n!" Charlie Spence swore. Hip-deep in a field of tall grass, gusts of wind shrieked and bent the yellow stalks sideways.

"This doesn't concern us," Jacob said. "Knock it off!" He wanted silence so he could think, though he sensed it would avail him nothing—there was no sense in what lay before them. *Why here? This place ain't military.* Dust billowed off the road as the Mexicans fled into the howling storm. Jacob raised the glass again and looked for answers on their backs but found none. The savagery with which the *rancho* had been wasted signified something deeper than partisan loyalties in an imported war—something older, something primal but the message was writ in the language of an alien culture and its meaning eluded him. Snow slapped at his face; shafts of sunlight fell and disappeared as the troubled sky churned. Jacob watched until the riders slipped from view behind a *ballena*—a fold in the landscape, so-called for its resemblance to a whale's humped back. Then he rose and walked down to the *hacienda*. An old man's body lay sprawled across the road; another lay in a big, dry canal on their left—both had been shot at close range. The Texans fanned out and discovered other bodies near the main house and the barn. Some were badly burned; others were glassy eyed, fixed on eternity. Goats lolled in red pools between the clumps of rabbitbrush, most of them dead but others maimed and bleating.

Near a corner of the main house, Hardy discovered two women bodies, one wrapped in a vain gesture of protection around the other, and he swore. "More over here!" he shouted. "Jesus-H, what happened?"

Jacob surveyed the red-speckled fields; soot stains on the whitewashed adobes; the gray sky turned black. Snow began falling harder. He leaned on a fencepost and squinted as the road dissolved from view. Downhill, the river, brown and sluggish, slithered away into the desert. Straightening his frame, Jacob slung the gun over his shoulder and clapped his friend on the shoulder. *"Yo no sé."* Jacob waved the others down from the hills. "See this?" He gestured toward the destruction. "This is how Yankees conduct business! Back to the horses and don't say *nothin'* 'til I talk with Dad Green!"

Confederate Encampment, Town of Jarales, New Mexico Territory

———————

1 Mar. 1862—To-night the starched shirts are dining at the home of M. Otero and his S. Carolinian wife. Otero is a former Territorial Delegate to Washington and, being a practical man, has circumstantially sworn allegiance to Richmond and Washington both, contingent, evidently, upon whichever nation's army is nearest. Pretended to be ill so I wouldn't have to go—in no mood. Discvr'd another *hacienda* that had been sacked; found survivors—four women and their littles hiding in the *bosque*. They described their assailants as Mexican militia with army weapons. Said they did not know why the farm was hit, except that its owner had recently refused to sell to a rico from the territory's north. Ever'where the strong prey upon the weak. Yesterday Gen. Sibley & Lt. Col. Baylor questioned me, Briggs Hardy and Sgt. Cavett—the provost in charge of the executions in Socorro. Luckily, we'd rehears'd our answers in view of this day and were spared real trouble on two accounts: first, whomever reported me knew that I dismissed the police detail following the first hangings but *not* that I subsequently ordered Jose Garza released; and second, Sibley was powerful drunk. This greatly hindered Baylor's inquest. Baylor is a hard, intense man and was all fired to have me clapp'd in irons and hung, too. Praise God for human frailty.

Albuquerque, New Mexico Territory, March 2, 1862

Even as the Confederates moved north from Socorro, Union scouts rode ahead of them, warning of their approach. Apart from modest hauls in the villages of Lemitar and La Joyita, Texan scavenging parties came up well short of the provisions necessary to keep their army adequately fed. All the way up the Rio Grande valley, Federal troops were able to destroy or simply move anything useful farther ahead of the Rebel advance.

꿍

At the U.S. Army Depot in Albuquerque, Assistant U.S. Quartermaster Capt. Herbert Enos learned that Texans were occupying Belén, just thirty-five miles south, and ordered that several wagons be loaded with ordnance and ammunition. As night fell, he dispatched these heavily armed teams north to the safety of Santa Fe, hoping that reinforcements were en route to help defend the Union's enormous Albuquerque stores.

The next morning, woodcutters sent into the mountains returned with news that the Texans were only twenty miles away in Los Lunas. Realizing that no timely reinforcement would come, Enos wandered dejectedly around the dusty freight yard. He looked up and spied the Sandia Mountains' broad, snowy crest, painted red by the rising sun. He exhaled slowly and his breath hissed between his teeth. Of average height, with a carefully trimmed beard, Capt. Enos prided himself on the depot's efficiency. He considered the careful allocation of U.S. Army matériel an almost sacred responsibility. While his men continued transferring crates and barrels onto heavy freight wagons, his eyes left the mountain and fell upon the rooftops and church-spires of Albuquerque. *No way to save it all.* A pall of blue smoke hung over the valley as residents stoked their morning fires. All week civilians had nosed about, asking if they would be allowed to scavenge whatever was left behind. Repeatedly Enos had explained that he meant to destroy whatever he could not ship, lest it benefit the Confederates. Most had left dejected, though a few had narrowed their eyes and tilted their heads, suggesting either that they did not believe him, or that they meant to subvert his plan. Indeed, only the night before, heavily armed deserters from a native militia had ambushed another Army wagon train, killed two guards, driven off the others, and escaped with three vehicles loaded with artillery shells, rifles, powder, and bullets.

A native of Wisconsin and a West Pointer, Enos didn't much care for Albuquerque, thinking it overpopulated with bummers and malcontents. Looking past the large Federal warehouses he saw groups of men, Anglo and Mexican, milling outside the gates, watching and waiting. He conceived that they might riot and overrun his guards if they spied the mounds of goods, and so resolved to leave everything inside and set fire to the warehouses themselves. Walking through the long, narrow buildings, he noticed particular items—occasionally recalling even the dates on they had arrived. It pained him to lose these resources, brought here to world's edge at fearsome cost, but damned if the wretches outside would take them for sale or presentation to the rebels. Finding the warehouses clear of men, he called to one of his sergeants: "Jules, are we loaded and ready?"

"Mules are in their traces, Sir."

"Good. Grab those tins of kerosene and meet me behind number three." From the warehouse's rear entrance, Enos saw that the crowd outside the gate had grown. Despairing that soon they might overrun the depot, he ducked between the first warehouse and a corral and began to run. From the building's rear forward, Enos and the sergeant doused the walls with kerosene, soaking bundles of blankets and other flammable items. They repeated this process in all three of the long barns. When he reached the last door, he lit a dead-flame lantern and tossed it into the darkness. He shuddered at the sound of broken glass, and moments later telltale clouds of smoke began to pour from the windows. It was ten minutes after seven a.m.

Unhappy but satisfied that the destruction was underway, Capt. Enos climbed aboard a wagon and shouted commands as his small but heavily armed detail rolled through the gates. They turned north. Scudding clouds covered the sun and the air grew colder. A half mile up the road, he looked back at the depot. A crowd of civilians had converged on the storehouses and more were on their way. Even as flames began to consume the walls, men, women—even children—could be seen darting inside and emerging with armfuls of goods. Even once the house belonging to Col. James Carleton—whose ranch the government had leased for use as a depot—caught fire, looters braved the flames and emerged, their arms overflowing with furniture and other goods. Dejected, Enos left Albuquerque without looking back or saying another word.

Confederate Encampment, Town of Peralta, New Mexico Territory

—————◆—————

2 Mar. 1862—Lights of Albikirkie ahead. Word circulates that Pyron's advance is already there. Rest of the column will start at dawn and should arrive by noon. I hope that there is food; I have made several new holes in my belt, as my weight continues to drop. Spoke to Dad Green in private about concerns that we are moving too slowly and he frankly agreed. Then I made a mistake and criticized Gen. Sibley for his drunkenness and lack of leadership, at which the Col. became very huff'd. Said I'd no standing to complain; that for years the Gen. had soldiered bravely—the Seminole Wars, the Mexican War, jayhawker troubles in Kansas, and with A.S. Johnston in Utah, quelling the Mormons; that therefore the Gen. knew more about soldiering than I and it wasn't my place to question but to serve; and finally, that he expects more from me. Regarding Sibley's drunkenness, Col. Green issued no denial, but said that every man must struggle wi. his own demons and that God does not suffer us to judge their success or lack thereof.

P.S.—Left angry and embarrassed, but afterward considered what Green said and now see that he is right. My own failings are such that I can scarce dwell upon them for very long and neither would these, I am sure, be viewed wi. much charity were they set before my peers for inspection. Sibley is unlucky then, for he cannot hide his decay, whereas mine festers unseen. Still, when the Reckoning comes, like as not Gen. Sibley will have an easier time defending himself than I. Nights awake are hard but these long days on the road are a close second.

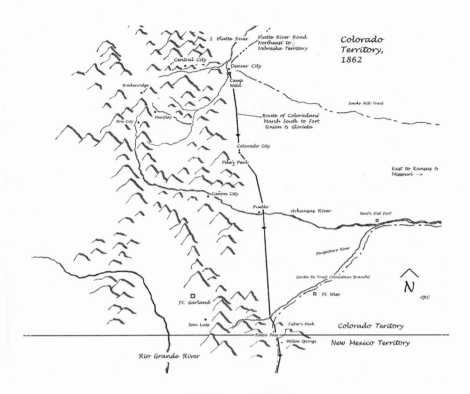

Colorado Territory, 1862

S. Platte River
Platte River Road Northeast to Nebraska Territory
Central City
Denver City
Camp Weld
Breckenridge
Route of Coloradans' March South to Fort Union & Glorieta
Smoky Hill Trail
Fairplay
Oro City
Colorado City
Pike's Peak
East to Kansas & Missouri -->
Cañon City
Pueblo
Arkansas River
Bent's Old Fort
Purgatoire River
Santa Fe Trail (Mountain Branch)
Ft. Garland
Ft. Wise
N
QKC
San Luis
Fisher's Peak
Colorado Territory
Raton Pass
Willow Springs
New Mexico Territory
Rio Grande River

4-1st CO MARCH MAP

Camp Anthony, Pueblo County, Colorado Territory, March 3, 1862

Gusts of wind made the tent's heavy canvas sides heave and sigh; a coal-oil lantern on the pole-rafter swung so that the shelter's corners were either brilliantly illuminated or cast into deep shadow—there was no middle ground. Reading under these conditions had given John Slough a headache. He paused between chapters and rubbed his temples. *On, off, light, dark—this lighthouse will wreck my eyes.* Like nearly every military officer at that time, Slough was studying a translation of Antoine-Henri Jomini's *Art of War.* Unlike his counterparts from VMI and West Point, however, his civilian background limited his ability to process this newfound knowledge. Slough's father had been a general in the U.S. Army and his grandfather the first colonel appointed by George Washington, but he himself had pursued a career in law and fallen into the military only on account of the war.

He stared at the page before him:

"Every point of the theater of war which is of military importance, whether from its position as a center of communication, or from the presence of military establishments or fortifications, is a geographical strategic point."

Fair enough. Then:

"A distinguished general affirms that such a point would not necessarily be a strategic point, unless situated favorably for a contemplated operation. I think differently; for a strategic point is such essentially and by nature and, no matter how far distant it may be from the scene of the first enterprises, it may be included in the field by some unforeseen turn of events and thus acquire its full importance. It would, then, be more accurate to state that all strategic points are not necessarily decisive points."

Again, Slough rubbed his temples. *What of this?* Every locale reachable from the front lines, no matter how distant wherefrom, must be protected? *Not by the feckless First.* Overwhelmed by the administrative and disciplinary aspects of herding the Coloradans down to New Mexico, the prospect of honest to God fighting had given him an ulcer. Once he found himself in battle, he hoped it would be among Army regulars and not his own unmanageable pack. He placed a marker between pages and closed the book. The folding desk was on uneven footing and the book slid until he stopped it with the heel of his hand. He sighed. *Can nothing work around here?*

There was a rustle at the tent-flaps. "Colonel Slough, you wanted to see me?"

Feeling beat, Slough sighed again. "Come in."

Major Chivington stooped and entered, too tall for the tent by a good six inches. Snow flurries swirled around him as he struggled to close the flaps. "Came as fast as I could."

"Getting worse out?" Slough was briefly tempted to leave him standing, though at last he gestured toward a folding wooden chair.

"Much. What we have here is a true blue-norther, straight down from the Pole." Chivington leaned forward, held his hands before the tiny woodstove, and tried to cook feeling into his fingers.

Slough laughed politely. "Since you're a parson, I don't know whether or not I should offer you a drink."

Chivington shook his head, dislodging crumbs of frost from his beard. "Appreciate the hospitality but no, thanks."

"Shortest road to warmth."

"Thanks again, but I do not travel that road." Chivington's disapproval was unmistakable.

Slough poured whiskey into a tin cup. "Suit yourself, but every surgeon *I* know prescribes a belt or two for health."

"You're probably right about that."

"Cheers." Slough threw back the shot and winced. "Look here, Major, our strengths may derive from different sources, but in many ways we are alike." Chivington said nothing and continued to warm his hands. "We hold to our convictions and neither of us suffers fools."

"Yes, Colonel," Chivington replied, and while the tone was army-issue, Slough questioned its sincerity.

"But make no mistake—I am in charge here. Me—one man to lead and that is me, understand?"

"Yes, Colonel."

Again with that tone! "If you disagree let's have it out here, because I'm certain Governor Gilpin and the other officers will back me in this."

Chivington shifted his weight in his chair, glanced at the book on the desk, and returned Slough's hard glare. "I've no issue with your leadership, Colonel."

As ever with Chivington, Slough felt painted into a corner. The major always said the right things, usually in the right way but the edge of his voice suggested otherwise. Of course, he was jealous of Chivington's popularity, unable to fathom why his own disciplinary efforts only provoked resentment, while the major's constant abuse of the troops made them love him more. Not that he needed the approval of border ruffians and bar brawlers, but why wouldn't they accord him any respect? The attorney in him resented being out-lawyered, always on the defensive, forever explaining his decisions. On the spot, he resolved to become harder with Chivington and his adherents: fair but firm. And if they still wouldn't go along, then they could return to Denver in irons. "You're an asset, John," Slough said, "but you must follow the chain of command—you *must* respect my rank. If the talk I've heard continues and it turns out that you are its source, the consequences will be severe."

Chivington, however, had never backed away from a fight and here in Slough's tent, he wasn't about to start. He'd preached all over the Midwest, tossing out drinkers, sinners, and copperheads in every sinful town he'd saved. More than once, he'd faced down mobs opposed to his ministry, one time confronting a pro-slavery gang in Missouri who'd meant to tar and feather him. Storming into the church, he laid open a Bible, framed it with two revolvers, and announced that by the grace of God and the guns he was going to preach. With that, the town's unsavory element had scuttled away. Seated there in the drafty tent, he'd almost laughed. By comparison, this was too easy. Slough's insecurity and prolonged absences had cost him the regiment, and more and more Chivington felt that it was *his* instrument—a hammer of Divine requital. Someday Slough would have to be removed, though Chivington guessed it wouldn't take much to tip the scales. "I abhor slander, Colonel—"

"I have ears," Slough hissed.

"—and gossip repulses me."

There! The right words but in that tone! "So tell me, where do the rank-and-file get their mutinous notions?"

"They're only boys, Colonel," Chivington soothed, "and they're frightened—all I have done is tend to their spiritual needs. I tell 'em they mustn't joke about your inexperience, but admonishments only go so far. And it's nothing personal—already they know they'll be under regular Army command at Fort Union."

"Goddammit!" Slough was tired. His eyes hurt and he was sick of punching in the dark, always missing his target. "Keep it up and I'll have you court-martialed—clear?"

Chivington let the blasphemy pass unremarked but he dropped all pretension of civility. "Perfectly."

"You may leave." Slough poured himself another cup and glared over its rim. Chivington stood and saluted, but Slough noted that he did a half-assed job of closing the tent-flaps as he exited. The colonel moved from the table to his cot and turned out the lamp as he went. The isolation and loneliness in that shelter was suffocating, and it frightened him to think of the dangers that lurked outside. A waning moon shone brightly. He pulled the blanket up to his chin and saw blown snow worm its way inside the tent, searching out every corner. Back at Camp Weld, one of the captains reported that soldiers wanted to kill him and then there was the incident in Colorado City—the idea that he might be assassinated terrified and infuriated him. He fumbled in the dark for his Colt navy pistol, checked that a round was chambered, and pulled it under the folded coat that served as his pillow. As he drifted into uneasy sleep, his last thoughts were of Chivington: *Not once did that bastard call me 'Sir'.*

Fort Marcy, Santa Fe, New Mexico Territory, March 4, 1862

Louisa Canby dodged several overloaded wagons and threaded her way between plodding mule teams. Her destination was a nondescript adobe warehouse on Fort Marcy's far western side. Dressed in a blue Basque bodice and double-layered skirt, she was conspicuous as the only woman there. To her left, the hillside fell away and she enjoyed a commanding view of Santa Fe, past the speckled Cerillos Hills, all the way to midnight-blue mass of Sandia Peak. On other occasions, she had marveled at this view, but just then she was preoccupied and it escaped her notice.

At the quartermaster's office, she knocked on the door. Hearing no reply, she opened it. Across the room, Maj. James Donaldson rose from his seat. "Sorry, Mrs. Canby—didn't hear you. Pandemonium out there. You aren't staying in Santa Fe, are you?"

Louisa stepped over the threshold and glanced around the office. "I'd understood wives aren't allowed to accompany the menfolk to Fort Union."

"That's right, ma'am. I assumed you'd strike for Taos or Colorado—you can't stay here!"

"Yes, I can," Louisa said. "From appearances, I presume you will not?"

"No, Ma'am." Donaldson answered. "Department's supplies have been concentrated here, and I haven't enough men for defense." He pointed to the bound documents he'd pulled from the shelves. "Mind if I continue?"

"You go right ahead."

Donaldson mumbled thanks and moved toward a glass-fronted cabinet. He unlocked two security irons, removed several leather binders, and placed them into packing crates.

Louisa glanced outside as a teamster swore at his balky mules. *Finally, an honest reaction.* Donaldson glowered darkly at the outburst, but Louisa ignored the driver's tantrum. "Will Dr. Connelly accompany you?"

"The Governor's already gone." The major laid out another set of binders. "Rode with the territorial records up to Las Vegas this morning, Ma'am."

"How prudent." Louisa smiled but there was no mirth in her expression. The sound of distant gunfire carried through the open window. Both the major and Mrs. Canby stopped and listened, but nothing more was audible above the commotion inside the fort.

Donaldson resumed his chore. He set the volumes within separate crates—one each for contracts, land records, payroll, and so on—until each was full. Then he padlocked their lids and repeated the process. After a prolonged silence, Donaldson glanced up again. "You should head for Taos, Ma'am—Santa Fe won't be safe for Northern folk."

"Perhaps," Louisa murmured. She looked past the major and out the window. "Personally, I'm most concerned for families with children. Mother Hayden has offered them shelter at the convent—I hope there's enough food. In all honesty, I came here to ask whether or not you'd heard from my husband."

Donaldson shook his head. "Sorry, Ma'am—communication with the Territory's south has been cut off for weeks."

"I know." Louisa gathered her skirts and tried to navigate between precarious stacks of paper. She rounded the table's corner, faced Donaldson, and crossed her arms. "Forgive my ignorance, Major, but since I cannot speak with Edward, I wonder if you'd educate me? Is there any plan to oppose the Texans, or is everyone simply going to fly before them? In and out again—no fight at all?"

Donaldson exhaled sharply and set a bundle of papers on the table. He was exhausted and irritable from stress and the intense labor of stripping the post. Even though Mrs. Canby's question was insulting, she was also the wife of his commanding officer, and he chose his words with care: "Ma'am, hundreds of Americans paid full-price at Valverde—*hundreds,* and probably twice that number were wounded. Those fellows—your husband's men—took an even larger swipe at the rebels. No one can say that the Confederates have gone unopposed."

"Oh, of course not." Louisa's eyes reddened as she fought back tears. "I apologize, Major—I am beside myself! I do not know whether Edward's dead or alive, and seeing the Army depart has depressed me."

"Me, too, Ma'am but the curtain's fallen. Now we are engaged in a bloody game of chess, and all we can do is move our pieces to safety so that they may be used again."

Louisa smiled. "My husband likes that analogy."

"He's who I borrowed it from, Ma'am." The major snapped a lock on the last crate of papers. There was a rapping on the doorframe as soldiers arrived and began to remove boxes and bundles from the office.

Again, the sound of gunfire carried through the window, closer this time, and it drew Louisa's attention outside. After studying some activity on the parade ground, she uncrossed her arms and pointed. "Major, are you aware that your soldiers are chopping down the flagpole?"

Donaldson craned his neck to look through the window. "On my orders, ma'am. First thing the Texans did in Albuquerque was run up their banner, and that will not happen here—not now."

"Very...thorough."

Donaldson rubbed his eyes. "Spiteful, really but Col. Paul told me to leave nothing except food for the women and children. You need anything before we go?"

Louisa shook her head. "You'll deliver those goods to Mother Hayden at the chapel?"

"Three wagons are already enroute."

"Good. The rest of us will manage."

Donaldson handed a crate of papers to a waiting private who carried it out into the cold sunshine. "Pray the Pike's Peakers come soon—without 'em, we'll be stretched pretty thin."

"No word from Denver?"

"A full regiment set out four days ago but they were overrun by bad weather." Anxious to depart, the major held the door for Mrs. Canby. "If they're slowed even a little bit, they may be too late."

Louisa nodded, grimly aware of that the Union's hold on New Mexico Territory was slipping. "Godspeed, Major."

"Be safe, Ma'am. God save the Union." Donaldson closed the door and locked it out of habit. He waved a line of teamsters out of the yard and fell in behind them. Within the hour, the U.S. Army's last units were gone, and Santa Fe lay exposed.

Bent's Old Fort, Southern Colorado Territory, March 5, 1862

At twenty-nine, Samuel F. Tappan had travelled to the Colorado Territory to write about the Pike's Peak gold rush for Horace Greeley's *New York Tribune*. Later, he had worked for Denver City's fledgling papers before he moved up to Central City to open a hardware store. When news of the Secession broke—and as the son of rabid New York City abolitionists—he'd eagerly recruited two companies of volunteers, earning, at age thirty-two, the rank of lieutenant colonel for the entire regiment. Tappan was short and wiry, hard as iron, and he kept his curly black hair and moustache neat. His dark eyes flashed with intelligence and pride, and he was fastidiously organized. Governor Gilpin could have made no better choice. In early February, Tappan led three companies to Camp Wise in the territory's southeastern corner and drilled them meticulously. On March 1, word of the Union's loss at Valverde arrived, and they had set out in a blinding snowstorm south toward Fort Union.

Three days later Tappan's battalion crossed the frozen Purgatoire River at Hull's Ranch and rendezvoused with Slough's men under the square crown of Fisher's Peak. There, an Army express delivered a message from Fort Union confirming Canby's losses at Valverde, and declaring that everything north of Albuquerque was now threatened. This last message left Slough nonplussed. Was Fort Union already under attack, he wondered, in which case was it prudent to set a defensive line at Hull's Ranch? Alternatively, was the threat still distant and the note merely an entreatment for them to act with dispatch? With nothing but an aggressive constitution as his guide, at assembly Slough announced that to have any chance of saving the "honor and prosperity of the Republic," let alone Fort Union, the First Colorado would have to accelerate their pace with forced marches. With only a few pack mules and light buckboards to carry supplies, they followed the Santa Fe Trail over Raton Pass and emerged from the mountains at Willow Springs, New Mexico Territory. In this fashion, despite a two-day blizzard that left deep drifts across their path, their speed improved tremendously.

Not all was well, however. Behind his back, many junior officers complained that Slough was unfit to command, and rebellion simmered. In camp on the Cimarron River, tense and exhausted from an all-day slog of more than thirty miles, Lt. Col. Tappan was startled in the early morning hours to discover that the soldier assigned to guard Col. Slough's tent was not at his post. In the search for this derelict, he overheard other soldiers discuss who among them would be first to shoot Slough. Tappan drew his revolver and stepped into their circle. "Holy God," he swore, "there's no call for this, understand? None!"

Tappan counted neither Slough nor Chivington as friends—indeed, he took Slough for a blustering fool and the Fighting Parson for a conniving bullyrag with more ambition than sense—yet it was clear that the First was dangerously unwell. Tappan said nothing to anyone about this episode, though for insurance he did write out a list of the conspirators' names and hid it among his effects.

North Bank of the Cimarron River, Northern New Mexico Territory, March 8, 1862

Around midday, a second dispatch arrived, this time from Denver. Colonel Slough read the message and handed it to Tappan. "Interesting," He shifted his weight, sore after only one day in the saddle, having spent the first leg of their trip in the relative comfort of a coach.

"Gilpin's out?"

"Recalled to Washington to answer for those bogus sight drafts." He turned away from a vicious spit of snow.

"Who's his replacement? Teller?"

"Lewis Weld will keep the chair warm until Lincoln can appoint someone new."

"What's your opinion of him?"

"Lincoln?"

"Weld," Tappen clarified.

"Hardly know him, but he's bid us to hasten forward and I like him on that basis alone."

"What's your sense, then?" Tappan glanced north, where columns of infantry could be seen struggling across the frozen prairie.

Elated by the news of Gilpin's departure, Slough tried to sound nonchalant, "No one's lurking over our shoulders now, so things just got a damn sight easier."

"Hallelujah."

"And to keep the boys happy, tonight we'll announce the results of their company elections. Five new sergeants. Clark Ault, John Baker, and James Hay will be promoted to lieutenant, Scott Anthony will lead Company E, and though I wish they hadn't, evidently the Irish boys have elected Peter MacInnes as their captain."

145

City of Albuquerque, New Mexico Territory, March 8, 1862

Morning broke slowly and a brilliant orange sun pushed long blue shadows ahead of every rock and tree. The air was soft and Sandia Peak loomed white beneath a fresh cloak of snow. Everywhere, the sound of meltwater in the *acequias* was like music. Riding along a lane, Col. Green patted the neck of his horse. "Few days' rest, we'll be good as new." Though his leg was heavily bandaged, his injuries had begun to heal and the day's beginning was so beautiful that nothing could dampen his spirits—not even the columns of heavy black smoke rising from the city's center.

Behind Green rode other officers of the Texan Fifth Regiment, including Green's adjutant, Joe Sayers; Lt. Col. Henry McNeill—at twenty-four years, the so-called 'Boy Colonel'; Maj. Metzger; Lt. William Wood; and the regimental chaplain, R. W. Pierce. Beyond a series of cry canals, the habitations grew denser and the fields between them diminished. The Texans followed poplar-lined lanes leading to the town's center, past Mexican, Indian, and Anglo families standing silently before their small adobe farmhouses. A few wore friendly expressions, but most were as blank and frozen as stones, clearly wishing this monstrous gray snake would quickly slither out of their lives.

Green grew increasingly cheerful. "Smells like molasses—everyone smell that? Burnt molasses. Vinegar, too."

"Not good." Metzger did not share the colonel's cheerful outlook.

"Sir, have the abolitionists destroyed the stores here, too?" Chaplain Pierce, a considerable man who had traded for larger

146

horses twice since leaving Texas, kept his eyes focused on the pillars of smoke.

Green was too far ahead to hear, so McNeill turned in his saddle. "Tried to, Chaplain. Torched what they couldn't pack and locals swiped the rest."

"These people," Metzger groused, but did not elaborate.

Lieutenant Wood looked stunned. "How can we continue without those supplies?"

"Bill—" McNeill started, but Wood could not be silenced.

"General Sibley said we would be welcomed as liberators, fed, and sheltered, but I haven't seen one friendly face since we left Texas. And now the supplies on which our hopes rest are gone?"

"Problem'll solve itself," McNeill said. "We'll get food somewhere, somehow—"

"By God, *how?*"

"Well, the Indian pueblos, comes to it. And don't discount windfall—"

"Is there good news?" Pierce leaned forward in his saddle.

"Last night we captured twenty-five wagons headed to re-supply Fort Craig." McNeill pointed east toward Carnuel Pass. "Guess they hadn't figured we'd get this far this fast."

Metzger nodded. *"Herr* General sent parties to confiscate what the looters seized."

Green overheard this much of the exchange and relayed even more good news: "Speaking of which, Pyron's men have gone to Cubero to bring in a big cache of Federal arms and ammo." A series of muffled booms echoed over the treetops and puffs of white smoke rose into the bright sky. They continued in tense silence but heard no more shots, only the sound of wind in trees and their horses' hoof-falls.

"Is there resistance still—is that what we're hearing?" Pierce glanced warily toward the town's center.

"Likely a salute," Green said. "Bill Scurry's gonna raise our flag on the plaza today—probably all that was."

McNeill wound the reins around his left hand and tried to unfold a map with his right. "Damn this thing." He struggled to keep it open in the breeze, finally clamping it between his thigh and the saddle horn. He traced its roads and rivers with a gloved finger. "Colonel Green, where's Cubero? Ain't on this map."

Green waved toward the west, where low volcanic mesas and brown mud hills stretched away toward an indistinct horizon. There the clouds there had lost their golden hue and were building into white cumulus ramparts, softer now but still brilliant against the steel-blue sky. "Sixty miles," he said. "Navajo country. You'll love this—four civilians demanded the post's surrender and the Yank officer in charge complied—no shots fired. Nice haul, too—sixty weapons, three thousand rounds, boots, medicines, et cetera. One of the four—a doctor—rode here all by himself to let us know."

"See? There's good news!" McNeill closed the map and slapped it against his knee. "Has anyone told the general?" Prolonged silence followed, broken only when horses' hooves splashed in adobe mud.

Green tipped his hat forward and scratched his head. "Anyone seen our general?"

"Went through with Lieutenant Colonel Scurry," Wood said.

"Doubtless drunk," Pierce whispered a little too loudly.

"Lieutenant," Green exhaled, "go find his ambulance and relay that we're expecting those munitions."

"Yessir."

McNeill whistled and pointed as a Confederate banner—a canton with thirteen white stars on a blue background, two red field-stripes, and one white—rose above the treetops to the apex of a tall pole. Wind snapped it taut and there it stayed, a sure sign that the territory's governing order was changing.

"Sir," Wood said, spurring his horse abreast of the colonel's. "Anything else I should tell him?"

McNeill caught Green's attention and pointed to the flag.

Transfixed by the sight, Green forgot about the instruction that he'd given to Wood. He removed his hat and the others did likewise. "Gentlemen, ain't that pretty? The whole world is ours!"

"Sure is," McNeill agreed.

Again, Wood leaned forward to ask his question, but the colonel was so visibly distracted that he stopped.

"Lord, I feel *good!*" Green said. Replacing his hat, he pulled out his canteen and drank. "Professor Metzger, what's on today's syllabus?"

"What, Sir?" Metzger had fallen behind and barely heard the colonel say his name.

Green pulled out a tobacco pouch, packed his jaw and spat. "You taught college, right?"

"Dalhousie University—one year only."

"Where's that?" McNeill said.

"Halifax, Nova Scotia. High German, Latin, classical Greek, *und* the geologic sciences."

"Nuts, what are y'all doing here?" Wood asked him.

Embarrassed by his troubles in Maine, Metzger ignored the question.

McNeill came to his rescue: "Y'all German or Canadian?"

"Texan," Metzger answered emphatically.

"Never could understand you," McNeill laughed. "Say something in Latin."

"Nemo qui aliquid scit stultus negare potest omnes naturaliter liberos nasci."

"Wait, I know that! Say it again, but slower this time."

Metzger complied.

"Milton?"

"*Ja.*"

"'No man, who knows aught, can be so stupid to deny, that all men were naturally born free'" McNeill recited, recalling an old primary-school lesson. "How about another?"

"Pax Coelii eis qui gladios in bello tam justo dignoque adripiunt."

"Cato? Tacitus? I got 'heavenly peace' but the rest threw me."

"'The peace of Heaven is theirs that lift their swords, in such a just *und* charitable war.'"

"Hell and snakes—" Green spat tobacco juice onto the dirt "—more Shakespeare."

Tired after months of the same stories, Chaplain Pierce exhaled through clenched teeth. "For pity's sake, boys, don't get him started. Last week he tried to tell me that the earth is more than five million years old—"

"Colonel, Sir," Wood interrupted, "is there anything else you want me to tell the general?"

"Wait—what?" Green looked puzzled.

"Those weapons? Cubero?"

Green glanced backwards and saw that Metzger and Chaplain Pierce had begun to argue in earnest. Exhaling heavily, he turned back and nodded to the lieutenant. "Yes, do—and bring me his reply once we're in camp."

Wood saluted and turned down a side road as Green, McNeill, and the others spurred their horses forward. For the rest of their short ride, Green could think of nothing except the paltry state of their supplies, but once he and the others reached camp a little after ten a.m., within minutes he'd handed off his horse, shed his boots, and collapsed into deep and dreamless sleep.

Fort Marcy, Santa Fe, New Mexico Territory

8 March, 1862—Santa Fe at last. Part of the third group to enter after Phillip's Brigands tore in two days ago and ran wild, robbing the Union officers' wives and cabbaging anything not bolted down. Calmer once Maj. Pyron arrived and downright dull since I took quarters. Briggs, Lt. Wood, Capt. Jordan of Company K, Capt. Ragsdale of Company D and I all share an adobe barracks within Fort Marcy. Gen. Sibley, Col. Green and the bulk of our force is still in Albikirkie; others are up in the Sandias, where we hope there is more grass for the mules.

9 March, 1862—Duties include scouting for Yanks and hunting for supplies, with great emphasis on the latter. Here only a couple of days and already I am restless and bored. Never thought I would miss being on the trail. No word whether the Yanks mean to reinforce from St. Louis or California but we don't worry overmuch, as either place is considerably farther from Denver than we. More Whites in Santa Fe than I expect'd but they are as near to unfriendly as the natives. This whole territory is of No Account and I am glad we will be leaving leave soon. Attendance compulsory at a party scheduled for the 11th.

ভ

On March 10, returning from a fruitless search of the ranches along Peñasco Creek, Jacob and his fellows had almost reached Fort Marcy when they overtook a slow-moving carriage just north of the city's limits. Its driver was uninteresting—a wizened man who looked neither left nor right but one of two passengers caught and held the young Texans' attention. Seated beside an old crone dressed

151

in black was a young woman who, like the driver, at first refused to acknowledge the Confederates, even though every one of them tipped their hats in an effort to attract her interest. As the trailing riders began their pass, she looked up and locked eyes with Jacob Stark. Her cheeks flushed. She covered her mouth with the end of her silk shawl but did not avert her gaze.

Jacob, for his part, looked elsewhere once Hardy and others took note and began hazing him. His heart pounded for a long time after the carriage departed the main road—indeed, well into the evening and all throughout dreams in which the beautiful girl featured.

Fort Marcy, Santa Fe, New Mexico Territory, March 9, 1862

———◆———

Well into second sleep, Jacob awoke, bathed in sweat despite the cold. He rose, padded softly through the dark toward the low table and a washbasin crusted with ice, and punched through its skin to the water beneath. Dipping both hands, he ran them over his head and shivered as droplets fell from his hair onto his shoulders. Through a small transom window, a thin sliver of moon hung clear against a velvet sky. Turning, he threw another stick into a small woodstove and studied the reflections on his glistening fingers. Back on his bunk, he sat on its edge and stared at the pure, clean blade of the moon as it cut across the dark heavens. He'd been dreaming about his daughter, Jenny, sorry that he'd known her for such a brief time; and about the girl's mother, Sarah, who for all her faults had been better to him than he'd deserved; and of things he'd done and wished he had not. Nothing he'd done since Jenny's death had lessened his anger—indeed, most of the things he'd done had made things worse. He fumbled with the gutta-percha writing guide that he used for his journal, turning it over and over in his hands. He recalled the girl in the carriage, wondered who she was, and dismissed her pleasant memory as something he did not deserve. He set the guide down on the table and leaned forward to look at the moon.

From across the room, Hardy shot Jacob an unseen look. "Talkin' in your sleep again."

"That right?" Jacob said but there was no point in objection or explanation. *We've known each other since we were fifteen. No matter how I might try and convince him that everything's set square, still he would know better.*

An hour later, it was still dark outside. Then a bugle sounded, and he didn't have to think about anything for another whole day.

North of Fort Union, New Mexico Territory, March 10, 1862

Dawn broke without much light and still the First Colorado marched. They were now only twenty-two miles away from Federal Fort Union.

Between the rugged hills and mesas, northeastern New Mexico was astonishingly flat: bare patches of dead grass stretched like long shadows wherever an erratic boulder or clump of ocotillo forced wind-lashed snow around it. Drifts five and six feet deep and hundreds of feet across—each of which had to be breached before the column could advance—covered segments of the Santa Fe Trail.

&

Edward Wynkoop pushed his horse forward to the edge of a bluff and watched lines of footsore men slog past. For three days out of Bent's Fort, the captain had worn a long wool coat with the collar turned up full, and still snow had worked its way inside. Indeed, every man in the regiment was allowed to protect himself however he could. Boots had been double and triple-wrapped with burlap rags, and there wasn't a single Army-issue forage cap anywhere, all having been supplanted by square-crown bowlers and slouch hats—anything with a full brim. As the column's tail came into view, Wynkoop recognized a handful of Pinebark Independents and spurred his horse down the slope. "Captain MacInnes?"

Lieutenant James Hay lifted his eyes at the sound of Wynkoop's voice and shielded his face from the blinding snow. "Sorra, Sir—wha'?"

"Where's Capt. MacInnes?"

Hay gulped. "Sir, he bid we stay in the column like—those were his only orders."

"You don't know where he is?"

Hay *did* know, but did not answer.

Wynkoop looked north into the strange half-light. The unbroken whiteness made it impossible to gauge distance and made him feel sick and disoriented. He wiped snow from his beard and moustache and shook the moisture from his hand. "The minute he shows, you tell him that the colonel has ordered him to report." Then Wynkoop rode south to find Slough. He regretted having to report MacInnes's continued absence to their mercurial colonel. *I don't know what is afoot here, but Maj. Chivington will twist it into something it is not. Lord knows he borrows trouble.*

&

As Wynkoop rode south, the snow let up enough that patches of blue were visible overhead. After several minutes, the captain spied a group huddled beside a wide furrow in the snow. Lieutenant Col. Samuel Tappan and captains Samuel Cook, Richard Sopris, and Samuel Logan were listening as Slough finished speaking: "...at this pace, we'll be there by nightfall. Our spacing's good—only a few stragglers in the ambulances today." He turned and shielded his eyes to look at Tappan. "Well?"

Wynkoop shook his head. "No sign."

Slough glanced at Logan. "Wasn't I just saying that I should've folded them into another company? Shouldn't have left them unattached." He looked again at Tappan. "Wouldn't desert, would he?"

"No," Sopris interjected, "those boys'd sooner kill each other than part ways."

"Probably true, Colonel," Tappan concurred.

"Well, notify me if he returns—there's nothing we can do now. Go tell your companies we will rest for fifteen minutes at one p.m. and then push hard into the evening. Fort Union will not fall because we weren't there." The others dispersed and left Slough to brood alone. The farther they got from Denver City, the more unsettled he felt.

How this melancholy lashes me! The courier's message at Fisher's Peak had been so unclear as to be worthless. Were they marching toward Texan conquerors, well equipped from Fort Union's armory? Or had the past several days' pain and exhaustion been unnecessary? Either way, Slough imagined that blame would fall on him. Others were acting strangely, too. Conversation ceased whenever he approached, and on the one occasion when they had drilled with live ammunition, Sam Tappan grew visibly agitated seeing him approach. Maybe it was paranoia, but the Ides of March was near and ignoring omens certainly hadn't helped Caesar.

Now a very strange letter had come down from a civilian in Denver, and its subject—Peter MacInnes—was missing. The colonel pressed his horse north, counter to the regiment's progress.

In the pre-dawn darkness, Chivington had come to Slough's tent and announced that he was taking men back to the baggage train for blankets; soon after, MacInnes had disappeared—the coincidence was too great to overlook. Slough still suspected that Chivington was behind much of the recent unrest, but even the reverend had his detractors and it was hard to tell which companies were in his thrall: B, D, G, and I, certainly—now MacInnes's independents, too. Lines had been crossed—something had to be done.

༄

Peter MacInnes broke directly for the solitary figure beside the trail. Snow had begun to fall again, even heavier this time, but he was sure he recognized Col. Slough. "Wanted to see me, Sir?" Peter shouted. He slowed his mount to a walk, reined in opposite the colonel, and saluted. Nearby, Capt. Charles Marion led K Company; eighty yards beyond were James Hay and the Pinebark Independents, stopped to re-cover their frostbitten feet.

The colonel walked his horse around so that his back was to the wind. "Where you been?"

Peter pulled the collar of his sack coat tighter. "Sir, my company's ill-fared. I have the only mount, so I rode for boots and rags."

"That's a job for the quartermaster, a blacksmith—anyone but the goddam company captain!"

"Meant to retour quickly, I did, but this weather—"

"Shows poor judgment, Captain—really."

"Yes, Sir."

The colonel glanced at Peter's company, floundering in the snow. "Look here," he said, "did you ride alone, or were you with Chivington?"

"Wha?" Peter recoiled. "No! Jaysus, no!" He swallowed hard and hoped that the colonel could not read his expression. Fortunately for the boy, falling snow made it impossible for Slough to keep his eyes open for more than a few seconds at a time.

"Others know you left the column, so I have to respond. *Have to,* and if you acted alone, then the consequences are going to be severe. However, if someone else sanctioned your absence, then of course I will be more lenient. All I require is a name."

"Name?"

"Which sentinel passed you out? Whoever permitted your absence had no authority—"

"Sir?"

"Chivington is against me—I *know* it! Or has Downing put you up to this?"

"Sir?" Peter's stomach churned, and he answered carefully, "I went for boots—only boots. Spoke with a sentinel, the skinners, and *no other body."* Only this was a lie: in the darkness near the wagons, Peter had very nearly collided with the major himself.

Slough glanced around to make sure that no one was near. "Chivington went back to the wagons this morning, too—how is it that you didn't see him?"

"Don't know." Peter's heart thudded painfully within his chest. "Didn't see him."

"Downing, then? What about Kerber?"

"No, Sir—the Dutchmen keep themselves apart." *Which you would know,* Peter thought bitterly, *if you ever came around.*

"You're saying you never saw Chivington?"

"Yes." Another lie: at the wagons, Chivington had subjected Peter to questions so similarly odd that he'd wondered whether the two senior officers hadn't fabricated their rivalry as a peculiar test of regimental fidelity.

The colonel sat up straight in the saddle. "Look, the only way your company stays together is if you level with me, understand? Otherwise, I'll have you arrested—"

"Sir—"

"Do you understand?"

"No, Sir, I don't—I don't know what ye want!"

"I want *answers!*" More than a hundred yards distant, the last of the Charles Marion's K Company disappeared into a swale. With the Pinebark Independents busy tying rags and vulcanized canvas strips around their boots, Slough and Peter were effectively alone.

"Wait," Peter said, alarmed and confused all at once. Where had this misunderstanding come from? The Pinebark Independents had tried to stay clear of both Slough *and* Chivington, and Peter was staggered to think that this reticence was the thing that had got them noticed. What chance did they stand against the Texans in the face of such discord? And how had he come to the verge of a court-martial on account of some harmless errand? Hadn't he been told—by Slough himself—that his company's welfare was his responsibility? Anger welled up inside him and his mind went blank. "Sir, you're way off—"

"Mick, you *will* swear that Chivington ordered the theft of arms from the wagons, see? If you refuse—"

"Can't do that, Sir!" Peter said. To the west, his company had resumed marching south.

"Stop—I'm not finished, see? Do you know Daniel Conroy? That name ring a bell?"

Peter was so shocked that he could not speak.

"Fellow sent me an interesting letter," Slough continued. "Says you're the devil's own—says he thinks you and your friends have enlisted in my regiment. What do you think I should tell him, *Captain?*"

MacInnes drew his revolver from its saddle holster, raised the weapon, and locked the hammer.

Colonel Slough inhaled sharply. While his mind boiled with suspicion and rage, for several moments he kept still, watching, waiting. When at last Peter shook the snow from his brow, the colonel drew his own weapon and the muzzles of the two Navy revolvers practically touched. "Put it down, Mick!" the colonel roared. "That's an order!"

The next several moments passed slowly as neither man moved—neither said anything as the wind shrieked and hard, heavy snowflakes struck their coats. The colonel's horse whinnied and stamped at the frozen sod, and despite the cold Peter could feel sweat soaking his clothes.

"Put it down or I'll shoot," Slough seethed.

The young captain could see no way forward except to press his luck. "That will not save ye—"

"Quiet!"

"—will *not*. Ye will have furnished proof that ye mean Chivington ill."

"There—*see?* You *have* spoken with him!"

"Already there is a target on your back—"

"Stop—"

"—and my friends will not leave the matter—*ever.*"

"I said *stop!*"

"Said ye wanted the truth, *Sir.*"

Slough made no reply and fell to brooding. Lord, but the kid was right: if word got out that he had shot one of Chivington's proxies (into whose camp the colonel had just driven MacInnes), he would be courting certain death.

Despite having committed a hanging offense, and despite the revolver still pointed at his chest, Peter felt strangely confident. "Look," he said, "I want no trouble."

"That's some way of showing it," Slough said. Disgusted, he wiped the snow from his beard and shoved his weapon into its holster. "No trouble for me, either."

"And what shall I say—?"

"Nothing! Say *nothing!*"

"You said that the others already know—"

"Anyone asks, I'll say you were authorized to go for shoes. So long as you do not cross me again, I am prepared to drop this matter entirely." Slough batted at the fresh swipe of snow on his hat-brim. "Satisfied?"

"And that letter? You'll tell Mr. Conroy that he is mistaken—that he is mistaken?"

"Yes," Slough said, "again, provided you never speak of this again." He suddenly felt a little sick. Saddle leather creaking in the cold, the colonel shook his horse's reins and walked the beast away from Peter's. *"Never.* Lord, give me a reason—anything whatsoever—and you will wish you hadn't! Treacherous dog, you are never to speak to me again, understand? *Never!"*

Slough spurred his horse into the pale gloom, and Peter stared after. A moment later, he grew aware of a pain in his shoulder and realized that the revolver was still in his hand. Slowly, carefully, he lowered the weapon and re-holstered it.

༄

Five minutes later, Peter finally overtook his company.

"Thanks for the boots, Captain," Sammy Douglas said, even though his fresh pair was already soaked. "A cheer for Pete!" he called, and while his gesture was sincere, fatigue and the howling wind dampened the others' enthusiasm.

"P-P-Pete," Hay chattered, "did our lief colonel ride past?"

"Don't ask," Peter cautioned.

Mike Maher waded into a knee-deep drift. "What did ye say to him, Pete?"

"Does he know that we are better shots than Kerber's boys?" Matt Maher laughed.

Close behind, Peter and Hay exchanged looks. "Boys, that's enough!" Peter called, and the joking ceased. Despite the swirling gloom, they saw that they had nearly caught up with Company K.

"Anything I should kn-kn-know?" Hay asked quietly.

"Better that ye didn't." Peter said, and his friend knew better than to press. "Maybe later." Over the next several hours, Peter's mood swung between elation and darkness. He was fired with new hope that their troubles with Conroy might finally resolve, yet nervous thinking that they had been forced to choose between Chivington and the colonel. *Troubles, always, no matter where we turn.* God only knew whether Slough would honor his word. Peter certainly hoped so, but several times that afternoon he thought he heard hoofbeats—a provost for certain, come to arrest him—only to realize that this sound was nothing but a queer trick played by the incessant wind.

Hacienda Carrizo, Santa Fe, New Mexico Territory, March 10, 1862

Alone in the darkness, Adria listened to the sounds of the house settling around her. Footfalls went past the door of her room, softly, quietly, which told her it was one of the servant girls. Maybe Petronila, maybe Rosanda—though *she* had a bad foot and her gait was unbalanced. Petronila, then.

Adria traced the edges of the exposed beams above her, dark against the whitewashed ceiling. They looked like the bars of a cell. She turned on her side and thought about the young Texan she had seen on her trip into town and wondered who he was. She could picture his face clearly, but could not recall whether he had green eyes or blue.

She rolled onto her back and listened for crickets, her favorite nighttime sound. Hearing none, she guessed that they were all still asleep beneath the dirt. *Are crickets already out in Texas,* she wondered? What were things like there? Did the boy she had seen miss his home, or was he glad to be somewhere else? Of course, he and his fellows had come to New Mexico to spread the sickness of slavery—that was what one of the nuns at Loreto Chapel had said. Strange, to risk one's life for such a terrible thing. She knew that her father had bought poor debtors' accounts at auction, and that these people then repaid him with their labor—was that the same thing as slavery? If so, none of the nuns at Loreto or anywhere else had ever said anything about it to the don. Hardly anyone stood up to the don.

The fireplace in the room's corner was still warm—too warm, she thought, and she threw off the first of three blankets spread across her bed. *He was very handsome,* Adria thought, remembering the way his eyes had bored into hers as they passed—how he'd sat so straight and tall in the saddle. Maybe he was a wicked boy, but he certainly hadn't looked it—not to her. Regardless, she decided she wanted to see him again. There was a dance scheduled for the following evening, and she knew that some of the Texans were invited. Maybe he would be there; maybe she could introduce herself. She turned again, tangled in her bedclothes, and pictured his face again. *Blue eyes, I think.*

It wasn't until many hours later that she finally fell asleep.

Fort Union, New Mexico Territory, March 10, 1862

Around three p.m. the wind picked up and drove the Coloradans to despair. Ground-blizzards flayed their frostbitten skin and still they marched. The sun was halfway behind the Sangre de Cristo Mountains when their lead companies spotted Fort Union, just eight miles off. A confused murmur spread: the Federal regiment's few veterans were astonished to find that the fort they had remembered was gone. Landmarks were familiar: nearby hills; stagnant, alkaline Wolf Creek—in winter merely a series of frozen puddles in a bed of dirty sand; and the deep, converging ruts of the Santa Fe Trail's Mountain Branch. The fort itself, though, was changed.

The old post had been little more than a cluster of log and adobe buildings near the roots of a two hundred foot bluff. As an officer of the U.S. 2nd Dragoons, Confederate Gen. Sibley had once been its commander, and his memories of the place had convinced him that its capture enroute to Denver would pose no great challenge. However, the new Fort Union—built the previous summer on Edward Canby's orders—rose above a sloping plain a quarter-mile east of the old. Shaped like an eight-pointed star, it was surrounded by deep ditches and steep parapets topped with sharpened log abatis. Artillery pieces were set within the ramparts and inside there was room enough for five hundred men and huge stores of food, clothing, and ammunition. Heavy siege guns set on the bluff could have fired over its walls but since the Texans had no such weapons, the new redoubt was substantially more formidable than the old.

Night fell. Weary marchers unfurled their flags and drummers pounded what martial cadences their cold-stiffened fingers allowed.

A delegation from the fort rode out to meet them, nearly delirious with relief. Colonel Gabriel Paul, the fort's commanding officer and a career soldier, stood in awe of what the Coloradans had just accomplished. He sent notice that tents would be set up for the infantrymen and hot food prepared within the hour. Incredibly, Col. Slough vented his pent-up frustrations by refusing Paul's offer. "Thank you, Colonel—that won't be necessary."

Riding alongside, Paul blinked, certain that he had misunderstood. "We've more than enough tents and though the cooks may not speak well of me, hot sop-and-biscuit is the smallest thanks we can give!"

"These are mountaineers, Colonel—hewn from solid oak. They're used to hardships of every kind."

A West Pointer and Mexican War veteran, Paul sensed immediately that William Gilpin had sent him an incompetent. "Colonel, they've marched four hundred miles in thirteen days. There's no need to test their fiber now—let them rest!"

But fuming in the hours before they had reached the fort, Slough guessed that everything the Irish boy-captain had said was true: the boots did indeed want to murder him, and disaffection was so pervasive that there was no longer a way to root it out—and for this, he meant to make the regiment pay. What did it matter, anyway? "No, thanks. That march was nothing—no more to them than a ten-mile walk would be to soldiers back in the Old States."

Perplexed, Paul tugged on the crop of white whiskers on his chin. "I see." Known as a firm but fair leader, Col. Paul was at a loss. "I'll let you make the announcement."

෴

Huddled around their fires that night, the Coloradans were miserable—none more so than Peter MacInnes, who guessed that their fix was largely a result of Slough's anger with him. James Hay returned from a trip to the post's woodpile and threw a few sticks onto the coals. Other than Peter and Hay, only Sammy Douglas was still awake. The others were laid out like railroad ties—some with their heads toward the fire, others their feet, but all of them achingly cold beneath thin blankets.

Hay stared at the flames, listening as pinesap boiled and sparks flew away on the wind. He poured himself a small cup of whiskey (provided to each company by the post sutler—at Col. Paul's insistence—in an effort to forestall any rioting by the exhausted and enraged Coloradans), drank it down, and winced at the cheap, metallic taste. "Come on, Pete," he said at last, "we are friends and so you *must* tell me what happened."

Peter stood and looked past the fire toward Fort Union. There, a forest of torches was blazing as teamsters unloaded the tons of supplies brought up from Albuquerque and Santa Fe. He exhaled and gave his friend a brief account of his confrontation with the colonel. "Now Slough's got us in his sights," he concluded. "Maybe I should go back."

"Aye, right," James scoffed. Turning to study his friend, he saw a look of weary resignation that he had never seen before. "Pete, *no*—I winna let ye."

"Conroy would be satisfied."

"No, boyo—he winna." Peter shrugged but Hay was adamant. "There is no easy road, so walk with us. Each one of us sees things that the others do not and so together we are stronger."

Peter thought for a long moment before clapping his friend on the back. "Ah, yer right."

Hay forced a laugh. "Aren't I always but?"

"O, brother, we shall see: right now it's every company for itself." Peter kicked an ember back into the fire.

"God help us," Hay whispered.

Peter puffed out his cheeks and exhaled heavily. "Pitiful thing to say, but only the devil looks after us now." Then he walked over to a patch of dead grass near the fire, laid down, and tried to find whatever wretched sleep the ferocious cold would allow.

Officers' Mess, Fort Union, New Mexico Territory, March 11, 1862

At supper the following evening, Col. Slough discovered quite by accident that his appointment to the rank of colonel had been processed one month prior to Gabriel Paul's, which meant he therefore outranked the fort's regular Army commander.

Mortified, Col. Paul set his knife and fork down and glanced around the table. "What will you do, Sir?" he addressed his new commanding officer.

Though Slough's mind was racing, he stayed silent for fear that he might laugh. *Dear God—full battalion, better weapons, Chivington's power diminished—hallelujah! Gilpin meant only for me to bring the First Colorado here, but damn him, now it is mine and all laurels accrued will be mine. Lord, You have delivered me from my enemies!*

"Colonel?" Paul said, and Slough realized that he'd been silent for too long. All eyes were upon him—including those of the governor, Dr. Henry Connolly, who had said practically nothing the entire evening.

"Said I'm not sure," Slough huffed and he well knew how tactless it sounded. "What was Canby's original plan?"

Colonel Paul swallowed the last of his wine. Seated around his table was a cadre of regular officers who'd stayed true to the Union (even as others in the West such as William Wing Loring, Henry Sibley, James Longstreet, and Richard Ewell had resigned their commissions and declared for the Confederacy), as well as capable Coloradans including Sam Tappan, Edward Wynkoop, and Richard Sopris (Chivington, MacInnes, and several others were absent on patrol). Paul desperately wanted to protect his men from Slough's rash incompetence, but his mind was a churning void and he couldn't see how. Duty bound, he was compelled to give Slough an honest account of the situation—but carefully, so that the bitterness he felt didn't inflect his voice: "Colonel, *my* plan was to march twelve hundred Americans and four guns down the Pecos River, east of the Rio Grande valley, and bypass the Texans. We'd have joined Canby's forces at the village of Anton Chico."

"When?"

"Rendezvous was set for the end of March. Kit Carson would've re-organized the native militias and brought them by a third way."

"How many will remain to protect Fort Union?" Slough stared at his plate and took another mouthful of peppered beef.

"Fort Union would've been abandoned—all four hundred of us here would've marched south. Our stores here are better than those at Fort Craig, so we'd have stripped Union and freighted everything to the rendezvous. Separated as we are we cannot deal effectively with the Texans, but combined we could destroy them."

Slough continued to chew. "Very well. Let the boys rest another day and we'll decamp the following."

Paul shook his head. "Canby *had* agreed to my plan but he changed his mind. He believes Fort Union's strategic worth makes it too important to abandon—we *must* stay here."

Slough rested his fork and raised an eyebrow. "Rebels are strung out between Socorro and Santa Fe, no?"

"Correct."

"Then why not attack now? Why wait until they've concentrated?"

"Sir, Col. Canby knows every corner of this territory—every strategic asset, every potential trap. However his orders arrive, I'm confident they're correct."

"Was he correct at Valverde?" Slough rapped the table and made his fork bounce. "Thanks, but I want to see those orders." Accustomed to Slough's brashness the officers of the First Colorado were embarrassed but not surprised; Col. Paul's veterans and career officers were aghast.

Paul stared coolly at Slough but said nothing. He motioned to an aide seated along the wall behind him. "Cal, go get Col. Canby's last express. It's on top of the pile in the safe." The aide departed through a side door. Paul rose from his chair. "Gentlemen, I'm confident that within the month we'll be rid of this plague. These rebels," he quickly added. "On behalf of every regular, let me say to our guests that it's an honor to make your acquaintance. Now if you will excuse us, Col. Slough and I need to plan. Governor Connolly, won't you please stay as well? Gentlemen, good night."

~

The three men moved their chairs nearer to the huge adobe fireplace. None spoke until Paul's assistant returned with the orders.

"Cigar?" Paul offered.

"Thanks." Slough lit one and scanned Canby's dispatch. Connolly declined the cigar but poured another glass of port.

"There's a nice sauternes, too, if you'd prefer," Paul said. Tapping his glass, the governor smiled and shook his head. Paul exhaled a plume of smoke. "His message says 'Fort Union must be held to maintain communication with the East'."

A knot exploded in the fireplace. Both Connolly and Slough looked up but said nothing.

"Further," Paul continued, "I recall he ordered me not move from here until he could advise our route and point of junction."

"Hard to set store." Slough set the letter aside and scratched his chin. "We leave now, we can stamp out this rebellion before it crosses the mountains."

"That's right," Connolly added, blindsiding Paul.

"Gentlemen, my orders—*your* orders—are clear."

"Says we're to 'protect the fort'," Slough set the letter on the table before pointing to a single line, "but see, we are 'not only to protect Fort Union but also to harass the enemy.' That's a call to action if ever I heard one."

"Then you don't know Edward Canby," Paul objected. "He is deliberate and thorough in everything he does. Leaving Fort Union would be a gross violation of his instructions. Worse, if things go badly, it might also result in the entire loss of the territory. With due deference to your judgment, Sir, I insist that we hew to the letter *and* spirit of those orders."

Slough glowered. "You've tallied losses even before a single shot's been fired—faint wonder this department's been stung these past few months."

Again, Paul started to protest but Connolly interrupted: "Gabe, I understand your view but here I reckon John's right—the Texans are disorganized, and waiting for ever-more favorable circumstance seems unwise. I don't expect that this slight difference of opinion between you two will lead to unfavorable results."

"The difference is not slight, Governor," Paul said, staring into the flames. "Colonel Canby has *ordered* us to stay and defend Fort Union."

"'Harass the enemy'," Slough said.

"Indeed." Connolly drained off the last of his port and tapped his glass on the table. "I vote to strike while we may, rather than once we must."

"This is the Army," Paul said, "we do not vote!" Not only no voting but, for him, no questioning orders—doing so was anathema. Appalled beyond measure, he could scarcely comprehend what was happening yet he felt powerless to stop it. Slough was, after all, his superior.

"To me," Connolly ignored him, "it seems that Canby's orders contemplate this opportunity and we mustn't waste precious hours parsing his intent. To aggress now is our best defense."

Feeling trapped, Paul tugged on his beard. "Gentlemen, I intend to follow the colonel's orders as honor and experience tells me I must."

"And what does that mean?" Slough eyed him with suspicion.

"It means that I will not allow varied opinions to jeopardize our stake." Paul felt disembodied, as though someone else were speaking through him. "Colonel Canby says we are to act in conjunction, which suggests to me that Fort Union should serve as the base for local actions. Colonel Slough can take the field while I remain here."

"Split our forces?" Slough wondered. "How is that conjunction?"

"Both actions would protect this installation, yours by finding her attackers at distance—'harassing the enemy'—and mine by repulsing the same should they get this far."

"Sure," Slough said, "I like that." Elated, he stared at the fire as his mind buzzed with possibilities.

"Our likeliest course," Connolly agreed.

His whole world upended, Paul stared glumly at the tabletop. Paralyzed with fear and remorse, he just wanted Slough to leave. *If the Texans rout the Pike's Peakers, then I will evacuate the fort and rejoin Canby down south anyway—no point arguing now.* "Gentlemen, now I think we have a plan, but there is paperwork I mustn't ignore. Disciplinary actions, invoices—that sort of thing, but it piles up rapidly. Sir, I'll be in my quarters if you require anything further."

Slough did not so Paul bid him and the governor goodnight.

Slough and Connolly remained. For a long while, the colonel stared at the door through which Paul had exited. Once it was clear that they were alone, he turned and searched the governor's face. "Think my plan is sound, Governor? Think I'm doing the right thing?"

Dr. Connolly stayed silent, certain he'd heard wrong. Studying Slough's expression, however, he perceived a hint of panic in the man's features, and suddenly the governor understood Col. Paul's apprehension. "Yes, and by God, so should you!"

༄

Alone in his quarters, Col. Paul stared at the blank paper before him. His hands shook. Never had he written a letter like the one he was about to, never had he contravened an order, and his stomach twisted itself into knots. Then he thought about Slough and his anger flared. Working quickly, he penned a letter to the adjutant general of the Army explaining what had transpired, so that once things went wrong it would be clear who was at fault. "*Responsibility,*" he wrote, "*for any disaster which may occur should rest on the right shoulders.*" He also asked for an immediate promotion. Once signed, he sealed the envelope with wax and set it on his desktop. For a full twenty minutes, he stared out the window at the moon, trying to imagine a remedy for the situation. He felt lost, aware that promotions took time, and that until one came through—*if* it came through—the department; the fate of two territories—*hell, the whole West*—was in the hands of an armed rabble from Colorado and its neophyte colonel.

That night and for weeks afterward Gabriel Paul slept terribly. In the morning, he awoke with a ferocious headache.

Santa Fe, New Mexico Territory

Just as Slough and Governor Connolly had guessed, at that moment the Texans were thoroughly disorganized: Sibley's brigade was thinly spread between Albuquerque and Santa Fe, where Maj. Charles L. Pyron and no more than three hundred Texans held the territorial capital. The General and Col. Green had returned to Albuquerque with most of Fifth Regiment—whose mounted companies patrolled east and west from the city to watch for troops from both Fort Union and Fort Craig—and most of the Fourth.

Principally, however, the Confederates were engrossed in a dire hunt for supplies. Every company was desperate for food, clothing, supplies, ammunition, and livestock. The loss of numerous wagons at Valverde—and the barrenness of the country through which they had travelled—had crippled their efforts far beyond anything Sibley had imagined possible.

At that moment, the Army of New Mexico was neither prepared nor able to undertake further offensive action. Despite the unchecked string of victories that had carried them to Colorado's doorstep, their hold on New Mexico was tenuous at best, and it was growing clearer by the hour that unless they captured Fort Union's supplies, and quickly, all that they had gained would slip from their grasp.

PART FOUR

ONCE AND FOREVER

Santa Fe, New Mexico Territory, March 11, 1862, 8:15 p.m.

———————•———————

Jacob Stark and Briggs Hardy were lost. Santa Fe was a warren of narrow lanes and alleys fronted by featureless adobe walls, making navigation difficult by day and nearly impossible at night. Happily, the crisp air was fragrant with wood smoke and with luck, the young Texans eventually found the large, fine plaza, bedecked that night with Confederate flags and flickering torches. Hacks and fine carriages arrived to deposit well-dressed citizens and Texan officers before the gates of the Palace of the Governors while the boys held back to observe these new arrivals. Jacob leaned with one boot jacked up against a tree; Hardy filled a pipe and lit it. Neither had much to say.

Occupying an entire block, the Palace was a complex of single-story adobe buildings built in the early 1600s as government offices, courtrooms, storage, shelter, and meetinghouses. Facing the plaza was the Portal, an open portico supported by log beams that ran the building's entire length; here small knots of guests had gathered before going inside.

After he'd smoked a while, Hardy tapped out the spent fill against his bootheel. "Get this over with?"

Jacob glanced at the moon and exhaled heavily. "Yeah. Shit—yeah."

೬

The Armijo brothers had paid to have the Palace's largest room decorated like a Southern plantation, complete with white faux columns along the walls, fabric camellias, and dried Spanish moss draped from the great *vigas* supporting the roof. Candles and oil lamps cast a golden light throughout the room. In one corner, musicians played waltzes, polkas, and other dancing music. The large room was warm and crowded: Texan officers and local dignitaries stood in groups of five and six, eating and drinking as if the world might end.

Immediately Jacob felt out of place. "You said you saw *girls,*" he hissed.

"Here somewhere." Hardy forced a polite smile at a passing couple. "Keep movin'." In a long gallery, they found Col. Green cornered by an elderly New Mexican man.

"Gentlemen!" Green nodded solemnly. "Been looking for you! I'm here only until tomorrow and we need to talk."

"Sir?"

"Beg your pardon, friend," he said to the man beside him, "but I need to speak privately with these two."

"Of course," the man replied in hoarse, heavily accented English. "Colonel, I am honored to make your acquaintance—consider what I tell you, please. *Buenas noches.*"

"Buenas noches." Green turned and limped along the gallery, smiling at every civilian he passed. Once they reached the empty courtyard, he breathed a sigh of relief. "Starting to think I was the only Texan here."

Hardy pointed over his shoulder. "Everyone's in the main room, Sir."

"Cold air feels good. Look, I don't have anything for y'all—just couldn't seem to shake that fellow on my own."

Hardy scratched his ear. "Who was he, Sir?"

"Nobody—a rancher. Wants compensation for cattle he thinks we've taken but he's from somewhere we haven't been so I know that it wasn't us—I think he's a schemer. You boys need a drink?"

"Yessir!" Hardy nodded with enthusiasm.

"Wait," Green said, "you don't, do you, Jacob?"

"Not anymore, Sir—kinda got the best of me there for a while."

"Well, don't jump back in on my account." Green waved to a server, who returned shortly with two generous whiskeys and a glass of murky water. "Cheers," he said and raised his glass, "to our beloved Texas." They drank and set the empties on a windowsill. The colonel gestured toward the main room. "Come to think of it, we *do* have something to discuss. A merchant here has agreed to sell us supplies at-cost and I'd like you to bring these in tomorrow—let's go find him."

⁓

After a short search, Green spotted a portly man in a black suit and high, starched collar. Noticing the colonel, the man bowed. "Sirs," Green said with some formality, "this is Don Carrizo. Don Carrizo, these are two of my regimental officers—Captain Stark and Lieutenant Hardy." Both smiled politely and shook the don's hand. "Recall," Green continued, "we met one of the don's business partners in Peralta—Don Miguel Otero, the Territorial Delegate."

"Yessir," the boys answered in unison.

"Don Carrizo has agreed to sell us wagons and mules on friendly terms. *Señor,* with your permission, tomorrow Captain Stark and company will retrieve these."

"This is acceptable," the hacendado said, and Jacob thought he heard disdain in his voice. "My stables are below town on the river-road."

As the two older men bowed their heads to discuss details, Hardy leaned away to whisper: "Why is Daddy kissin' this one's ass? Why don't we just *take* the mules?"

"He's a 'don'," Jacob whispered. *"Muy rico."*

"Don't matter if he's got funds enough to burn a wet mule," Hardy retorted. "He's still a greaser."

Starting to grin, Jacob had to compose himself quickly as the stunning girl he'd glimpsed in the carriage suddenly stepped out from behind another Texan. Trailed closely by an older woman in a black dress, she took the don's arm and smiled sweetly at the Texans. Green noticed the pained expression on Don Carrizo's face but the younger men were simply awestruck. "Colonel Green, this is my daughter, Adria." The don's tone became scolding and he squeezed

179

her arm: "Pardon her immodesty—she shouldn't interrupt us like this."

"Good evening, Miss Carrizo. It's an honor." Green bowed and kissed Adria's gloved hand. "Permit me to introduce two of my officers, Captain Stark and Lieutenant Hardy."

"Evening, Miss," both said, eyes wide with genuine adoration. Jacob knew he had gone bright red but could do nothing for it. When his heart began to race, the girl appeared to recede as though the world around her had dissolved. *Her,* he thought, and forever after there would never be another.

"Gentlemen," Adria said and followed with a shallow curtsey and a soft smile. Her eyes lingered on Jacob long enough that everyone noticed. "Papi," she said, "if I'm asked to dance, may I say yes? Benéfica will stay close."

"That depends." The *hacendado* narrowed his eyes and glanced warily at the Texans.

Green, who had daughters himself, sympathized. "Sir, upon my honor, every Texan here will acquit himself as a gentleman, or I will deal with them myself."

"*Gracias,* Col. Green." The don smiled weakly. "I'm sure it won't be an issue. *Hija,* please, go enjoy the music with your friends."

"*Sí,* Papi," Adria sighed. "Excuse me, gentlemen." With a rustling of silk skirts she departed, *chaperona* in tow, but not before glancing over her shoulder at Jacob. Mercifully, this time the don did not notice.

Green leaned on his cane. "Beautiful girl, Don Carrizo."

The don nodded grimly. "Thank you, Colonel."

"You're lucky," Green said. "Many her age do not listen to their fathers—think they know everything."

"Yes, well, we are very traditional here," Don Carrizo said, glaring sidelong at Jacob.

"An admirable quality, sure, and rest assured that the Confederate States respect your right to remain so." His eyes locked on something across the room. "Say, won't you boys excuse us? I want the don to meet Bill Scurry and General Sibley." Here the colonel turned and tapped Frederick Metzger on his shoulder. "Major, I want you there as well."The younger officers nodded as Green, Carrizo, and Metzger turned and waded into the crowd.

Seconds later, Hardy clapped his friend on the back. "Jesus Almighty, it's *her*—the girl we saw yesterday! And, shucks if she ain't sweet on you!"

"She came over to talk to her father."

"Stupid, she don't care about him *or* Dad Green."

"Well, 'Dad' told us to behave ourselves."

"I'll not suggest otherwise but if you don't ask her to dance, I will, and we both know how those things go."

"Coarsest man I know, Briggs."

"Certainly, but think where you'd be without me."

Jacob glanced over at Adria, who was laughing with other gentlewomen her age. Close by, her fearsome *chaperona* caught him looking and murdered him with her eyes. "Jesus," he whispered. Still, Jacob couldn't help but stare at Adria, radiant in shimmering golden silk. She was beautiful, certainly; a nonpareil, the prettiest woman he had ever seen, but she was Mexican and for that, he had to remind himself that she was different, separate—*less*. But despite the conflict this presented, he began to consider that it had no basis—by what perverse calculus could *she* be unworthy of *him*, when in fact he believed just the opposite? How could she be anything but perfect when he wanted her with every fiber in his being? Moreover, if all the biases he had accumulated, all the things he held true no longer applied, then what did he know about anything? Suddenly he was lost, cut free from his past, and frightened, except that when he looked at her—which he continued to do despite her *chaperona's* open hostility—he saw a way home.

"Jake?" Hardy said, letting Jacob know that he'd been almost catatonic for several seconds.

Forever, he thought and stepped away from the wall. "So what, right?"

Hardy gave him a friendly shove. "That's it."

Halfway across the room Jacob passed by Metzger, who took his elbow and spoke quietly: "Be gentlemanly, Captain—those wagons we *need.*"

Santa Fe, New Mexico Territory, March 11, 1862—10:40 p.m.

Jacob stood nearby while the don and Lt. Col. Scurry exchanged pleasantries. Seeing him there at last, Carrizo gave a perceptible start. "Yes, *Capitán?*"

"Sir, may I ask your daughter to dance?" The boy watched as a series of expressions—none happy—ghosted across the man's face. He guessed he had pushed the boundaries of propriety or whatever passed for it in this strange place and held his breath; several moments of awkward silence passed.

The don inhaled slowly. "One dance."

Green reappeared and took the don's elbow. "General Sibley's free now—do you have a moment?"

"Yes, of course." Turning, the don gestured emphatically to Benéfica, but Briggs Hardy's pathetic yet insistent misuse of Spanish upon another young woman had distracted the old *chaperona.*

Donning a borrowed pair of white gloves, Jacob jostled his way across the room. A picket of ancient Spaniards parted and there she was, so beautiful that it took all of his concentration just to make his legs carry him forward. "*Señorita?*"

"Oh, hello, *Capitán.*"

Jacob bowed. "*Señorita,* if you'd honor me, I've been cleared for a dance."

"'Cleared?'" Adria teased. "Goodness, maize and hides are 'cleared' down at the Customs House. Do you think yourself a commodity, too?" Her friends laughed but hoped also that soon other young men would ask them to dance, too.

"Meant that your dad doesn't mind."

"Oh, he certainly does, but my answer is still yes." She curtseyed and rewarded his persistence with a dazzling smile. She took his hand, and together they threaded their way toward the room's center. Musicians in the corner began playing Johann Strauss's *Alice Polka*. Merely happy to be away from the *rancho*, Adria was ecstatic to find herself paired off with the handsome soldier she had seen the day before. "Thank you, *Capitán*—this is nice."

Jacob agreed that it was.

Adria looked into the Texan's eyes and felt her heart skip a beat. "Where are your people from, *Capitán*?"

"Texas, mostly."

"Anyplace in particular?"

"Lived all over—Mount Pleasant, Nacogdoches, Indianola, and Brownsville—far south, where the Rio Grande meets the sea."

"Do you have family in those places?"

"Don't know. Doubt it—on my own since I was fourteen. You?"

"Here all my life. Unlike you—you've seen so much. You weren't hurt in the fighting down south?"

"No," he lied.

"Those bars on your collar are because you are a *capitán*?"

"Yes, ma'am." Jacob had borrowed the coat from John Shropshire, who had money enough to have a new one made upon his promotion to major. "That's a pretty necklace."

"Thank you for noticing." She smiled. "English jet and seed pearls—very fashionable in London right now."

Jacob feigned polite comprehension as they whirled around the room, making small hops and chassés. Adria had so many questions she wanted to ask but Jacob spoke first: "You dance beautifully, Miss Carrizo."

"As do you, *Capitán*. Do you attend parties where you're from?"

"Not lately."

"Of course." Adria smiled wistfully. "Here, all the young men are away fighting and no one holds dances anymore. Is it the same in Texas?"

"Might be," Jacob said. "I just don't go."

"Why? You're very good."

Jacob's mind felt disconnected from his body, buoyed by intimations of happiness he hadn't felt in years. Between his fatigue and wondering how much longer the music would last, he answered carelessly: "My wife doesn't like 'em." The effect was subtle but Jacob felt the distance between them increase. Belatedly realizing how his words had registered and desperate not to lose her, he looked into Adria's eyes and lied: "I *was* married—my wife died a year ago."

"Oh, no—," she renewed her clasp, "—I'm sorry for your loss."

"Sorry I upset you." The music slowed and they came to a stop. He released his embrace and bowed again. "Thank you for the honor."

She glanced across the room. "I know we should part now—I do—but I'd really rather—"

"Your *padre*—"

"Oh, I haven't this much fun in such a long time, please!" For a long moment, Adria thought that Jacob would turn and walk away, but at last, he bowed and took her hand. The musicians began to play the *Spanish Waltz* and the couple danced again. Around the room, others paused to watch them glide gracefully across the floor.

"I love this tune," Adria said and Jacob said that he did, too. As they spun, Adria felt a pleasant disorientation stealing over her senses. Lights whirling past like fireflies in the dark, the music's sweet stirrings, and the faces passing in a blur, all made her lean in closer than propriety allowed. The Texan's voice and mannerisms were different from the other Anglos she'd known. Tall, with strong hands. Quiet—difficult to read. His scent was a mixture of smoke, sage, and wool, and perhaps he was a little coarse, but even this distinguished him from the over-mannered men who had dominated her life. "Do you want to know something scandalous about me?" she whispered, wishing she could draw him out again.

"You don't have to." Jacob leaned back and looked into her dark amber eyes. She was so lovely he felt light-headed, awkward, unworthy; never before had he felt the way he did then and he quickly looked away.

"There's no one else I can tell."

Sensing the girl's loneliness and cognizant of his own, Jacob surrendered.

"For months," she whispered, "I've done all I can to sabotage the marriage my father has arranged for me."

Jacob kept his gaze fixed over her shoulder.

"He wasn't my choice to begin with—I never consented to the match and I think I should have a say in the matter, yes?"

"I do, but I'm no authority on what passes for normal 'round here. One of these fellows your fiancée?"

"No, he has been missing since early February—no one knows where he is."

"Is that why your dad's so unhappy?"

"Partly," she said and lowered her eyes. "But mostly that's simply how he is." They continued to waltz in a smooth line around the floor's perimeter. They stepped quickly and their bodies rose and fell in time with the music. Many admiring glances—and a few disapproving ones—followed as they whirled past. Adria looked into Jacob's eyes and this time he returned her gaze. "Evenings like this are so rare—I pray the war ends soon."

Jacob thought of his company, freezing in the mountains above Albuquerque, and suddenly felt foolish.

"Isn't it romantic," Adria continued, "all this excitement?"

"No." Irritated, Jacob glanced at the ceiling. "War is drudgery, nerves and cruelty—nothing more." He looked into Adria's soft eyes and relented. "Maybe sometimes right before the shooting starts, exhilaration and anxiety get mixed up beyond anything I ever felt back in Texas, but there's the limit." She listened as he tried to explain the euphoria that had swept him and his friends into the army, but which now seemed as tiresome and bloodless as his old life had before.

"You've defeated the Americans, though," she said at last, "aren't you proud of that?"

"It was only a few disorganized companies."

Adria shot him a puzzled look. "Why belittle your accomplishments?"

"Because we haven't done anything yet—unless this rebellion succeeds, none of this in-between will matter."

Adria did not entirely understand, but she tried to sound sympathetic: "These days, we are all of us a little mixed up."

Observing her expensive dress and fine jewelry, Jacob had to check the bitterness that rose in his throat. "Some folks might think so, but personally I can't see it."

"Everyone goes to war," she said. "Everyone."

"Not to the same extent, then. We fight to preserve a way of life—to protect sacred freedoms."

"So do I," said Adria, her voice suddenly serious. "Must I live as an ornament?"

"Hardly the same thing," he scoffed.

She narrowed her eyes. "There's more than one way to die."

Jacob suddenly felt foolish, having picked a fight with someone who did not deserve it. *"Señorita,* I'm sorry. My behavior..."

She stared into his eyes. "You needn't apologize, *Capitán*—I'm not offended."

Jacob wasn't so sure. "Been on the trail too long. Left my manners on the desert, I reckon."

"Honestly, *Capitán,"* she laughed, "I am not offended. We are but two friends having a spirited discussion. You don't think me too bold for saying that we are friends, do you?"

Jacob said he did not. Then he smiled and again she felt her heart flutter.

"You said..." she began, before pausing to search for the right words. "You say that you are alone in Texas—isn't there anyone there who is worried about you?"

"No." Jacob looked over her shoulder. "Not anymore." As the violins drew out the song's last notes, they slowed and stepped away from the room's center. Near the end of their program and eager to go home, immediately the musicians began their next piece and the lilting sounds of one final waltz filled the hall.

Adria drank some water and smiled at Jacob. "How brave are you?" Others around the room began to murmur.

Jacob thought for a moment before extending his hand. The long-forgotten feelings she had stirred were both pleasant and confusing to him. "We'll see." He took her hand and they whirled slowly across the narrow room and back. They said hello as they stepped past Hardy and the girl he'd plucked from the crowd.

Adria bit her lip. "Truly, you think no one cares for you?"

"It's no big deal."

"What about your friends?"

"That's different."

"Why?"

He shrugged. "They're in this, too." Adria's dark hair was pulled back, held in place by a jet and silver comb, though a few curls spilled to frame her delicate features. She was so lovely that it made his lonesome soul weary for her touch, her smile, and in that moment he thought that no sacrifice would be too great to remain by her side. She smiled at him then—a curiously sad expression, he thought— and his head swam.

"*I* will worry," she whispered, "every minute until the war is over."

∽

Colonel Green spotted the couple from across the room and pursed his lips, irritated by Stark's recklessness. He leaned toward Frederick Metzger. "You said he didn't care for her kind."

"*Gott im Himmel!*" Metzger said, "Look at her."

A grin softened the colonel's expression. "That kind of pretty gets a man in trouble. You see her father anywhere?"

The major cast a wary glance through a doorway and into an adjacent room. "No—a moment ago he was with *Herr* General."

Green turned and looked the other way. "Hell, here he comes now. Hold my drink, will you?"

∽

Don Carrizo entered the main room and immediately saw what had happened. He cast a withering look at Benéfica, but the old *chaperona* was fast asleep in a chair along the wall.

Green seized his elbow and pulled him aside. "Don Carrizo, Major Pyron returned keys to the *Gazette's* printing plant today."

Furious, the don began to stammer even before Green had finished, "N-no...oh, *yes!* Yes, I heard. It has become rabidly pro-Union, anyway."

"Well, no longer, and if you and other merchants advertise again it would help others understand that things are returning to normal." Saying this, Green followed the don's gaze toward the dance floor. Despite his initial irritation, he couldn't stop a grin from ghosting across his face. *Young and in love—I remember.*

Before the don could reply, Louisa Canby stepped in front of the two men and curtseyed. "Good evening, Don Carrizo. You look well."

Green saw the muscles along the don's jaw tighten. "Colonel, these are my neighbors—they are Federal officers' wives. This is Mrs. David Morris, Mrs., ah..."

"Ford," Louisa prompted, "Garrett Ford."

"...and Mrs. Edward Canby." He bowed stiffly. "Ma'am, I'm so glad to see you."

"Likewise, Don Carrizo," Louisa said sweetly. "Such interesting visitors. Are they friends of yours?"

Carrizo sighed. "Ladies, permit me to introduce Col. Green, an honorable son of Texas."

"Good evening, ladies. It's an honor."

"Colonel," Louisa said brusquely, "can you tell me whether or not my husband is still at Fort Craig?"

"Colonel Canby, Ma'am? So far as I know—he was there when we left."

She put a hand to her lips and an audible sigh of relief escaped. "Oh, thank God—thank *God!* Forgive my rudeness, Col. Green, please. The mails are halted and rumors rampant—for weeks I've been overwrought with fear."

Green leaned heavily on his cane. "My sympathies, Ma'am."

She turned to face the don. "Don Carrizo, too—please forgive my appalling manners."

"There's no need, Mrs. Canby, though in turn I must beg you to excuse me. It is late and my daughter and I really must be going.

Ladies, good night. Colonel Green, I'm looking forward to our next conversation." He spun on his heels and went to find Adria, who'd parted from Jacob and joined her friends against a far wall. Earnestly wishing to avoid a scene, the don escorted her out into the night.

Green turned back to Louisa and her friends. "Ladies," he said, "with your permission, I, too, must be going."

"Of course," Louisa smiled. "But Colonel, will you take some friendly advice?"

"Ma'am?"

"That young man who danced with Adria Carrizo? Watch him closely."

"Beg your pardon?"

"Oh, I mean no slight. It's only that her father is exceedingly protective—excessively so."

"Oh," Green laughed, "my men will be far too busy—"

"They're young," she countered and the colonel exhaled.

"You're right, of course. Say, if you'll let me know of any developments on that front, I promise I'll send an express to your home if I receive any news of your husband."

"Thank you, Colonel—I accept those terms."

Green took Louisa's hand and kissed it even as her friends whispered behind her back. "Good night, ladies." He turned and limped toward an exit, followed by Metzger and others. Jacob Stark was among the last to depart. His head was swimming and he was genuinely sorry to leave a place of such unexpected happiness.

Santa Fe, New Mexico Territory, March 12, 1862—12:07 a.m.

———

"Louisa Canby!" Nell Ford clucked her tongue. "I was prepared a joke about Adria Carrizo giving aid and comfort to our enemy, but aren't you being a trifle careless yourself?"

Louisa made a face. "Nonsense—how else will I learn of Edward's situation?"

"Well, it's a sin to Moses, treating these people like old friends."

"And now I must watch out for Adria Carrizo. Her father's a snake—a perfect brute."

"Poor thing," Nell said. "They were handsome together."

"Troublemakers, both of you!" Letty Morris scolded. "She's promised to one of her father's creditors."

Nell shook her head. "Her fiancée led native guards down to Fort Craig. It's said the militias fared poorly there and not all have returned—goodness knows what's become of him."

"Let's drop the matter," Louisa said. "Adria has troubles enough without our gossiping behind her back."

"Indeed." Letty stifled a yawn. "It's late. Shall we go thank the Armijos?" Nell agreed and took Letty's arm, but Louisa stayed behind, worrying, as was her habit. Fatigue had dulled her senses, though, and soon she followed her friends out into the night air. As they waited for their drivers, the women agreed to meet later in the week and parted with kind words and warmth. Inside the hour, each was home safe, but for their anxieties, none could sleep.

Fort Union, New Mexico Territory, March 12, 1862

Peter MacInnes pushed through a clump of a scrub oak, stepped clear, and listened for his friends. *Jaysus, where have they gone?* Not once in the last three hours had he seen another human, and while walks alone in the woods did not alarm him, never had he gone out with a view to killing those he might find. He clambered up a low ridge above Tecolote Creek, running cold and clear between red sandstone walls. As he climbed, rocks rolled loose and splashed into the shallow water. Overhead, despite great exertion, small birds could make no progress against a steady wind, finally peeling away to ride the current eastward.

Colonel Paul had suggested temporarily attaching MacInnes and the Pinebark Independents to the Fifth U.S. Infantry to give the least-experienced volunteers a chance to observe the habits of professional soldiers; eager to isolate the First Colorado's most-restive elements, Colonel Slough had quickly agreed. Thus, the Pinebark Independents and Samuel Barr's veterans were paired and sent to scout the roads between Las Vegas and Anton Chico. By all accounts, this arrangement had proved satisfactory, though nothing Peter witnessed gave him hope that the campaign would end well: daily Col. Paul's regulars openly defied Col. Slough; several companies of the First had brawled with their Federal counterparts; and because of the First's rampant thievery, the post's sutler had closed his store. Not once had Chivington made an effort to discipline the guilty and Slough's response had been to bar himself inside his quarters. Meanwhile, travelers on the Santa Fe Trail spoke of horrors up and down the Rio Grande. Everywhere banditry was

191

on the increase and with the Army preoccupied, Navajo and Apache bands had begun to raid the outlying settlements.

From the hill's crest he looked into another empty valley—*Nothing*. Nothing but bare branches and dry grass, tossed by a rising wind. Indeed, Peter would have been surprised only if someone *had* been there. New Mexico's great emptiness unnerved him; he couldn't imagine a less-likely place to wage war—no cities, no mines, no industry—nothing. All they had found in the *despoblado* south of the fort were farms and *ranchos* deserted in evident haste: tables set for meals, trunks filled with clothes, livestock broken from their pens and running wild. It was as if the whole population had been raptured away on a wind that never stopped.

⤲

Peter crouched at the base of a ponderosa. Furrowing a carpet of matted needles with his fingers, one of the needles stuck and the sight of bright red blood suddenly carried his thoughts back to the year he had endured in Maryland. *Daniel Conroy—by God, so wicked and weary. Bonded James and me out of jail, tied us down with crooked writs, and then paid off the courts for insurance. Chopped wood every day; tended the pigs and cattle. Great hemp-fields, flax, wheat, corn, and tobacco—and still we starved. Not Conroy, though—never him. Different rules. He beat Tink Jones bloody over nothing more than a pilfered crust of bread; lashed him so that poor Tink never got up again. Rye-meal poultices and iodine tinctures availed the boy nothing and he died on a Sunday.* He held his hands side by side and studied a scar that continued across the backs of both. *Black or white didn't matter, neither—Con beat old black Robert out of habit, Hyrum, too. Loundered anyone he pleased—and Christ, the girls had it the worst. Con's da was rich and that is all the authority he needed to behave like a beast. Might've died there like Tink. Did what we had to, then—there was no other way off that farm. No other way.*

⤲

That Sunday morning in August 1860 was a blur: Daniel Conroy and his father, Dodd, had returned from their customary ride and Dodd struck Neil Wilson with a rake-handle. Though Wilson had been unconscious, Con wouldn't stop kicking him. Blind with rage, Peter stayed hidden until Dodd drew near and then from behind brought a mattock down on the old man's skull. Con yelped and broke for the woods but James Hay and Bill Storey had given chase and caught him in less than a quarter-mile. After Wilson came around—minus three teeth—he and Peter followed the others back to where they had left Con, except that he wasn't where he should have been.

"Bill!" Hay shouted, "Was he under that tree? Or another?"

"Here!" Storey shouted back. Wide-eyed, he pointed to a bloody smear on a sycamore's trunk.

Peter looked around wildly. "Quickly, boys, find him!"

Hay jumped into muddy water and groped beneath the creek's overgrown banks.

Shaking with fear, Peter spun, took a huge gulp of air, and pointed. "Bill, Neil, go downstream—I'll go up. James, stay here case be he returns."

They had found nothing, however, and so they ran. Day and night, they crossed woods and climbed hills, and with great luck, eluded a posse assembled to track them down. Sleeping in coal sheds and fighting dogs for scraps, first they had gone through Greensburg, Pennsylvania; then Zanesville, Ohio; crossed Indiana and Illinois to Bonne Terre, Missouri (where they lasted just two weeks as lead miners, but also where they helped Sammy Douglas and Michael and Matthew Maher out of a similarly nasty scrape); and finally, after ten months on the road, to the Colorado Territory. During their first nine months there, they had gone undetected among the destitute thousands who'd quit the old states once the rumored gold strikes north of Pike's Peak had proved real. Then Bill Storey's name had made the papers, which certain parties had chanced to see, and so Conroy had crawled up from Hell to collect.

Despite having stuck for over a year, Peter hadn't dared to imagine that he and his friends' bonds would last. Con wasn't after Douglas or the Mahers after all—there was no reason they should continue to risk their necks, and yet they *had*; could've gone anywhere they wanted, and yet they had *stayed*—Wilson and Storey had *stayed*. And though Hay had been against enlisting, even *he'd* seen the benefit of sticking together. The realization struck him like a thunderbolt: his fellows were there still. It'd never occurred to him that friends could be a family—or as close to one as he'd ever known. Until that moment, he hadn't believed in the permanence of anything. At once, he stood and walked downhill.

꙳

A quarter-mile below, Hay, Mike Maher, and others came suddenly into view on the far side of a thicket, and when they shouted to the others that they had found him, Peter felt his eyes water and his throat tighten. Embarrassed by such tender emotion, Peter waved as though nothing was amiss and motioned for them to continue south. The air grew steadily colder. Broken clouds rolled across the sun and sunlight speckled distant hills—wild and beautiful country. At the ridge's terminus, Peter walked down a scree-covered slope and just as soon as he set foot upon the valley floor, it began to snow.

Fort Marcy, Santa Fe, New Mexico Territory

———— ● ————

12 March, 1862— All-day patrol east on the Trail. Left at dawn, turned back at the crest of Glorieta Pass, east of Canyoncito and re-cross'd the Plaza in darkness after six o' clock. Herders at Johnson's Ranch say they've seen no Yanks for more than two weeks, which means that we still have time still to rebuild our strength—if only there was more food.

13 March, 1862—Three days of splendid weather, now snow. In quarters much of the day. Mail arrived: Doc Miller's reply and a letter from Lydia Sams saying that she and her family are well but that Gabriel may enlist in a new company being formed in Brownsville. A note from Adria Carrizo as well. The don was in such a state after the party that Col. Green ordered me to stay back while Hardy and Fisher went to fetch the wagons. Carrizo needn't worry: expect that we will move forward tomorrow and that will be that.

14 March, 1862—Still at Fort Marcy with nothing to do. According to the latest Commissary Report, we've provisions enough for 40 days, warehoused mostly in Albikirkie. Companies are strung out between there and Santa Fe so as not to stress forage for the animals or precipitate a revolt by the natives, as we've confiscated an awful lot. First Regiment is over the mountains east of Albkrke; the Third is a little further north, guarding our dwindling beef herd. Hardy has gone to our company camp at La Cienega and will march the Guards here before taking them to our new posting on the road east of Los Cerillos. Am staying another day, as I rec'd another note from A.C., hoping that I am well, &c. and asking if I'd like to meet. Believe I would.

15 March, 1862—Spent an agreeable morning in Santa Fe wi. Adria Carrizo and her chaperona. A.C. is as captivating as this City is peculiar: mud architecture, burning candles and painted Saints in every room. Little distinguishes most cities: Brownsville is like Velasco, Velasco like Indianola, and so on. Santa Fe, tho, is different: built of soil itself, everything here feels ancient. Queen Elizabeth I had only just died and Shakespeare was still alive when the Spaniards established their territorial capital here. Amused at the intensity wi. which A. insists that she is _Spanish_—not Mexican. Lord but these people are more obsessed wi. mestizo miscegenation and blood fraction than those white planters who straddle the Color Line.

16 March, 1862—Met Adria again on the plaza before daybreak and this time it was just stray dogs, street sweepers, and us. She asked how long we would be staying and I did not have an answer. Falling for her. Parted company o' the noon bells, returned to Fort Marcy, and frankly spent all afternoon thinking about her. Am troubled to reflect upon my inclinations; very quickly, this has become rather complicated.

Willow Springs, New Mexico Territory, March 17, 1862

———— ◆ ————

Major Chivington shook gobs of wet snow from his coat and stepped into the stage company's office.

A company scribe looked up from his paperwork and gestured toward a pot-bellied stove and a coffee pot in full boil. "Anything?" the gray-bearded clerk asked.

"Not yet," the major said and poured a splash of coffee into a tin cup that was minus much of its blue enameling. "What about here?"

"No." He coughed and adjusted his sleeve so that he did not smear the figures he had just made in a ledger. "All quiet. Warehouse is filling with goods, bales of wool just waiting for the road to re-open. Oh, and some fellow here says he wants to speak with an army officer."

"Who's he?"

"Wouldn't say. Some foreign nabob—civilian. Rode down from Denver after the weather cleared. Been here two days."

"Where?"

"Up top." The clerk pointed to the one-horse log hotel on the hillside above.

Chivington looked out the window at smoke coming from the hotel's chimney. Tufted sage and mountain mahogany had begun to emerge from the deep snow, but it would be weeks before the ground was clear, and meanwhile the roads were sucking quagmires of mud and clay. "You told him to wait?"

"Told him the army has prohibited southbound traffic until further notice but that every few days a patrol comes north from Fort Union, so he said he'd wait."

"He comes down, you may tell him that I will be here until our horses are fed—"

"Here comes his majesty now." The clerk pointed. Chivington glanced out the window again and saw a short, thickset man navigating the slippery path down from the hotel. Mid-thirties, probably. Well outfitted for travel, he wore gold-rimmed glasses, worsted wool pants, a brown wool overcoat, and vulcanized boots. Another man, tall and powerfully built, followed him. The major downed the last of his coffee, strained the grounds with his teeth, and spat them onto the freight office's muddy floor. He thanked the clerk, who resumed his bookkeeping, and stepped outside to wait. The snow had tapered off and the clouds were broken so that patches of blue were visible.

"Good day, Sir!" the man hailed as he climbed the short set of steps to the freight platform.

Chivington scraped gobs of mud from his boots. "Good day."

"Name's Conroy, and I'd like your help, see? Are ye one of them that come down from Denver?"

"What can I do for you?" the major asked, deciding immediately that he didn't care for this poltroon. Five of the twenty soldiers Chivington had taken on patrol appeared at a corner of the building, but he gestured for them to wait by the stables. Taking this cue, Conroy nodded and his own man ducked inside the freight office. Chivington coughed and spat onto the road. Conroy approached until he stood but a little ways apart, which forced him to look up at the major, who stood a full head taller.

"Sorry, friend, I didn't get your name."

"Haven't given it."

"Of course," Conroy said, visibly annoyed. "But look, my business is important and I'd like your help, see? I have it on good authority that criminals have taken refuge within your ranks—"

"Oh?" Chivington smirked.

"Four boys," Conroy continued. "Their names are Peter MacInnes, James Hay, Neil Wilson, and Bill Storey. I've come a terrible long way to find them, see? They must be detained."

"What makes you think that they're here?"

Conroy's eyes swept the trail back toward Raton Pass. "In Denver a clerk showed me their names on your rolls."

"Your needs do not outweigh this army's."

Conroy stared at the major, alert to the swelling antagonism in the big man's voice. Indeed, he'd travelled far and at great cost, and despite several false starts had seen proof that the boys had recently signed one hundred and twenty-day enlistments with the First Colorado. But though this was basis enough for Conroy, all but one of his hired companions had abandoned him: one had struck for Fort Bridger north of Denver; two others had stayed in Denver; and a U.S. Marshal, whom he'd hired to serve fugitive-labor warrants sealed by a judge in Missouri, had doubled back to Nebraska to pursue other—in his words—"slower" quarry.

"Please understand," Conroy said, trying hard to control his voice, "these gadabouts have done me and my family terrible injury, see?"

Chivington scratched his beard. "Those names are unfamiliar."

"Sir, this is no small matter! Warrants have been sworn out for their arrest and return—"

"To which jurisdiction?"

Conroy exhaled, annoyed by the huge man's intransigence, confused by his overt hostility. "Seems I've offended ye, Sir, and that is *not* my intent—"

"We are preoccupied," Chivington said.

"Assuredly, sir—assuredly so. Perhaps at Fort Union I can speak with someone who isn't so busy—"

"You may not—we are all preoccupied," Chivington repeated.

"Indeed? Then how long must I wait?"

"Can't say."

"Sir, it is considerable of a sum those boys owe, see?"

"Is that right?"

Conroy exhaled heavily. "Sir, the truth—," he said, "—the truth is most wretched. Their debts go beyond mere monies—they are murderers. Killed my father—tried to kill me." He removed his glasses and gestured to a series of scars that ran at right angles between his left eye, ear, and jaw. "They set upon us like dogs—attacked without provocation!"

"And how are you acquainted with these fellows?"

"I own their debts, see? Let 'em work off the balance, which benefits them and us, both."

"Of course," Chivington said and looked through the window to the freight office interior. Conroy's man was there, staring back at him.

"Sir," Conroy said through clenched teeth, "you must appreciate my position. They are murderers—I will *not* turn away. Sir, I *cannot.*"

Chivington held silent. He still didn't care for this dandy—his tone, his fancified riding clothes—and he couldn't help but think that a great deal had been left unsaid. Neither, however, did he like what he'd heard, though if anyone cared to, much of the First could be brought up on the same charges. *Criminals, the Irish. Still, if anyone can shepherd them into God's fold, it is I.* Remanding them to a fool bent on revenge would be an abdication of his responsibility for their souls. He stared at the pines above the station and watched gusts of wind strip snow from their gnarled branches. "Let's see that warrant."

Conroy let out an enormous sigh. "In truth, I no longer have it—the marshal I'd retained demanded that his fee be doubled and quit the territory before it could be served."

"Where it was issued?"

"Greene County, Missouri."

"Don't think I can help—these days, Missouri is a devil's den." Chivington coughed so loudly that a few of his men glanced around the corner.

Despite having nearly depleted his funds, Conroy fell back on the one tactic that had never failed "I'll *pay* for your co-operation, see? You've been inconvenienced and it's perfectly reasonable that I should re-imburse your for your time. Is fifty dollars sufficient?"

The major halted mid-stride. "I said I cannot help you."

At this, Conroy's face went red. "You cannot deny me! This is a matter of *law*—"

"Mister, out here I *am* the law!" Chivington thundered.

Conroy spat on the ground. "I will not be treated like some common vagabond! I am going south and there's nothing—"

Chivington grabbed Conroy by the collar of his coat and began to drag him through slush and snow toward the far end of the platform. Barely able to breathe, Conroy could manage little more than a strangled cry: "Gibbs, man, *help!*" Revolver drawn, Conroy's hired man emerged from the office and took steps toward Chivington. At the building's corner, soldiers stepped from behind the warehouse, let the major and his captive pass, and then closed ranks behind him. Faced with muzzles that looked big enough to sleep in, the hired man dropped his weapon and raised his hands. Descending a short flight of steps, Chivington pulled Conroy to the rim of a wooden horse-trough, thrust his head through a skin of ice and into the water beneath. Conroy struggled and lost his glasses; tried to shout; wriggled free from his coat, and came up for air. He managed a quick, wheezing gasp before the major's enormous hand wrapped around his neck again and dunked him a second time. After several violent seconds, he inhaled a smart chance of water and thrashed so that his shirt and trousers were torn on the trough's edge. At last, the major let him go and he lurched backward, coughing and shivering, into an enormous snowbank.

Chivington leaned down until their noses nearly touched, and every time Conroy coughed, he expectorated water onto the major's beard. "You will be judged," he growled, "and He does not suffer your like."

"Bastard!" Conroy sputtered, "by what right—"

"Shut up," Chivington snarled. He gestured for Conroy's hired man to be marched forward. "You," the major said, "take him with you. If I see you again—either of you, today, the following, or ever after—I will kill you. Is that clear?"

Looking sheepish, the hired man nodded before turning to help Conroy retrieve his spectacles from the bottom of the trough.

"Sir, *please!*" Conroy whined but when Chivington made a gesture to punch him, his mouth snapped shut.

"I *know* what you are." The major dropped his voice so that only Conroy could hear: "Understand that when God calls you to account, I *will* testify at your trial. Perhaps those boys *did* injure you, but it sounds as though they had righteous cause and so I condemn only their failure to finish. Now, hie over yonder mountain and never come back, understand?"

Deflated, Conroy turned—using one hand to keep his torn britches suspended, the other to keep his bent spectacles perched upon his bleeding nose—and hastened up the path, hired man entrained, toward the hotel. Chivington waited until they were inside before calling for his soldiers to saddle up for their long ride back to Fort Union. Within a quarter-hour, each party had set off in opposite directions and stillness returned to Willow Springs.

As the sun dipped toward the mountains, the company clerk looked out the window and lit an oil lamp on his desk. He retrieved the revolver he kept in a desk drawer, checked to see that it was loaded, and set it atop a stack of papers. *Better safe than sorry—these days, only God knows what is out on the roads.* Then he began a new column of notations in his ledger.

Santa Fe, New Mexico Territory, March 18, 1862

———◆———

"Pendejo!" the don snarled, looking up suddenly from his notebook. "You are *weak!* How could I have made such a mistake?"

"Don Carrizo," Felix pleaded, "I'm afraid for my *soul!* This burden is heavier than anything I could've imagined."

"You are *weak,*" the don repeated. "No man admits such things—"

"Those people appear in my dreams," Felix said. "They ask me *'why'* and I have no answer."

"They are *dead!* They need no answers—your imagination—"

"I cannot help it," the boy said miserably.

The don glanced sharply across his desk. He'd called Felix out to the ranch to discuss another job, and here the boy was faltering, claiming that he was unfit to continue. With the Texans poised to depart, Don Carrizo was anxious to attempt another forced sale before the cover they provided disappeared—most anxious, yet here was a confidante, weeping like a child. "Is it the money?" His attempted purchase of La Rinconada had fallen through, and with it went the fee that he'd promised to the boy—it wasn't unreasonable that Felix expected to be paid, though if these tears were a deliberate tactic, well, that was shameful. *Unmanly.*

"No," Felix sobbed, "it's not that."

"What then? Must I call in someone else?" This posed all manner of problems, of course, for the boy knew everything—names, dates, *everything*. A constable from down south had contacted Santa Fe's chief magistrate with questions about the devastation of Jorge Luis's *rancho*—this much he knew, but whether or not there were connected threads was harder to say. To expand the cast now was to invite more tongues to wag, and that was decidedly unwise. No, there was no choice but to hold the boy's feet to the fire—gently perhaps, but certainly. "We will talk about this later. Have you heard anything from your brother?"

Felix shook his head but did not speak.

No surprise there, the don thought. It was widely known that the territorial militias had collapsed at Valverde, and while the don had a theory about who was to blame, Felix's breakdown had made him wonder if there wasn't some basis in fact for the slurs. "How are your parents, then? I've not heard from them for some time."

"Papí is still across the mountains in Colonias. My mother stays locked in her room, mourning for Sílo."

"They must know, then."

Felix brushed angrily at his face with his sleeve. "I think we all do."

"However upsetting, it is better that they accept the truth. The sooner they do, the sooner we can discuss whether or not you and Adria are suitable." The don paused. "Do you not agree?"

Embarrassed to have revealed his feelings, his weakness to the don, again the boy wiped his eyes. *I am caught,* he told himself. The don, a man who wants for nothing, only wants more—indeed, to the extent that even his only child was merely a token for barter. *A way to take from me that which is mine and I have wanted her for so long that I haven't thought of anything else, haven't thought clearly.* To have Adria was to surrender his birthright—*that has always been the unspoken price, redoubled now that Porfino is dead.*

"Felix, do you not agree?" the don repeated.

Caught, the boy thought again, though this time he nodded in agreement. "Yes, Don Carrizo. What do you need me to do?" In that moment, he began to hate Adria Carrizo nearly as much he had always wanted her.

"You're sure?" Cautiously relieved, the don tapped his ring finger on the desktop.

The boy thought about the bottle of whiskey in his saddlebag and shook his head to clear it. "You can trust me, Don Carrizo." His head ached, but he wanted to get back on the road and prove his worth.

"Good—it is not so far this time." He reached for a map and indicated a village south of Cerillos. "Not nearly so far," he said, though for as distant as it sounded to Felix, he may as well have pointed to a mountain on the moon.

Fort Marcy, Santa Fe, New Mexico Territory

17 March, 1862—Light snow, melted by ten. Ordered Hardy to Cerillos w.o. me. Ev'ry morning, I am certain that we will march east but then it is foraging parties and patrols. Am so accustomed to getting up o' nights that I don't mind it much and would as soon start for Ft. Union now as eat supper, but we are mired here. Frozen. Do not know what keeps us but fear that the Brass knows of impediments that we do not, and which must therefore be serious. Must leave soon, or it will be too late.

18 March, 1862—Every day I grow softer, my fires banked. Adria's father is gone down to Belén for five days, so I think I will go and pay her a visit.

Fort Union, New Mexico Territory, March 18, 1862

———————◆———————

The weather was sunny but cold. Eyes closed, James Hay leaned against a slab of blood-red sandstone and listened as wind drove down the dead grass. Since noon, it had blown up from the south, bending trees back against their usual inclinations. For thirteen days various companies had made longer and longer probes—some cavalry units had gone as far south as the town of Anton Chico—in search of an enemy that evidently lacked the potency to venture beyond Santa Fe. *Frost-burnt haste to get here and—for what?* Rocks clattered nearby, but he did not open his eyes.

"Lieutenant Hay?"

"Quiet, heathen."

"Sorra," Sammy Douglas lowered his voice, "ye weren't moving."

"By design, eejit." Hay still found it strange to hear friends address him by rank, but not so strange that he did not enjoy it. He raised a hand to shield his eyes. "We are too far ahead."

"But they've caught up—"

"To the lane?" Hay said.

"Well, *nearly.*"

"Don't bother me until they're in the four-roads." He resettled against the warm stone and closed his eyes. "Tell me if ye see Peter, though." Despite his initial resistance, Hay had fallen quite naturally back into soldiering. His father had served—and died—with the British Army in India, and though among his friends only Peter knew it, for eleven months Hay had been a sailor aboard a U.S. Navy Home Squadron steamship (his unauthorized absence from which being the reason he'd ended up at Dan Conroy's farm).

Down in the valley Company A was following a track alongside the creek, enveloped in red dust. Comanche scouts—the first Indians Hay had ever seen up close—rode behind as a rear-guard. "Cloudy above the mountains?"

Douglas glanced over his shoulder. "Aye."

"More snow, then."

Douglas watched Company A's progress until another knot of volunteers appeared on the ridge's crest. "Wilson and the Mahers are here—O'Dowd, too."

"Call 'em over." Hay opened his eyes and hoisted his musket.

༄

"Nothing," Mike Maher said, picking his way between the rocks. "Not a soul."

Hay looked disgusted. "'Course not—they're well over those mountains."

"They're coming, boyo—regulars say they must have Fort Union's stores."

Hay yawned but even before his mouth closed he noticed slips of movement in a clearing farther down the valley—men on horseback, picking their way along an arroyo. *Four, five, six,* he counted quickly before they disappeared from view. Mexicans by appearance but who bloody well knew what a Texan looked like, so he turned to the others: "Mike, throw a flag to Cap'n Barr—horsemen on the road there. Everyone else, *get down!*"

Maher pulled a square of red fabric from his pocket and waved to Company A's scouts down on the valley floor. Those men scattered rapidly, as did the Pinebark Independents on the canyon's opposite rim. Senses engaged, Hay glanced around a boulder.

"How far?" Mike Maher felt his hands growing slippery with sweat.

"See there? Three-fourths of a mile—six of 'em."

"Texans?"

"Dunno," Hay said, "be quiet." He squinted over his musket's five hundred-yard leaf and acquired the foremost rider in his sights: a dark-skinned man with a scraggly beard, deerskin leggings, and a coarse-woven blanket across his shoulders. A shotgun was balanced across the bow of his saddle. Down below, a Federal waved frantically to the men on both hillsides. After a few seconds, he crossed his musket against his free arm and then ducked back into a clump of scrub beside the track. "Boys, don't shoot—understand?" Hay tried to sink even lower into his concealment between the rocks. The riders were within three hundred yards, so he lowered the No. 5 sight-leaf in favor of No. 3. Glancing to his right, he saw Matt Maher staring blankly into the distance, musket rested across his knees. "Busy, Matt?"

"Can't see hyne away."

"Matt's eyes are bad," his brother explained. "Needs glasses."

"Christ," Hay said, "watch the ridge, then."

Matt rolled onto his back and squinted uphill.

⁓

Someone on the valley floor shouted for the riders to halt. En masse, the Federals rose along both sides of the road with muskets raised. The riders in front pulled up hard and shouted to one another in Spanish but the rearmost pair wheeled hard and spurred their mounts toward the trees.

"*Stop 'em!*" Capt. Barr shouted, and musket began to crackle. Broken pine boughs showered the road and smoke blanketed the hillside. One of the riders slumped over his horse's neck but he did not fall and his animal did not stop.

"Got one!" Sammy Douglas crowed. "Boys, I got him!" His shot had only grazed its target, though, and the riders continued their frenzied flight. Barr called to the men on the hillsides, anxious to learn whether more were coming. From their lookouts, Hay and Peter MacInnes both signaled that the road was now empty. A Federal sergeant lowered his weapon, held up a hand, and approached the Mexicans. A conversation ensued, too far away for Hay and the others to hear.

"Who'd Sammy shoot?" the boyish O'Dowd gulped.

"Come on," Hay said and scrambled downhill so that he might hear some of the exchange. "What of them?" he said, gesturing after the Mexicans.

"They're not important." Barr inhaled dust and coughed. "You see those others?"

"Not well," Hay admitted.

"Mexicans said they are Texans who fell in with 'em near Bernal this morning. Said right now there are only a couple hundred Texans in Santa Fe." A Comanche scout reined up in front of Barr and they conversed rapidly. *"Wahaatu taibo"*—two whites, was all Hay heard them say, but these sounds meant nothing to him. Soldiers on the road stood aside as six more Indians thundered after the Texans.

Hay wiped sweat from his eyes. "What now?"

Barr pulled out a notebook. "Hasten back to Las Vegas and send an express to Fort Union."

From the opposite slope, Peter MacInnes's squad descended. "All clear, Cap'n," he said. "No one for five, six miles, certain."

Barr finished his notations, closed the notebook, and tucked it into his jacket. "Good. Captain MacInnes, we will head back uphill. Keep a weather-eye behind you, but we must emphasize speed over safety to get this news to Fort Union." Thirty feet away, Douglas was still talking excitedly about his shot.

"Were they Rebels?" Peter asked.

"Appears so," Barr answered. "We'll see if our Indians return with anything."

Hay stared into the green-speckled distance. Clouds of dust filtered upward through the pines, though whether these marked the Texans' progress or that of their pursuers he could not tell. He shouted for the others: "Come on boys, hurry—Lord, we must hurry!"

⁓

As Barr would soon learn, Lt. Col. Manuel Antonio Chaves—the leader of a native militia—had already reached Fort Union with reports of Rebel scouts east of the mountains. By the time Barr and MacInnes's companies reached Las Vegas, already the First Colorado and several Federal companies had sallied forth. In the small hamlet of Tiptonville, Barr, MacInnes, and their companies reversed course and fell in with the column without opportunity to rest or re-fit.

Hacienda Carrizo, Santa Fe, New Mexico Territory, March 18, 1862

Hacienda Carrizo, or as it was formally known, Rancho de los Cerros Verde, was nestled within the low hills that separated the Santa Fe River from the Arroyo de las Truchas. Jacob rode along a lane for twenty minutes before he realized that everything he'd seen since he'd crossed the river—every building, every field—belonged to Don Carrizo. *My God, he owns half of the territory.* To the southeast, Jacob saw laborers guiding ox teams hitched to single-furrow plows, turning over the fields in anticipation of spring. Robins hopped between the dirt clods, searching for worms.

Reaching the main house, he dismounted and tied his horse's reins to a wooden pillar. Standing before a large, ornately carved door, he knocked four times before it creaked open on wrought-iron hinges. Removing his hat, he smoothed his hair as a servant escorted him to a plain pine bench and asked him to wait. After what seemed like hours, Adria appeared at the hallway's end, dressed in simple green cotton. She had a finely knit shawl thrown over her shoulders and Balmoral boots on her feet. Her dark brown hair, held back with a silver comb, framed her smooth forehead.

He rose. "Afternoon, Miss Carrizo."

"*Capitán* Stark." She extended her hand, which he kissed. "I hope I haven't kept you waiting for too long."

"No." He shrugged.

"I have, haven't I? I'm sorry."

"Wasn't gonna leave."

She smiled and he studied her face: narrow nose, delicately rounded; her chin tapered to a soft point below full, beautiful lips. *Lord, she is perfect.* Her smile produced small dimples below the corners of her mouth and eyes like polished jasper glittered above finely chiseled cheekbones. Looking at her made his heart ache. *Be smart,* he thought, and then *Hell, if you were smart you wouldn't be here.*

"Please follow me," she said and then Jacob didn't care whether it was smart or not. "We'll be in the drawing room," she announced rather loudly, though as far he could tell they were alone. Afternoon had stolen across the valley, so a servant appeared to light candles and oil lamps and then quickly disappeared. Jacob walked behind Adria and admired her form as she moved through angled beams of dusty sunlight. Moments later, he heard shoes clacking on the tile floor and realized that Benéfica was behind them, wrapped in her habitual dark dress. They entered the drawing room with a huge billiards table at its center.

"Wine cellar's locked. Would you like water, or tea?"

"Tea's fine."

Adria said something in Spanish and Benéfica stepped away to summon another servant for the tea. "Do you play billiards, *Capitán?*"

"No. You?"

"Only when my father's away," she said. "He says it's vulgar for women, though as I see it this is the far edge of the earth and it's only practical that we should know the same things as men, no?"

"Maybe." Jacob shrugged. "Not everything's worth knowing."

"Like what?" Adria walked around the table to retrieve a pair of cues from a rack. "Drinking and fighting?"

"That's two," Jacob said and glanced out the window, where blue shadows were beginning to pool beneath the hills. "I'm pretty good at both but neither helps me sleep no better."

Rounding a corner of the table, away from Benéfica's sight, Adria reached out and briefly rested a delicate hand on his arm. "Did you come here alone?" she asked.

"Yes."

"Your friend isn't waiting outside? The blond boy with the sad face?"

"Briggs? No, he's leading our company to a new post." Thinking of his friends brought on waves of guilt, but then Adria smiled and he began to forget about them and everything else.

A huge fireplace dominated the sumptuous room's northern wall. A male servant recharged the hearth with pine logs, while a girl entered from a side door carrying a fine silver tea service. Jacob noticed that neither would look directly at him.

Standing beside the table, Adria turned a cue in her hands and made sure there was no warp. "Shakespeare mentions billiards," Adria said," but my father's European guests call it *carom*. Funny word, *carom*." She broke and commenced to sink a succession of shots.

"Believe I'm in over my head," Jacob laughed.

"A resourceful soldier like you? You are only being modest." Saying this, she missed a shot. Jacob took the other cue and lined up his first effort, off by several degrees. "Or maybe you weren't," she laughed. "Do you need help?"

"I'd appreciate it."

Adria stepped around the table, placed her hands on his, and helped him position the cue. His hands were warm and his touch thrilled her, so that she had to bite her lip to focus. "Like so," she said, "aim just to the right of that one there—you'll get it." She broke contact and stepped away from the table.

Jacob drew the cue back and botched the shot. "Definitely in over my head."

"It's all geometry," she laughed. "The relationship of one thing to another—the potential for one body to affect another."

"That much I understand—it's actually doing the thing correctly that's hard."

Out in the hallway, shoes clattered on the tile floor. Blank faced, Benéfica gestured through the doorway. "Will you excuse me?" Adria said. She followed the older woman out into the hall and Jacob heard them converse in Spanish. Moments later, he heard Benéfica's fading footsteps in the hallway. Adria saw that he was looking at her and she smiled.

"We in trouble?"

Adria retrieved her cue and promptly made another shot. "No."

"She don't look happy."

Adria shook her head. "She only wants to protect me."

"From me? I'm harmless."

"From myself. And you, *Capitán*, whether you believe me or not, are the most dangerous thing I have ever brought into this house."

"Should I leave?"

"No."

Nodding, Jacob leaned against an armchair and propped the cue between his elbow and hip. He glanced at the tall bookshelves flanking the fireplace and whistled softly. "Lot of books."

Adria glanced after Jacob before resuming her study of an angle on the table. "Papi says that was his worst mistake, giving me an education. There's a saying here—*'A woman's place is in the home, with a broken leg,'* and it dismays him that I am not so traditional."

"My step-dad always said that books were the devil's work."

"Do you read much, *Capitán?* You can read, can't you?" She put a hand to her mouth. "Oh, I'm sorry! I didn't—

Jacob grinned. "Reasonable question—most of my fellows can't. I can, though. Even wrote and set type for our town's paper."

"Is that your profession?"

"Lately. I've fished some, broke horses, carpentry—a little of everything, I guess."

Hands trembling, Adria took a shot and missed. Jacob managed no better, so he sat and watched intently as she lined up another. She caught him staring. "What are you thinking, grinning at me that way?" She tried to focus on her next shot.

"I like your fearlessness. And I think that if I wasn't so much wiser than I used to be, I'd really like to kiss you."

"Maybe I don't want a wise man." She laughed, and Jacob thought she sounded like a songbird. "May I call you Jacob?"

"Wish you would." He maintained his gaze. "Sounds nice on your lips."

Adria leaned on her cue and beamed. "We'll have to be careful, Jacob—*very* careful. Half of Santa Fe is on my father's payroll and the other half wants to be." Once again, she leaned over and made her shot.

Outside, the setting sun washed the valley floor with golden hues; higher, the peaks shone rose-red from the day's last strong light. Jacob rose from his chair and stepped around the table. "I'd risk anything for you."

She glanced out the window, where wind tossed empty branches in a fit of pique. "This will complicate things," she whispered.

"I'll stand for that."

Light played across her face as she turned toward him. He drew near, closer, closer, smelling her hair, her skin—not daring to close his eyes for fear that the moment would vanish. With tender haste, he leaned in and kissed her, and her lips were even softer and sweeter than he'd imagined. For the rest of their lives, each would remember that moment when nothing else had existed beyond the span of their embrace, and how they had entwined with a fierceness that had left them breathless and aching for more.

"Despite our want of every necessary provision, I say that we <u>must</u> continue north to Colorado. No matter how painful that way, it is less fearful than the wasteland we have left behind."

—Colonel Tom Green, Fifth Texas, in correspondence, March 1862

Albuquerque, New Mexico Territory, March 21, 1862

A fire was blazing in the hearth, but still Gen. Henry H. Sibley shivered beneath a pile of blankets. His teeth chattered so hard that earlier in the hour he had chipped a canine. Near the head of the bed—strewn on top of tables, books, and piles of paper—were numerous green and brown bottles. A messenger stood by and held his breath against the sickroom smell while the general tried to focus on a dispatch concerning Federal troop movements near Fort Union. Of course, the general was drunk again—exceedingly so—but unknown to his troops this was, or had once been, more of a symptom than a disease: since returning to New Mexico, however, the two were indistinguishable. Over years, the accretion of hard minerals inside his kidneys and gall bladder had formed enormous, jagged stones, which left him in debilitating pain, often unable to sit, stand, or walk for longer than thirty minutes at a stretch. Toxins and dead cells had built up, slowly poisoning him from the inside out. Wracked by sharp, cramping pains in his back and sides, whiskey bottles had become his constant companions. Bouts with the chamber pot were bloody nightmares that left him weak and feverish, incapable of thought let alone speech—and since he vomited nearly every time he set a foot on the floor, anymore he rarely conducted staff meetings. Some wondered why such acute debilitation hadn't resulted in his removal, but because the New Mexican campaign had been his sole creation and because the other officers' competencies offset his lack, he remained the Texans' titular head.

In the feverish gloom of his quarters, Sibley rose up on an elbow, coughed, and handed Pyron's dispatch back to the courier. For a

216

moment, he regained a shadow of his former vigor and ordered the soldier to make notes for distribution to his staff: "Lieutenant Col. Scurry will move Fourth Regiment back over th' pass again to find more grass for their animals. Colonel Steele should take Seventh Battalion there as well. They must rest and recover their strength but stay ready—step up patrols to watch for movement from the east. Colonel Green and Fifth Regiment will come here and remain at the ready until he hears from me. Won't be long." He paused and looked outside the window, where a strong north wind had blown in ahead of a black storm front, blanketing the town with dust. *This pernicious dust.*

"Yessir."

"I want 'em prepared to move in haste." A wave of pain convulsed his features and he sank back onto his cot.

"Sir?" the courier asked, confused at this apparent contradiction.

Sibley looked through a bright, square window that framed nothing but the overcast sky. "Dear God," he whispered, "we are running out of time."

Fort Marcy, Santa Fe, New Mexico Territory

21 March, 1862—Eli Fisher is missing since Wednesday last, disappeared on the road above Galisteo. Our sentries caught Mexican bandits—Yankee deserters, we believe—with his weapon and haversack, and though they claimed to have found his things beside the road, we shot them both. Don't know why Fish had gone to Santa Fe alone, but friends there said he told them he was setting out for our camp, so I do not believe that he was deserting—Fish is devoted to Texas. This, however, leaves injury or Death as the only possible outcomes. It grieves me to think like this. Is he hurt somewhere, lying beside the trail? This country is lonely enough for the living and I would guess that dying here is worse. If our old friend is gone, does he lie unburied—fodder for animals and the elements? How do I convey the news to his family? Will writing now cause them unnecessary grief, or is never knowing even worse? Would that he might walk in from the night and lays these worries to rest. Briggs reports that the company is in an uproar, and he has asked me to quit Santa Fe and return to camp. I know I should.

22 March, 1862—Strangely warm all of a sudden. In the valleys, anyway—snow still covers the hilltops. Ystrday Adria sent a note that her father will be in Taos for another day or so. None of my superiors has so much as inquired about our situation, so I reckon I will stay here a little longer.

North of Santa Fe, New Mexico Territory, March 22, 1862

Adria sat with her back against a stone. Jacob lay stretched to his full height and his head rested on the gathered skirts in her lap. She held his gaze—though inverted—and ran her fingers across his brow. Leaning forward, she kissed him again and again. Her thoughts raced in time with her heartbeat and she took pains to speak slowly for fear that she might say something entirely at odds with her intentions: "I cannot believe we are here, you and me. Never in a thousand years."

"I was thinking the same thing," he said. "This is something, sure." He reached up and tucked a loose strand of hair behind her ear.

She kissed him again and he reached up with both hands to pull her mouth toward his. Her hair brushed against his cheeks and when she finally opened her eyes, she saw that he was looking at her. "What?" she said.

"What I said before—this is *big*." His boots sent a stone clattering down the hillside and he leaned forward to listen. He was so intent for so long that she guessed he'd heard something more out in the woods.

Her heart beat even faster. "Jacob, is someone there? If there is, we must go—we cannot be seen together!"

Jacob listened carefully and scanned the trail leading into the closed ravine where they lay. Wind hissed in the yellow grass but beyond this, there were no other sounds. "No one here but us," he decided and pulled her down next to him on the blanket. "No one in the world. We are safe—for a little longer, anyway."

"No one but us," she whispered and kissed him again.

Village of Galisteo, New Mexico Territory, March 24, 1862

Galisteo was too small to have a plaza. A simple adobe church consecrated the three roads that met at its center, though none of the Confederates there believed that any blessings had come to them. Camped in deep, muddy snow, the entire company was viciously unhappy. Their daily routine consisted of rotating sentries between posts outside town limits and moving their horses from one overgrazed pasture to another—that was all. Drills had been suspended due to a shortage of ammunition, and attempts at forage had already stripped the locals of everything useful. Orders arrived every day from Santa Fe, though their perfect monotony had turned these into an acid joke.

Briggs Hardy was particularly resentful, having spent the previous several days laid up with a wracking cough. *A thousand miles for this.* Quarantined in a commandeered home, he'd done nothing but lie abed and fret over their lack of progress. Only within the last twelve hours had he felt well enough to step outside, though his pace was quite slow and his breathing labored. Surveying the dry cedar flats and low, surrounding hills, a geologic oddity just north of town caught his eye—a stone crease in the earth's surface: seventy feet high, a quarter-mile wide, and at least ten miles long. The road north followed Galisteo Creek through a water-worn notch in this *habra*, past the village of Los Marias, and the ancient ruins of an Indian pueblo. Hardy stared at the breach, supposing it needed to be watched in case the Yankees bypassed Santa Fe. *Even with that assist, we couldn't fight 'em off—not now.*

They were hopelessly mired and despite exercising considerable mental energies, he could not imagine how they were ever going to recover their momentum. Repeatedly, they had saddled up and stood down; patrolled the same roads over and over; asked for papers from the same poor Mexicans again and again—all for nothing. The boys had laid better odds on a return south to Doña Ana than an attack against Fort Union. *Or starving to death.*

That morning someone joked that between the Texan army and its horses, more than ten thousand rib-bones were standing at attention, except that no one laughed. He felt as if he was losing his mind. It wasn't just their want of food and supplies, but the weather, too. They had been hammered for five days by wet spring snow, freezing winds and mud—too deep and viscous for their few remaining draft animals and wagons. Illness was rampant and worst of all there had been no leadership from general staff—no explanation, no directions except to sit and wait. *And for what?*

Now some Mexican girl had gotten Jake so turned around that he'd abandoned his responsibilities as their commanding officer. *All he thinks about now is her.* Right there was the problem with women: a wink and a sigh were all that it took to deprive a fellow of his common sense. *No,* Hardy corrected himself, *that's the problem with men.* He coughed and spat in the snow.

And damn these leaky boots, too.

୬

Another twelve hours later and Hardy was able to walk for five minutes without coughing, though his outlook had not improved. Jake was in camp for the first time in days, though he'd brought neither news nor encouragement. Indeed, his mood was as black as anyone's, and everyone could see that he was preoccupied. Hardy hobbled over and found him talking with Charlie Spence—newly elected to replace Eli Fisher as first sergeant. "Charlie, I need to borrow our captain for a few minutes."

Jacob looked annoyed. "Hold on," he said and Spence nodded in agreement.

Hardy, however, would not. "Big news? Somethin' new?"

"No—"

"What, then, Jake? What?"

Both Spence and Hardy stared at Jacob—at one another, too—each contending for his time and after a just few moments of this, Jacob had to fight an urge to walk away; from Galisteo, certainly, but from the Army of New Mexico as well—he was sick of it. Sick of the whole enterprise. Here he was, fighting for a cause in which he did not believe, bedeviled by concerns he did not share, and all of which were keeping him and Adria apart. Again he thought to leave. He took an involuntary step north, away from Texas, but Hardy grabbed his sleeve.

"Only take a minute, Charlie."

Spence was a huge man, but he deferred to Hardy's tone. "I'll call assembly."

"Fine," Jacob said and pointed to an open field beside the church.

Charlie started toward the tents, where most of the company sat gnawing on hunks of plug tobacco or fishing bits of bread and dried apples from their haversacks. The two officers turned in the opposite direction, vaulted an adobe fence, and crossed another field. They paused on the sodden banks of Galisteo Creek, knee-deep in the wet grass beneath an enormous cottonwood.

"Briggs," Jacob spoke first, "we've been *amigos* since forever so say whatever you want, but don't you *ever* challenge me in the front of the others, hear?"

Hardy glanced west to make sure that none of the others could hear. "Ain't my company to lose, *amigo.*"

"Correct—"

"It's yours, 'cept that you have ignored every obligation—"

"I was delayed."

"*Three days*, Jake!" Hardy began to cough and for nearly a minute could not stop.

As he waited for his friend to recover, Jacob glanced at the creek. Swollen with snowmelt, it was flowing for the first time that year—brown water over rounded stones, and his thoughts were just as turbid.

"Three days," Hardy rasped. "What would Fish say?"

"I don't know," Jacob said, and he meant it. He knew he'd picked a bad time to stumble—no argument there—but try as he might he couldn't force himself to feel differently. He should have cared intensely, should've been outraged to see his friends suffering—he *knew* this—but he was distracted and weary and did not. Could not.

Hardy, on the other hand, was full of righteous indignation. "I'll tell you, then: he was hot, Jake—Fish was so angry seein' us fall apart that he went to Santa Fe simply to put some sense into your head. You are destroyin' this company!"

Jacob looked over and saw their friends were standing around talking, smoking pipes, laughing. It was a placid scene, no turmoil evident, yet he knew that trouble was lurking below the surface and that he was its cause. "If that's how you feel, then I'll resign my commission," he said. "Y'all deserve better. I'll recommend to Col. Green that you replace me—"

"The hell!" Hardy said. "They don't listen to me the same way!"

"I'm no good now."

"Yeah?" Hardy snapped. "And where will you go?"

"Santa Fe, to see if she'll have me."

"Don't be simple—her father wants you *dead* and frankly, son, I reckon we're owed some loyalty: who dusted you off after Reynosa's boys killed Jenny? After Sarah left? Who got you on with Doc Miller? Who has *always* looked out for your interests? I'll remind you: me and Fish, that's who."

"Briggs, what do you want?"

"Your best, Jake! How many people have to die before you get it right?"

"Take that back."

"Fish went for *you!*" Hardy shook with rage. "To prop you up once more, and you think you can just quit? His blood's on your hands—"

"Take it *back!*"

"No, pard, I won't!"

Jacob clenched his fists. *"Take it back, Briggs!"*

"Know what, Jake? You *should* go—you're bad news! First your daughter and now our dear friend. That Mexican girl had better watch out—you are death itself." Faster than Hardy had thought his friend could move, Jacob closed the gap and threw a wild punch at Briggs's head. Turning sharply, the lieutenant tripped and sat heavily on the ground. Shaking his head to clear it, he scrambled backward in the mud, even as Jake came after him again.

"Shut your goddamn mouth!" Jacob's eyes blazed but he found that his knuckles hurt so badly that he couldn't close his fingers.

Hardy spat blood onto Jacob's boots and backed farther away. Once his tattered soles found purchase, he stood and wiped his face. "I'm right and you know it."

"Go to hell!"

The lieutenant felt the adobe fence behind him and swung a leg over its rough-plastered top. "Nice to know where we rate, *friend.*"

Jacob watched him turn and walk across the field. Moments later, he called his friend's name, but Hardy kept on as though he hadn't heard. *Just as well,* Jacob thought, for if Briggs had hesitated, he wouldn't have known how to respond—too much had already been said.

Santa Fe, New Mexico Territory, March 24, 1862

Even as it began, the Confederates' ceremony was a disappointment. There were far fewer attendees than Sibley, Col. Green, or the newly promoted Col. Scurry had expected, and most of these were transient Anglo teamsters. Hardly any of the city's leading citizens were present—far more were conspicuous by their absence.

∾

Sibley's aide, Lt. Thomas Ochiltree, stood in the bed of a wagon, faced the plaza, and read from a single broadside:

"To the People of New Mexico:

The signal victory which crowned our arms at Valverde on 21 February proves the truth of the assertions contained in my first proclamation in regard to our powers and ability to accomplish the purposes therein declared. Those of you who volunteered in the Federal service were doubtless deceived by designing officials and interested citizens. The militia were driven from the field by force of arms. Under these circumstances I deem it proper and but just to declare a complete and absolute amnesty to all citizens who have laid aside or may within ten days lay aside their arms and return to their homes and avocations.

The conduct of this army since its entrance into the Territory of New Mexico attests the honesty and integrity of our purpose and the protection it has and can afford to the citizens of the country.

Return then with confidence to your homes and your avocations and fear not the result.

This proclamation is given by Brigadier General H.H. Sibley, Commanding, Confederate Army of New Mexico."

Ochiltree stepped down, and the crowd dispersed. Granted, the same document had been posted weeks before in Albuquerque, but somehow the general had believed it would show Santa Feans—who had lately been less free with their credit—that the Confederates were firmly in control and deserved their support. Don Carrizo—returned only that morning from Taos—Adria, and a pair of the don's servants, stayed longer than most. Turning, the don spotted Louisa Canby and Col. Green; Green was limping badly and Carrizo noted the pained look on his face.

"Good morning, Mrs. Canby." He bowed politely to Louisa before smiling broadly at the Texan. "Colonel Green, *Señor,* you look unwell!"

"Señorita." Green lifted his hat to Adria before turning to face the don. "Don Carrizo, I've been better, certainly."

"Nothing serious, I pray?"

"No, but I'm slowed some and Col. Scurry will have to take this army forward." The group looked across to the portal where the colonel was talking to the *Gazette*'s new publisher. Scurry noticed the attention and replied with a polite nod.

"Mrs. Canby," Carrizo said, "the colonel and I have something to discuss in private. Will you accompany Adria while my man, Tircio, fetches our carriage?"

"Certainly." Louisa took Adria's arm. "We'll follow the lane." As the men departed, the women crossed the plaza toward San Francisco Street, and paused before a fine home's tall gate. Peering between the round wooden pickets, Adria saw rows of flowering peach trees in the courtyard, their fragile blossoms already set in the unusually warm air. Leaning against the gate, her shoulders sagged.

Louisa realized then that Adria had tears in her eyes and she laid a hand on her young friend's arm. "Adria, what's wrong?"

Embarrassed, Adria wiped her face with both hands. She looked away from the flowering trees and forced a smile. "They're leaving, aren't they?"

"The Texans?"

"Yes, and I must stay here with this false weather—warm enough now to deceive these blossoms, but of course it'll snow again—it always

226

does—and all these lovely flowers will die." Adria turned, draped her arms over Louisa Canby's shoulders, and began to cry harder.

Louisa held the girl and stroked her hair. Adria composed herself somewhat, and Louisa handed her a lace handkerchief. She squeezed the girl's hands. "Cold gives way to warmth—always. Spring is God's reward for the winter."

"That's just it." She wrapped her hands around the pickets and leaned heavily against the gate. "Never have I known such heat and still I am heartsick!"

"Adria—"

"What will I do once when winter returns?" Louisa put a hand on Adria's back but said nothing. Adria wiped at her eyes with the handkerchief. "My father openly gloats. *Dios Mio,* the moon and stars have all gone out!"

Louisa Canby withdrew her hand and tucked a curl of hair behind her ear. There was no point in arguing—indeed, she felt essentially the same way about her own beloved. Edward was rarely home for long, and her mood rose and fell accordingly—elated to see him walking up the steps and reduced to ashes when he left. Vanished into the territory's wilds, he disappeared as completely as a pebble dropped into a well. Still, having steeled herself time and again, she had one advantage that Adria did not—she knew that she could endure. Of course, Adria was young and could not know that real love was never truly gone—not entirely. Of this, Louisa was certain; every time a vireo warbled outside her window or the wind soughed in the pines, she was reminded that she and Edward's fates were inextricably bound. "Adria, the moon and stars are forever," she said, "except when we refuse to see them. You mustn't worry about things you cannot change."

"What did I do wrong? Why does God grant such happiness, only to take it away?" Adria looked at Louisa—the truest maternal influence in her life—and shook her head. "Everyone I have ever loved has left me!"

"No one is promised happiness, Adria."

"So it seems. " Adria stood up straight and turned away from the gate. "If he leaves, I'll have nothing!"

Louisa touched her rested a hand on the girl's shoulder. "Your friends love you. Your family—your father..." She exhaled.

"He wanted sons," Adria whispered. "He regrets that I was even born."

"Darling!" Louisa glanced toward the plaza but saw that they were still alone. "That is untrue—you are a likely, clever woman and that will not change no matter what he or any other man thinks."

Reaching the plank sidewalk's end, Adria took a few hesitant steps away from the plaza. For days, she'd thought of little except she and Jacob might leave Santa Fe together, but the shackles of fear and tradition were on her still. She looked helplessly at Adria. "Is there no other way?"

"Your Texan cannot stay—don't ask him to."

Adria looked east, where mountains held back the clouds. "I don't want him to *stay*—I want to leave with him!"

"Adria!" Louisa laughed softly in spite of herself. "Where would you go? What would you do for money?"

"I don't care about money—that's my father's province. Jacob and I could go to Fort Union. He can surrender there, and the army will parole him after he swears not to fight again—I've seen it done!"

"Do you really know that he would?" Alarmed at the hazards Adria was contemplating, Louisa shook her head. "There's no certainty in it. However capable our soldiers, Fort Union may yet fall and if this Texan—"

"Jacob—his name is Jacob."

"Jacob, then. If Jacob is captured by his fellow Texans, the best he could expect is the stockade—more likely they would hang him."

"What about Fort Craig, then? Will you help us?"

At the mention of Edward's prison, far behind enemy lines, Louisa's heart caught in her throat. Blinking back tears of her own, something inside her shifted. "You realize what you're asking?" She thought her own voice sounded like another's, but as she spoke, she found that the shaking in her knees subsided. A sensation of lightness washed through her: "I will see it done. No one may tell us—" On the block ahead, the Carrizo's servant, Tircio, rounded a corner, spied the two women, and turned back to wave toward the plaza. Quickly, Louisa took Adria's hands and squeezed them. "However quixotic, it will be done. Not a word to anyone, or else our plans will be for naught, agreed?"

"Yes, Mrs. Canby," Adria whispered, fighting back tears. "Bless you."

"Patience—there is much to be done." Adria returned the lace handkerchief. Moments later a driver guided the Carrizo's carriage around the corner and Tircio climbed onto a platform behind the backstay. The vehicle stopped, and the don disembarked. He handed the reins to Eulogio, his driver, who kept silent and his eyes fixed straight ahead.

"Ladies," the don said, "discovered at last. Mrs. Canby, thank you for your time. Adria, get in the carriage—I want you to go home. I have an appointment now, but I'll return in time for supper and evening Mass."

Adria climbed onto the seat but leaned out over the curb. "Papi, may I stop at Vitalia Castillo's house? She has some fabric and notions I've been meaning to pick up."

"You've been out all morning," the don said, "and the roads are unsafe. These men occupying our city are little more than common criminals."

"But Papi, it's on the way!"

"No, Adria!" the don thundered. Tircio stared coldly at Louisa Canby, who was in turn glaring at Don Carrizo—only old Eulogio, the driver, kept his eyes on a distant horizon. "Do as I say! Eulogio?"

"*Sí, Señor?*"

"*Hacer no punto, y hacer no perdido.*"

"*Sí, Don Carrizo.*" The old man flicked the reins and Tircio had to grab the backstay to keep from falling onto the street. Adria glanced back at Louisa Canby but made no other sign before the carriage rounded the corner.

The don bowed to Louisa. "Good day, Mrs. Canby. I must be going." Then he started walking, south toward the warehouses that fronted the Santa Fe Trail as it entered town.

Santa Fe, New Mexico Territory, March 24—2:30 p.m.

Louisa watched the don walk away until some rankling voice inside told her to follow. Carrizo had a half-block head start but Louisa's stride was longer; when at last she caught him, he was startled but otherwise made no acknowledgement and continued down the lane. "That proclamation was interesting," she said, her forehead flushed from exertion. The don cast a sour, sidelong glance at Louisa and barreled ahead in silence. "Especially that part about conducting themselves honorably and protecting our citizens, when every day we hear of fresh outrages. Personally, I believe that the bandits plaguing us are largely opportunistic deserters. What is your thought on this, sir?" Louisa followed doggedly and ignored the red mud that clung to her thin leather boots. They waded through tall grass to avoid a collapsed wall that had strewn broken adobe bricks across the path.

"Mrs. Canby," Carrizo finally said, "I don't have time for this."

They crossed a small wooden bridge above an *acequia* in which water from the high hills was already flowing. A quartet of heavily loaded wagons rolled past and showered them with fine red dust. The don brushed at his clothes. Two drivers were singing—badly—"Do They Miss Me at Home," while the fourth whistled a fair version of "Ellen Bayne."

"Colonel Green tells me he's returning to Albuquerque," Louisa said.

Abruptly, the don stopped. "Yes, I understand you two are quite close." He cast a withering glare at Louisa, who had to shield her eyes from the sun.

Louisa felt her cheeks flush with anger. "We've spoken twice—*in public*—and he's been kind enough to inform me of Edward's situation. If these limited exchanges qualify as friendship, fine."

"Mrs. Canby, your affection for Southerners is well known." Here he was referring to the fact Louisa was a distant cousin of the Confederate Gen. Sibley's wife, as well as a false rumor that Edward Canby had been the best man at Sibley's wedding. True, Sibley and Edward had served together in New Mexico and Utah in the decade before the Civil War, but speculation about a non-existent bond between them had led some to believe that they had conducted their campaigns in ways meant to keep from embarrassing one another. In truth, any affection Louisa harbored for the ragged Texans was born of compassion for the hungry and ill clothed, not conflicted loyalties—or worse.

Her eyes blazed at the suggestion. Taking a breath to calm her nerves, she gestured over the don's head. "Pray the weather spares these flowers."

Don Carrizo blinked, certain he had misheard, until he looked up and saw that they had stopped beneath a flowering crab apple. *Peculiar thing—is she mad?* Not that it mattered. Even after all these years, the Anglo mind was a mystery to him. "Indeed," he said and set off once more.

A block later, he realized that Louisa was following again. "Don Carrizo—" she began but he brushed her words aside.

"Mrs. Canby, how long do you intend to keep this up? Your behavior is most odd."

"I want to speak with you about Adria—" she said, but this time his interruption was even more abrupt.

"*¡Aquí estamos!* Don't you dare—don't you *dare* interfere!"

Louisa stopped and crossed her arms. "I don't know what you mean."

"Do you think I'm stupid? For years you've tried to poison her against me."

"She isn't set against you! She's confused—"

"Confused because you've filled her head with *lies!*"

"Don Carrizo, I only want to help—"

"Now?" The don placed his hands on a fence rail and watched another wagon roll by. "You want to help *now?* Where were you when Irinea died? Why did no one come and—"

"Don Carrizo, Edward and I did not live in Santa Fe then—"

"Yes, *you are not from here!* You are not Spanish and you are not family, so leave us alone!" He turned again and hastened along the road.

"You'll lose her!" Louisa said. "You will lose her." She adjusted the shawl across her shoulders and started back toward the plaza.

೧

She'd made it the length of the block before Don Carrizo overtook her. "Woman, how *dare* you!"

She whirled and faced him there on the path, surrounded by sprouting grasses and chamiso. "How dare *you?*" Louisa fairly bristled herself. "Your mistreatment of her is scandalous!"

"No, *your* behavior is the scandal! Comforting your husband's enemies while he sleeps out in the cold, suffering so that your kind can stay home and gossip—have you no shame?"

"Are you ashamed of your daughter?"

The don cast a withering look of contempt. "How can you live alongside us and still know so little?"

"She has no one to talk to! The world outside confuses her—"

The don rolled his eyes, but his voice was calmer. "Teresa and Benéfica look after her."

"Everyone knows Teresa's unwell—"

"That, too, is none of your business!"

"—and Benéfica is past seventy and never married—they cannot help her now."

"You aren't so young yourself, Mrs. Canby."

Louisa ignored the insult. "Why do you refuse help?"

"Why won't you leave us alone?"

"See? You *still* don't understand—"

"No, Mrs. Canby—" Don Carrizo stabbed the air between them. "—it is *you* who does not understand! You indulge the Texans because you can—I oblige them because I *must!* One false step and they will destroy everything I have—won't even have a dog to bark at me. *That* I understand!"

"Have we been unneighborly?" Louisa crossed her arms. "We have treated Adria like a daughter—"

"I never asked you to."

"Because you are too busy, you mean. You are obsessed with money, yet no sum will ever buy you another day with her—"

"What about my money?"

"Don Carrizo—"

"You want me to apologize for what I have? Well, I won't, see? Money is the only thing that protects me—it's the only reason you people accord me respect. Without it, I am merely another Mexican!"

"Honestly, this is absurd." Louisa spun on her heels, intending to walk away.

Swiftly she realized that the don was trailing her now, more furious than ever. "Believe me," he raged, "if your husband ever returns to Santa Fe, we will speak about this!"

She stopped. "He'll agree with everything I've said."

"This explains your lack of tact. Because he is a powerful man, you think you can say whatever flits into your head, but you *cannot!* Mrs. Canby, women like you are repellent!"

"And what of men who trade shamelessly with their enemies, who profit from the misery of others—"

"Oh? Pray, tell me, who are my enemies?"

She shot him an incredulous look. "You cannot be serious? You are an American citizen and the Union is owed your loyalty."

"I am not American by choice."

"By the grace of God, then!"

"No one from Texas has taken my property without first paying for it—something I cannot say about your people."

"Never taken—? You yourself opposed the annexation! Now the same belligerents have overrun New Mexico and you say that you don't care?" Disgusted, Louisa turned and walked away.

"At least they don't hide behind smiles and handshakes!" the don roared. Two laborers walked past, their arms loaded with ropes and tools. They stepped off the curb with downcast eyes and when the *hacendado* hissed at them, they quickened their pace.

"Your treachery is staggering," Louisa called over her shoulder, "when all nature knows you've fattened yourself on Army accounts—"

"*You!*" the don sputtered and hastened after her again. "You think your anemic contracts made me rich? What ignorance! Twenty-five years ago—before Yankee guns 'bought' this territory from Mexico; before my family's lands were confiscated under a treaty *we did not sign;* before Anglos came here and seized the government for their own enrichment—maybe then I was rich! Today, I own a fraction of that granted to my forefathers by the King of Spain. The *King!* And still no one in Washington will listen to me. Look, I do not believe that Richmond will prove any better, but how can you be shocked that I do not love your United States? Indeed, do you know why the native militias abandoned your husband at Fort Craig? Because they wanted only to return to their homes and work their fields—as stubborn as this land can be, still it is more reliable than your government. You have taken my wealth, thrown me crumbs in return, and yet you expect gratitude? Ha! That will *not* happen!" His peroration concluded, the don stopped walking, still some thirty feet from Louisa.

She loathed him then like no one she'd ever known. "You think you have nothing," she began, "because you do not appreciate the treasure you have. You have spurned you daughter's love, destroyed her trust, and cannot even *see* it! If ever she has a chance to leave this place—even with a *Texan*—rest assured that I will help her in any way that I can!"

Carrizo checked an impulse to chase after Louisa and strike her, but on this point, he knew she was at least partially right: others had reported seeing the young Texan at his rancho, though none of his servants would corroborate this. Still, it was dreadfully expensive to keep these rumors from the Ortizes and the don was looking forward to the Confederates' departure. "The boy," he scoffed, "can do nothing. Soon the Texans will leave and no matter which road they take, the Yankees will kill him."

However, this pronouncement unintentionally buoyed Louisa's spirits: since the start of the invasion, this was the first time she'd heard anyone suggest that the Texans were incapable of domination *ad infinitum*. Confounding him, she smiled sweetly. "Thank you for the welcome news, Don Carrizo—thank you and good day." For the last time, she turned and walked away, humming softly in the pleasant afternoon sunshine.

Watching her depart, the don had an all-over sensation that he had just given away some vital intelligence, but which for the life of him he did not recognize. *Strange, strange woman.* Before he turned away for good, out of habit the don lifted his hat as a courtesy toward Louisa, though his thoughts about her and the things she'd said remained pitch-black. He finished his errands in such a mood that afterward everyone with whom he'd bargained complained that he'd done so with malice.

Village of Pajarito, New Mexico Territory, March 25, 1862

———◆———

The old man regarded José Garza with a mixture of curiosity and contempt. "Boy, why would you want anything to do with those people?"

It was a fair question. Garza's mother's family had given him no end of grief when he'd announced that he would ride down to Mesilla to greet the newly-arrived Texans, and the Texans themselves had greeted him with little more than indifference. He had no answer for the old man, no answer for himself; in truth, he did not know where he belonged. His mother had been a washwoman for *ricos,* his father a white trader from Illinois. He'd grown up between cultures, haunted by whispers and furtive glances, lost even inside his own skin. Riding with the Confederate Brigands, for the first time he'd felt as though he was part of something. Many of them were mere criminals, but they had taken him in and shown him rude principles by which he might live—principles that did not factor his parentage. After the botched raid in Paraje, he fled north, only to be caught hiding in a barn outside Socorro. There, the Texans would've executed him as a deserter but for the intervention of Jacob Stark.

Working at their hospital in Socorro, he'd ample time to reflect on these events and decided that this *capitán* must have somehow sensed his innate worth. He'd even imagined that they might have some basis for friendship, though whites had scorned him in the past and he was justifiably leery. Garza exhaled and looked around the plaza. He'd just turned seventeen and felt that at last his life was unfolding as it should—that soon Stark and the Texans would accept him as an equal. *That* was why he had left the hospital and gone north; gone looking for the Texans before they marched on Colorado. Even if they did not yet know it, *he* did: they were his future.

"They are going to run this place," Garza said at last, "and I want to ride with the victors."

Above Tesuque Pueblo, Near Santa Fe, New Mexico Territory, March 26, 1862

Morning broke clear and cold. Every tassel of grass wore a thick frost jacket; every tree threw a heavy indigo shadow across the snowy forest floor. Up north, feathery clouds spilled over the great Sangres' crest, fading from the brilliant red of sunrise into peach, then gold, then cottony white above deep green slopes. Jacob wrapped himself in a blanket as he'd seen Indians do. Indeed, had he climbed a little higher on the ridge he could've enjoyed a fine view of Tesuque Pueblo. Instead, his eyes were riveted south. His heart thudded painfully against his ribs and his head felt as though hundreds of fires were burning inside it.

ം

Fifth Regiment had orders to return promptly to Albuquerque, as inexorable as a turning tide. Once begun, Jacob guessed that he would be borne away like flotsam atop floodwaters, with no view to a return. One step south was as good as a million, and it was with immense reluctance that he sent a message instructing Briggs Hardy to break camp and prepare the company for a return along the La Joya road. All night he'd wrestled with the bright and dark angels of his conscience, though in the end, neither had prevailed. At intervals, he'd favored one course of action above another—sometimes highly—only to reverse himself thereafter, and on it went. At five a.m., he decided that if Adria arrived on a strong horse they would ride for Denver, with California their eventual goal.

Ten minutes later, a sentry passed him out of Fort Marcy. He rode north, fired with enthusiasm and certitude until after seven o'clock, when he rummaged through his saddlebag and found a deck of cards that Eli Fisher had given him. Why this talisman was freighted with such power he couldn't say, but having seen it his plans went to pieces and he felt like an imbecile for having come so close to abandoning his friends. Since leaving San Antonio, death, illness and desertion had whittled the Cameron Guards' ranks from sixty to forty-seven— forty-six if he left, too—which course he now abjured.

A rider emerged from the *barranca* some three miles distant and his nervousness increased tenfold. A slight figure on a white horse—*Her.* Certainly was. Despite her nearness, however, he began thinking about finding and rejoining his company, of apologizing to them, and whether or not they would even want him as their captain. His capriciousness was sorely embarrassing. He especially regretted his fight with Hardy—regretted that he hadn't apologized since. Having retreated from the brink, it shamed him to think how near he'd come to discarding their friendship. Not the first time he'd run from his responsibilities, but for once he hoped that the damage might be repaired instead of admitted as inevitable. All his life he'd lived like an animal, concerned only with self-preservation. For once, he resolved not to run.

༽

As Adria drew near, Jacob saw how her dark eyes smoldered— whether from anger or excitement, he couldn't tell but he was certain she'd never looked so lovely. Again he wavered, appalled by his own weakness. She said his name and his heart leapt, but when he reached out to take her hand, she recoiled.

"What's wrong?" He searched her eyes.

She studied his face, unable to tell exactly who stood before her. Part of her wished that a gust of wind might carry them away together, while another screamed for her to tap her heels against the horse's flanks and leave. "How *could* you?" she said.

"I don't—" He wondered at the fire in her voice. "What did I do?" She leaned forward, took his hand, and stepped down. At once, she wrapped her arms around his waist, pinned his arms to his sides and leaned heavily into his chest. So sustained was her hold, so unyielding that immediately he absorbed some of the tension in her frame. He worked his right arm free and returned her embrace. "Adria?"

"Don't let go—not yet."

"No," he said, but then she released her hold and took a backward step. She shivered and brushed at her arms as if trying to rid herself of his touch. "What are you doing?" he asked.

"I don't know—*I don't know*. You have me so twisted I've almost forgotten how to breathe."

"Adria, there's something I have to say—"

"I'd thought you'd saved me," she cut in. She wiped her cheek with the heel of her palm.

"What?" He wanted to kiss her so that they wouldn't have to talk, but again she stepped back.

Her hair had come loose from a tortoiseshell comb; a few long curls fluttered across her face. She stared into his eyes and shook her head. "My father told me everything."

He exhaled, thinking he understood. "Fifth's re-assigned to Albuquerque—I have no choice."

"No." Her eyes flashed. "He told me about *you*. Are you still married?"

The color drained from Jacob's face. "What?" In an instant, the bittersweet parting he'd imagined had turned into something else, something far more tempestuous. He did not know whether to concede every point to ensure a swift and complete break, or try to explain himself fully. While expedience favored the latter, he allowed that he cared deeply and was unwilling to let her walk away hurt. "It ain't that way."

"And how is it?"

"An unhappy situation—complicated."

"*¡Dios Mio!* You *are!* Married, and all this while you let me think otherwise! I thought we belonged together. You *lied*, Jake—everything you've told me is a *lie!*"

"Wait," he said but she would not.

"You said your wife was dead but she *isn't*—you were living with her up until the day you started here—"

"That's not true!"

"—and maybe you believe you're so far from Texas that the rules no longer apply, but believe me, they do! Here more than anywhere else! *"Dios Mio,* I have risked everything for you!"

"Adria, my wife left me." He couldn't bring himself to look into her eyes. "My daughter died and Sarah was badly hurt. She wouldn't talk to me afterward—not even to berate me or tell me that everything that happened was my fault. Shunned me completely. Nothing but silence, and it drove me mad! She left Brownsville last summer, and I haven't heard from her since. No papers, no letters—I don't know what else I can do. I know *I* ain't still married."

"And what happened after? Is that true, as well?"

Jacob winced. "They murdered my little girl; what was I supposed to do?"

"You found her killers?"

"Near enough. Adria, I was out of my mind—"

"My God," she whispered and put a hand to her lips. Turning quickly, she waded through the frosted grass to catch her horse's reins. She set one foot to a stirrup, grasped the saddle, and pulled herself upward in a swish of skirts. "I don't know anything about you, do I?"

"You don't believe that."

"I don't know what I believe."

Jacob took hold of her stirrup and held fast. "Who told your father?"

Adria looked up at the boiling clouds, some already bearded with snow. "Does it matter?"

"Yes." He inhaled sharply, and the cold air made his lung ache.

"A Texan from your company—I don't know his name."

"I do," he said. "Will you let me explain?"

"I don't want to hear any more."

Jacob let go of the stirrup and took a backward step. "You won't let me explain?"

She looked at him and the cast in her eye was the most wretched thing he'd ever taken. "Don't you care for me at all? Am I unworthy?"

"Unworthy? My God, Adria, you're everything any man could want—everything to me!"

"Yet you're leaving."

"Only for now. This is huge—I can't back out now."

"You've made a fool out of me, Jacob!"

"Jesus, Adria, maybe I haven't been a perfect gentleman, but lives are at stake. I shouldn't have let this continue, shouldn't have talked about running away—I'm sorry about that. But there are things that I have to fix, see? *Have to*. For once I want to do what's right."

"But not by me? Why does no one ever think of that?" She watched a crow soar over the hilltop, lost in her helplessness. "I don't want to be engaged—not to Basilio! I'm not happy that he's missing, but I can't help hoping that he never returns."

"Where did he go?"

"A month ago he led a militia down to Fort Craig. No one knows anything more—he's simply vanished."

Jacob thought back to the hundreds of New Mexicans he'd seen slaughtered at Valverde and shook his head. "He ain't coming back."

"No one ever does."

Jacob watched as the cold wind tousled her hair. "Should I go?"

"I..." She squeezed her eyes shut. "I don't know."

"I should," he said, hating himself for it. He pulled the horse's picket pin and shook the tether loose from its rest atop a pine branch. "I'll come back and look for you," he offered.

"When?"

"Soon."

She opened her eyes. "Haven't I made you happy?"

"Yes, of course!" He felt so empty that if the wind had gusted then, he believed that it might've hurled him over the ridge. "But I cannot turn away from promises that I made before you and I met. Wasn't meant to be settled—I don't deserve it."

"And what if I do?"

"Look somewhere else," he said. Adria bit her lip and walked her horse around. Jacob rested a hand on the pommel of her saddle. "Adria, I'm *sorry*—"

Wind spilled her dark hair across her shoulders, and fear made her cruel: "You're a coward, Jacob—you wallow in your loneliness. Lying in the darkness, someday you will remember how much I loved you—how desperately, how completely—and that you cast me aside. Carry that with you—I don't care." Tears spilled down her cheeks.

"Adria—"

"You have ruined me, Jacob." She tapped her bootheels against the horse's flanks and guided the animal onto the road. Jacob watched her ride away and knew that she was wiping at her eyes.

By then gray clouds had begun to gather over the valley and he pulled the blanket tighter around his shoulders. He swore violently and wiped as his eyes as his horse descended the hill. *I'll never do better.* He hated Hardy, Fish, Tom Green—hell, all of Texas for refusing to release their claims upon him; hated the Yankees for starting this whole wretched affair, and the Confederacy for taking the bait; hated himself, most of all. *The body and soul do not die together.* Where had he heard that? His stepfather, maybe? At such times, *he* would have counseled that the only way forward was to submit to Jesus, but having seen how selectively this could be done, Jacob had never felt the call. The world was full of pharisaical bastards—*that* population had no need of increase. He did not think it was impossible to start anew—only that most people never figured out how. But if past failings could not be undone, then all that remained was to go where they did not weigh so heavily on his aims. He couldn't quite speculate how this might be done, but he could well imagine the swiftness of his decline if he did not change.

Riding back into town, Jacob paused just long enough to sight in and shoot a crow that had perched atop one of the snowy trees. This tantrum, however, did nothing to salve his anger, and for a long time afterward he'd felt perfectly wretched.

Village of La Bajada, Below Santa Fe, New Mexico Territory, March 27, 1862

Colonel Green unbuttoned his wool coat and wiped his brow with a bandanna. *Damned unnatural weather will not settle!* Green and the bulk of Fifth Regiment were returning to Albuquerque to guard the brigade's meager stores and stay ready if ever the previously defeated Federals emerged from Fort Craig. Before dawn, their horses had broken through thin skins of ice along the river's edge but by noon, the temperature had risen well above eighty degrees. The Texans began shedding layers of clothes, consigning more and more gear to the battered wagons that trailed the column. Few were pleased with their assignment—especially since their comrades in A and B Companies had stayed in Santa Fe to bolster Charles Pyron's attack on Fort Union. Neither were they pleased that a dust storm had blown in and drawn veils of sand across the sky; the only remedy was to cover their faces as best they could and turn to shield their eyes.

These tribulations notwithstanding, a tired carnival atmosphere hung over the procession. Shouted conversations traveled up and down the column. A few persistent souls even sang, played coronets, or drummed. Green himself hunched over his saddle and tried to shut out the world, though the cacophony bled into his subconscious and set his teeth on edge.

෫ৄ

Staff officers were halfway across a wide, sandy channel when some commotion erupted on the rim behind them. "Colonel Green!" someone shouted, "someone direct me to Col. Green!" His horse's sides flecked with foam, an express descended the washout's edge and pushed toward the procession's head.

Green and his coterie stopped, turned aside, and strained to hear over the wind. Joe Sayers, Col. Green's adjutant, put fingers in the corners of his mouth and whistled loudly. "Private," he shouted, "over here!"

The dust caked rider coughed for several minutes and then his words poured forth in a flood: "Sir, Col. Scurry requests everyone you can spare—everyone! There's been a fight east of Santa Fe, Sir!"

Green shook his head to clear the fog. Unaware of any Federal force capable of attacking, he and the others were thunderstruck. "The hell, son—who fought?"

"Major Pyron's men and a full Yankee battalion."

Green glanced north, where the tops of the Sangre de Cristos were barely visible above the wash's rim. "And the result?"

The courier looked pained, as though he imagined he would be punished. "They whipped us, Sir!"

Those assembled began to shout so loudly that Green had to wave his arms for silence. *"Stop that!* We will *never* run!" He turned to face the messenger. "Now, tell me what happened." The boy took a gulp of water, wiped his mouth, and relayed the details of a sharp action just east of Santa Fe. With growing impatience, Green listened until he could no longer keep silent: "The outcome, son— what is the outcome?"

The courier panted and took another gulp of water. "Major Pyron's men are in full flight." Green pondered this news while other officers peppered the boy with questions about locales, tactics, and personnel. Farther back in the ranks, others set to talking and within ten minutes the entire column had been infected. "Our howitzers," the boy volunteered, "was useless on account of the narrow canyon and all the trees. And those devils'uz led by a giant—seven-feet tall, with pistols in each hand. Couldn't set nothin' on *him*."

Green frowned. "Anyone know who that might be?" The others tried to recall the Northern officers with whom they had served and shook their heads.

"Jayhawkers," one suggested, using a derisive term for the Kansas anti-slavery militias rumored to be marching to Fort Union's defense. Quickly it was decided that this giant had to be a Coloradan and the regimental grapevine bore fresh rumblings.

"Don't matter—," Green dipped into his tobacco pouch, "—we'll whip them, too." The colonel's tone was infectious: a new current flowed up the column and the ranks began agitating to turn around and fix flints for the last time. For a long minute, Green let this buzz persist. Adjusting his chaw with a finger, he leaned forward to speak with the courier: "Jayhawks bring cavalry, too, or boots alone?"

"Cavalry, too, Sir." While the courier appreciated the Fifth's enthusiasm, having seen this new enemy firsthand, he did not share their confidence. "Mixed Yankee regulars and Jayhawks. There at the end, we crossed a gulch, wrecked the bridge behind us and still they jumped it—it'uz all we could do to get away."

"How many we lose?"

"Believe about one hundred and twenty."

Green winced at the total—more than a third of Pyron's force—but tried to maintain an air of confidence. "Others headed north?"

"Colonel Scurry's full command—smaller posts from the villages around Santa Fe. He requests everyone you can spare."

Green turned to confer with his staff: "Albuquerque is wide open—without those supplies, well, let's not even consider that."

"Can't," Joe Sayers murmured, thinking back to their collection. "Just can't." Slumped in his saddle, he chewed on a pencil and spat small pieces of wood and plumbago into the weeds.

"Gentlemen, this is an emergency," Green said. "Maj. Metzger, I want you to take C and D Companies north. The rest of us will continue south as before."

Metzger, a silent observer until now, turned and glanced north. "Colonel, Sir, another company is needed. Scurry has a thousand men now, *und* Pyron but two hundred. If those Jayhawks were detached, fifteen hundred Yankees there may be —Sir, more men are needed!"

Green studied the backs of his gloves and worried a thread of tobacco between his front teeth. "Someone!" he shouted, "Find Capt.

Stark." Wood turned and departed just as another blast of sand-laden wind struck the valley. "We'll be okay," Green reassured the others, who were shielding their eyes with their hatbrims. Despite his sore leg, the colonel stood in his stirrups, seeking the best possible view along the road. "We'll be fine." As the gust died, Green raised his heavy cavalry saber. "Texans, listen! C and D Companies, Artillery Company B! Colonel Scurry needs reinforcement. East of Santa Fe— you will have to move fast! All others will continue on to Albuquerque as before." The colonel sank back into his saddle. When Jacob arrived, Green motioned him aside and shouted at the others: "Major Metzger, Lieutenant Bradford—you have the right-of-way. Form up!"

The whole regiment cheered, and calls of "Hurrah! Hurrah! *Hurrah!*" shook the valley. Comrades slapped one another on the back and wished each other well. Some were envious; others relieved— secretly glad to be marching away from this new front.

Metzger waited until the tumult subsided. "Captains, you have your orders! Quickly, now!" He wheeled his mount and walked north to help extract companies from the column.

Jacob waited next to Green. As men rushed to the wagons to retrieve rucksacks and jackets, the colonel leaned over and shook hands with the young captain. "Your head on square?"

"Sir?"

Green spat on the ground. "Want you to take your Guards back north with Metzger." He wiped his chin with the back of a gloved hand.

"Yessir."

"Look, I know you've been chasing Don Carrizo's daughter—I knew it and I let it go, thinking we'd be gone before it mattered. Now you must stop, hear? You've got to set these things aside."

Jacob felt his cheeks flush and his stomach drop. "Yessir."

"Son, I've been where you are, fixated on something I wanted beyond all reason. But this, *this* is everything—*everything's* at stake."

"Yessir." Jacob bit the inside of his lower lip and drew blood.

"Need your word."

"We broke things off, Sir. You can count on me."

"Shadows across the way—no distractions, hear?"

"Yessir," Jacob said.

With the artillery carriages turned, James Bradford shouted: "Sir, Company B is ready!"

"Colonel Green—Company C is ready!" Denman Shannon echoed.

Green gestured toward Jacob's company. "Don't let them down, son—don't let *me* down."

"I'm in, Sir—in all the way."

"Company D is ready, Colonel!" Dan Ragsdale called.

"Good." Green rested a hand on Jacob's shoulder. "I trust you, Jacob. Some day we will look back at all this and raise our glasses— drink to the good fortune that sprung from this very moment. Now, go do what you must—Godspeed, son, and good luck." Jacob saluted before riding away to find his company. More cheers went up as the detachment started north. For a good while after, Green and the others stayed and watched—watched until their companions disappeared within clouds of red dust. Then the colonel reined his horse around so that it was headed south again. He adjusted the brim of his hat and scanned the long horizon. "Captains, let's move—I want to reach Bernallilo by sundown!"

Apache Canyon, New Mexico Territory, March 27, 1862

As the Confederate messenger had said, on March 26 a nasty little skirmish in Apache Canyon, ten miles east of Santa Fe, had ended in a Union victory—their first since the start of the invasion three months earlier.

That morning had been foggy and cold, with hosts of sparrows pinwheeling between the pines. Salmon pink clouds dissolved to reveal whitened trees high above the Santa Fe Trail, but lower down the frost began swiftly melting. Texan Maj. Charles Pyron set out with three hundred men and a two-gun artillery section, uphill through deep, shaly mud, to meet Federal raiders reportedly advancing on Santa Fe. Indeed, on the eastern side of the pass, Maj. John Chivington was leading four hundred men as rapidly as possible toward the capital, intent on engaging the small enemy force that his scouts had reported garrisoned there.

In the pre-dawn darkness, somehow both forces' scouting parties had ridden past each other. Doubling back from the summit of the pass, four Confederates rode directly into the midst of a twenty-man Union detachment and surrendered without firing a shot. From these prisoners, Chivington learned that the Texans were near and ordered his men to hurry forward.

Descending the pass's western side, the Coloradans stumbled upon another small knot of Texans. Caught off guard by a numerically superior force, all thirty members of this Confederate advance, too, were surrounded and disarmed without a struggle. While a Union messenger ran uphill to relay this news to Chivington, suddenly the main Texan force came into view. Throwing their knapsacks,

249

canteens, and coats aside so that they could fight unencumbered, the Coloradans charged.

Having lost their scouts, the Texans had no warning, but in less than a minute Pyron had set a defensive line and ordered the howitzers unlimbered. Pyron also recognized that the two forces had collided at the narrowest part of Apache Canyon and set his artillery so that any advance along the road would have to pass directly before their muzzles. His gun crews drew what looked to the raw Coloradans like an impenetrable curtain of exploded iron; sheets of flame spurted from the Texans' muskets; the canyon quickly filled with mustard-colored smoke. The first Coloradan fell.

❧

Chivington felt his adrenaline surge. "Men! Enact God's will! Shoulder arms! Have no fear and do not falter!" He threw his arms wide to encompass the whole of his command and his eyes flashed with fury. "Muskets ready! Prepare to fire—"

Then, practically in unison, a hundred voices cried out as a Confederate shell sailed directly toward him. Unsure where to turn, Chivington had done the only thing he could and ducked as the hissing canister passed inches from his skull. The missile—a dud—bounced harmlessly off a sandstone boulder and his astonished troops bellowed again. Confident that the Lord had protected him for some greater purpose, Chivington began to shout: "Trust Him, boys! Trust me! Now, for God and the Union: volley and advance—*fire!*" Chivington stepped aside and his Coloradans unleashed a rolling broadside.

Barking like dogs, the Federals quickly dispersed into the rocks and trees above the trail. Meaning to flank the Texans on both sides of the canyon, they climbed higher and higher until the Texans couldn't elevate their howitzers' barrels to reach them. Perched safely on the canyon's walls, they began to pour deadly fire upon the gun crews.

Hastily, Pyron ordered his skirmishers and artillery to withdraw westward, down Apache Canyon. An eighth of a mile downhill, they set up a second strong front, partially protected by a huge sandstone fin that projected from the canyon's north wall. Moreover, they were now west of a deep, narrow arroyo that entered the main canyon from its northern side. Pyron judged this barrier impassible. "Come'n git yours!" he hissed as the Coloradans renewed their advance. "There's plenty here!"

Watching the Texans setting up, Chivington ordered his infantrymen to repeat their flanking maneuver, but this time told Samuel Cook's cavalry to remain alert and charge if the Texans could be made to withdraw their artillery once more. Recovered from his brush with death, Chivington did everything he could to drive his command forward. For more than an hour, he ranged back and forth, shouted orders, and praised anyone whose advance he noticed. Occasionally he paused to squeeze off rounds from one of the four revolvers he carried. The Confederates targeted him repeatedly but to no avail. Easily spotted on account of his great height and full officers' regalia, never again did anything they threw at him come close.

A creeping sense of unease began to afflict the Texans. Watching Chivington stride boldly across the road, Maj. Pyron emptied both of his revolvers in the minister's direction. "Bastard's leadin' a charmed life," he complained. He gestured frantically to Adolphus Norman, his acting artillery chief. "Set case atop that one's head, okay? He can't keep this up forever."

Pouring sweat, Sergeant Norman ran his burning eyes along the Union front. He raised his hands in frustration. "Can't put *nothing* where we need it—can't depress the stocks any further, can't elevate the barrels!"

"Rake the field, then!" Pyron tugged on his long beard and pointed up the canyon. "Goddammit, keep 'em off the road!"

"Ain't on the *road!*" Norman shouted. "They're up in the *trees!*" Then, underscoring the sergeant's point, one of his gunners took a bullet in the throat, sank to his knees, and toppled forward. Norman dashed away to help remove the body.

Pyron shook his head in frustration. "Damn it," he said, watching blue forms moving swiftly between the trees on the canyon's north wall. "Damn it all to hell."

꙰

High above, the Coloradans continued to work their way west, by then nearly abreast of the howitzers. Realizing that they were in danger of being flanked again, Pyron called to Norman and ordered him to re-limber the cannon for withdrawal.

Uphill, Chivington spotted this movement and whistled for Capt. Cook's riders to charge. Shouting, these horsemen thundered downhill, firing at the confused Texans. Rounding the huge sandstone outcrop, concealed Texans fired and struck Cook twice in the leg. While the Texans scrambled to reload, the Coloradans regrouped under Lt. George Nelson and renewed their charge against the main Confederate line. Unprepared to volley, the Southerners reacted by throwing timbers off a narrow wooden bridge spanning the arroyo.

"Don't stop!" Nelson commanded, "full bore!" Ignoring the smoke and thunder swirling around them, the cavalry reached full gallop and leapt the arroyo. Landing squarely among the panicked Texans, slashing indiscriminately with their heavy sabers, they set off a rout. High upon the scree-covered hillsides, Capt. Jacob Downing's infantry company, too, began to run as fast as the steep terrain would allow, trying to cut off as many stragglers as they could. In this manner, they killed dozens, cornered twenty others in a box canyon, and took them prisoner. Though shots continued for a good while longer, with each one fainter than the last, it was clear that the Texans were in full flight back to Santa Fe.

ᦸ

Near sundown, Chivington halted pursuit and ordered his men back to Kozlowski's station, east of the pass. Pausing at the summit, Chivington turned and looked west. He closed his eyes and began to pray. For several minutes he remained motionless, undisturbed by the long lines of men filing past. When at last he reopened his eyes, he saw that the sun had nearly vanished; pools of darkness were overflowing the spaces behind the scorched rocks and trampled grass. Brimming with gratitude, he felt certain that this opportunity, this blessing from *Him,* was a sign that *He* viewed their errand with favor. Again, he prayed: *Lord, I will labor until the stain of Southern slavery is wiped clean, this menace wiped away. I will not stop until Your favored civilization is safe to flower in these barren wastes—until a new Eden blooms in the fields that we have prepared for You.* Then the wind gusted hard and scourged his face with sand and gravel, forcing him to hunch sideways and pull his hatbrim down for protection.

Hacienda Carrizo, Santa Fe, New Mexico Territory, March 27, 1862

Don Carrizo was in a terrible hurry, so he spoke as he walked: "Hasten north to Taos, then. A deputy magistrate from Valencia County is in Santa Fe now, asking questions about a man named Juan Aguilar—you know him?"

"Aguilar?" Felix Ortiz asked. "*Si*, though I haven't seen him since the business at La Rinconada—I heard he found bad trouble down Bernardo way."

"Well, he didn't find it soon enough. *Pendejo* evidently ran his mouth and now authorities from *Rio Abajo* have come north with questions. Many questions. Are all the others accounted for?"

"Yes, Don Carrizo—they're on the Pecos with the other *caballeros*, watching my father's herds."

"Will you not be going to Colonias this season?"

The boy kicked at a pebble in the road. "My father doesn't want me there."

"Honestly, Felix, I am a little disappointed in you myself—I thought I could trust you." Breathing hard, he stopped at the back of an elegant coach and set the box he'd been carrying inside the boot. Felix handed him a second box, which the don also placed inside the vehicle.

"Aguilar always was a little erratic."

"Then why on earth did you take him? And I thought I told you to watch your liquor—you've been drinking again, haven't you?"

Felix exhaled. There was no point in lying.

The don stared at the boy for an uncomfortable duration, filled with regret. *He knows so much.* Only weeks ago his ties to Felix and the Ortizes had seemed so crucial and now here he was, sorry that he'd entrusted such a greenhorn with so many important tasks. Sorry, too, that the boy seemed to have fallen out of favor within his own family—perhaps marrying him and Adria was no longer a surefire means of insinuating his way inside the Ortiz's circle. Still, the don did not believe in mourning the past and he told himself that there was still time to bring the whole situation to a satisfactory close. "Get up to Taos until I decide what to do. I want you there by tomorrow evening, *comprendé?*"

Felix nodded but did not speak, angrier and more frightened than he had ever been in his life.

Southeast of Santa Fe, New Mexico Territory,
March 27, 1862

———————

By late afternoon, the weather had turned sharply colder on the back of a strong wind from the north and Confederates began to regret leaving their coats and blankets with the regiment's teamsters. At five o'clock, rain showers spattered the dusty track, and by six, spits of wet, heavy snow began to fall. For three hours Metzger, Stark and the other officers led their companies on a double-timed march, skirting the city's southeastern edge. Nearing Santa Fe, they ran counter to a tide of civilians fleeing with their valuables and livestock in anticipation of a battle on the capital's streets.

Major Metzger was the first to grow frustrated, tired of pushing against these multitudes and their dumb, clumsy beasts. "Ma'am!" he shouted at a well-dressed Anglo woman in a chauffeured cabriolet heaped with boxes and bags. *"Was sie ist machend?* Go home!"

Before answering the major, she commanded her driver not to stop. "The Yankees have whipped our boys!"

"Go home *und* stay inside! Get off the road!"

She shook her head emphatically as they passed and called over her shoulder: "It's said they'll murder all Southerners, so no, thank you—I will take my chances out here."

Unbidden, a Mexican leaned across his saddle to offer more intelligence: "Señor, you'd best run, too. The Yanks are shooting Texans—even those who have surrendered!"

"Shut up!" James Bradford snarled and shook his fist. "Get out of our way!"

The man shielded his eyes and spurred his horse forward, unwilling to confront a long file of angry-looking men.

Disgusted, Metzger shook his head as a rickety, mule-drawn *carreta*, loaded with furniture and wide-eyed children, trundled slowly past. "*Idioten!*" he swore and crossed the road.

Bradford kept his voice low: "Hear that, Jacob? Think it's true?"

Stark's head swam from all the pointless clatter and he exhaled slowly before answering: "No—only rumors and noise."

"Hope so," Bradford said. "We'd best find Col. Scurry."

"*Ja*, I will send an express!" Metzger called before riding ahead.

Bradford quickly detailed one of his gunner's mates to follow the major. "Company A, move ahead!" he bellowed. "Anything gets in your way, push it aside—*we must move faster!*"

Jacob peeled back a quarter-mile and repeated this message to his company. Near the column's tail, he slowed to speak with Briggs Hardy—their first conversation in days: "How they holding?"

"Okay." Hardy reined in his horse. "Could use some water, but otherwise no problems."

"You?"

"Glad to be movin' again—damned glad. Think we all are."

"See what I can do about the water. There's a good well at Arroyo Chamiso." Jacob looked ahead and saw that the gun carriages had stalled again. Traffic was backed up in three directions and he craned his neck for a better view. "Shit, what now?"

"Jake!" Hardy spurred his mount to catch up. "I want to apologize—"

"No, you don't. I'm the one—"

"Shut up and accept mine first, won't you?"

"Sure, if you'll let me say that I'm sorry I punched you."

Despite a split lip, Hardy grinned. "Pshaw, son—once a week some girl or another hits me harder'n that."

"So we're good?"

"Think we are."

"Good." Hearing loud shouting up ahead, Jacob nodded to his friend. "Wanna help?"

Hardy touched the brim of his forage cap. "Ready."

ᘏ

For two hundred feet the road narrowed between low adobe stores so that carts and caissons could only pass single-file. Complicating matters, the lane was drifted with items cast off by southbound refugees. By the time Briggs and Jacob reached this bottleneck, a scuffle there had nearly turned bloody. Jacob could see a knot of infantrymen, but not what they had surrounded. Halted in the lane, a team of mules hitched to one of the gun carriages jostled his horse aside, and by this accident, his view of the commotion improved. A quartet of Mexican civilians—young men in their teens and twenties—stood with their backs against an adobe; two were brandishing knives, the third a rimfire .22 pistol, and the fourth was empty-handed. Opposed were members of Ragsdale's Company C—some with bayonets fixed, all with their hammers locked. Both factions were braying at one another in a hash of English and Spanish so that neither group could understand the other. Around them, terrified travelers were scrambling for safety, which added immeasurably to the pandemonium.

"Texans!" Jacob shouted, "stop!" He searched the crowd for Ragsdale but saw that he'd been cut off from returning by snarled traffic. Bradford and Metzger, too, were nowhere to be found, so he quickly pushed forward. "What's this?"

One of the infantrymen gestured at the Mexicans. "Shoved past us in the narrows—we told 'em to wait, Sir! That one swung at me, and then his *amigos* got their hackles up."

Jacob pointed at the young Mexicans. "Stand aside," he said. "You can't cross us!"

Two of the teens dropped their knives and inched away. Finding the building's corner with their hands, they turned tail and vanished into a narrow breezeway. The third ducked into a crowd and was gone, but the one with the pistol glared at Jacob.

"Stand aside," Jacob repeated. "Now."

"*Gringadas* should never have come here!"

"You're short several friends, *pelado*. Clear off now or I'll turn 'em loose." Jacob drew his own revolver and rested it across his left forearm; from behind, the click of a hammer told him that Hardy had done likewise.

The Mexican dropped the pistol and spit in the dirt. *"Pendejo,* the Yankees will give you everything you deserve!"

Jacob narrowed his eyes. "Kill him if he says another word." Grasping the futility of his stand, the youth backed along the adobe wall and ran after his friends. Satisfied, Jacob nodded. "No one can stop us—push ahead!" Slowly the foot soldiers shouldered their weapons and shoved their way clear to the crossroad.

Hardy tapped one of the infantrymen on his shoulder. "Hand me that?" The private reached down to retrieve a blade that one of the Mexicans had dropped—a long, D-guard Bowie knife—and handed it to the lieutenant. "Always wanted one of these," Hardy said.

"Those are useless in a fight." Jacob grinned and spurred his horse forward.

"Sure," Hardy admitted. "Looks boss as hell, though!"

༄

It took near thirty minutes to unsnarl all the traffic and free the column from the constricted thoroughfare. On the village's other side, the road was still crowded as it snaked between scrubby piñon and juniper trees, but there were fewer obstructions and these were better managed, and once again they made good time. By sunset the column's lead elements had reached the crossroads village of Arroyo Chamiso, which was nothing more than a small adobe church, a sawmill, mercantile, and a loose cluster of mean adobe farmhouses. Here, the column slowed. Heeding reports that water was scarce up on Glorieta Pass, the mules and horses were allowed to drink their fill, and each soldier topped off his canteen at the well.

While the Cameron Guards took turns at the well, several mule-drawn wagons hove into sight on the upper road. News spread that these were Confederate teamsters freighting wounded Texans down from Apache Canyon. The vehicles were in terrible shape, yet each was fully loaded with ragged and bloody cargoes.

Lieutenant Bradford rode alongside one, talking with the driver until they met the first ranks of Jacob's company. Bradford shot them a troubled glance. "More coming."

Jacob touched the brim of his hat as the first wagon rolled past. "How we doing, boys?"

The driver shook his head. "Right on the edge, Cap'n."

"Hold fast—help's on the way."

"Muchas gracias. If you would, Sir, keep 'em back until we round the chapel."

Hardy shouted for others to step aside so that the wagons could navigate. A second ambulance rolled past, rocking on its springs as its wheels jumped in and out of the track's well-worn ruts.

"Give 'em room!" Jacob seconded.

Behind the three small wagons came two larger ones, both of which had difficulty completing the tight turn. Before the intersection, Jacob halted his mount across the track, forcing the men of his company to peer around him. "Hang on, friends," one called to the blanket-wrapped forms lying in the bed of the fifth wagon. "You'll make it!"

From his seat, the teamster—an older man with a tattered leather vest and felt hat—expressed mild surprise at this benediction. "They all dead."

Jacob rested a hand on the well-wisher's shoulder. "God bless 'em, then."

The old teamster raised the brim of his slouch and gestured toward the dark mountains. "Reckon He has, Sir. Others still missing up there—no food, no water, no blankets."

Jacob cut the conversation short and ordered his company to sort out raveled civilian traffic. Ten minutes later, they were underway once more; beyond the crossroads, the track lay open toward its junction with the Santa Fe Trail. Jacob's company increased its pace and soon caught up with the artillery. Just after sundown, snow began to fall.

సⴰ

Jacob's was the last company to pass one last road that led back to Santa Fe; from a quarter-mile away, Jacob, Hardy, and the others could see a carriage halted there. A small, stooped form—wrapped in dark blankets and spattered with snow—was standing beside the vehicle. Attempting to interpret this spectacle, Jacob missed seeing Charlie Spence approach.

"Sergeant," Hardy asked, "who's that?"

"Mexican woman, askin' for Cap'n Stark. Should I tell her to leave?"

Jacob and Hardy exchanged looks. "Get her name?" Briggs asked.

"Didn't," Spence replied. "Tried to ignore her."

"No one I recognize" Jacob said. "Not at this distance, anyway."

Spence grinned. "She's old, Cap'n—sure don't look dangerous."

Jacob shook the snow from his sleeves. "Keep 'em moving then while I see who it is."

Hardy and Spence rode ahead while Jacob stopped and allowed the last marchers to clear the intersection. He did not recognize the man in the driver's seat but saw in an instant that the woman was Benéfica, Adria Carrizo's old *chaperona*. Feeling his heart surge, he walked his horse forward, stopped below her perch on the cutbank, and removed his hat. *"Hola,* Benéfica, Ma'am. *Buenos tardes. ¿Qué quieres?"*

"Hola, Capitán Stark." Benéfica pulled her heavy black shawl tighter around her shoulders. She continued in English: "You look well, praise God."

Jacob inhaled. "Lord, sorry—I didn't think you spoke English."

"French and German, too, if you please. Have you said anything that you did not want me to hear?"

"Plenty, if memory serves."

"All is forgiven, *Capitán.*" She coughed into a lace handkerchief, revealing tobacco-stained teeth. "The weather turns, so I'll hurry. It is a tremendous favor I ask: please, sir, you must help Adria leave Santa Fe—tonight, if possible."

His heart leapt into his throat and he looked into the carriage. "She here?"

"No." Benéfica pointed toward the city. "I was not certain we would find you."

"Can't take her with me—not now."

"She is in great danger, *Capitán.*" Jacob tried to speak, but although his mouth moved, no sound came out. Benéfica glanced back toward the lights of Santa Fe, nervous even at a remove of some several miles. "The don no longer thinks clearly—more and more, his rage falls upon her. He knows about you—some things, anyway—and I am afraid that he will do something terrible to preserve the family's honor."

"How can I answer, Ma'am?"

"Please, *Capitán!* I did not think she could cry so much—*please!*"

Already the column's tail was a hundred yards up the road. "We were half-way to Albuquerque this morning—how did you know I'd be here?"

"I knew who was watching you—that and my luck held."

"Y'all shouldn't have left the city—it's too dangerous," Jacob glanced toward the city, and then back toward his company, out of view as the road dipped into a ravine.

"You will help her, yes?"

"We aren't going that way."

"We'll come east, then. I have family in La Cañada—there's a school there. Tonight, ten-thirty—please don't forsake her."

He wiped his mouth with the back of his hand. "I can't—"

"No, *Capitán,* you are the only one who *can.* Eulogio and I try to protect her, but we are old—we dare not confront him. We are practically strangers, you and I, but frankly, I would rather entrust her to Fate than the devil I know. I am certain that she cares deeply for you, and I pray that you feel the same way—truly, she must run and never look back. Anywhere else will be better."

He stared at her, unsure how to answer. *There is nothing I can do.*

Later, he wondered if he'd nodded then or said something that he could not recall, for Benéfica had smiled as she returned to the wagon. If he'd signaled in any way that he would go to La Cañada—a tiny settlement in the hills above the Santa Fe Trail—he hadn't meant to, and he hoped Benéfica would tell Adria that the no-account Texan had refused. He was sorely vexed thinking about her predicament, but there was nothing he could do. *Certainly not—mustn't look back.* He stayed and watched as the carriage turned in a weedy field and started up the road, lingering even after the buggy had vanished. The city's lights were shining—bright stars against the inky blackness of piñon-clad hills. Staring at those bright pinpoints, so near yet so distant, he wondered if Adria was beside one of them, looking back out the window for *him.* Jacob thought about her hair, her skin, and how her kisses tasted, and he felt as low as he had at any point since leaving Texas. Spurring his horse, he rode to catch up with his company.

∽

Having recognized Benéfica and certain that Adria was therefore involved, Hardy could not contain his surprise at Jacob's return: "Hey, you're back! Good!"

Jacob shot his friend a quizzical look. "You really think I was gonna leave?"

Briggs shrugged. "Reckon you were tempted. What did she want, pard?"

"Nothing."

"The don didn't send her?"

"Exactly the opposite, in fact."

Hardy eyed Jacob as they rode and saw that he'd assumed his customary slouch and locked his spurs in the cinch for the long ride ahead—coasting, they had called it in Texas. His friend seemed well enough, but there was no way to be sure. Still, he had returned and that there was something. Hardy offered his canteen and rolled his shoulders to try and work some of the stiffness out of his joints. It began snowing again.

Jacob returned the canteen. "Sure wish that was bourbon."

"Haven't heard you say that in a while. Once we're past all this," Hardy offered, "we'll go on a natural bender—I reckon we've earned it."

They pressed their horses uphill into the deepening gloom.

Apache Canyon, New Mexico Territory

———————

27 March, 1862—Found Col. Scurry's command about half-past ten and were immed. sent to guard the ranch's western approach. Told the fellows they'd five hours to sleep, after which we'd receive a new assignment. Troops that arriv'd earlier to-day have dug shallow entrenchments and felled trees for abatis. Snowing hard; shin-deep now. Bulk of the company is fast asleep on the ground under what cover the trees do afford, tho I don't think I will be so fortunate. Could make La Cañada if I left <u>NOW</u> and am wretch'd both for thinking that I <u>SHOULD</u> and for knowing that I <u>CANNOT</u>. Mindful that duty now binds me, or rather, that I am late to acknowledge those bonds that have long existed. Lord, protect Adria from him and grant us strength in our trials. Forever bestow Your blessings upon Texas. Victory in Your Name.

Federal Encampment, Bernal Springs, New Mexico Territory, March 27, 1862

"From Bernal Springs the Santa Fe Trail turns west and crosses the Pecos River. Skirts the ruins of the Pecos mission church, begins to climb, first across broad, rolling foothills south of the Sangre de Cristo Mountains, and later beside Glorieta Creek until it reaches the pass. From the summit, it turns sharply south and drops into Apache Canyon. It arcs northwest for a few miles and then due north, right into Santa Fe. Forested much of the way and in places it's quite steep and rough." An old, garrulous U.S. Army regular relayed this information to the Pinebark Independents as they huddled around their campfire.

"Room enough for a battle?" Sammy Douglas wondered.

The old Federal scratched his chin. "Not really. It'd be an Indian fight—wicked."

Matt Maher kicked a stick back into the fire. "How far is Santa Fe, then?"

"Thirty-odd from here, twenty from the top of the pass. You boys Irish, right? I was a marlinspike seaman on a coaling ship—called in Waterford in '52. Always liked you people."

"Waterford's away south." Neil Wilson waved his hand in that direction. "We are Ulstermen from the north—Protestants. My family's from Strabane, County Tyrone."

Douglas stared into the fire. "Antrim—atween Ballymena and Slemish."

"Carnlough," Hay mumbled.

"Belfast proper," Matt Maher said, "greatest city in the world." The others groaned.

Matt's brother, Mike, offered up the coffee pot and the old soldier poured himself a scant half-cup. He took a sip, stood, and turned up the collar of his sack coat. "Take courage, boys. Been shot twice in my life and still I am here to say so. Once things get hot, stay low and stay on one stick—only advice I got that's worth a damn." He finished his coffee and threw the dregs into the snowy grass. "That and no matter what leadership says, sometimes there's no shame in running. G'night." He turned away, melting swiftly into the snowy darkness and for several minutes none of them spoke as each tried to imagine their futures.

Finally, Bill Storey broke the silence: "Are we going back t'Fort Union, Pete?"

Wrapped in a rough woolen blanket, Peter MacInnes stepped into the red firelight. "Don't think so—Col. Slough won't stand for it."

"Our brave colonel," Hay mocked, "leading from his tent."

"Have we numbers for all 'at?" Storey said.

"We'll see."

"Chivington's boys said the Texans broke an' ran."

Peter threw his grounds into the snow. "Not quite: we outnumbered 'em two, maybe three for one—merely lucky is all." As their fire began to gutter, the fearsome cold regained its strength. A few of the boys crawled beneath their blankets and tried to sleep. Despite their fatigue, the others were too nervous to close their eyes.

"What of us?" Wilson wondered.

"Will we go with Chivington?" Douglas added.

"No—he is going south to try and flank 'em." Peter's teeth chattered. "W-w-we'll be in the main column. Boys, let's do like that oul' son said—come hell or high wind we must stick together. We'll come through—see? Now, sleep while ye can." Then he stepped away into the darkness.

Hay and the others stayed and stared into the fire, each man lost in his own thoughts. Once the coffee was gone, one by one they drifted off into cold and fitful slumber.

Johnson's Ranch, Apache Canyon, New Mexico Territory, March 27, 1862

East of Santa Fe, Johnson's Ranch straddled the Santa Fe Trail for nearly a mile, its headquarters set where a wide arroyo branched away from Apache Canyon. A prosperous operation (but deserted: staunchly pro-Union, Anthony Johnson had fled with his family into the mountains, mere hours ahead of the Confederates), the main house was surrounded by barns, stables, dairy houses, loafing sheds, and chicken coops. Tucked into side-canyons were the homes of Johnson's various hired men. Anticipating that the Federals would attack them there, Col. Scurry's Texans had constructed crude fortifications and set rough juniper abatis all across the spread. Teamsters needed ropes and improvised block-and-tackle to help their jaded mules pull artillery pieces up the steepest portions of the trail; upon reaching the ranch, they rolled these guns onto ground protected by more juniper slash. By ten o' clock, eight inches of snow had fallen and the Confederates, few of whom had tents or adequate blankets, lit dozens of enormous bonfires to try and ward off the cold.

Jacob's company guarded the ranch's western approach. There the Santa Fe Trail left Apache Canyon and entered the heavily wooded hills that girded the capital. They were all of them glad for this assignment, as there had been neither trenches to dig nor construction to complete (the Federals weren't expected to arrive from the west, after all). Most had quickly fallen asleep. On first watch, their sentinels had stopped three freighters who'd meant to overnight at Johnson's and ordered them to return to town—but not before confiscating several choice food items. While most of

Scurry's regiment choked down stale hardtack and coffee, the Cameron Guards had cooked ham steaks and fried biscuits in the fat. Afterward a jug of apple cider went around and to a man, they agreed that it had been the best meal they had enjoyed since Mesilla, three months earlier.

"Good to be from Cameron County," Charlie Spence said before going to look for a place to lie down.

Then on second watch, Jacob, Hardy, Cyrus Dupree, and Bob Turner played cards for a pouch of tobacco that Hardy had liberated from a four-up driver. Dupree won. Feeling generous, he'd passed it around until it was gone and they all enjoyed their first smoke in weeks. They argued over Fort Union's likely defenses; declared what they would do once they reached Denver; and debated whether the black-sand streams in Colorado truly flowed over beds of pure gold. Finally, the conversation lagged and most drifted off to sleep.

At two a.m., George Orth waded downhill through the snow, looking for Hardy. Jacob asked if there was trouble, but when Hardy assured him that everything was fine he went back to his writing. Hardy and Orth walked quietly between the trees until they found a sentry, standing in the middle of the Santa Fe Trail. The sentry pointed west, where three Texans were guarding a small buggy, its dark curtains pulled tightly closed. A large square of white fabric hung from the vehicle's roof and hitched to the rig were two enormous draft horses, exhaling prodigious clouds of steam.

"Big things," Hardy said.

Orth spit into the snow. "They ain't the half of it, Jimmy." Arriving at the barricade, Hardy greeted the sentries.

Behind the rig, Charlie Spence motioned him aside and glanced around to make sure they were out of earshot. "Jacob still on the barricade?"

"We catch a spy?" Hardy asked. "Or is it that old lady again?"

"She ain't old," Spence said quietly. "Says she wants to see Jake."

Hardy stepped up, peered between the buggy's drapes, and then stepped away. He turned to the others. "Roust him out—tell him to meet me at that barn above the spring. And don't say nothin' to no one else."

Orth saluted and slipped away in the darkness.

Hardy spoke with the sentries before he took one of the horse's bridles and guided the team onto a narrower fork away from the main trail. For five minutes he walked the giant horses—Belgians, Percherons, he didn't know the difference—uphill toward the barn. The snow had almost stopped and the woods were silent, save for the muffled clop of horses' hooves and creaking iron springs. He turned onto another road, partially overgrown with sagebrush. The driver pulled aside one of the buggy's curtains, and Hardy cast a backward glance. He lifted his hat. "Lovely weather for a ride."

"Where are you taking me?" Adria Carrizo coughed and adjusted a heavy buffalo-hide blanket around her shoulders.

Hardy ignored the question. As the horses plodded forward, again he looked back. *I'd have thought this a dream, except there she is.* He shook the snow from his hat and whistled softly. "Drive this rig yourself?"

"Only from La Cañada."

"With the drapes closed like that?" Even in the dark, most horses can follow a trail without guidance, sometimes with better results than if their rider or driver is handling their reins—though here this was not the case.

"I only closed them to stay warm after your men stopped me."

"Ain't my men—they're Jeff Davis's first, General Sibley's second, and Jacob Stark's third. Lots of prior claims—why'd you come here, anyway?"

"To let him go." Adria looked up at the silvery moon. "I am no thief."

"We'll see." Hardy, who did not know many women, nor particularly trust those he did, could hardly guess what she meant. The horses plodded ahead and broke through crusted snow. With dark and silent woods drawn tight around the road, the atmosphere was as hushed and intimate as an opera box. Around a curve in the road at the edge of a deep arroyo loomed the wreck of a two-story barn. Set atop a foundation of cut sandstone flags, mortise and tenon held its ancient and massive framing timbers together, though the rearmost third had collapsed. Notched into the hillside above, their outlines indistinct beneath snowy mantles, were a puddled adobe house, its roof long caved, and a tumbledown stone cellar. Hardy guided the horses into the yard before the barn's lower doors. Glancing downhill through the clouds, he saw the faint outlines of the Confederates' main camp. "You know Jake loves you, don't you?"

Adria, who had grown increasingly nervous the farther they went into the woods, was slow to answer. "I—I'd hoped so, but now nothing is clear."

Hardy nodded. "He does."

"Has he said so?"

"He don't talk that way, but he's acted such a mess, that must mean *somethin'*." At this Adria began to cry, leaving Hardy more nonplussed than ever. "Oh, hold on!" he said. "Sorry, I can't ever put my thoughts into words. You and Jake, this dream you inhabit ain't nothin' but air, nothin' but a wave upon sand. 'Course, sometimes the wind and waves have their way. I've seen the damage storms can do—pulled bodies down from trees and helped fight a fire or two, but I don't want that here, see?" He looped the horses' reins over a cross-brace before returning to the cab and offering his hand to Adria.

Turning to face him, she hesitated. "So I cannot see him, then?"

"What? No," Hardy exhaled heavily. "He'll be along shortly."

"You just said—"

"Jake loves you," he continued, "more than us, more than life itself. He finds you here, I expect that's it. He'll leave, and we brothers—now fifty of the seventy-five that left Brownsville—will have to weather this storm without him."

"But if you're afraid that he will leave, then why not keep us apart?"

This time Hardy hesitated. "He's my best friend," he said at last. "I'd rather see him happy than stand on principle."

Despite her tears, Adria smiled. She wiped her eyes, took Hardy's hand, and stepped down from the buggy.

Hardy pushed open a small Dutch door and accidentally broke the rotten stile as he did. "Watch your step." He pushed aside a pile of debris with his boot and helped Adria inside. He struck a match and lit a tin dead-flame lantern that he'd removed from the buggy's backstay. That portion of the barn that was still intact was cool and smelled of adobe dust and rotting wood, but it was dry. To one side was a separate room with a flagstone hearth, an old table, and a couple of plain pine benches. Strewn across the table were sardine tins and champagne bottles, all empty. Hardy threw damp kindling in the hearth and tried to light it with a spill of paper (one of the broadsides bearing Sibley's proclamation, as it happens), but the burning paper expired and the kindling refused to catch. "Up here earlier tonight," he explained. "Hearth's wet, though, and it's doused the coals. All this snow, I guess."

She exhaled slowly. "Lieutenant...Hardy, is it?"

"Briggs."

"I cannot control the events now unfolding—though I suppose that in some small way I am trying. I don't want to make trouble."

"What's comin' at us is so big, I don't know what matters now."

She tried to swallow the lump in her throat, but it wouldn't budge. "I only want to see Jacob again...before tomorrow. What do you think will happen?"

Hardy was nothing if not confident. Sprung from a combination of experience and expectation, he'd no doubt whatsoever that they were about to sweep aside the last Yankee resistance between them and Denver City. "Honest? I 'spect we'll knock 'em all down tomorrow or the day after, and that'll be that. We'll take Fort Union's stores and leave this awful place for good—no offense. Jake can say he saw this thing through and then he's all yours—won't anyone have the wind spilled from their sails."

"I can wait," she said, her hopes renewed. "You'll watch out for him?"

By then, Hardy had gone through all the kindling so he stood and brushed dirt from his hands. "As best I can. We made it this far, right?" He looked around the space, but for the feeble lamplight saw nothing else that might burn. "Sorry, Señorita, but it won't re-light."

"Thank you for trying. And please—my name is Adria."

Air played across the smoking embers, but the hearth stayed cold. "Okay, Adria. Need anythin' before I go?"

She said she did not, and noticed that she could see her breath.

Hardy's eyes remained fixed on the dying coals. "Don't normally set stock in prayer, but maybe you'll remember us in yours. Pray that we meet again, far away from here." He picked up his waterlogged hat. "You and Jake, me and some silly, shameless thing with loose morals. Goodbye, Adria." He took her hand, meaning to kiss it as he had seen Col. Green do, but she leaned forward and hugged him instead. Pleased and embarrassed all at once, he went out into the cold.

❧

A hundred yards below the barn, Hardy spotted Jacob wading through the snow. "Morning," he called, and his friend waved in return.

"What now?"

"Stopped another one." The clouds had begun to fray and a full moon cast shadows beneath the pines. The wind gusted and skiffs of snow tumbled from the branches, coating the buggy's tops and sides until they shone like silver.

"Orth said to bring water." Jacob carried a bucket drawn from a deep well down by the trail. "For those brutes there, I guess?"

"Big damn things, ain't they?"

"Wait—" Jacob recognized the horses as Don Carrizo's. His heart surged inside his chest, but his friend merely clapped him on the shoulder and continued past.

"Go see for yourself."

Jacob stood fast and watched Hardy until he disappeared. Then he held the bucket until the animals drained it and stepped through the Dutch door.

❧

Adria rose from her seat and hurled herself into his arms. For what felt like an age, neither spoke; the only sounds were of their rapid breathing and the low hiss of a dying fire. "You didn't come to La Cañada." She buried her face in his chest, drawing so near that she could hardly breathe.

"Adria, I'm sorry," he said, "My God, I'm so sorry."

She looked up at his face, but it was so dark that she could barely make out his features; words poured from her mouth in torrents: "Some saint has doused those flames, else you'd see how I blush now to speak. Do you love me, Jacob? Truly? You need not answer—I think that now I know your mind. But, if you say yes—"

"Yes, Adria, a hundred times, yes!"

"—I'll accept your word. The road we are traveling, so rough and obscure—how we have stumbled! And might we again? My love, have I been rash with my affections? Do you think I am silly, following you this way? Too bold? Perhaps. Maybe I *have* been reckless—"

"No," he said, "I am the only fool here."

"I shouldn't have been so careless," she said, "but how could I—? The feelings—they are nothing I've known before—how could I have known? Please, don't doubt me when I say that I love you. I'll swear my love for you is real, you'll see."

"Adria, I know it's real—your love has led me out of darkness." He leaned down, kissed her and for the first time did not fear the things that threatened to separate them. He leaned away and looked into her eyes. "I should have stayed."

"I shouldn't have asked you to." She buried her head against his chest and tried to inhale his soul into hers. *Perhaps I do not know him so well*, she thought. No matter—she loved him anyway. She closed her eyes and shut out the darkness and desolation that loomed beyond their embrace. Beyond this moment, nothing else mattered—nothing ever could. "Hold me," she whispered.

"Forever," he said.

Over his shoulder, she saw that now even the embers in the hearth were dying. "I can stay for a little while—can you?"

Gently, he slipped her grasp and moved the lantern to a stone flag. "A little while, yes."

She touched his arm as he moved past her to stir the embers. Studying his movements, she admired his strong hands and handsome profile and wished that they had years together instead of hours. *Already we have wasted so much time—what conceit, asking for more!* She leaned forward to speak, and even as he tried to light the kindling he listened intently, transfixed by her voice: "Seeing you there, I can hardly breathe. I forget every pain, every sadness— everything that came before. And while we are nearly strangers, I know you'd leave with me if you could—"

"Yes, I would."

"—though I was late realizing why you mustn't." She rested a hand on his shoulder and he laid his hand across hers. "I cannot keep you."

"Adria—"

"Our minutes must now be like hours—and I'll never regret being with you, no matter what tomorrow holds." In the fireplace, faint sparks began to glow. Jacob rubbed his free hand on the sides of his trousers, turned on his knee, and wrapped his arms around her. He kissed her face, her neck, and clasped her hands as tightly as he dared.

She shivered and rested her head on his shoulder. "Last I saw you—"

He bowed his head. "Forgive the things I said."

"It doesn't matter—"

"It *does* matter, Adria! It does! I must explain myself, all the things that you've heard, and while I do not believe that afterward you will think better of me, you deserve to hear the truth."

Shaking her head, she pulled him closer. "Another month, another year. Some distant day when we are far from here and we've run out of things to say—tell me then."

"What if we don't get that chance?" Jacob's eyes traced the limits of the lantern's light; everything beyond eluded his perception. "What if this is all?"

"I haven't been this happy since I was very young," she answered. "Nothing you say can change that."

"Don't bet on it."

"This is what I want—only this." Outside, wind drew on the chimney, but the kindling merely continued to smoke and the room grew steadily colder.

He wanted to believe her, but trust did not come naturally. Still, she'd sought him out—at risk to her own safety—and surely that was something. "Ask me and tonight I will leave with you." He closed his eyes and kissed the top of her head. "Otherwise how can I protect you?"

"Protect me?"

"Adria—"

"No one but God can protect me." She closed her eyes. He stared morosely at the flickering lamp. "And things aren't so bad that I cannot look after myself."

Abruptly Jacob slipped her grasp and took hold of her shoulders. The strength of his grip startled her and she opened her eyes. "Soon, then! Soon as it's over, I will run to you—then no one can tell us how we're supposed to live."

She smiled at the promise. "But how—"

"I'll resign. Enlisteds are in for the duration, but officers can resign their commissions. Dad Green won't need me to chase after Jayhawks, anyhow." Imagining the possibilities, he began to speak faster: "Denver City, San Luis, anywhere—I'll find you. Come April, if I haven't heard from you, I'll come back here."

She shook her head. "My father—"

"He cannot keep us apart. Needs be, we will meet somewhere down south and go from there. This can work!"

"But how will I find you?"

"You'll know," he said, and kissed her. "I'll send you a message—somehow you'll know. Say you'll have me and I'll never stop looking—not for a thousand years!"

"I will," she said, but her body began to shake. She laid her head on his chest and tried to burrow into his embrace.

Jacob held her even tighter. "Sakes, how you shiver!"

"I'm freezing," she confessed.

"The fire..." he trailed off. "You have blankets in the carriage?"

She said she did, so he went outside. One buffalo blanket was in fine condition but the others were of rough, moth-eaten wool—miserable things, though better than nothing. When he returned, he draped the best one over her shoulders and kissed her again. Together they sat on the bench, arms enfolded, and she kissed him back.

He hesitated, aware of how much of the trail was still on him. "I'm awfully dirty."

She kissed his stubbled cheek. "I don't care."

"You sure?"

"I need to be near you—to breathe with you."

His hands moved unhurriedly along her arms and down her sides. He pulled her closer, tighter, so that he could trace the curves of her hips. He kissed the soft, olive skin along her neck and throat and felt her hands tug at his hair and ears as he did so. Slowly he reached up, undid a single button on the front of her dress, elated, and terrified that this might abash her but she herself undid the second. He kissed her there on the newly exposed skin below her collar and felt her back arch into his embrace. His nose and ears were frigid. She whispered his name once and again, and afterward she'd remember how those syllables felt on her lips—how his rough hands, cold at first, had held her gently, and how for once she felt complete, as though for the first time her soul beheld one of the miracles for which it had been created. Her breath quickened in the feeble lamplight and he struggled to keep the blankets from slipping off their shoulders. Across the room, indistinct against the rough sandstone, faint, conjoined shadows played across the wall, until the lantern guttered out, throwing the room into complete and sudden darkness.

༄

Adria stood and re-buttoned the collar of her dress as Jacob, still seated on the pine bench, held tightly to her waist. Resting his head against her hip, he looked into the hearth for embers and saw only sparks. He guessed it was near to four a.m. "Adria, will you marry me?" he said.

Startled, she pressed her fingertips to her lips. "Do you mean it?"

"I do." He squeezed her waist. "Come summer, we'll get married."

She bent to kiss him again and placed her cold hands upon his cheeks.

"Then nothing will separate us." He stood, helped her pull on her coat, carefully folding the collar around her chin. He groaned and pulled her tight again. "Must you go?"

"It's late," she whispered, "and bribes only go so far."

"You bribed Benéfica?" Jacob laughed.

"She bribed Eulogio to drive us to La Cañada—I must return before they wake."

He shook his head in amazement. "Never in my wildest imagination." Outside, it was unclear whether snow was falling from the sky or merely blowing down from the trees. A few stars shone through gauzy clouds and the silverwhite moon had sunk low—except for its light, the world was lost in darkness. He helped her into the buggy, and she took the reins, turning it expertly within the open yard. Jacob climbed in the other side and stared in amazement at the horses' broad backs. "You can handle these brutes?"

"More readily than mules—they're perfectly docile."

"Full of surprises, Miss Carrizo." He rested a hand on her knee as the buggy descended through the woods.

Returned to the barricade, Jacob saw that Briggs Hardy and George Orth were the only two still on watch. He waved. They returned the gesture and motioned for Adria turn west toward the city and safety. Jacob stepped down and walked around to Adria's side, grateful to see that his friends were standing at a discreet distance. He planted one foot on the running board, leaned in, and kissed her again. Then he stepped back and took hold of her hand. "Darling, I will love you until the stars fall right out of the sky."

"And I love you. Bond strength with resolve so that sorrow cannot touch us."

"The tide's running now—two weeks at most. After we clear the field tomorrow, I will send a message about where to meet—Denver, Peralta, or Franklin. You sure you can get away?"

"Yes. Promise me you'll stay safe?"

"Don't worry." He jumped onto the running board, kissed her one last time, and whispered again that he loved her.

"You have my heart—don't forget."

"Never." The giant horses strained against their harnesses. Though they were staring in snow on an uphill lie, the little vehicle was well within their strength. He watched for a full five minutes until the rig slipped seamlessly into the mirk.

❧

Near the barricade, Jacob fell in alongside Hardy, who had just returned from a small pile of firewood they had pulled off a cutter's wagon. He reached out and took a few sticks from his friend's arms. They scuttered and slid in silence until Hardy cast a sidelong glance at his friend. "You okay?"

Jacob said that he was.

"Glad you stayed."

"Wouldn't leave—not now." Jacob looked out into the forest. "Remember when you convinced Doc Miller to hire me on at the ranch? After the troubles?"

"Sure."

"First night there, Fish lit a big fire in one of the fields, remember? That other hand—what was his name? *Ray Stennis!* Ray had that bottle of mescal and Lord! How we roostered! Feels like that tonight, too. Not the drunk, of course—like I'm on a new path, headed toward something better."

They walked into camp. Orth greeted them warily and looked to Hardy for guidance. Unseen by Jacob, Hardy winked, and so Orth began to speak. "More news."

Jacob threw his load of sticks onto the fire. "What?"

Orth produced a tin box that contained a fair portion of stewed pork, still warm.

"Good Lord, who pulled mess at this hour?" Jacob marveled.

"C'mon," Hardy laughed and pulled a fork from his haversack. "This ain't no campfire meal! George here lifted it off some poor woodcutter about a half-hour ago. Fellow's wife probably made it for his lunch, but it seemed wrong that one man should enjoy so much when we've made do with so little."

Jacob handed the fork to Orth. "Your catch, George—you go first." Within a few minutes, their meal was concluded and Jacob looked up the road, north toward Santa Fe and for a happy future with Adria. "Ain't so bad up here, huh?"

Hardy and Orth exchanged grins, supposing that Jacob had enjoyed the last several hours more than they had, but both agreed that it was an extraordinarily fine meal.

PART FIVE

GLORIETA

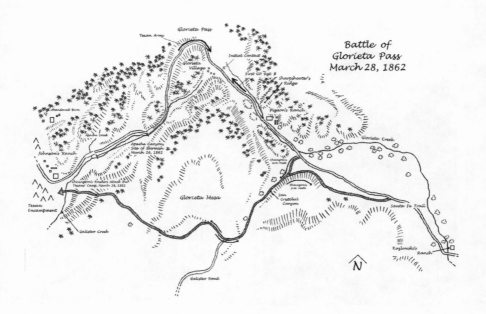

Battle of
Glorieta Pass
March 28, 1862

5-GLORIETA MAP

Pigeon's Ranch, East of Glorieta Pass, New Mexico Territory, March 28, 1862

———————————

Early the prior decade, Alexander Vallé—Pigeon to his friends—had emigrated from France to New Mexico Territory and secured a land grant on the east side of Glorieta pass. There he'd constructed the largest and best-appointed hotel anywhere along the Santa Fe Trail. Wedged into the narrowest part of Glorieta Canyon, there was room only for the hotel, Glorieta Creek, and the Santa Fe Trail. In fact, to step off the covered porch was to step squarely onto the Trail itself. Roofed with tin, five chimneys crowned the main building. North of this were dozens of corrals, sheds, and stalls, encircled by a thick adobe wall about four feet high. Farther afield were variously sized tracts for pasturage, each delineated by a split-rail fence. Surrounding hills were dotted with piñon, juniper, and mountain mahogany; only along the gulches was there moisture enough for willows, alders, and cottonwoods. Indeed, water was the single greatest scarcity at Vallé's ranch. Two springs behind the corrals barely met domestic needs and though he'd dug a well, it was scarcely reliable. Autumns were especially dry, forcing Vallé to import water by wagon from the Pecos River—some five-miles distant—at a substantial cost.

For two days, men wounded during the skirmish in Apache Canyon had been taken to Pigeon's hotel, filling the building well beyond its intended capacity, and with alarming rapidity, the main room had acquired patinas of blood, bile, and God knew what else. At first this upset him greatly, for he prided himself on cleanliness and order—traits that the Union surgeons did not seem to share.

Then Quartermaster Capt. Herbert Enos had assured him that the U.S. Government would pay for use and damages at double the normal rate, which had lessened the sting.

∽

On March 28, Pigeon rose late and took his coffee on the porch. The hilltops were lost in cold mist, but down along the creek, spring's imminence was writ certain in the willows' pale green buds. Better days were ahead: soon his pear and peach trees would blossom, and by summer, there would be pies and preserves—morels, wild strawberries, and currants in the hills above. In peaceful times he'd have seen teamsters in the yard, battening loads before they began—depending on their direction—either the last day or the second of many more days on the Trail. Of course, times were no longer peaceful, so instead he watched Yankee soldiers mill about and stack their rifles. Clustered around the well, they elbowed each other for a turn at refilling their canteens. He pulled a watch from his vest pocket—*twenty-five minutes past ten o'clock*—and wondered how long they had tarry. With the trail closed, there had been no other business for days, and while he enjoyed their ribald stories, the presence of heavily armed men in his front yard left Pigeon deflated and nervous. He took a sip of coffee and watched a stream of infantrymen marching up the trail. He realized then that he had not seen the huge Coloradan, Maj. Chivington, since his return from Apache Canyon two days prior. Surely, this was an augury. Pigeon hailed a mounted officer from the porch.

Captain George Howland, one of Col. Paul's regulars from Fort Union, recognized the hotelier and reined his horse to a halt beside the porch rail. "Mr. Vallé, good morning."

"*Capitaine* Howland!" Pigeon smiled broadly. "*C'est* good to see you! Welcome! *Capitaine*, two days ago I see *les gros une*. Today Chivington is not...*voici?* Ah, present, no?"

Howland knew that Vallé was solidly pro-Union, so he'd no fears about sharing what little he knew. "Major Chivington is away on assignment. Departed the trail at Kozlowski's, but where he is going, I cannot say. How are the fellows inside?"

"Les plaie? Most fare better. Of course, *ils sont bienvenue*—all are welcome here. Sadly, a few others have died and were buried last night."

"I heard." Howland touched his hat brim.

"Sad, yes."

"Yes. This is probably the last you'll see of us for a while," Howland said and tapped his spurs. "Take care, Mr. Vallé."

Pigeon watched Howland canter west to rejoin his fellows as they continued toward the pass. He turned opposite and saw a mounted coterie of senior officers and their staffs in the field east of his hotel. Perhaps one of these was Col. Slough, about whom a few of the wounded in his dining room had spoken. He took another sip of coffee and glanced at his watch—*thirty-five minutes past ten o'clock.* As he reached down to pick up a scrap of paper, a crackling sound rolled down the canyon. A strange sound, as if the air itself had split. A dull boom shook the porch rail, but this he felt rather than heard. *Tonnerre?*

Pigeon leaned out from the veranda, glanced skyward and saw nothing but a dull, gray shroud. Then a commotion farther up the trail caught his eye, and he saw one of Howland's companions barreling toward the hotel. While many in the yard stared in slack-jawed wonder, Pigeon well knew what this meant and ducked back inside the hotel. *"Les chiens ont été libéré,"* he murmured. He strode along a hallway, pulled employees into his train, and refused to let any return for belongings. Once out the back door, they ran for the stables, mounted horses that had been saddled as a precaution, and departed in haste, east toward Kozlowski's station.

⁓

Howland's rider raced past the hotel at full gallop. "Kick out the frost!" he shouted, "Texans in the woods, this side of the pass! Here they come!" Within seconds, a thunderclap of grape and shell confirmed this news. As Pigeon and his employees streamed east, Federals who had been making fires for coffee were bugled into lines. Another blast of grapeshot cut the treetops and showered the hotel's yard with dust and splinters.

Colonel Slough and his staff galloped across a field and tried to fix the Texans' positions. "Let's go, let's *go!*" Col. Slough yelled. "Hit 'em back! Tappan, take yours left, into the woods! Have Ritter and Clafin bring their guns forward now! Go! Sopris, Robbins, to the walls! Support the artillery! Move, boys, move! Everything depends on speed, so *move!*"

Upper Glorieta Canyon, New Mexico Territory, March 28, 1862

Less snow had fallen east of the pass, yet the ground there was a muddy, sodden mess. After the Texans' initial salvo, the Coloradans rushed a quarter-mile west, found themselves in an indefensible position and so their buglers sounded a retreat. Confounding the Texans, they ran some three hundred yards back east to the safety of the trees and re-set their lines. In all this haste, they committed several errors: first, the infantry's sudden withdrawal left the Federals' battery of heavier cannon alone in a salient with a single company of Coloradans in support. After several anxious minutes, Capt. John Ritter's gun crews re-limbered these guns and dragged them back inside the Union's line. Second, and nearly as calamitous, Quartermaster Capt. Enos—still dejected over the lost Albuquerque stores—had brought two ammunition wagons forward, and the retreating Coloradans had overlooked these, too. "Damn you," Enos swore at his drivers, "bring those wagons up or burn 'em—the Texans can't have 'em!" With the Confederates closing fast, Enos's men were prepared to set fire when three civilian teamsters stepped forward and managed to free both vehicles, mere seconds ahead of the onrushing Texans. Though disaster had been averted, little else slowed the Texans as they crossed an open field and charged the disorganized Union front. Gray-clad units swarmed into the breach created by the Coloradan's withdrawal and blood began to spill.

Texan Bill Davidson was one unfortunate actually hit during this wild initial skirmish. A minié ball had ripped a jagged hole through the middle of his left thigh; unable even to stand, his comrades had left him behind.

"Oh, no, son of a *bitch!*" Despite his physical situation, Davidson was still well prepared to curse his luck. "Son of a bitch, I'm tired. Shit, shit, shit—no, no *no!*" Newly arrived units were puzzled to find Davidson seated squarely in the middle of the Santa Fe Trail, struggling to tamp tobacco into the bowl of his pipe. His musket lay nearby but he was shirtless, having removed the garment and torn it into strips for a tourniquet.

Captain Issac Adair of the Seventh Texas Regiment knelt and put a hand on Davidson's shoulder. "Help's coming, pard—how you fixed?"

"Goddamn Yankees ruined my pants—tore two big holes in 'em!"

Adair glanced east. "You see where they went? Five minutes ago, all Colorado was standing right here." Adair scratched his chin and listened to the sound of muskets discharging in the woods on his right.

"Thus," Davidson said and gestured toward the pale sun. He tore another strip from his shirt. "Hell, I don't even know where I am right now—is this Santa Fe?"

"Useful as a four-card flush," Adair muttered to another officer. "Hey Private, where is Sergeant Carson?" Adair knew that Davidson and Carson were friends, and hoped that a familiar name might jog the man's memory.

"Big Jim's with A Company, Fifth Texas. Still in Santa Fe, I reckon." The pool of blood beneath his leg continued to spread.

"Take care, Private. Stay right here." Adair and signaled for his command to move ahead.

"You're welcome, Sir," Davidson shouted after. "Tell Big Jim I'd have done my part, but the goddamn Yankees tore my britches! He'll understand."

೨೦

From the Confederates' headquarters on the hill above, Maj. Frederick Metzger stood between two giant trees and sketched a map of the valley—its hills, gulches, and stands of timber. Working quickly—and glancing up frequently before smoke obscured the field—he saw Col. Scurry ascending. Holding his pencil carefully, Metzger snapped off a salute but the colonel waved for him to continue working.

After a moment, Scurry lowered his field glass and studied Metzger's drawing. "That's real good—Tom Green told me you had a gift for reading landforms."

"Thank you, Sir." Metzger continued his work.

Scurry pointed to a series of concentric pencil lines on Metzger's map. "What of that hill? South of the ranch buildings?"

"Die strassen hier?"

"I don't follow," Scurry frowned. Though he had grown up in New York State among German immigrants, his memories of their language had rusted from decades of disuse. "Aren't *strassen* streets?"

"Roads, yes. Upon those roads, behind the *Wänden*—there they will stand."

Scurry brow stayed knotted. *"Wänden*—what's that?"

"Sorry, Sir—walls," Metzger grunted and continued his labors. The din in the valley was terrible.

Scurry studied the captain as he worked, but the younger man was wholly absorbed. The colonel scratched his own ear and spat. "Wall Hill, then—there's our objective."

"Wald'? Distracted, Metzger thought Scurry had used the German word for forest.

"Yeah, walled. We take that hill, we'll control the valley—now, how do we get there?" On their left, Bradford's artillery thundered and shook their bones. Wild cheers of indeterminate origin echoed out of the scrubby woods on their right.

Metzger paused and studied the hill that had caught the colonel's eye. It was the major's twenty-seventh birthday and although he wished he were home with his wife, his mood was unusually buoyant. He put his finger on the paper and traced various arroyos and flats to a single point. The field was hourglass-shaped, with a high, narrow waist where Glorieta Creek had cut through a transverse ridge. He pointed. "Sir, here—here they cannot defend without severing their lines."

Scurry squinted to see through smoke that had already begun to obscure the field. To his right, Charles Pyron's troops were firing at their Federal counterparts; to his left, Maj. Raguet's troops were similarly engaged. Grasping the soundness of Metzger's observations, he slapped the major's shoulder and started downhill toward his tethered horse. "Then there, my friend, is where we'll attack."

&

From another prominence, Bradford's artillery blasted the Federals' line with cannister. This fire was especially hazardous for George Howland's company of regular Union cavalry, who had dismounted and sought shelter in the pines north of Glorieta Creek. Within minutes of their deployment, three of their number were killed and two others wounded. Though Confederate units straddled the Santa Fe Trail, none had yet pushed north of the creek. Of his own initiative, Coloradan Charles Kerber decided to flank the Texans here and silence their artillery. Lieutenant Kerber had only recently been named to lead Company I—German immigrants and farmers recruited from settlements around Fort St. Vrain, north of Denver— and he guessed that a deep ravine leading away from the main creek offered their best chance to bypass the Confederates' deadly guns. Crouched at the gulch's mouth, he waved the men of Company I past; one by one they scrambled upward over the brush and loose stones that littered its narrow floor.

Texan skirmishers spotted this movement and relayed a frantic message to Col. Scurry. Scurry, in turn, ordered Captain Charles Buckholts, a thirty-eight year-old Galveston lawyer, to lead a detached infantry company north. Pulling a twelve-pound howitzer, they dashed across a closely shorn hay meadow and attracted immediate Federal attention. Several were killed or wounded before they reached protected positions above the draw. As Buckholts' men paused to catch their breath, they could hear Kerber's men below, swearing in German as they attempted to navigate the narrow, rocky ravine.

Among these Texans was nineteen-year old Ben White, whose formative years in the swamps back of Galveston had left him more than a little wild; he'd joined Sibley's Army of New Mexico for sole reason that he'd always wanted to kill someone. With his back against a boulder, he double-shotted the barrels of his two guns and nodded to his childhood friend. "Bud, ol' pardner, they will hate what I'm about to say."

Sweating profusely, Buddy Elliot's hands shook as he struggled to re-load his heavy revolver. "Need to hear it, though." In the ravine the Coloradans continued west, unaware of the Texans above. Other Federal companies tried to warn Kerber's men, but already Company I was too far away and the battle too pitched for them to hear.

Captain Buckholts signaled his company, pantomimed the act of shooting, and began waving his arm in a slow and silent countdown. When he reached two, Ben White stood, turned both shotguns down in the ravine, and fired. Still hunched over in a scramble, four Coloradans were hit, three of them fatally. The rest of the company could not have been more thunderstruck if an earthquake had leveled the surrounding mountains. White's exultation was short lived, though, for even as his comrades rose and opened fire, one of Kerber's Germans aimed carefully and put a minié ball into White's stomach. White tumbled backward and landed beside the boulder that had only just sheltered him. There he laughed a little and remembered the sound of his mother's voice before quickly and quietly bleeding to death.

The Texans' howitzer raked the gulch with cannister, exacting a ghastly toll. Yelling and firing as they leapt, the Southerners poured over the ravine's lip. One lunged at a gray-bearded Union soldier and killed him with two shots from his revolver. He took the dead man's musket, clubbed a wounded Yankee with it, and then dispatched him with another shot. All along the gulch, desperate hand-to-hand fighting broke out as Kerber's company struck back with bayonets, revolvers, knives—even fists and rocks. Exchanging shots with gunbarrels crossed—so close that muzzle-flashes ignited clothing— men on both sides fell and died in the brush, slowly, painfully, from their wounds. Within three minutes, the overmatched Coloradans were driven back toward Union lines and several more were shot as they fled. Achieving nothing for their efforts, Company I retreated having sustained a casualty rate of almost fifty percent.

❧

Minutes later, a second Federal assault on the Texans' right stalled and the Confederates counterattacked hard. Major Pyron sent two waves of gray-clad infantry hard against Capt. Jacob Downing's Coloradans and earned a measure of revenge for his losses at Apache Canyon two days before. Returned from his triumph at the ravine, Texan Capt. Buckholts led one of these frenzied charges up the wooded slope, only to be killed on the point of a Coloradan's bayonet. By eleven a.m., forty-two of Downing's sixty-man Company D were casualties, sniped or struck down by endless barrages of grape and cannister from a howitzer the Texans had masked within the woods.

As a brief lull settled over the field, the entire Union force withdrew another two- hundred yards east toward yet another defensive position. Watching this retreat, the First Colorado's Col. Slough gritted his teeth and gripped the pommel of his saddle. Once his troops were re-set he rode forward, and his adjutant and several messengers had to ride hard to catch him.

"Colonel," one shouted, "where to?"

Slough stopped to observe Capt. Ritter's gun emplacements, now set behind the adobe wall surrounding the hotel's yard. They had just commenced shelling the Texans' batteries across the field and the noise was terrific.

"Colonel?" the messenger said, nauseated from the reek of nitre.

"Hell if I know," Slough nearly choked with rage. "We don't kill more Texans, they will run us back to Denver!"

❧

Scurry's chief artillerist, James Bradford, shouted for his crews to drag their howitzers forward to support the Texans' next attack. Of average height but hard and lean, the boyishly handsome Bradford strode calmly behind the three pieces and watched their five-man crews perform an intricate ritual. Even at breakneck a pace, something about this routine's exactitude comforted him. First, his gunners barked out ranges and the type of ammunition they wanted—that day mostly cannister, though battery number one, rotated to engage the Union's artillery, had switched to explosive case-shells. At the limber chests, these orders were repeated and each gunner's mate cut fuses in corresponding lengths. The gunners shouted: *"Load!"* Other mates approached the muzzles, inserted rounds, and rammed them into place with long, wooden rods. At the tubes' backs, the gunners sighted each piece with an instrument called a pendulum-hausse and turned an elevating screw to adjust its range. Bradford noted that one crew operated short-handed, as Federal sharpshooters in the southern woods had taken one of the mates down. Despite this, their operations were smooth and steady. *Splendid work.*

Next, the gunners called *"Ready!"* Lanyards were attached to primers and inserted into the vents. Bradford leaned away and covered his ears. He knew that the command to fire would come next, and that even at fifteen yards away the discharge would rattle his teeth and jangle the watch fob attached to his coat.

"Fire!"

The guns roared—a slightly hollow sound, as if pulled from the barrels by each shell's violent expulsion. On the hill above the ranch there was an orange flash and blossom of dirt as one shell detonated; the other two cut into knots of Federal infantry with lead and iron. Bradford stepped aside as the nearest piece was run back into position, pleased that the Yankees could not advance, pleased that the adobe wall that surrounded the hotel was beginning to crumble. He lost himself in thought as his crews busied themselves. He had decided to have the mules brought forward so that the pieces could be moved again when his eye fell upon a commotion across the valley. His face went white. *"Purcell!* Look! There, ten degrees north! They have moved and now they see us! They've moved, Sergeant—*hurry!"*

George Purcell of Victoria, Texas—thirty years old and four years removed from a vicious political feud in Florida—adjusted his wire-rimmed glasses and struggled to see through the acrid pall that obscured the field. Not until the wind thinned this haze could he see what had so alarmed Bradford: Union gunners had moved their pieces from concealment between the hotel and a barn. These guns no longer addressed the Texans' infantry; now they faced directly toward their artillery. They fired. One shell sailed overhead and exploded in the trees behind them; a second crashed through a stand of pines, fell between loose rocks, and blew a small crater in the forest floor.

Frantically, Purcell shouted new orders. One mate took a handspike and pushed laterally on the hot barrel; others strained against the wheels to move it around. Newly aligned, Sgt. Purcell called out an intended range and the firing sequence began anew.

"*Load!*" Purcell bellowed, and another Mullane was rammed home.

"That's it!" Bradford called. "We'll get 'em now! Faster, boys, *faster!*"

"*Ready!*" Once the primer was fixed, the crew leaned away from the piece, even as Bradford leaned forward in anticipation. The lanyard had just been attached when one of the gunner's mates standing near the gun's front fell, sniped by a Coloradan from across the meadow.

"Goddammit!" Bradford raged. "Re-set! Come on, boys, *come on!*" The other two guns discharged, but their aim was low and the shells tore harmless furrows in the field near the creek. Captain Bradford screamed at their supports to provide suppressing fire into the woods while Purcell and his remaining crewmen struggled to remove their comrade's body—slumped over a trunnion, wedged against a wheel—and re-orient the piece. Bradford took two quick steps toward the ditch-bank where their supports were crouched. He pointed to a copse where glimpses of blue were visible between the trees. "There!" he shouted, "shoot 'em! *Shoot 'em now!*"

Bradford glanced back at Purcell at the exact moment that a Federal round detonated above the first howitzer, ten feet over the crew's heads. A visible shock wave ripped through the smoke and dust; hot metal shards cut down the men and their draft animals, shattered the carriage, and destroyed the piece. Within a fraction of a second, an even larger concussion followed as the powder and rounds in the battery's limber box exploded. The resulting fireball slung mangled debris for a hundred feet in all directions, trailed by tendrils of mustard-yellow smoke. For the entire world, it looked as if a huge, hideous chrysanthemum had suddenly bloomed on the hillside. Horrified, Scurry and his staff spurred their horses wildly downhill to reach the burning wreckage.

❦

When Bradford regained consciousness, he found himself wrapped around the splintered trunk of a juniper. It hurt to inhale and he struggled to rise. Brushing the dirt from his trousers, his hair, his face, he was vaguely aware of a burning sensation in his right hand. Looking down, he saw that an iron shard had ripped the flesh from between his third and fourth knuckles, splitting his hand halfway to the wrist. Misshapen thoughts filled his head—*Am I left-handed? Have I always been this way?*—until he realized that he couldn't hear. Neither could he see out of his left eye due to the blood that flowed from a deep gash above his eyebrow. His head felt heavy and he struggled to maintain his balance. "Purcell," he whispered, "run 'er back. Hurry."

Other Confederates ran toward the survivors, stamping out spot-fires in the scrub as they went. Among these rescuers was José Garza, who had ridden north from Socorro, alone. Using a false name, he had re-integrated himself into an unwitting unit of the Texan Fourth Regiment under Maj. Raguet. At the Socorro hospital, he'd gleaned a very rudimentary medical knowledge, but anyone at all could've seen that Bradford was in serious trouble.

The captain gestured as Garza approached. "Find Scurry! We must move these guns and no one will help. *Load!*"

Garza forced Bradford to sit on an upturned crate as he tore long strips from a dirty canvas sheet that lay crumpled on the ground. With these he bound Bradford's injured hand and made a sling. "Easy," he soothed, but the blood that trickled from the lieutenant's nose and ears suggested a concussion or worse—sometimes there was no telling how scrambled that kind of injury might leave a fellow.

"All dead," Bradford whispered conspiratorially. "The Lord said this day would come." Garza nodded and continued his treatments. New arrivals helped re-set the two remaining guns. Others came forward to cut harnesses away from dead draft animals and relocate the remaining caissons and limbers. Garza couldn't stanch the blood flowing from Bradford's scalp, in part because his patient would not cooperate. "Damn it, let me go!" the captain moaned. He gestured frantically toward a makeshift gun crew as it struggled to return fire. *"Ready!"*

"Sir, hold still!"

Bradford was beyond coherence. "Can't hear you!" he screamed. "Goddamn Yankees, bound for hell!" With this, he slumped forward, and if Garza hadn't caught him, he would have fallen into the dirt. The former Brigand called for help, and swiftly Bradford was loaded onto a buckboard ambulance and driven over the pass to the Texans' field hospital at Johnson's Ranch.

Garza approached another man and asked where he might find Jacob Stark and the Cameron County Guards. This fellow had pointed south, but then an officer ordered him to help carry the dead, and so Garza did not start that way for several hours more.

᠅

Ten minutes later a solid projectile struck one of the Texans' remaining guns squarely in the barrel. Though the howitzer was destroyed, there was no similar loss of life. Cursing that the Yankees had found their range, Scurry ordered the remaining piece withdrawn and for a brief duration, the Texans pressed their attacks without artillery.

Pigeon's Ranch, New Mexico Territory, March 28, 1862

All morning Col. Slough had crossed and re-crossed the field on horseback, periodically calling up reserve units to suture gaps in the Federal lines. Far beyond his or anyone's expectations, the Union center and left had withstood repeated frontal assaults, while their right—in the forest above Pigeon's Ranch—had hardly been touched. This was just as well, for he'd barely enough men up there to set a thin skirmish line. His men were fighting hard, and for this he was grateful, but any notions of Union victory were slowly slipping away. Instead, the battle had devolved into a series of delaying actions as endless ranks of Texans had poured over the pass and driven his forces east. *How can we be outnumbered? Our damned spies said...* He resented Chivington's insistence on a separate command, and while the battle had absorbed nearly all his energies, in the back of his mind there were nagging sensations about its...*necessity*, for want of a better term. As events began to turn against them, he recalled with some chagrin Gabriel Paul's reluctance to leave Fort Union. Belatedly, he realized that had they stayed there, in all probity they could have beaten beat back this gray horde with fewer losses. Now both time and numbers were against them, and it was all because he'd parsed Canby's orders to suit his own needs. That he'd once believed in the correctness of an aggressive move on Santa Fe no longer mattered. Here the First Colorado was, dissolving bit by bit, and for which—*Provided I survive this day*—he might be court-martialed.

A staff officer jolted him from this grim meditation: "Sir, Lieutenant Colonel Tappan requests that Ritter's artillery be moved left one hundred yards. How do you want to respond?"

Slough glanced up the canyon. The air was blue with billows of smoke and dust. Gradually the Union line had given way, bent back all the way to Pigeon's Ranch. There it wrapped around the base of a large hill abreast of the ranch buildings—extending even across the flats south of that prominence. It seemed dangerous to him to invest anything more on the far left, for even if the Texans shifted that way, still they would have to cross rugged terrain and the deep bed of Glorieta Creek to reach the Santa Fe Trail. On their right, however, he'd seen and more and more gray in the woods above the ranch and he feared losing the highly defensible ground there. "Tell him no. We will move Clafin's guns higher on the hill, but I want Ritter's pieces exactly where they are. Tell Tappan to charge the instant Chivington arrives. Won't be long now, so hurry back—*go!*"

The express saluted and ran off in the direction of Clafin's battery.

Captain Charles Walker, a regular cavalry officer who had served with distinction at Apache Canyon two days earlier, stepped forward and gestured toward the south. "Tappan is requesting to have Cook's men moved lef—"

"Colonel! Here they come again!" his adjutant shouted. "Left, left, *left!*"

Slough raised his field glass. For the past two hours, Texans had made repeated probes south of the creek, and it was these forays that were driving Sam Tappan to distraction. The Confederates' latest charge had erupted from the scrub on a slope between two hills, and though smoke quickly obscured Slough and Walker's view, again the Union lines held. Several tense moments later, Slough heard wild cheers from Union positions upon the hill and he vented a sigh of relief. "We held! Thank God, *we held!*"

"Sounds that way," Walker said, but already Slough's mind had returned to the problem of protecting the artillery at the center of his line.

"Cook's down—who's his replacement?"

"Nelson, Sir."

"Well, there I agree with Tappan. Have Nelson move up the ridge, but leave Sopris where he is to support the center."

Walker removed his hat and scratched his head. "Hotter'n hell in front of Clafin's guns—real dangerous chore."

Slough thought for a moment before pointing to another messenger. "Robbins will move fifty yards south and bring up the reserves. Bill Wilder's company—Peter MacInnes's, too. Set those Irish kids at the foot of that hill—let them know they *must* hold. Got that? Hold that hill at all hazards—everything depends on it! Go!" The messenger saluted and rode east. Then an abrupt lull settled over the field, so quiet that Slough could hear Capt. Kerber shouting in German to soldiers hidden among the imbrecated rocks above the hotel.

"Unnatural," Walker said. He peered toward the Texans' lines. "What does it mean?"

"Has Chivington arrived?" Slough looked up the canyon and prayed that the sudden stillness augured confusion within the Confederate ranks. For almost thirty seconds this silence held, so clear that they heard crows cawing high overhead. However, this was only a breath—a collective inhalation as the contestants steadied themselves for new onslaughts. With a roar, the Texans' muskets broke the calm and Capt. John Ritter's two twelve-pound cannon fired into the gray ranks advancing on his position.

"Not yet," Walker said of Chivington, "but Sir, he departed Kozlowski's station on schedule. Cobb *will* find him. He will drop in behind 'em at any moment." From the right came the sounds of an intense fight on the rocky ridge above the hotel—evidence that this time the Texans were probing the Union right.

Slough clenched his fists in frustration, wondering when or even if the Fighting Parson might consent to grace the field with his presence. Suddenly his mind was given to dozens of wild conspiracies: *had Chivington taken his men back to Fort Union, or even Fort Craig? My God, he will do anything to undermine me!* "I...I shouldn't have sent him. He doesn't show soon, we'll have to withdraw."

"Sorry?" Walker asked, straining to hear above the artillery.

Slough watched a single Union soldier stand, discharge his musket, and then duck for cover behind a log so that he could reload. Things weren't going awfully, but it wasn't clear how much longer his forces could hold out. Their artillery was heavier, they had more ammunition, and their infantry, though raw, was better supplied and fighting hard. Walker and the others were standing by expectantly. *Look at 'em, still so confident.* He nodded. *Can't tell 'em otherwise—not yet.* "I said we're strong in the middle and good thing, too—that's where they'll strike hardest. Inform Tappan that whenever he sees fit, he may summon his reserves on the center-left. But Ritter's guns stay. If anyone needs me, I'll be up on the ridge." Then Slough, his adjutant, and several couriers dismounted and climbed for a better view from the steep, rocky eminence behind Pigeon's Ranch.

୬

Frederick Metzger took a new sheet of paper from his saddlebag and tucked its corners beneath the canvas anchors of his field tablet. He had spotted a ravine within the Confederates' lines that he believed might serve as a means of shuttling units east without exposing them to the Yankees' artillery. As he began to sketch this potential advantage, he heard voices in the thin woods on his left. Believing that part of the field to be vacant, he looked up, curious to see whether he recognized anyone there. A flash from within the trees and a thud on the left side of his chest registered simultaneously and he fell, scattering his maps across the hillside. His wife never received a letter that he'd written to her and tucked inside his coat pocket.

୬

The Pinebark Independents had spent the entire battle guarding the Federals' supply train, parked a quarter-mile east of Pigeon's Ranch. Then at 4:50 p.m., a courier arrived and told them they were needed, double-quick. Peter MacInnes, James Hay, and the rest of their small company followed Capt. Bill Wilder and G Company uphill through the ranch complex. They bypassed lines of skirmishers that were preparing to move up and support the heavy artillery, which was blasting away at the Texans' center. They saw maimed and wounded men—some horribly so—carried or limping past.

"*Goradh mhór!*" Matt Maher whispered as a union solider, his jaw shot away, was helped into the hotel. Seeing this patient's bloody handprint on one of the porch columns, Maher turned ashen. "Jaysus, boys, did ye see that?"

"Don't think on it!" Lt. Hay bellowed. "Keep up!"

The whole company was wide-eyed with amazement at the sound and fury of battle. Fearful and nervous, each could feel his own heart thrashing. Heavy smoke stung their eyes. Surrounded by friends, of course none wanted to falter—or even appear to—and even as the musketry and explosions grew louder and the screams of the wounded more shrill, none hesitated as they stumbled ahead, hard on the heels of the man before them.

⁓

On a thin sliver of land between the trail and the creek, Lt. Col. Sam Tappan stood like a railroad yardmaster. He waved some men forward and halted others so that Lt. Ira Claflin's lighter mountain howitzers could move along an old logging road, up the hill immediately south of the hotel. "Wilder! MacInnes!" Tappan bellowed. "Follow me!" G Company shuffled forward, followed by the Pinebark Independents.

Hay looked at Peter. "Louder'n hell up here!"

"Gonna get worse. Stay tight, now—don't get separated!"

They turned south, entered the narrow bed of Glorieta Creek, and forded its muddy shallows. They climbed over the shoulder of a large hill that loomed above the Santa Fe Trail and then descended to a flat. Here they deployed in a long arc, wrapped around the hill's western footing; Wilder's G Company was emplaced on the hillside above them; higher still were Claflin's howitzers.

The Coloradans were growing cautiously optimistic. Across the creek to the north, Capt. Ritter's heavy cannons were set behind the adobe wall that encircled the ranch's yard and corrals. Since mid-morning, this wall had given the Federals excellent protection from the Texans' muskets: their supports had been able to rise, fire rounds, and then drop to reload in relative safety—a fact that alarmed and infuriated the Confederates. Colonel Slough set his new headquarters on the ridge above the hotel. In the woods higher to his right were a few understrength Federal companies, including the survivors of Charles Kerber's ill-fated maneuver along the gulch. Based on the steepness of the terrain there, the Federals had gauged that there was no way the Confederates could execute an effective assault. Reversing his earlier assessment, Slough sent more and more of these men to reinforce positions farther south.

Middle Glorieta Canyon, New Mexico Territory, March 28, 1862

Col. William Scurry hated his nickname, Dirty Shirt, earned during the Mexican War of 1848. However, on a cool spring day in northern New Mexico Territory, once again, dirt and powder residue covered his white blouse and gray frock coat, and both of these were streaked fore and aft by runnels of sweat. It was two o'clock in the afternoon and he was sick with frustration. Serial assaults south of the creek—into the Federal center and left—had been repulsed with significant losses. Just as troubling, several of the Confederates' best officers had been killed or badly wounded, including Charles Buckholts, artillerist James Bradford, and engineer Frederick Metzger—taken by a sniper's bullet within minutes of Buckholts.

His throat raw from smoke, the colonel shifted in his saddle and coughed. Glancing south, he saw Charles Pyron galloping toward him. What happened then was too quick for Scurry to apprehend; as he blinked, Pyron and his horse disappeared—simply vanished within a cloud of dust. In fact, a Union bolt had struck and decapitated Pyron's mount; he and the animal's carcass had fallen together in the tall grass. Scurry held his breath until another soldier rushed forward and helped Pyron stand. Unsteady at first, the crusty rancher had merely brushed off his clothes, removed two pistols from their saddle holsters, and staggered through sagebrush toward the colonel.

"My word, Chuck—you hurt?" Scurry called.

"I'm fine," Pyron said through split lips, "but that was my favorite horse."

"Bad luck," Scurry said, but Pyron merely scoffed.

"Hit me, *that* would'a been bad luck."

"Speaking of which, what's it gonna take to improve our fortunes on the right?" To their left, the re-formed Confederate artillery was attempting to lob rounds onto Union guns near the ranch—trying to cut away the adobe wall that was shielding them. One Confederate bolt struck the hotel's thick upper wall; its adobe bricks were shoved nearly a foot into the dining room, showering the surgeons and patients inside with dirt, dust, and soot.

"What's it gonna take?" Pyron repeated. "Hell, more men." He winced as one of the howitzers discharged. "Every half-hour we probe their lines but they just fire and fall back."

"Goddammit, we outnumber these jays two-to-one—what in deep, hot hell's going on?" Scurry was right, but dense, gray smoke had made an accurate count impossible; there was no way he could see that some six hundred Confederates on the Texans' right were being impeding by just two hundred and forty Coloradans . Superior Union artillery, difficult terrain, and superb Union musketry had thus far kept the Southerners in check, but if a breeze had cleared away the smoke, Scurry might have seen the truth and ordered an all-out assault.

Remembering the Coloradans' flanking attempt in the gulch that morning, all afternoon Pyron had been watching the northern fields. Now he was sure that there were fewer blue uniforms in the hills north of the creek, and it was for this reason that he'd gone looking for Scurry. "We can hammer 'em up there," the major said, "I'm sure of it."

"What about that big hill in the center?"

"Bad ground—crossed every way to Sunday with ditches, roads, and walls. Every time we move forward, the bastards pop up and unload into our flanks. Then they fall back and we start all over again."

"Fall back too often, they'll run out of ground," Scurry said

"Maybe not before we run out of men."

"What about farther south—those high flats?"

"Poor ground, and they keep extending their lines and curving back. Don't know if we can outrun 'em."

"Can't extend forever."

"Yeah," Pyron agreed, "but with internal lines shorter'n ours, they move units quick-like from one place to the next. Speaking of which, I came here to tell you that they're moving again up in them hills."

Scurry glassed the hills north of the creek and saw the First Colorado's emaciated skirmish line. "Raguet's there?"

"Yessir—crossed the creek 'bout five minutes ago."

"Then take yours, too. Hammer 'em, hard and mean. First get organized—then once and for all, I want you to take down that battery at the ranch." Just as Pyron saluted, a low-pitched whir filled their ears and Scurry's wide-brimmed hat flew backward; only a chinstrap kept it from sailing off his head. "The hell was that—grasshopper?"

"Early for locust," Pyron said and watched as the colonel retrieved a spent lead slug, still warm and slightly flattened on one side.

Scurry inspected the bullet before handing it to Pyron. "Ringtail—.54 caliber Sharps."

Pyron returned the talisman. "Seems we've got some luck yet."

"Roll on." Scurry dropped the bullet into his pocket. "No safer back here. Press 'em off that ridge and we'll bust up the middle. I want this over by sundown." Pyron saluted and ran back across the clearing.

∽

Scurry turned his horse and found Jacob Stark standing beside him. Jacob saluted, and Scurry nodded in return. "How are we on the right, Captain?"

"Sir, not well." Jacob was dirty, sweat-stained, and covered with welts and scratches. "We can't see 'em in there. In the last half-hour, my company alone has lost four."

"Those goddamn walls..." Scurry's voice trailed off, and he clenched his teeth so hard that Jacob could see his jaw muscles moving beneath his beard. Scurry's eyes blazed as he scanned the hill before them. Smoke billowed between its trees like a volcano's exhalations. It was a brutally tangled landscape, seemingly impossible to climb, nevertheless under fire—but of course, no place on earth is so rugged that men will not fight there and Scurry was certain that they needed to control it. "Metzger said as much," Scurry murmured.

"Sir?" Jacob said.

"Long as they hold that hill, it's gonna grind us down. Awful, bushwhacking kind of fight, but the goddamn thing sees too much—we *must* have it."

Jacob grasped where their conversation had gone. "Crosson, Adair, and I are all in place, Colonel—we are ready."

"Get to it, then." Scurry spat, pointed to the hills north of the ranch, and spat again. "Pyron and Raguet are up there—I'll take everyone else to the center. Crosson has overall command. Tell him to stay where he can see me—stay in contact—but I want you three to take the right. Keep those howitzers from turning on our center."

With these words, our graves are dug. Jacob looked up at the hill's inscrutable face and inhaled. All afternoon it had chewed through wave after wave of Texans and the assignment seemed like an order to commit suicide. Less than twenty minutes earlier he had helped drag Maj. Shropshire's body back inside their lines, and had personally seen Denman Shannon captured and marched away at gunpoint. Still, it was a necessary thing the colonel was ordering them to do and his friends were there waiting, pressed behind anything that afforded any degree of cover—rocks, trees, fence rails—and if they were going to survive, they would need to be shown the way. "Yessir," he saluted, but already the colonel had begun to walk his horse north, across the creek, toward a fresh eruption of smoke.

"They'll want to turn toward the center, Captain. Goddammit, they'll want to, 'cause I'm gonna punch 'em right in their shitstained teeth. But you're gonna keep 'em occupied."

"Take the pressure off each other," Jacob offered.

"That's right," the colonel shouted. "You see the Yanks' center collapse, then there's your authority. Go plant our flag on that peak so everyone can see that we own this place. Let's end this."

"Yessir."

"Run 'em off and run 'em down. That ranch, heaven or hell."

Pigeon's Ranch, New Mexico Territory, March 28, 1862

By four o' clock, the sky had taken on the ugly aspect of a badly blackened eye, turning noticeably bloodier as the sun began its descent. Halfway up the hill, the First Colorado's Company G took positions behind a low wall of drystacked, irregular boulders, while Peter MacInnes's company found shelter inside an empty *regardera* that snaked around the hill's base. As Peter ran to get into place, he tripped on a root and nearly fell. Catching himself on the ditchbank, he pushed off at the last second. Stopping beside a small wooden headgate, he checked his revolvers to see that they were ready. Alongside, his company busied themselves with their weapons; all kept weather-eyes out for any sign of a renewed assault.

High above, Claflin's three mountain howitzers pounded away at unseen targets (unseen by the Pinebark Independents, anyway) across the field. On the right, Union batteries at the main ranch house were dueling with Confederate gunners nearer to the creek. In the northern hills fresh clouds of smoke indicated that the fight there was growing hotter. For nearly ten minutes, Peter's company of Coloradans lay in the snow and mud within the ditch. Hearing the melee up north, they wondered why things had suddenly gone quiet in their sector. Concealed behind an irregular berm, their muzzles masked by great mounds of chamiso, they were nearly invisible— even to their Union comrades above, and *they* knew where to look.

The air pulsed with cold energy, trees glowed with late afternoon light, and the smoke that drifted across the field was tinged yellow. Even the heavier clouds that rolled in from the north stayed high enough to permit well-formed rays of light to penetrate the haze; behind every feature, shadows of the deepest blue began to pool.

Sammy Douglas was hyper-vigilant and refused to look away from the arroyo that crossed the field about forty-five yards in front of the Coloradans' position. "They're in the burnie," he said over and over to those nearest to him. Partially overgrown with yucca, mountain mahogany, and low, scrubby cedars, and if the Texans were indeed within the gulch, they were entirely hidden from view. "Thon burnie," Douglas repeated.

Hay looked away and rolled his eyes. "Where are they?" he asked, already tired of their little adventure.

"Thon burnie," Douglas insisted.

Farther right, Matt Maher leaned away from his musket and so that he could whisper to his older brother, "What'll we do, Mike? Out front like this—"

"We will be fine," Mike said.

"Och, aye?"

"Aye, believe it." They clasped hands. Before he looked away, Mike Maher spat in the dust beyond the ditch. "Remember that I loved ye, brother." He clapped a hand on Mike's shoulder and returned to his makings. Working quickly, he placed a charge of buck-and-ball atop cotton wadding and rammed these to a temporary repose inside his rifle.

James Hay took his eyes away from the field and glanced at Peter. "Are ye ready?"

"Aye." Peter exhaled and tired to steady his nerves. In truth, he was miserable and wished he was somewhere else—anywhere at all, but also accepted that there was no turning aside—not now. *Lord,* he prayed, *if Ye will let me live...* He did not get to finish. Perhaps the mixture of elation, fear, and nausea that he felt had sharpened his senses, for just then he noticed movement among the backlit cedars along the gulch. "Boys!" He elbowed the men next to him and Hay quickly turned his head. "Steady the now!" All along their line, Coloradans quietly pulled hammers back above percussion caps. Their eyes fixed upon the gray-clad soldiers that clambered out of the arroyo; sweat beaded on every brow. *"Steady!"* Peter whispered again.

Across the meadow, the Texans began a stately advance. They moved from rock to fence to bush, scanning the hillside and its cloak of trees. Though Peter and his companions did not know it, this was the fifth assault the Texans had made across this meadow and they were disinclined to repeat the headlong charges that they had made earlier in the day. Closer and closer they crept: forty yards, thirty-five, thirty... Twenty-five yards in front of the ditch and still they couldn't see Peter's company.

"How can they not?" Hay whispered, so softly that even those nearest to him could not hear. Despite their fears, the boys in the ditch grew almost giddy with anticipation.

"Steady!" Peter whispered one last time before Claflin's hilltop battery opened up and spat three rounds of cannister into the field. The Coloradans heard hundreds of lead balls thudding into the snow and mud around them—the copper sabot from one shell event pinged loudly off a rock near Bill Storey's head. One Texan was killed, several others wounded, and suddenly there was chaos immediately in front of the ditch. Targeting the smoke from Claflin's guns, the Confederates raised their muskets and discharged a rolling volley into the hillside. Sheets of orange flame leapt from their muzzles, illuminating the field like a photographer's fulminate. The rocks and trees there shook. From high on the hillslope, Capt. Wilder's G Company began to pepper the meadow and so the Texans crouched to reload.

Peter MacInnes rose to a knee and lifted his revolver. *"Fire!"* Point-blank in some cases and from nowhere farther than twenty-five feet, the Pinebark Independents unleashed a single, cruel volley into the Texan's static line. In an instant, ten Confederates lay dead or dying and an equal number wounded. The flash and roar were so swift and terrible that even those Texans not physically hit were stunned. One man was struck thrice by the same bullet as it passed through his arm, into his hip and out through the opposite hand. Surgeons later noted powder burns on the hands and faces of the wounded. Though the Coloradans' surprise was total, and though they had completely stoned the Texans' advance, they were so badly outnumbered that just as soon as they fired, every member of the Pinebark Company turned and sprinted uphill. Blinded by smoke, the Texans had no idea where the devastating volley had come from and the two forces retreated in opposite directions. As they passed into and through G Company's line, not a few of the Coloradans were laughing—not from mirth but out of sheer terror, thrilled to be alive, like schoolboys fleeing the scene of some horribly dangerous prank. A few Texans recovered enough to fire into their backs, and while every Pinebark Volunteer made it to the rock wall, Mike Maher was struck in the back of his head and fell, dead even before he hit the ground.

御

Jacob Stark's Cameron Guards had been part of the Texans' assault on the big hill. They had only reached the woods at its base when it seemed as if the soil itself had exploded—the men on Jacob's right and left were killed, and their advance was stopped cold.

Jacob's senses were brutally overmatched. There was a roar that he felt more than heard, a sledgehammer blow to his chest, and then his breath was gone. His ligaments thrummed, supple tuning forks struck on hard metal, and he fell—fell and it seemed as if he might never stop. Unspeakable pain, vivid in every fiber, jolted his nerves. The muscles along his spine convulsed as violently as snakes dropped on hot sheet-iron and his bladder voided like it had when he was seven and a stray dog had bitten off much of the smallest finger on his left hand. Lungs burning, he bit cleanly through the inside of his lower lip. *Breathe!* Was his only reflex and still he could not. Panicked, suffocated by nitre-stained dirt, there was nothing he could do. Spittle trickled from the corners of his mouth. Thick, coppery blood spilled down the back of his throat as half-thoughts, pale reflections on dark glass, flitted through his mind: intimate moments with Adria; his daughter's laugh; important things that he'd never quite known how to say. Unable to lift his head, unable to see, Jacob had laid quivering, burning, certain that he was either dead or dying, until hands grabbed his jacket, rolled him onto his back, and dragged him back to life.

❧

Wide eyed, Charlie Spence was standing over him, searching for a wound.

Wiping blood and dirt from Jacob's mouth, Spence assumed that his captain's injured breathing meant that he had been shot through the lungs. Instead, Charlie found only small quantities of blood on Jake's shirt and decided therefore that he would simply hold Jacob's hand until he could inhale.

At last, Jacob's breath came in one enormous gasp, quickly followed by dozens more. "Gonna puke," Jacob whispered, though he managed, with Charlie's help, to sit upright. He spat a gob of bloody mud onto the bark of a pine tree.

"Got bit, huh?"

"Hard." Jacob winced and felt gingerly along the right side of his chest. He pulled open his shirt collar and felt a hard, raised welt four inches in diameter immediately below his collarbone. "Shit."

"Ricochet," Charlie judged. "Didn't enter, praise God, but it's raised blood right smart. Cracked a rib, maybe."

"Can't breathe." The sergeant pulled Jacob onto unsteady feet. He looked around and saw men from Adair's company organizing themselves for yet another assault. "How are the others?"

Spence glanced into the darkening woods and tears began to stream from his eyes. "Feller, Lamb, and Stanhope are dead. Orth, Dupree, and Irwin are wounded, but Bossard is the worst—had most of his face shot away, yet he lingers. And you, of course."

"I'm fine, though." Jacob put a hand on Spence's shoulder and leaned heavily as he took his first few steps.

Charlie wiped his eyes with a dirty sleeve. "You sure?"

"Think so. What about Briggs?"

"Not a scratch—he's leadin' now. Tore him up to leave you, but someone had to rally the others. I told him I'd stay with you unless... no, *until* a surgeon—"

"I know—it's okay. Where'd everyone go?"

Spence pointed left toward a gulch leading up the hillside, halfway between the meadow and Glorieta Creek. "Still need to clear that hilltop."

"Glad they pushed ahead." Jacob rotated his right arm to try and loosen it a little, but the pain was almost overwhelming. "Oh, God, let's go find 'em."

Pigeon's Ranch, New Mexico Territory, March 28, 1862

North of the creek, Maj. Pyron and Maj. Raguet led forces against a small but well-concealed Federal defense consisting of dismounted regular cavalry and the remnants of Charles Kerber's I Company. Still emplaced near Pigeon's hotel, the Union artillery's view of the northern hills was blocked by a tilted sandstone ridge projecting from the canyon's north wall. This feature spared the Texans' left flank from the galling fire that had scourged Scurry's repeated forays against the Federal center.

Only Raguet's death—sniped by a rifleman lying on the rocky ridge—slowed the Texans' charge. As his and Pyron's men regrouped at the ridge's base, this momentary calm lulled Col. Slough into making a significant tactical mistake. Assuming that the Texans' assault north of the creek had failed, he ordered all regular cavalry down from the ridge to saddle up for a counter-attack. This move would leave only a few skirmishers atop the rocky eminence to repulse repeated Confederate attacks.

At a little past three that afternoon, both sides realized the Coloradans could not sufficiently extend their line to repel the Texans. Pyron's force advanced. They worked higher and higher into the woods until the Yankee's rifles' went slack. Then they regrouped and descended en masse against Kerber's perilously thin blue line. Completely overwhelmed, these Coloradans broke and fled down the ridge's sloped eastern side. Caught unprepared, Slough and his aides hastily abandoned their observation post directly above the hotel. Unopposed, Pyron's Texans moved southward until they found themselves directly above the main Union battery. There they unloaded with everything they had. Realizing that he could no longer hold his position behind the adobe wall, Ritter, the Federal's artillery chief, ordered their cannon limbered and moved a half-mile east of the ranch. As the Union right and center collapsed, Slough ordered his entire force east so that a new defensive line could be set.

On the big hill south of the ranch, however, this order never arrived. Sam Tappan and half the Union force were still in their lines, unaware that the dam had broken or that a gray flood had begun pouring down Glorieta Canyon.

Atop Glorieta Mesa, New Mexico Territory, March 28, 1862

Beneath a brilliant blue sky, Maj. Chivington halted and watched his troops work their way across dry, stubbled flats at the head of San Cristobal Canyon. The narrow track they followed alternated between mud and sharp, volcanic talus, and their pace had been discouragingly slow. Almost five hundred strong—fully one-third of the force that had set out from Fort Union on March 22—Chivington's command left Slough and the main column at Kozlowski's station around eight-thirty that morning. By noon they had nearly crossed Glorieta Mesa—a wide, flat-topped hill that paralleled the Trail for miles. The Second New Mexico Volunteers' Lt. Col. Manuel Chaves and that regiment's Roman Catholic chaplain, Reverend Alexander Grzelachowski, had served as capable guides. At a faint and unfamiliar crossroads, they stopped.

Though some of the other officers groused, Chivington did not mind that Chaves and Grzelachowski conversed almost exclusively in Spanish. Rather, he faulted the others for failing "to cast scholarly nets both far and wide." Though the wind was gusting hard, the major could understand a few words—*mogote* for an isolated clump of trees; *desconocido* for unfamiliar; and *creo que está tan*, which meant, more-or-less, "I believe so." While their guides re-oriented themselves and the others crabbed, the major chewed happily on a piece of dried beef. He scanned the towering mountains to their north. In that direction, the forest thickened toward what he assumed was the canyon rim, though he could not be sure—the mesa's corrugated top concealed its northern edge from observation.

Chivington's plan had been to split off his command, cross Glorieta Mesa, and fall upon the Texans' flank—essentially the same plan that had worked so well in Apache Canyon two days prior. With Slough's and the Confederates' forces entangled, the Coloradans believed that the shock of a surprise attack would throw the Texans into chaos. As each man was desperate to be rid the other, both men declared the plan brilliant—despite protests by Army regulars, who suggested that the rough ground above the canyon made such maneuvers easier to plan than to execute. Still, the Coloradans were in charge, so this became the plan.

‹›

"Major?" His conversation with the padre concluded, Lt. Col. Chaves walked his horse to stand alongside Chivington's. He thought that the burly reverend seemed calmer than usual. *Perhaps he does not know what we face.* "Major?" Chaves repeated, but Chivington continued to appraise the monstrous green ramparts north of the pass.

The sun reflected brilliantly off these high peaks, blindingly white against a cerulean sky. It was an awesome, humbling view, wholly unmarred by "progress," and to Chivington a direct testament to God's unfathomable power. Whispering, he recited first lines of Psalm 121: "I will lift up mine eyes unto the hills, from whence cometh my help. My help cometh from the Lord, which made heaven and earth." Then he grinned at Chaves and gestured for the New Mexican to follow him toward the column's front. Reaching another crossroads, Chivington reined in. He signaled for his troops to halt and they leaned on their muskets and stared with rapt attention. "First Colorado," he shouted, "eyes and ears!" As the major began to speak, the wind increased, and soldiers just a few ranks back struggled to hear him over its plaintive howl. "Lieutenant Colonel Chaves, how far now?"

Chaves glanced at Padre Grzelachowski, who cleared his throat before answering: "A quarter-mile, Major. North past the *ceja*—ten minutes, at most."

Chivington faced his troops. "Hear that? Ten minutes. Anyone care to stay here? I'll not judge those who do, but all who go north with me must pledge to God that they will not stay their hands until every Texan in that valley is slain!"

The first ranks cheered wildly, which made the rest of the column press forward, desperate to understand what'd been said. As word filtered back, some held their muskets aloft and shouted; others stamped their feet and whistled, louder and louder, until the noise reached a crescendo. Then Chivington raised his hand for silence and the column flattened itself further—those in the back pressed forward hardest so that they might hear. He raised both hands in benediction and ordered his troops to bow their heads. "Almighty God, we are here in your name to stamp out a pestilence—a pollution that degrades everything it touches—a sin that must be scourged with fire and lead. As we pull this failed crop from your fields, grant us victory, O Lord! These rebels are stunted and sick in their understanding of your ways, unfit to sow their seed upon your creation. You have set our feet on solid rock, and our trumpets will tear down their walls of iniquity! Captains, soldiers, will you shoulder this burden?"

Samuel Logan, Ed Wynkoop, and the other Coloradans responded according to their own religiosity. Many called in reply: "Yes, I will," "Amen, Sir!" or "Hallelujah!" while others stared in silence.

As the wind died, Chivington ordered Chaves's New Mexican scouts and a detachment from William Lewis's infantry battalion ahead. Following an old logging road, this advance hurried north and disappeared into one of the gullies that crossed the mesa's top. Once again, the major addressed his command: "Some of you have never seen the inside of a church, and maybe you think that everything I say is hogwash. About that, I do not care—so long as you do your job! Others may wonder if the Texans, too, have asked God to grant them victory, but know this: He doesn't hear them! When sinners spread forth their hands, He hides His eyes, and when they pray, He doesn't listen, for their hands are full of blood. Men, you are covered in righteousness and clad in the armor of God! He has ordained your weapons! Soldiers, raise the sword of the Lord and kill His enemies!" Again, a cheer erupted, but already Chivington had wheeled his horse and started north. The others broke ranks and ran after him, surging around rocks, trees, and shrubs. With the noise they made smothered by a howling wind, this blue tide rolled north, unchecked and undetected.

∽

Within a hundred feet of the mesa's edge, Chivington learned that Chaves's New Mexicans had captured two Texan sentinels who had been asleep beneath a huge ponderosa. Upon seeing the major, Chaves had bowed slightly and gestured toward the canyon. "Sir, you are right on top of them."

The officers crawled forward in silence. From the top of a cliff, they spied a long, pine-and-scrub-covered talus slope that steepened as it fell into the upper reaches of Apache Canyon. Chivington recognized it as the western entrance to the pass over which he'd ridden just two days before. What they saw stunned the Coloradans: tents and wagons covered every level patch of ground—wall-to-wall on the valley floor, and even into the surrounding trees.

"My God," Samuel Logan said. "My God."

Chivington looked at Chaves. "Where's Slough? Where's the battle?"

"No sé." Chaves shrugged, genuinely puzzled. "No sign."

The Union officers spent the next half-hour in grim conversation. Chivington personally questioned the captured Confederates, trying to learn more about the situation below, but they were sullen and uncommunicative except to promise that the Yanks were in for a sound thrashing. Chivington smirked and punched one in the chest. "Take these traitors to Kozlowski's. They give you any trouble, shoot em!"

Try as they might, the Coloradans could not make an accurate count of their foe. Were the tents empty or occupied? There were breastworks hacked into the hillsides and abatis below, but no troops behind these improvements. There was a hospital tent, corralled draft animals, and a single six-pound mountain howitzer atop a low rise beside the trail. Still and all, no battle.

Chivington paced back and forth, the picture of concentration, absorbed by the myriad possibilities. If more Texans were inbound from Santa Fe, or if the contingent that was battling over the pass suddenly appeared, there would be no chance of retreat. Then again, another opportunity to destroy the Confederates' entire wagon train was unlikely to present. He stopped pacing and stood within the shadow of an enormous cedar. Several times, he tugged at his beard. Wynkoop, Chaves, and others noted that he no longer appeared tranquil. At last, the major strode briskly over to the group and knelt. "Get your ropes—first ones to those trees above the rockslide, tie off so there's something for others to hold on that steeper pitch. Once I say go, get down as fast as you can—spread out so you aren't bunched up. Captain Lewis—down on the valley floor, it will be your operation. Now, *hurry!*"

Pigeon's Ranch, New Mexico Territory, March 28, 1862

By four o' clock, the Texans occupied most of Pigeon's Ranch and everything north of Glorieta Creek and they had driven the hated Union artillery from its protection behind the adobe wall. Elsewhere, fragmented companies of U.S. Army regulars and Coloradans retreated east in good order, pausing frequently to fire at the cautiously pursuing Texans.

South of the creek, Lt. Col. Tappan had set Peter MacInnes's Pinebark Independents as a screening force to the right of Claflin's batteries. This had given them a perfect view of the Union center's slow collapse. Supposing that Slough had set a trap to envelop the Confederates, the Volunteers had fired with enthusiasm into the passing Texans' flanks until they noticed that their counterparts north of the ranch were gone.

Neil Wilson ran south from unit to unit until he'd found Sam Tappan.

Tappan saw the young private coming, knotted his brow, and wondered why he was away from his company. "You—get back! Get back in your line!" he shouted even before Neil Wilson arrived, panting and breathless from his run.

"Permission t'retreat, Sir!" Taking a gulp from his canteen, he'd looked Tappan in the eye and pointed east. "We are flanked— *overrun!* The Texans—"

"No." Tappan pointed north. "You must stay where you are! Don't move until I hear from Col. Slough."

"The Colonel's gone, Sir!" Verging on panic, Wilson didn't care that he'd sprayed Tappan with spit. "Ranch is overtaken and

Slough's flown east—if ye haven't heard from him, ye won't now!" As an afterthought, he turned and looked west. "Where's Major Chivington?"

"On his way," Tappan snapped, "any moment." Then he noticed that all artillery had gone silent—for the first time since breakfast, he could hear magpies calling harshly from the treetops. He glanced toward the setting sun, downhill through gold-shrouded trees, and noticed that the trail was swarming with men. *What has he seen?* He grabbed Wilson by the elbow, shouted for his adjutant to follow, and ran north.

As they passed other companies, their captains begged for instruction, but Tappan could only shout at them to remain where they were. "I'll return! Stay in your lines—stay where you are!"

They crossed the logging road that Claflin had used to bring his small howitzers forward and saw a second set of tracks signifying their withdrawal. All along this route were gunners' accoutrements: fuse punches, a leather water bucket, a tompion, fuse gimlets, a broken limber chest—evidently dropped in great haste. Shaken to pieces, Tappan ran faster, over the rocks and fallen timber that carpeted the ridge's crest, fearful that they had already been trapped, desperate to learn the truth.

"See?" Wilson practically sobbed, and Tappan began to run faster.

Sounds in the gloom betrayed where Peter's company had taken up a skirmish line behind another low rock wall. Most were busy with their makings; a few muskets crackled and flared. On the hill's crest, Tappan finally saw what had happened—and saw hordes of Texans preparing to charge the hill once more. He shouted for the Pinebark Independents to fall back. Then he and his adjutant ran south again to rally other companies for similar actions. "Trail gets cut," Tappan cried, "head for the flats above! We'll re-form there and move east together!"

Hay fired his musket, and though he'd hardly bothered to aim, he struck a Texan support in the hip and knocked him down. "Pete!" he shouted, "they'll kill us!"

"Go, man! *Go!*" Peter looked over the hotel yard and saw that the Texans had unlimbered two howitzers and were working to elevate the barrels. Not eager to face artillery at less than sixty yards, he shouted again before others had even reached their intended positions: "Don't stop! Christ, they're upon us! Through t'the ditch!"

"Where away?" someone shouted, and Peter gestured wildly in reply.

"Uptail, now! *Now!* Fall back, boys—*back!*" Peter glanced over his shoulder as one of the howitzers flashed and threw a case-round into the trees ahead of their retreat. The Coloradans flung themselves to the dirt seconds mere before the shell detonated; all of them felt its heat and heard the heavy summer hail of leads balls striking the dirt. Two of these found Neil Wilson: one passed through his right hand, breaking bones as it went, and though another struck his skull and knocked him unconscious, it did not penetrate. The others scrambled to their feet and crested the ridge before the Texans fired their second gun. "To the ditch!" Peter barked. "Together! *Dogs and devils are upon us!*"

Within a minute, most had reached the defile and tumbled in. Some paused to reload, while others fired uphill at scatterings of Texans who'd shown themselves before swiftly retreating into the trees.

༄

The Union artillery that had tormented the Confederates all afternoon was gone—fled east, evidently, and the woods had fallen almost silent. Wheezing in the cool, scrubby shadows between the pines, Jacob watched Hardy and Spence reload their muskets and walk northeast into gathering darkness. A single artillery round had detonated in the woods to his left; suddenly alone and unable to see over the ridge, he'd tried to make sense of the sound. Exhaling painfully, he began to wade uphill through dense brush. Rounding the trunk of a large ponderosa, Jacob paused at the edge of a deep furrow in the forest floor and his eyes widened: at his feet were dozens of Yankees. Turning, he saw that others were filtering down from the ridge. Those before him had their muskets ready and eyed him expectantly. *Holy God!* His feet froze to the earth and he lowered his revolver in deference to their number. Then he looked at their captain—a thin, young fellow who stood over the prone forms of his men.

The Yankee pointed west. "Here they come, Cap'n—get in."

Jacob nodded even as his mind reeled. *Clothed in blue—I am invisible to them.* He crouched and leaned against the enormous tree's base. "No one behind me. Where do you think they are?"

Peter MacInnes could scarcely see this stranger's face, but he'd come from the direction in which Tappan had run only moments before. Wasn't as though he knew all the regular officers, anyway, and this one's voice was perfectly level. "Over away, Cap'n—north and west."

Jacob and Peter stared at one another for several seconds and in the poor light, Jacob couldn't be sure if the Yankee lieutenant had merely squinted or if some understanding had passed between them. "Have they taken the ranch?"

"Aye—are ye with Major Chivington?"

"No," Jacob said, "haven't seen him." This was true, of course, as Jacob didn't know who Chivington was. He stood. "I'd best go find my company. Boys, you'll want to hasten east now." The last Pinebark Independents arrived with Neil Wilson's body, unconscious and bleeding, and lowered him into the trench. These men paused, unsure what to make of the stranger who stood between them and their comrades.

"Get in!" Hay shouted. "They're seconds away!"

But Matt Maher—half-mad since his brother's death an hour before—stared hard at the stranger. "Who's this?"

Quickly, Peter climbed back out of the ditch. "Stop, Matt."

Holding still, Jacob fought to remain calm.

"This one's a Texan!" Maher said as he scanned the darkened woods with red, watery eyes. "Quare locks wearing blue, but ain't none of 'em ours. Sammy killed one earlier—this one's sesech, too!" Maher's wariness was justified: twice that afternoon Texans in Federal blue had confused the Coloradans under Tappan's command, as they had assumed that these soldiers were part of Chivington's long-expected force. Only at the last minute had the truth been discovered and disaster averted.

"Matt," Peter said, aware of the odd tone in his friend's voice, "leave him alone."

Maher held perfectly still, stared hard at Jacob, and the Texan's knees began to shake.

"Matt, listen t'yer captain!" Hay barked. "Can't see nothin', anyways!"

"I see well enough," Maher bristled, but Peter reached out and pushed the barrel of Matt's Springfield toward the dirt.

"Come away, boyo—into the ditch."

Maher spat on the ground and brushed hard past Jacob before jumping down.

Peter look at Jacob for a few silent moments. "Be careful out there," Peter said before he, too, turned and stepped toward the ditch.

Then Jacob's instincts failed him, for rather than turning and running, he waited until Peter drew even. "Thanks."

Peter stopped and looked squarely at Jacob. As expected, he saw nothing evil there—merely someone who looked an awful lot like himself and the wretchedness of their situation struck him full. *We are but men.* "Go home," he said at last, "I can do nothing more." Then he stepped around Jacob, jumped back into the trench, and shouted to his company to re-load.

As Jacob stumbled away, at the thicket's edge he glanced backward. Already dusk was so deep and the forest floor so crossed with long shadows that he could see nothing, and he turned again and plunged into the brush, completely unaware that Matt Maher had shouldered his musket and taken aim upon his back.

Devastated by his older brother's death at the conclusion of their first encounter with the Texans, since then Maher had scarcely thought about anything else. For an hour, he'd fired and reloaded mechanically—even walked through a vicious crossfire to drag the wounded Neil Wilson to safety. Now, despite Peter's orders to leave the stranger be, he drew a shaky bead on the man's back—hindered by poor eyesight but aided by Jacob's silhouette against the setting sun—and locked the hammer. *Texan*, he thought, *certainly*. Exhaling to steady himself, he began to pull the trigger, until a sudden rustling in the brush made his target lurch sideways.

A second figure stumbled out of the darkness, moving directly toward Maher and the Coloradans. "Stark!" the man screamed, *"run!"* Jacob stepped forward in response but tripped and fell headlong into the undergrowth. The stranger passed within feet, yet for the gloom and the swiftness of his passing, Jacob could not guess his identity. There was an odd familiarity to his voice, but because it was entirely out of context, Jacob could not place it. *"Run!"* the stranger shouted again, but when he fired at the Coloradans his aim was too high and the bullet sailed harmlessly.

With the advantage of last light, Matt Maher was the first to return fire and his shot caught this cipher full in the chest.

More and more figures began to appear in the red light between the pines' long shadows, and so the Coloradans volleyed in earnest. Crashing muskets brought a steady drizzle of needles and twigs down upon their heads. Salvo after salvo split the darkness; billows of smoke filled the air; and every discharge lit this cumulus from within, so that the hilltop woods pulsed like a stormcloud in summer. Jacob took cover behind a stout trunk, his pistols untouched within their holsters. Waves of Texans crested the hill and fired—every shot a skyrocket in the gloom. The crossfire was withering; several times Jacob heard the ziiip of passing bullets and one even gouged the tree trunk just above his shoulder. He felt bloodless and weak, and while he knew he *ought* to move, he found that he could not; his only role would be as witness to this pitched battle between light and the gathering weight of darkness.

Inside the ditch, Peter's Pinebark Company held fast. Flames sought them from two directions, but because they were so well set in the ground, no Coloradan was hit. Still the Confederates kept coming and Peter knew there was no way they could stem the tide forever. Shouting for one last volley, he raised his revolver and fired twice.

From behind another tree near the ditch, Charlie Spence saw shadows moving upon the forest floor. He lunged forward and fired from such close range that although the ball missed, burning powder struck Peter MacInnes's right eye full and destroyed it. Bellowing in pain, Peter crashed backward against the ditch's far wall. As Spence reached for the knife that he kept tied to his belt, Matt Maher swung his empty musket and connected, breaking a bone in the big Texan's hand. Spence managed to scramble away on his three good limbs while Jimmy O'Dowd and Sammy Douglas grabbed Peter by the arms and lifted him to safety. Immediately, James Hay began to shout commands.

The Coloradans volleyed again. Half-blinded by flares within the gloom, the Texans regrouped again and tried to advance; several were now within sixty yards of the ditch. Unable to solve the holdouts' location they fired again and again, hoping that sheer volumes of lead would atone for the lack of clear targets.

To James Hay, it looked as if all of Texas was closing in upon them. "Again, boys—*again!*" Muskets crashed but by now the Coloradans' volleys were less organized—rapid, random firings continued all along the ditch's length, as each man struggled to reload in the darkness. With shots now coming from within fifty yards and voices in the woods calling for a bayonet charge, the Coloradans despaired that soon they would be overrun.

"James, thare's too many!" Bill Storey shouted. "We canna stay!"

"One minute more!" Hay shouted, praying that Tappan might deliver them from disaster.

Crouched beside Storey, Matt Maher shook his head but couldn't clear it. Despite the roaring sounds and flashing lights that never stopped, he could not put his brother's image out of his mind. Tears streamed down his cheeks and he knelt to tamp another ball into the blisteringly hot barrel of his musket. He thought of Mike lying dead in the woods, somewhere on the other side of a vicious swarm that God had not seen fit to limit. He thought of their mother, father, and two sisters, all dead in a far-off land, and something inside him broke. Of all the people equipped to wander the earth alone, he knew he was not one. He looked at Storey, who'd just reloaded his own musket, and stood. "Give me that."

Storey paused, the weapon halfway to his shoulder. "Mattie, whit for?"

Matt wrenched the Springfield from Storey's grip, set his foot upon a rock, and crawled up out of the ditch. He took one step forward and then the darkness devoured him. Catching one Confederate completely unprepared, he fired with the muzzle just inches from the man's torso. Then he dropped that weapon and ran toward the last flash he had seen. Half a dozen carbines opened up in his direction, but as none of them struck him, he kept on running, braying like a wounded beast. Thinking that he'd spotted another form in the half-light he had started to raise his musket when a flash and roar from the right spun him around. Seeing stars and his brother's face, he struck the ground and did not move again. Frightened Texans closed in from all sides, and for several moments beat and stabbed at Matthew's body, not knowing that by then there was no need.

The Texans' standard-bearer had nearly reached the ditch when he was struck and fell. Seizing on the chaos before them, the Coloradans bolted eastward into blackness; a few fired as they ran and that was enough. As James Hay began to run, his last memory of Glorieta was of a crimson flag and its white star, lit by flashes as it fluttered to the ground.

෫

In the darkness and confusion that followed, the Pinebark Independents escaped. They tripped and fell more than they ran, and many tore their clothes and barked their shins on unseen rocks. Several nearly impaled themselves on tree limbs. Bill Storey, too, nearly lost an eye when he ran square into a dead juniper's ragged branches. Only by turning as he fell did he sustain deep scratches across his temple and cheek instead. On and on they ran, away from the creek, across sage-choked flats, and into the starlight shadow of Glorieta Mesa. Mercifully, none of the Texans followed. At last, their noisy flight alerted Tappan's rear-guard and once their identity was confirmed, the larger force welcomed them as prodigals. Together, they hurried east in search of Slough's command.

ᕬ

The chaos in the woods quickly ebbed. Jacob pushed away from the tree trunk and held onto a low branch to keep from collapsing. It took him ten full minutes to regain his equilibrium. He shut his eyes and clenched his teeth until his jaws ached. He felt hollow, as though he'd been inflated with air, and his chest hurt so badly that when he coughed he doubled over. At last, he recognized the voice that he had heard in the thicket and set off in darkness toward the ditch. There he searched for a full half-hour until he found José Garza's body. Garza had been struck twice—by Matt Maher's shot and one other—and was as cold as the bloodstained ground on which he lay.

Confederate HQ, Pigeon's Ranch, New Mexico Territory, March 28, 1862

Even though the Scurry's Texans could hear the last Union wagons creaking eastward on the Santa Fe Trail, they were exhausted and in no condition to pursue. Shortly after sundown, they halted at Pigeon's ranch. As the U.S. Army had before them, the Confederates commandeered the hotel's main dining room for use as a hospital, and their short-handed surgeons administered what care they could. The senior officers walked between the tables, shook hands with the sentient, and prayed for the dead and dying. Of these there were many: Shropshire, Buckholts, Raguet, and Metzger among them. Bradford wavered between life and death, and Issac Adair was lying on a table, comatose from the bullet in his brain. Watching a surgeon use a hooked probe to pull a jagged wad of lead from an un-anaesthetized soldier's left shoulder, Maj. Pyron had nearly vomited. The major had entered the building in good spirits—satisfied, if not elated. Once inside, however, the gore and cries of distress had injured his mood, and he'd stalked its hallways in grim silence.

࿇

Colonel Scurry entered a room at the back of the hotel. Chairs scraped and forks clinked against plates as his officers stood. "As you were." Scurry settled into a chair so that an aide could help him remove his boots. The colonel grabbed a glass of wine and raised it to toast his staff. "Damned proud of your work today."

The others lifted their glasses and returned the compliment.

The colonel glanced unhappily at a plate of biscuits and beef gravy that had been set before him and cleared his throat. "So how does the wind blow? You weren't sitting in silence before I arrived. Major Jackson?"

Alexander Jackson, a former Territorial Secretary, swallowed the last of his coffee. "Colonel, we were pondering our next step."

"Oh?" Scurry moved his fork from one side of the plate to the other.

"Tonight, Sir, if possible." Jackson glanced around at the others and cleared his throat. "Don't mean to talk out of school, but I vote to press 'em hard, right now, and end this quick-like."

"Major Pyron?"

Covered with grime, Charles Pyron blotted a weeping cut under his left ear and nodded. "I'm with Jackson."

"Two votes for pursuit. Captain Crosson? Captain Stark?" Both concurred with their predecessors, as did others, until Scurry pointed to the last two men at the table's farthest end. There, lieutenants Pleasant Oakes and James Noble agreed, too.

"Sir, my vote's yes," Oakes enthused. "We whipped 'em bad."

"We can support, Sir," Noble said, "but they fit awful hard at the end. My company's cut up pretty good, so mine's a qualified vote in favor."

Pushing his plate aside, Scurry exhaled heavily. "Counsel's appreciated, gentlemen, but your votes don't count. Best I can tell, more than a quarter of our number is dead or wounded. The boys may be in good spirits, but they are spent. Our food and kit are back over the pass—won't be here for two hours, at minimum. No—we'll entrench here and wait for reinforcements."

A low murmur rippled around the table's far end until Maj. Jackson raised his hand and called for silence. He faced Scurry. "Sir, what shall we say if the boys ask when we'll move against Fort Union?"

"How many days until Denver?" Pyron added.

Scurry pushed his wine glass away and motioned to aide who stood along the wall. "Get me some water?" Tapping his fork against the side of his plate, he turned back to face Jackson. "Not before our train arrives. Once everyone's fed, we'll need to get burial details together—" A loud, insistent knocking at the door made him stop and turn his head.

Oakes drummed his fingers on the table and grinned. "That's Abe Lincoln, come to surrender." A few of the younger officers laughed, but the opened door revealed nothing more than a tired and impossibly dirty boy.

"Colonel Scurry here?" he said. "Lieutenant Taylor sent me."

The colonel tugged on the courier's sleeve. "Here, son—what's the message?"

"Sir, Lieutenant Taylor asked that I give you this information in private. May we step out into the hall?" As the boy glanced around the room, a few of the officers noticed that he was on the verge of tears.

Exhausted and irritable, Scurry exhaled heavily. "Honestly, son, I don't care—"

"*Sir!*" the boy said, startling everyone else in the room. Among the Texans, Col. Scurry's intolerance of familiarity and insubordination was well known.

For a moment, the colonel continued staring at the boy, until finally he pushed away from the table. "Come on." He strode briskly out into the hallway and the courier followed, closing the door as he went.

Inside the room, the other officers began talking excitedly, speculating as to whether the news was good or bad. For several minutes the door remained shut, and several of the officers stood up and began to pace. A sense of unease slowly stole over their deliberations, and at length a few of the lieutenants even began to argue about one another's perceived shortcomings. Even once Col. Scurry re-entered the room, their bickering did not cease—if anything, it only grew louder.

At last, Scurry banged on the table with his plate for quiet. "Shut up, all of you!" Jackson and Pyron noticed that the colonel had gone deathly pale and their hearts began to race. "Sit down," He said, staring down at his knees. "This is...the news is not good. Jesus Christ, I don't even know where to start."

෨

A few hours earlier, Coloradan Ed Wynkoop had been halfway down the slope when, for the first time that day, he heard artillery. It sounded low and distant and seemed to come from the east. The captain paused and there it was again: dull echoes off the sandstone cliffs that confined Apache Canyon and Galisteo Creek. He slid a few feet more, and though he stopped on a narrow ledge, loosened talus continued to tumble downhill. Texans at the hill's base looked up and saw that the hillside swarmed with blue-coated soldiers. Both sides were so astonished at seeing each other that for several moments neither said a thing. Wynkoop broke the silence: "You fellows, who are you?"

Tim Nettles, a young sergeant, threw aside the book he was reading and ran toward the howitzer. "Texans, goddamn you!" He vaulted a log and shouted to his fellows: "Arm yourselves, brothers! Awake!"

From the canyon's rim, Chivington ordered Wynkoop's thirty-man detail to provide covering fire as the others slipped and skidded down the lower slope. Although Nettles and his short-handed crew reached the howitzer, they struggled to turn it toward the onrushing Coloradans and managed only two ineffective rounds before the Federals were upon them. Two guards were killed and the others ran for their lives.

The two hundred sick and wounded Texans in camp mounted a feeble, chaotic defense. Nothing they did slowed the Coloradans—not even the white flag that Episcopal Pastor Lucius Jones waved before he was accidentally shot in front of the Confederate's main hospital tent. Everything that Scurry's thirteen hundred Texans owned was burned: weapons, clothing, blankets, food, forage for the livestock, supplies, ammunition, gunpowder, medicines, personal goods, all manner of correspondence—including Jacob Stark's journal—and more. In less than half an hour, the lightly equipped Texans were left with nothing but that which they had carried with them that morning.

Penned in a side canyon were hundreds of horses and mules and for some time the Federals debated whether to kill them. However, this prospect was so disagreeable and time so short that they decided to turn the animals loose instead and stampede them into the wildlands down Galisteo Creek. This was quicker, more humane, and as dozens of locals were standing around the camp's fringes, come to loot what they could, no doubt rustlers among them would quickly disperse a good many of the freed animals. Once the destruction of the Confederate's wagon train was complete, the Federals, along with seventeen able-bodied prisoners, clambered back up the mesa. By the time they reached the top, clouds had built in and it had begun to snow. Like a fish tossed onto the shore, Wynkoop's chest heaved from the exertion. He watched a guard-detail march the prisoners east along the logging road.

"Worried about our main force," Chivington confided. "Hope they haven't been run off."

"Those men—," he panted "—the men we freed all say that Slough is standing firm at Pigeon's Ranch."

"Maybe, but for how long? You think he can hold?"

Padre Grzelachowski returned on his huge white horse.

Wynkoop brushed at the grime that covered his features without result. "No matter what happens over the pass, here we've left 'em with nothing. Either they must return to Santa Fe for resupply or try and freight everything up from Albuquerque—either way, they're on the run."

"Provided we have men enough for pursuit."

"Slough will stand."

Chivington eyed Wynkoop with curiosity, not altogether happy at hearing him express confidence in their colonel's abilities. "Pray so. Look, we'd best get back ourselves—Padre, can you lead us in the dark?"

"God willing," Father Grzelachowski replied, "I travel this way many times and my horse it know the roads."

Anxious to get away, Chivington temporarily forgave Wynkoop's breach of faith. "Good—Ned, wait five minutes and bring up the rear. See that no one is left behind."

⁓

"Those that could rode or ran for their lives," Col. Scurry concluded. "The rest are probably dead."

With this, the young courier, who had stood by while the colonel informed the other officers of the Texans' losses at Johnson's Ranch, burst into tears.

A seething tension enveloped the room and the messenger's choked sobs drove Scurry slightly insane. *"Boy!"* he exploded, "go to the kitchen. Grab a plate and wait there." Just as soon as the private exited, again the men around the table erupted and again Scurry had to pound on it to restore order. As their eyes fell on him, he exhaled and stared at his uneaten meal. "Hell and Maria," he muttered, "they shot Pastor Jones! A *reverend!* Goddamned Abs have lost all sense of humanity!"

"Ain't right," Pyron concurred, but the others remained silent.

Scurry stood and cast around the room for signs of strength. "First, let's gather our dead. I need someone to press those bastards for a cease-fire—give us time to regroup. What have we got for a white flag?" The men looked all around the room but no suitable cloth was found. Already the surgeons had claimed every scrap of the hotel's bedding for tourniquets and dressings.

"Nothing," James Noble concluded.

Scurry slammed his fist on the table and made the plates and cups bounce. "Goddammit! Someone tear off your shirt tail—we must have a white flag!" Sacrificing a trophy he'd found, Lt. Oakes surrendered a white silk handkerchief that some Yankee had dropped on the road. Scurry studied the fine cloth before handing it to Maj. Jackson.

Jackson wrapped the fabric around his left hand. "How long?"

"Forty-eight hours. We must make Santa Fe before they know we're gone. Form details to scour the near-hills. Get the wounded indoors—it's snowing again, damn it. Go."

Chairs scraped and Jackson led an exodus from the room. Last to leave, Jacob Stark paused beside the colonel and cleared his throat.

Slumped in his chair, Scurry pushed a sodden biscuit across his plate with his knife. "What?"

"Sir, do you want an inventory of arms and ammunition?"

Scurry mashed the biscuit into pieces and took a sip of water. "Tonight?"

Jacob blinked, unsure what to make of the colonel's tone. "So that we are ready once the truce's expires."

Muffled shouts from outside the hotel and the anguished cries of a patient on one of the surgeons' tables punctuated the silence that followed. Scurry looked up and studied Jacob. His hair was matted with dirt and a rill of dark, dried blood from a gash on his chin had stained his collar. He looked tired, worn, and like a ship that had taken on water he listed to the right. Despite this, his eyes burned brightly, which Scurry found consoling. The hard set of the colonel's jaw softened and he permitted himself the merest fraction of a smile. "No, thanks—go send the dead to their rest."

Jacob did not protest and went to find his company.

Scurry exhaled and shoved his plate toward the middle of the table. He reached into his pocket for his watch and when he did, a metallic wad rode up on the back of his hand and fell to the floor. Puzzled, he reached down and recognized the mangled bullet that had struck his hat late that afternoon. He dropped this relic onto the tabletop and glanced at his watch: 9:20 p.m., Friday, March 28, 1862—four hours and an eternity since the Confederate Army of New Mexico's last advance of the war.

Bernal Springs, New Mexico Territory, March 29, 1862

Trudging toward Kozlowski's in the dark, James Hay held out his canteen. Up ahead, bonfires and the low murmur of conversation signified that they had nearly reached the First Colorado's encampment.

Peter leaned heavily on Hay's shoulder and took a drink. "Thanks." His right eye was ruined and his head ached horribly beneath layers of bloody cotton bandages. The rest of his body was scarcely any better, having been dragged through the rock-strewn woods at a breakneck pace—the blind leading the blinded.

A hundred yards down the road, Hay whispered to his friend, "That one in the woods was Texan, Pete—why'd ye let him go?"

Peter did not immediately answer. "Can't say."

"Not saying you were wrong," Hay pressed. "I'm only trying to make sense of it all."

Peter took another swig of coffee and handed back the canteen. "We'd ambushed his fellows at the bottom of the hill. Dunno—felt wicked."

"Better them—"

"He'd done me no wrong and I just couldn't do it. Overmuch like murder, I guess."

"Could've taken him prisoner."

Peter stumbled a little, and Hay had to catch him. "They had nearly pinched us—remember?"

"Odd we let him away, is all."

"Maybe so."

Hay slung the canteen over his shoulder. "How d'ye feel?"

"The worst, James—the worst."

"Still here."

"To the most part. Was this worse than your turn in the Navy?"

They took several more steps before Hay answered: "Aye. From the below decks, I ne'er saw who we fought, but up there, tare-an'-ouns—I saw things I wish I hadn't."

Though Peter agreed with this last bit, he said nothing more all the way into camp. Hay and others stacked their arms and lay down on the frozen ground to sleep, while an Army surgeon did what little he could for Peter's burned face and ruined eye.

&

Around midnight, the air grew colder and heavy snow began to fall. In the forest's dark corners, many of the undiscovered wounded froze to death.

So many of the Texans' horses had been lost that all remaining animals were press-ganged to pull the few serviceable wagons; cavalry companies such as Jacob Stark's were permanently converted to infantry. Moreover, when they finally inventoried their remaining ammunition, Scurry discovered that with the train's loss they had fewer than twenty rounds per man and no more than a dozen rounds for the artillery—barely enough for a brief skirmish.

&

Developments in the Union camp weren't as grim, but just as startling. A little after ten o' clock, Chivington's raiders returned to Kozlowski's with their incredible news about the Confederate's wagon train. Believing that the advantage had swung back to their side, the rank-and-file called for the renewal of hostilities at daybreak, but their officers demurred.

Following Chivington's victory at Apache Canyon, Slough had written to Col. Canby—still at Fort Craig—to say that he intended to move against the enemy with his entire force. Canby sent an urgent counter-dispatch ordering Slough to return to Fort Union and avoid an all-out battle. Canby had been so adamant about this that he had strongly suggested that Slough would be court-martialed if he left Fort Union. On March 29, when an express rider rode into the Coloradans' camp, Slough accepted and read this message in the presence of his staff. Thus unable to pretend that he had never received it, he resigned his commission on the spot. The next day, as Union forces marched back to Fort Union, Slough departed for Denver. That night, by popular acclaim, the Reverend John Chivington was promoted to colonel (vaulting in rank over Sam Tappan) and assumed command of the First Colorado.

PART SIX

RETREAT

Fort Marcy, Santa Fe, New Mexico Territory, April 1, 1862

Unable to transport their wounded, the Confederates left them with what little medicine was available (this having been obtained from U.S. Quartermaster Capt. Herbert Enos in exchange for Union wounded who'd been left at Pigeon's Ranch during the Federals' retreat) and retreated west toward the capital. Unsure whether the force that had destroyed their wagon train was still in the field, they went cautiously. Bitter weather impeded their progress and strung out their column for several miles. Though the first Confederate units reached Santa Fe at daybreak on March 30, the last would not arrive for another thirty hours.

*

Jacob's company entered the city around nine a.m. on April 1 and hastened back to Fort Marcy's ruins to seek what shelter they could. After they'd slept for a few hours, the men fanned out to scavenge food, and by nightfall had found enough for a few days.

Seated on an adobe wall overlooking the city, Briggs Hardy chewed on a heel of dry bread and watched as other units and individuals arrived below. He struggled to swallow a morsel and coughed. "That might've gone better."

"Goddammit, we should've posted more guards." Jacob leaned his elbows on the wall and laced his fingers together. He looked south and there, where the city thinned and fields prevailed, the earth was greener, softer; the sky was blue and everywhere he heard the sound of meltwater in the streets and ditches. *No human catastrophe can stop the seasons.*

"Should've brought our wagons forward to the summit."

Jacob watched other companies set out to beg, borrow, and steal whatever they could from the city's terrified citizens. "Now we're fixed."

"Your boots in good shape?"

"Not really, no."

Hardy cast a sidelong glance at Jacob. "Think you'll go look for her?"

"Don't know if she's even here." Jacob looked west but couldn't see over the hill that loomed above the fort.

"Think you should," Hardy persisted. "I sure would."

Jacob glanced at his friend and tried to gauge his sincerity, but already Hardy's attention had drifted elsewhere.

⁓

As Scurry's force returned to Santa Fe, Col. Green and the remainder of Fifth Texas left Albuquerque with what flour and cornmeal they could carry, but it hadn't been nearly enough. Moreover, all the additional bodies had increased the pressure on Santa Fe's food supply.

Moved by news of the Texans' plight, on April 1 Louisa Canby went to visit the wounded in their makeshift hospital. Appalled by conditions inside the converted warehouse, she had gone to Col. Scurry and offered the use of her home. Also that afternoon, she had organized a company of nurses to help Maj. Powhattan Jordan—a physician—try to save the most grievously wounded. The next day, simultaneous with the First Colorado's return to Fort Union, Louisa herself travelled to the Glorieta battlefield to bring in more of the injured, including Capt. Issac Adair—comatose from a bullet in his brain but still clinging to life.

On April 3, Louisa helped secure a supply of government blankets and made quantities of soup in her own kitchen. As she stepped outside for a breath of fresh air, she saw that another wagon had arrived in the yard. Exhausted, she nevertheless waved to the driver and pointed toward a side door. "It's easier unloading from that side," she said. She tried to rise, but her aching knees buckled and she sat heavily in the chair. She took a sip of tea in the hope that it might revive her for the work ahead.

Other residents who'd volunteered to help had been astonished at Louisa's dedication. Nell Ford was especially supportive, baking dozens of loaves of bread, but by midnight on April 3, fatigue had dulled even her enthusiasm. Seated at the Canbys' kitchen table, she soaked her aching feet in a pan of warm water. "Don't know how you do it," she said.

"Have to." Louisa winced at the pitiable groans coming from the next room. Seated opposite Nell, she folded her arms and laid her head on the tabletop.

"Dear woman," Nell soothed, "what'll you have once you've given it all away?"

Louisa lifted her head and pushed away from the table. "It's these fellows who have nothing. I don't care that they're from Texas—I cannot lie about while they shiver and starve. So much suffering..." Then she rose and went to go see what else she could do.

੭ఄ

Outside the Canby's home, the teamster reined his mules to a halt and lifted his battered felt slouch. "Thank you, Ma'am."

Another soldier pulled back covers to reveal three wounded men, suspended in tent-cloth hammocks nailed at angles across the bed. "Tommy," he called to the driver, "I'll go get help."

Hat in hand, the young driver grunted in reply and stood shyly beside Louisa.

"How are they?" she said.

"Fair," he answered. "Grapeshot carried that un's foot clean away, but the other two are steady. This'un took his bullet in the arm— other one has Henry Shrapnel's iron in his feet, shins, and thighs."

"No sepsis?"

"No fevers, no."

"Good." Louisa walked around behind the wagon to unfasten the gate-latch. "At least they're down from the mountain."

The soldier helped lower the wagon's gate and stood aside as Louisa, hefting a stout earthenware jug, offered water to the patients. "Thank you, Mrs. Canby," he said. "I'll make sure folks at home hear about your charity."

Louisa held the jug to a wounded man's lips. "That's kind of you."

The driver retrieved a pair of pliers so that the improvised hammocks could be unslung and their contents carried indoors.

"Fellas, how y'all doing?" One man groaned and another made no sound at all, but the third waved with encouraging vigor.

Another soldier appeared at the side door with four of Maj. Jordan's orderlies, leaned toward Louisa and spoke softly: "Hope we can check their fevers—more have died that way than from Yankee bullets."

"Far too many," Louisa agreed sadly.

The orderlies lowered the first man—one of James Bradford's gunners, shot through the right shoulder (a slug had broken his collarbone and only barely missed his lung) and who'd nearly froze to death after the battle.

Hat in hand, the young teamster stopped and stood beside Louisa. "You've been an angel, Ma'am. Mrs. Ford, too. Let her know if I don't see her?"

Louisa offered him some water. "Tell her yourself—she'll only be gone for three days."

The Texan shook his head. "We'll leave Santa Fe. Soon as we's organized, likely."

"Quiet, George!" From across the drive, the young soldier shot his partner a murderous look. "No offense, Ma'am."

"None taken." Louisa glanced toward the road and noticed that another carriage had turned onto the drive.

"Ain't supposed to speak of...plans," the soldier explained.

Louisa merely clasped her hands and smiled. "Of course. Gentlemen, please excuse me." The Texans tipped their hats as she turned, skirted the porch steps, and started down the drive.

⁓

Many Santa Feans took pity on the suffering Texans—including Bishop John Lamy—and understood Louisa's actions. Others were less charitable. Some—Letty Morris among them—held that any aid or comfort given to the Confederates was tantamount to treason (though in fairness, she'd only just received word that her husband had been horribly wounded at Glorieta). Letty's driver pulled to a stop and she leaned out the carriage's window. "Louisa, I came to return some books but perhaps this isn't the best time." Behind Louisa, orderlies were lowering the second wounded man from the wagon and cursing one another foully.

"Good as any, Lett. How is David?"

Letty viewed the commotion with ill-concealed disdain. "Haven't you done enough for these people, Louisa?" She sighed and proffered the books. "Why do you exercise yourself this way?"

Louisa took the books. She glanced at the Texans, struggling to maneuver through the door with their patient. "What way is that, Lett?"

Letty scowled. "Can't imagine the Colonel would be pleased. I love you dearly, Louisa, but this is beyond the pale."

"Then you don't know Edward," Louisa answered tersely. "If saving the Republic is our aim, then these men are but wayward citizens. There's nothing to be gained by treating them badly."

"They treated my David rather badly, don't you think?"

"I'm sorry for his troubles, Lett—and yours. But, shouldn't we do what we can to foster amity?"

Letty leaned over and whispered something unheard to her driver before she stiffened her spine. "I will not feed or shelter our enemies, Louisa."

Louisa looked out to the main road and was relieved to see that a wagon there continued past her driveway. "Lett, did you know that on Friday our men loaned their tools and worked alongside the Texans to bury the dead?" Letty stared straight ahead. "If they can accord one another respect, oughtn't we to do so, too?"

She turned and cast a cold eye on Louisa. "They've earned that latitude."

Louisa searched her friend's face. "Friend or foe, every one of those boys is some dear mother's son. I hope you'll kindly consider the Coloradans once *they* arrive."

"Of course! They're *our* boys."

"And that," Louisa sighed, "is partisanship, not charity. I will pray for David's recovery. Good day." The orderlies emerged from the house to retrieve the last patient. Letty nodded to her driver and though she did not respond when Louisa waved, the colonel's wife hoped that someday their relationship could be mended.

Meanwhile there was work to do.

Hacienda Carrizo, Santa Fe, New Mexico Territory, April 5, 1862

Practically overnight the weather turned. After a huge lunch and siesta, Don Carrizo felt the urge to receive fresh air out-of-doors and for an hour, he sat at a table on the lawn and reviewed his ledgers. He felt better than he had in a long while, partly from the warm weather but also from knowing that soon the Texans would leave and with them, many of his most expensive troubles.

The day prior, Col. Green had paid a visit and very civilly conveyed his thanks for the don's assistance. It had surprised—and pleased— Don Carrizo a little that the Texan hadn't asked for anything more—food, wagons, money—before he departed, which confirmed the don's generally high opinion of him. He was irked, however, that only Green had accorded him this respect—the drunkard Sibley, the irascible Scurry, and the "Boy Colonel" McNeill had not. Still, this was of no consequence. His balance sheets had weathered the storm—that was the important thing. Moreover, with the Federal government's return, soon rich freighting contracts would be let and Southern-owned properties would head for the open market. He closed his eyes and enjoyed the warm sunshine on his face—so much so that he did not hear his servant, Nestor, approach.

"Don Carrizo?" Nestor said. *"Señor?"*

The don exhaled softly and opened one eye. *"Qué es así?"*

"Un visitante." The servant stepped aside to present Jacob Stark.

Don Carrizo opened both eyes and laid a pencil in the ledger's crease. "I thought you might come." The don waved at one of the

346

chairs across the table. "Bring *el capitán* a whiskey and *informe a* Tircio *que tenemos una huésped.*"

"Water's fine," Jacob corrected.

"Don't all Texans drink whiskey? Cigar, then?" he offered, but again the young Texan declined. Nestor reappeared with the water, handed it to Jacob, and then disappeared back inside the house.

"Don Carrizo—" Jacob began but the don raised a hand.

"You walked here?" Jacob nodded, embarrassed that after Glorieta his entire company had turned their horses over to the Seventh's teamsters. Don Carrizo pointed to Jacob's tattered blue jacket. "How are your supplies?"

"Wanting." Jacob felt his cheeks redden, so he lied: "Train's enroute from Mesilla, though."

The don pursed his lips. "I hear General Sibley wrote to Governor Clark asking for supplies, but was told that none were available."

"They'll come," Jacob said without conviction.

"No matter." The hacendado waved at a fly that buzzed around his head. "Heat's up early and where you're going I doubt that you will need a coat."

"Ain't going nowhere." This time Jacob's irritation was plain. "Soon as General Bee reinforces Mesilla, we'll continue as before."

The don took a cigar from a cedar box on the table, cut the end, and lit it. "Costs me a fortune to stay informed, *Capitán*—a fortune—but it is money well spent. '*Saber es poder*', as they say, and I have it on good authority that you are going back to Texas."

"That right?"

"Yes."

"Well," Jacob blurted, "then there's something we need to discuss."

"I *knew* it!" Don Carrizo glanced south, where the shimmering lavender valley rolled away toward the dark blue Sandia Mountains. "What does he want now?"

"Pardon?"

"Tell him another wagon will be ready tomorrow," he sighed, doubly glad that these locusts would be gone before his crops were in the field.

Jacob shook his head. "No, Sir—I want to take Adria with me. We'll do this honorably and get married—I'd like your approval, Don Carrizo."

"I see." After a long pause, the don stubbed out his cigar and pushed away from the table. "We should talk about this—follow me."

⁓

In silence, the two men walked along a drive that skirted the house. Stopping in front of the chapel, the don broke a twig from the trunk of a small, dead tree. He turned it repeatedly, snapping off pieces, none longer than his little finger. "A shame this one did not make it through the winter." The don dropped the last piece of wood in the grass and brushed his hands clean on the fronts of his brown wool trousers. "You love my daughter, yes?"

"Yessir."

"I think she loves you, too," Carrizo said, "but she is engaged to another, see? *Engaged,* boy. Can you not see how vulgar you have been? Or what you might've done to her reputation?"

"I understood that her fiancée—"

"No, boy, you do *not*—you do *not* understand. Your friend understood that you aren't welcome here, but you do not."

"'Friend'?"

"One of your men—"

"Yeah, Eli Fisher—I figured it out. You twisted his words all t'hell—you lied to Adria."

The don exhaled. "So what?"

"So I'm going up to Taos to find her."

"*¡Maldita sea tu madre!* You think you can go wherever you want?"

"Sure do."

"I will not have my daughter ruined by the likes of you!" Don Carrizo stood his ground even as Jacob took a menacing step forward. "*Pendejo*, she isn't for you. Nothing here is for you—nothing except death. She's engaged—"

"He's *dead!*"

"You don't know anything."

"I know how you abuse your daughter—"

"Texan, your presence is an abuse! We are descended from kings and who are *you?* Some *matón* in a stolen jacket, yet you have the nerve to ask for my daughter's hand?"

"Didn't have to ask."

"You think you have fooled me, don't you? Oh, I know you've been lurking around here—I know my own home. No, I should've been stronger, but you Texans had everyone fooled. Now that I see how weak you really are, you may rest assured that you will never see her again."

"You can't stop me." Jacob said, but glancing around, he realized how far they were from the road. Buildings on every side, he thought he saw furtive movements in the windows. His hand fell to his hip and he remembered that his holstered revolver was hanging on a peg in the house's entry.

Rather than speak, Carrizo backed toward a shed and whistled.

Jacob glared at Don Carrizo but caught another movement in the corner of his eye—Tircio, half-concealed in the shadow of a doorway, a rifle in his hands. The young men stared at one another, immobile, seething. *"Vamanos,"* the servant said. "You come with me."

Jacob fixed the distance between them at fifteen feet; between he and the don, half that. He continued to face forward but slowly rotated the tips of his boots to his left. "Where are we going?" he said, desperate for a few more seconds. Exhaling, his breath whistled between cracked lips.

Don Carrizo stared hard but betrayed no emotion.

"Vamanos," the servant repeated, startling into flight a crow that had been perched on the shed's parapet. When Jacob turned his head at the motion, the other two followed. As they did, the Texan lunged to his left, pulled Don Carrizo into a chokehold, and drove his knee into the side of the don's leg.

Nearly buckling from the strike, the don let out a strangled yelp. *"¡Mátele!"*

Simultaneously, Jacob lifted the don's head with his left arm and punched the small of his back with his right—the don's hips rolled out over his knees and he'd no choice but to stumble forward. Tircio lifted the rifle to his shoulder, but with the likelihood of striking his master, he stepped left, raised the weapon, and tried to club the Texan.

Toppling forward, Jacob released his grip on the don's neck and pushed even harder with his fist so that the don pitched into Tircio's knees.

Stepping backward, Tircio had no base for delivering a blow, so he gripped the weapon mid-barrel with his left hand and tried to punch Jacob with his right. *"¡Ai!"* he shouted.

Deflecting this clout, Jacob tripped over the don's legs, grabbed Tircio's lapel, and fell forward. His knee struck the side of Don Carrizo's head and he kicked as violently as he could to try to wrest the rifle from Tircio's hand. The young men rolled nearly into the doorway, each with one hand on the weapon, and Jacob ended up on top. At the same time his feet found purchase against a wall, he felt a tearing sensation on the side of his chest where he'd been struck at Glorieta. His hand slipped from the rifle. Unable to raise his right arm, Jacob ground that forearm into Tircio's throat and punched his face with his left. With one hand, Tircio tried to push against the arm that was crushing his windpipe and bludgeon Jacob with the rifle with the other, but the pressure on his throat was too great and all he could do was flail. He, too, let go of the rifle. In agony from the flare in his chest, Jacob gritted his teeth and put his full weight onto his right arm. He took hold of Tircio's right wrist and turned away from the Mexican's left, desperate to avoid more strikes to his eyes and nose. Even so, and despite a handful of dirt thrown into his face, he could feel Tircio's punches weakening, and he was certain that in a few more seconds the servant would lose consciousness.

Jacob extended his legs and pushed against the wall to increase his downward leverage. "You son-of-a-bitch!" he hissed and then a blow fell across his back and knocked the breath from his lungs. His right arm and shoulder went numb and he toppled sideways, aided by a feeble, reflexive shove from Tircio. For the longest time he couldn't breathe—couldn't *breathe!* And for the second time in a week, he felt as if he'd fallen headlong into his own grave.

Clutching the rifle's barrel with both hands, Don Carrizo staggered backward and coughed violently. He tied to kick Jacob's head but missed and nearly fell. *"Pinche* Texan," he wheezed, "I told you to stay away."

Jacob rolled onto his left side and tried to fix the don's whereabouts, but the spasms in his chest and shoulders wouldn't let him lie still. He pushed with his toes and with his left hand pulled on a windowsill until he was propped more or less upright against the adobe wall. Already his right eye had begun to swell shut. Blood pounded in his ears.

The don could scarcely stand from the pain in his back, so he stayed hunched over the rifle's breach and took a backwards step. With his sleeve, he wiped the blood that seeped from his nose and made a gargling noise that Jacob mistook for laughter.

The Texan's ribs hurt so much that he could barely breathe and he closed his eyes rather than watch Carrizo work the rifle's mechanism. He heard the lever click but as the seconds ticked by, he wondered why he'd neither heard nor felt a shot. Perhaps this was some unknowable aspect of death—maybe he *had* been shot and passed into another life, yet insensate to the transit. Then he heard voices. He opened his eyes (or eye—the right one having swollen closed) and saw that the don had dropped the rifle on the ground and sunk to his knees.

"You mustn't," Jacob heard him say, "you mustn't!"

Rolling his head against the wall, Jacob saw Briggs Hardy followed closely by Charlie Spence. Hardy had his revolver drawn and stepped carefully over Tircio's legs; Spence took no such pains and brought his rifle's butt-stock down on the unconscious man's skull.

"Jake!" Hardy shouted, "are you okay?"

"God, you boys are a welcome sight."

"Charlie, watch him." Hardy retrieved the rifle and leaned it against the building.

Spence raised the rifle over his head like a club. "Gonna beat you to death."

"Charlie, stop!" Jacob said as Hardy helped him to his feet. Looking around, Jacob saw no one else—merely empty lanes between the buildings and swirls of wind-thrown dust. He took a step forward, felt better than he'd expected to, and so continued on to the building's end. He stopped and looked back. Tircio lay motionless, facedown in a spreading pool of blood; Don Carrizo and Spence were glaring at one another; and Hardy stood with his back against the building, sweeping the lane with his eyes. He felt unspeakably tired. "He answers one question, I'll never come back."

The other three men turned their heads and stared, unsure just whom Jacob had addressed.

"Who's that?" Hardy said.

"Carrizo," Jacob wheezed. While it hurt to inhale too deeply, his legs felt well enough and the pain in his head was tolerable.

The other two Texans looked askance at the don. "Jake," Spence said, "you can't let him go—"

Jacob tried to lift his right hand as high as he could, which was only a little above his waist before a jolt of pain made him stop. "He still has a chance." He walked back and stopped in front of Carrizo. "He wants to live, he's gonna tell me what he and Adria know about Peralta."

"*Qué es?*" Confused, the don began to stammer: "W-w-what do you mean?"

"You heard me."

"Peralta?" Carrizo blanched and Jacob noticed that his hands were trembling. It is a village below Albuquerque—*Rio Abajo*. I have no dealings there," he added. "Not for some time, anyway."

"What else?"

"Nothing—your question makes no sense. Adria's never been there—why would you think she had?"

"Went through it coming up here—just thought I'd ask."

The don glanced at the other two Texans but neither appeared to know what their captain meant, either. "I don't understand."

"Don't matter. Look, I know you don't normally let things go, but this time you'd better, *comprendé?*"

Carrizo said nothing and glared with such malice that Spence took offense. "Don't put on airs—hear what he said?"

"Yes," the don hissed.

"Then answer."

"No one will follow you, *Capitán.*" Don Carrizo looked away, and Charlie struck him in the stomach with his rifle. The don gasped for breath and rolled in the blood and dust until Spence pinned him to the ground with his boot.

"Nigger, I'd have killed you," he said, but Hardy pulled the big Texan away.

"Come on, let's go. Jake, you need help?"

"I'm okay," Jacob answered. He took Tircio's rifle, slung it over his shoulder, and started north.

Hardy and Spence followed, walking backwards until they were well beyond the *hacienda's* last buildings. Once it was clear that no one was following, they turned and fell in beside Jacob. Less than two hours later, the trio had been passed back into the Texans' stronghold at Fort Marcy.

Armijo's Mill, East of Albuquerque, New Mexico Territory, April 8, 1862

A thunderous boom made Confederate Capt. William Hardeman abandon his meager cornbread-and-bacon breakfast, cross a court-yard, and run up a staircase. On the building's roof, he shouted at a pair of gray-clad figures crouched behind the parapet: "Can you see anything?"

Joe Roberts handed Hardeman a field glass and pointed. "Three guns," Roberts said. "Two there—there's the third."

"Goddammit, where are the pickets?"

A twenty-pound case-shell exploded in a vacant lot only fifty yards west. All three men dove for cover as a wicked rain of debris clattered around them. After a while, they raised their heads to peer through the trees. "Federals," Roberts coughed.

"Hot Jesus, you don't say?" Hardeman raged. *"Where are the pickets?"*

"Porter's boys are missing—probably captured."

"Just arrived myself," Bethel Coopwood said. He picked a jagged wooden splinter from his hat-brim and held out a piece of paper. "Sorry I couldn't find y'all sooner."

"What's it say?" Hardeman lifted the glass once more to scan the fields west of the city.

"The Abs have left Fort Craig, dot, dot, dot—left Kit Carson and ten companies of Mexicans to hold it, dot, dot, dot—twelve hundred strong, they're coming up-river—" Coopwood's report was interrupted as by a shell's detonation. The Confederate officers clapped hands over their ears as a shock wave and blast of hot air rushed over them. "—with artillery," Coopwood concluded. A shed adjacent to their post collapsed in a cloud of dust.

Hardeman stayed crouched behind the parapet and glanced northward. "Canby broke out of Fort Craig? Wish I'd known sooner!" Another shell exploded and toppled a slender cottonwood across the road, littering Coopwood's prostrate form with splintered wood. Though their ears rang, at last they heard the staccato crackle of small arms in the fields nearer the river.

Coopwood coughed. "Brought big guns, too." On the roads below, men were running uphill and there was considerable anxiety on the rooftop until they recognized these troops as their own.

"All right," Hardeman struggled to keep his voice even, "let's get down from here! Joe, send a fast dispatch to Col. Scurry and Col. Green. Tell 'em we are under attack—tell 'em to drop everything and run! Coop, get ours back behind that canal and goddammit, tell Reily to unlimber his guns and shoot back! Let's go!"

The three men ran across the rooftop, praying that more Federal shells weren't inbound. Within five minutes, the Confederates' artillerists were dueling with their Union counterparts. Farther west, the infantry re-formed defensive lines behind a network of irrigation canals gouged into the long hillsides east of town. Desperate to defend their meager supplies, even the sick and wounded rushed out from the Texans' hospital to fight.

⁓

On the river's eastern bank, Edward Canby lowered his field glasses and called toward the nearest battery: "McDermitt! Another dozen rounds at two-minute intervals—four per gun—then pause!" Uphill, smoke was rising, black on blue, and pillars of fire were visible above the treetops. Canby handed the glass to Maj. Thomas Duncan and fished around in his vest pocket for a cigar. "Damned if I can tell, Tommy. Three hundred, five hundred—I cannot tell." He began to worry the cigar between his teeth.

Duncan tried to peer through the smoke. "Unsure whether it's the same cannon being moved around or if they have ten pieces up there."

"Then it's not just me." A thunderclap sounded on their left and dirt erupted from an embankment as the Texans offered resistance. All three Federal guns replied.

Returned from a ride near Confederate lines, Duncan took a drink from his canteen and wiped drops of water from his beard. "Our scouts have probed above that big canal, but they haven't much to report. All shots have come from inside those buildings, so we cannot fix their number."

Canby checked his pocket watch and moved the cigar from one corner of his mouth to the other. "Knock over every damn one until we can." The guns fired again.

Duncan glanced uphill and saw men running between buildings. "Are these the ones from Glorieta?"

"No, Gabe believes those units are still in Santa Fe, licking their wounds." Over in the artillery pit he watched that crews run their guns back into place and start the loading sequence.

Duncan mopped his brow with a handkerchief. "Hot today."

"Summer's come early." The Federal cannon boomed again.

Captain Paddy Graydon, a Union spy, scout, and longtime resident of New Mexico Territory, approached with two ancient civilians entrained. "Hell of a fix up there," Graydon said. He turned to the older of the two men. "All right, grandad, tell Col. Canby what you told me."

Hadden Paar looked up at Canby and politely offered his hand. They shook and the old man spoke in a slow, raspy voice: "Texans will not let anyone leave their homes."

Canby looked up and saw that entire blocks of buildings were ablaze. "How do you mean?"

The second geezer, a retired blacksmith named Cleofas Lucero, nodded. "Said they'd shoot us if we did. We followed your captain's company as it went past."

Canby and Duncan exchanged concerned glances before Canby spat out the cigar's ragged remains. "How many Texans are here?"

Paar shrugged. "Hard to say—they come and go."

"Four, five hundred," Lucero added, "maybe fewer."

"Are your families up there?" Canby glanced uphill again, troubled by this news.

Paar shook his head. "Cleo's a widower, and I'm ugly. Women and children up there still, though, sure."

The colonel retrieved another cigar but did not chew it; instead, he tucked it into the grosgrain girding beneath the crown of his hat. "Thank you, gentlemen." He turned to Graydon. "Captain, have someone get these gentlemen some food." A strong easterly wind began to blow. Graydon and the old men left to find a commissary wagon as the Federal batteries paused.

Canby beckoned to Duncan and they put their horses forward a short distance so that they could speak in private. The two men stopped within the shade of a spreading cottonwood, already covered with new leaves. Canby took the cigar from his hat began to chew it. "Haven't fixed how many Texans hold Albuquerque," he said, "but now we know that civilians are trapped in an area that we've been shelling for the last thirty minutes. That about right?"

"Believe so."

"Hmmm. Travel by foot between Fort Union and Tijeras? What, three days, two days?"

"With forced marches, two. If it's those Coloradans we heard about, perhaps even sooner."

"And a little less from here to Santa Fe. A dispatch to Col. Paul, then—he should proceed via the Galisteo Road and meet us at Tijeras—"

"Evacuate Fort Union after all?" A hot gust of wind bent the brim of Duncan's slouch hat upward and made him turn his head.

"Sibley must pay attention to us first—we're the bigger hazard."

Duncan looked up toward Armijo's Mill, where muzzles flashed all along the Texans' line. Groups of men ran between burning buildings. "Do we invest here?"

The colonel chewed in silence, lost in thought for so long that Duncan thought the question would go unanswered. "No battle," Canby said. "Only want 'em to leave."

Duncan puzzled over what would become a constant complaint for the duration of the Texans' stay in New Mexico Territory: why didn't they confront the Confederates directly? "They're in wretched shape, nearly starved—shouldn't we attack now? Have Col. Paul march west?"

"I don't want a battle on the streets of Santa Fe."

Duncan looked west and saw that a low yellow haze obscured the horizon. "Sandstorm," he thought aloud but the colonel was still looking eastward.

"Send that dispatch." Duncan wrote on a small pad of paper. A Federal gun boomed and threw another shell over the canal. "Damn it," Canby shouted, "McDermitt, *cease fire!*"

"And the rest of our attack?" Duncan glanced over at the battery, where its idle crews stood confused.

"Halted for now." Canby wiped at his mouth with the back of a gloved hand. "But I don't want the Texans to know it. Tell McDermitt to aim for open and burnt-out areas. Make a show of digging in but keep all wagons loaded."

"Sir?"

A prudent man by nature, Canby was committing his force to a high-stakes bluff intended to draw the Texans away from Santa Fe. Counting on Gabriel Paul's columns of regulars and Coloradans to arrive within two days, he was betting that the Texans would have no choice but to evacuate, threatened by his larger combined force and the potential loss of their remaining supplies.

With the sun at its apex, the sandstorm began in earnest. Canby turned his horse away from the river. "Post the river road," he shouted, "and the way through Sandia Pueblo."

"Yes, Sir." Duncan shielded his eyes from airborne grit.

"Once their reinforcements are within ten miles, we'll start east over the pass—find Col. Paul and the Coloradans. The Texans will have an open road south out of Albuquerque, and then we'll shadow them to see that they don't loiter."

"Won't he attack Fort Craig then?"

"Hasn't got the strength. Like as not they'll cross the Journada south." Duncan scribbled in his notebook as the wind began to scream. Canby recoiled from a blast of windblown sand. "Come find me if anything develops."

ᘏᘓ

In Santa Fe, news that Canby had emerged from Fort Craig—and that their stores in Albuquerque were threatened—provoked an immediate response from the Texans. Col. Green ordered mounted units south along the river road, and quickly the rest of the Army of New Mexico prepared to evacuate their erstwhile capital.

Fort Marcy, Santa Fe, New Mexico Territory, April 9, 1862

The streets that funneled toward the Cerillos road were roiling; chaos reigned as once again soldiers and civilian sympathizers competed for space. Powhattan Jordan and other Confederate surgeons elected to stay behind and care for their sick and wounded, but all other Texans departed the territorial capital in haste.

Outside the door of his billet, Jacob sat in a chair and sharpened a knife with a small piece of native sandstone. Occasionally, as particularly noisy events occurred on the road at the foot of the hill, he would pause and look up. Otherwise, he persisted in his labor, even as his fellow Texans emptied the fort for the last time. Looking frayed, Briggs Hardy arrived at nine-twenty. Seeing his friend seated there, knapsack and rifle leaned casually against the doorframe, he chewed his lip in frustration. From the barracks, Hardy glanced downhill to the road, where several wagons, both military and civilian, tried to round a particularly tight corner. "Straight pandemonium."

"Briggs," Jacob said and returned to his sharpening.

"Company's assembled near the yard. Abels will stay and help at the hospital, though, so's he can look after Orth and Dupree. You ready?"

Jacob winced at the mention of Orth. "Surgeon took his right arm below the shoulder."

"Shame."

"Dupree ain't coughing so much now, though."

"Looked better," Briggs agreed. "You ready, Jake?"

Jacob looked up and squinted from sunlight that poured through a ragged screen of cloud. "Think I'll stay, too."

"Bad idea." Hardy looked down at the road.

"Can't leave her here—not now."

"Yankees'll kill you."

"Prisoner, maybe—they'll swear me out on parole."

"That's for surgeons and orderlies. They find you with a gun in your hand, they will kill you. C'mon, man—our pickets have fallen back and the Yanks have crossed Arroyo Hondo."

Jacob held the knife blade like a visor and looked at his friend. "I'll catch up."

"Son of a bitch, you'll run straight the other way for Taos!" Hardy retrieved Jacob's rifle and knapsack. These he balanced on his hip, opposite from his own gear. "Come on—Albuquerque's besieged and smoke's risin' in the east. Yanks don't kill you, Carrizo will." Jacob said nothing and resumed his labor. At the bottom of the hill, a fight broke out between two teamsters and several other parties rushed in to restore order. "Fine, wait it out in Mesilla." Hardy looped the canvas strap of Jacob's knapsack over the back of his chair. "Find her once the dust settles, but you can't stay here."

"Rather die than leave her behind." Jacob set the knife on top of the wall. His back still ached, but the swelling in his face had diminished and he could see out of his right eye.

Hardy leaned the rifle against Jacob's knee. "You're leaving Santa Fe, son. Whether with us—with prospects for a return—or boots-first; one way or another, you'll leave here today."

"Take this." He pushed the weapon toward Hardy. "I'll stay and help in the hospital, too."

"That's a lie."

Jacob threw his sharpening stone downhill, where it rolled and bounced until it came to rest under a spiny yucca. "Go on," he said. "The Abs will wash over town and then I'll head north."

"You saved my life in Brownsville, Jacob—now let me return the favor." From the east, there came the muffled sound of gunshots. Again, Hardy leaned the musket against Jacob's knee. "Can't stay here. Carrizo'll have you killed—no question."

"They've left the city—the whole family."

"His influence remains. Look—leave and it'll be four, five months until the water runs clear. Stay and you'll lose everythin'."

Jacob glanced at the street, where for the moment traffic was moving again. A pair of vireos swooped past, landed on a pine bough, and warbled to each other. Seconds later one of the little creatures took flight and vanished into the arroyo. He stood, slung the rifle over his shoulder, and hefted his knapsack and blanket roll. "I *will* see her." A gust of wind shook the trees and the second bird took wing.

"Damn right," Hardy said. He cocked his head to one side and strained to hear faint but persistent sounds of gunfire.

"This is only for now."

"Right," Hardy concurred.

"Everyone's ready?"

"They are." Hardy set foot on a path that led down into the city's heart. "Charlie got 'em well organized, so let's hurry, son—we really gotta hurry."

"Get 'em started, then. I need to deliver something and then I'll find you on the Cerillos road. And don't give me that look."

ഹ

As it happened, Hardy's fears of a slaughter were wildly overblown. Around three that afternoon, a few hours after the last Texan bellig- erents departed for Albuquerque, a single unit of regular U.S. cavalry escorted Governor Connolly and other members of his territorial government into the city. Two riders found the Confederates' hos- pital and informed everyone there of this change. Powhattan Jordan and Samuel Manley shook hands with these men before they went back inside to look after their charges. With that, Santa Fe quietly returned to the Union.

Farther south that same day, Canby's Federals stayed in their lines until scouts reported that fast columns of Texan cavalry had reached Bernallilo, just north of Albuquerque. To complete their ruse, Canby's forces built their usual campfires before stowing their kits and marching fifteen miles east over Carnuel Pass. Just before dawn on April 10, Gen. Sibley and most of the remaining Confederate forces straggled in after an all-night march of their own. Hardeman's troops welcomed these reinforcements with cheers and prepared for a counterattack. As dawn broke, however, Texan scouts discovered the Federals' deserted camp. In an instant, it was clear that there was no longer any possibility of sustaining their camp. Canby had slipped their grasp, and soon he would have the Coloradans—known to have left Fort Union—at his disposal. From Sibley and Green to the blacksmiths and teamsters, each and every Confederate understood that their dreams of conquest had been dashed.

Village of Talpa, Northern New Mexico Territory, April 8, 1862

In 1829, on his twenty-first birthday, Enrique Anton Carrizo (not yet a don) had purchased a small *rancho* above the village of Talpa, a few miles south of Taos. Over time, he expanded his holdings through the acquisition—legitimate and otherwise—of adjacent *suertes* and *ranchos,* and by 1860, these compromised nearly ten thousand acres of planted fields, rangeland, and forest. The ranch was efficient, albeit hampered—like most everyplace in that part of the world—by water problems: superabundance for one month in the spring and scarcity the rest of the year. It was nevertheless profitable and had served as the Carrizo family's refuge in times of crisis.

The first difficulty occurred in 1833, when an expensive shipment of goods from St. Louis had disappeared and an Anglo trading partner blamed Don Carrizo (unfairly, as it happened). When this trader put a bounty on Carrizo, he'd barricaded himself at the ranch and settled the affair with painful cash-diplomacy.

The second exigency came as the Mexican War and Taos revolt rocked the territory: this episode had been more serious by far. In January 1847, when Adria was two, Taoseños rebelled against New Mexico's takeover by the United States. Taos Indians violently resisted the new American officials; anyone with ties to the new government, including Don Carrizo, was a potential target—ironic, as he had armed several of the mutineers. Nearly lynched on the town's plaza, Carrizo himself had to ride to safety in Talpa. A mob had given chase and one intruder had been shot attempting to enter the *casa,* but armed vigilance forestalled the threatened massacre. Hundreds of rebels—including women and children—were not so lucky; at Taos Pueblo, nearly 150 men, women, and children who'd sought refuge in a church were killed by US artillery. Not until the shooting stopped—and nearly 30 rebels had been publicly hanged in Taos—had any member of the Carrizo family left the *rancho*, and not until a third crisis in 1852—the death of Irinea Carrizo and her stillborn son—had any member other than the don returned to Talpa.

Of these three events, Irinea's death had been the most ruinous, and from which it might be said the family had never truly recovered.

☙

Adria hated Talpa. It was queer, quiet, and impossibly rural, and no matter how often her father extolled its rustic virtues, traveling there annoyed her. Her latest visit was the worst. Isolated and aware that she was being watched, she read most mornings and sewed in the evenings. Her only reprieve had been long afternoon rides alone—the one thing for which the *rancho* was useful. Every evening she dreaded her return to the main house for supper.

One afternoon the horse had carried her higher and higher on Talpa Ridge, all the way to the head of Ojitos Cañon. Thinking about Jacob, she dismounted and wondered whether she would ever see him again. Of course, it was unlikely, and this thought made her pain feel as though it meant to be permanent. She looked across the valley at sage-covered flats that unfurled west from the mountains, neatly cleft by the Rio Grande. *Maybe there.* Within that defile, shadows crowded one another for dominion. Her head and heart ached, and when she looked down between her boots, it had taken reservoirs of restraint to keep from jumping into the Rio Chiquito narrows, four hundred feet below. *Maybe here.* A stone rolled from under her heel, hissed through the air as it fell and moments later made an enormous splash in the shallows. *Unchanged,* she marveled—despite this injury, the *rio* continued as before, it's course unaffected. Inhaling, she held onto hope and backed away; determined to know what had happened to Jacob, she chose to endure. She wiped her eyes and decided that although she would obey the letter of her father's strictures, as soon as possible she would leave New Mexico. Whether by one of the trails that radiated from Santa Fe, or by her own hand into some other dark wilderness, never again would anyone rule her world.

༜

Dinner that night was excruciating. Around the long dining table—built to seat twenty—were the don, Adria, Felix Ortiz, and Sol Cooper, one of the don's associates from Missouri. The older men huddled at one end of the table and discussed contracts, while Adria and Felix sat near its waist and mostly ate in silence.

"Pleasant ride?" Felix said. He was nearly as tired of Talpa, and just as resentful of its isolation. He raised a wineglass to his lips.

Felix had been drinking for hours; even from across the table she could smell his breath. "Winds drove me down from the ridge."

"Bad on the river road today, too—dusty." He nodded. "Any snow up there still?"

"Only a little." Adria picked at her food. "Dirty patches on the north-facing slopes. Have you seen Tircio lately?"

"The don told me he had an accident—went home to his family in Mora. Why?"

"Strange not to see him is all. I pray it's nothing serious."

Again, the pair lapsed into silence. He stared at her and studied her delicate features. *Why not?* He thought. *Sílo was suitable—why not me? My brother is dead and the don himself said I am the better man. My God, she is a lovely thing, too. Don Carrizo's daughter and his money—Joseph and Mary, the things I will do...* Before long, she caught his gaze and narrowed her eyes in return.

At the head of the table, the hacendado smiled graciously. "Felix, Adria—our business is done. Please, come be social." Felix glanced at Adria, who pushed away from the table and stood mechanically while a servant came forward to re-set their places nearer the table's head.

Adria made a small curtsey to her father's guest, a short man—shorter than Don Carrizo—with thick black hair, topped with a skullcap and a neatly trimmed beard. His teeth were a shambles but his eyes were kind, and he bowed politely in return. The don held his wineglass up to the light. "*Señor* Cooper says the trail east is clear again."

"Good," Felix said, eager to contribute. "Normal commerce can resume?"

"The Texans are leaving," Cooper said, "but the Indians have taken advantage of the Army's preoccupation. I lose most two of every thirty wagons that depart Independence."

"To Indians?"

"Not all," Cooper conceded. "The whole of Missouri is roiling now. Battles at Wilson's Creek, Lexington, and Belmont last year. Fayette this year—why, even now New Madrid is under the gun. Still, the Comanches and Kiowa account for most of my losses."

Don Carrizo motioned for a servant to clear the plates and leaned forward in his chair. "Once the graybacks are gone, the U.S. Army will move against the Indians."

"I wouldn't count on much help, Anton—I've had to arm my drivers to the teeth."

"Wise," Felix said.

"Solomon," the don interjected, "tell Adria what you saw in Santa Fe yesterday." He shifted uncomfortably in his chair—his back still ached from his fight with the Texan *capitán*.

Cooper struggled to recall anything of interest. "The flag?"

"Yes." Carrizo smiled at his daughter. Adria caught this attention and squeezed her hands tightly together in her lap. She recognized his posture as something he reserved for guests: smiles, inclusion— and though she smiled prettily in return, cancerous contempt grew inside.

"Not much happened," Cooper began, "except that Federal riders escorted Governor Connelly into the city and promptly lowered the filth-covered sheet that the rebels had hung as a parting gesture. Now our dear flag is flying once more."

"How wonderful," Adria murmured drily.

"This sort of talk probably bores you. I have two daughters back in St. Louis, one a little younger than you, and she tells me that she is positively terrified of Southern soldiers."

"Why is that?" Adria tone made the don wince a little.

"Oh," Cooper laughed, "because that's how I raised her."

The don laughed politely and looked at Felix. "Yes, I expect that soon things will be quieter around here—much quieter."

"Of course," Felix said. Servants brought in small berry *tortas* for dessert.

"Indians and banditry," Cooper continued, "are what the Army must now address."

"Bandits?" Adria asked innocently, "Are they a problem in New Mexico?"

"Oh, far worse than the Indians! Why, many of the worst are even deserters from our own militias!"

Adria noticed that Felix bend forward to study his plate. "Anyone you know, Felix?"

"No." He feigned indifference. "Some of our men went down to Fort Union. Others put aside their weapons—"

"As you did," she said.

"I have other responsibilities," he bristled. "And the Anglo officers don't respect us."

The don rested a hand on Adria's forearm but looked at Felix. "The past few months have been difficult for everyone—let's not bicker."

Adria entertained poisonous thoughts while Felix attacked his dessert. *Even poor Basilio*, she thought, *was man enough to resist the invasion.* For the very first time, she something like affection for her missing fiancée.

☙

Normally it was too cold to remain outdoors after dark in mid-April, but lately it had been unseasonably warm and so the party adjourned to a small patio on a hill immediately north of the main house. Over brandies, Cooper and the don contemplated another deal; Adria and Felix sought opposite corners of the terrace. At one point the don pulled Felix aside and asked whether he'd let slip about his work, particularly in Peralta and La Rinconada. Carrizo did not reveal that Stark had mentioned the former, and when Felix answered without evident guile, the don left him with an admonition to watch his alcohol. Then he crossed the patio and escorted his daughter onto a carefully manicured patch of grass.

"Warm already," he said. His back ached even worse than before and his movements were stiff. Thirty feet below, the path diverged: right toward the stables and left toward the hacienda's front door. Overhead a waning quarter-moon sailed across the sky and cast faint shadows beneath the chamiso. "Was your day pleasant?" he tried again and this time she answered.

"Yes, Papi—windy, but nice."

"Where did you go?"

"To the top of Talpa Ridge."

The don sighed. "I don't like you riding alone—I worry that you range so far by yourself."

"I'm always careful."

"Darling, these days one cannot be too careful. *Señor* Cooper's right about bandits—it'll be some time before this territory is safe again."

"I'll carry a shotgun, then."

The don shook his head. "Just stay close—weapons aren't anything for women to handle."

She nodded, except that she already knew how to use and clean the shotguns, rifles, and revolvers he kept locked in a room at the back of the house.

"Things will get better." He put an arm around her shoulders. "I've been too preoccupied to pay you the attention you deserve, and for that I am sorry."

She leaned against him, feeling some flicker of the closeness she remembered from her childhood. "It's all right, Papi."

"No, it's not." He looked out across the sage flats to a picket of tall cottonwoods. "I remember being your age; remember the exertions I put my parents through." He exhaled a little and continued: "Before I met your mother there was an Indian girl in Santo Domingo who caught my eye, but your grandparents would not suffer me to see her. I am sorry if this embarrasses you, but I say it only to let you know that I understand. And while you may not comprehend it now, as I did not then, my parents were right. Our traditions give us strength and our strength protects and keeps us together." He gestured with his free hand toward the darkness. "Out there are multitudes who would take everything from us—our land, our wealth, our history—some by force, others by deceit. Only by protecting ourselves from such people will we survive."

"Papi—"

"Adria, I only wish that you would realize your worth."

Adria followed his gaze. She traced the thin, pale line of the road as it followed the *bajada's* undulating terminations above the river. "Do you think that Felix has our interests at heart?"

"Whatever do you mean?"

"I don't trust him."

"The Ortizes are our friends." The don faced his daughter. "In time you may find Felix more to your liking."

Adria struggled to contain her revulsion. "Papi, he is repellent," she said and locked eyes with her father.

Don Carrizo raised a hand but quelled his impulse to slap his daughter. Adria flinched, and it pleased him to know that his authority remained. He let his hand drop and turned to look across the flats, where a coyote was loping between mounds of sage. "Tell me something, girl—have you ever accompanied me to Peralta?"

"Where?" Adria's lip trembled. "Never."

"Not with the Dueros? Or Don Alvarado?"

"No."

"This is important—*think!*"

"I've never been *Rio Abajo*—never been south of Albuquerque."

She sounded sincere, but it was dark and he could not read her expression. "Two days ago a Texan came to our house—"

"Who?"

"It doesn't matter, but he wanted to know if you'd been to Peralta. Any idea why he'd ask that?"

"Was it Jacob Stark?" she asked, unable to stop herself, knowing even as she said it exactly how this question would be received. "Is he well?"

"Adria Magdalena!" This time the don slapped her hard across her face; both Cooper and Felix looked up at the sound. "I am ashamed

of you!" he wheezed, having wrenched his back in the process. "Now answer me—why does that bastard want to know whether or not you've been to Peralta?"

Tears beaded in the corners of her eyes. "I don't know," she said.

"You've *never* been there?" He grabbed her wrist and squeezed.

"Never!" She shook her head. "I don't know what he meant."

"Believe me, you will rue the day you first saw him." He stared into her eyes, but this time she did not flinch and so he relented. He forced a wan smile. "Things will get better." He gave her a small hug and kissed her forehead. Then he escorted her down the stairs and went to bid Cooper good night.

৵

Near midnight, with the household abed and crickets chirping in the grass, she realized what Jacob had meant. *Darling, of course!* Her heart raced. She dressed quietly and packed a small bag. She grabbed a few foodstuffs from the pantry, a new J.D. Dougall ten-gauge shotgun and a revolver from the armory, and slipped out to the stables.

North of the Village of Las Trampas, New Mexico Territory, April 9, 1862

Adria pinched her horse's nostrils to keep it from nickering to the others on the road below. She leaned against the trunk of a huge ponderosa and wished for more cover—wished that locals hadn't logged the hillside so heavily. Now there was nowhere to run, no way to hide—she would be safe only if she held still and the two men there did not look up.

Her horse stepped on a branch and one of the men's mounts looked toward the sound. Its rider, too, looked up, swept the woods with his eyes, and lit on the incongruity of Adria's profile against a deep green backdrop. Quickly, he reined in and whistled to the other rider.

Adria stepped uphill of the big tree and pressed her back against the bark. *My God, why? Why did they follow?* Since daybreak, she'd been aware that men were behind her. When first she'd glimpsed them, they were almost five miles back, but within an hour they had gained on her despite the fact that she had pressed her animal hard. Now they had caught her on a hillside a few miles south of the small village of Las Trampas. She did not recognize the Indian who'd whistled, but she'd known that the other rider was Felix even before he'd turned uphill to look.

"Adria!" he called. "Come on, no one's gonna hurt you!" He dismounted and threw his animal's reins over a tree branch. The Indian rode ahead toward the mouth of the ravine that Adria herself had followed uphill.

"Leave me alone!" she shouted. She checked the shotgun to see that both barrels were loaded and dug in a saddlebag for the revolver, only to find that it was buried too deeply for quick retrieval. She glanced around the tree, saw that Felix had left his rifle tied to his saddle, and prayed that he wasn't carrying a pistol.

"Adria, this is silly," he yelled and walked straight uphill, directly toward her. He grabbed a branch to pull himself up a particularly steep stretch and his boots scrambled to find purchase in the deep carpet of pine needles. "Your father's worried about you—I'm worried, too. You didn't have to run." He stepped sideways in pursuit of a better view, unable to see anything more than Adria's left leg and shoulder behind the tree.

"I won't go back, Felix—I will not."

Felix stopped, the fronts of his feet balanced on a narrow rock ledge, his heels out over the short drop. "Why not? What do you have against me?"

"Nothing—leave me alone!" Adria's horse stamped nervously and pulled against its reins, anxious to get free.

He glanced toward the ravine into which his partner had disappeared and then back uphill. "Why are you doing this?" he said. "*Mire,* a storm's coming—we must get off this mountain. The don wants you home—I want you home. Why won't you listen?"

Adria, too, glanced over at the ravine and guessed that by then the Indian had attained the same elevation as she, though he was nowhere to be seen. She choked back a mouthful of bile and took a huge breath to steady her nerves. Her heart beat so rapidly that it hurt. "Leave me alone, Felix. Leave me alone or—"

"Or what? Girl, *you don't have a say!*" He took another step uphill and stood on a massive tree stump. "Hey, *tipo,*" he shouted, "bring your rope!"

Adria hugged the shotgun tightly to her chest, her palms slippery with sweat. Her horse whinnied and the Indian's animal answered, uphill and to her right. She listened for signs that Felix was moving. Hearing none, again she scanned the ridgeline. *Where had the other man gone?*

Felix yawned. He stepped down from the stump and walked sideways across the hill until he stood directly below Adria and the tree. "You don't like me, do you, *amor?*"

She could just see him out of the corner of her eye and judged that he was about forty feet away. Slowly she lifted the shotgun in parallel with her body so that when the need came she could aim it quickly. *There!* She saw a flicker of movement in the woods above but realized it was only the ears of the Indian's horse—she could not find Billy himself. A small rock skittered downhill on her left. She glanced in that direction, several degrees from where she had spotted the horse, but still there was no sign. *God, please, show him to me.*

"Adria?" Felix said. "You're a smart girl—too smart, really—and I know you don't believe what I've said. That's a credit to you, see? I could have made you happy. But now I'm done—done hoping that you'll give me the attention I deserve. Sílo didn't trust you either—know that? He knew you'd refuse your bit, but he never did anything about it. Well, I won't stand for that. Will not. You may be wild now, but I'm going to break you. *Mire,* I'm coming up there right now to bring you back—back down where you belong. Some scrapes and bruises along the way, maybe, but that's exactly what you need, *entienda?*"

"Felix, wait!" Adria screamed. Her breath came faster now, shallower, and she felt dangerously dizzy. "Let my father decide and I will come down." Another rock skittered downhill, bounced off a stump, and clattered loudly against the tree trunk beside her. She thought she saw a shadow move, but it was only a limb swaying in the wind.

Felix laughed. "You think that's wise? Think he'll be any—"

"Do you *promise?*" she screamed.

Felix thought for a moment. "Don't know," he said. "I, too, doubt the things I've heard—from both of you. Think I will come up there and sort this out myself." He stepped onto one rock and then hopped uphill to another.

As he moved from her left to right, he disappeared behind the huge tree—disappeared from her peripheral vision, and as she rolled her head to her right she saw Billy standing there, slightly uphill but no more than ten feet away. He had a rope in his hands but wore a surprised look, evidently having mistaken the shotgun in Adria's arms for nothing more than a stick.

"*Felix!*" he shouted, "she's got—"

Adria lowered the muzzle and pulled the trigger. One of the barrels emptied, severing Billy's right leg below the knee. He toppled from the ledge where he'd stood and rolled almost twenty feet until his arm hooked around the base of a tree. Billy screamed in pain, screamed for help but Felix, too, had stepped backward and fallen. Scrambling laterally in the dirt, he flattened himself against a tree trunk. He'd lost sight of Adria and glanced wildly from left to right, unable to locate her.

Adria stepped out from behind the ponderosa, sat, and slid down the steep slope as best she could. Her skirts caught on rocks and branches and when she dug her heels in and stopped on par with Felix, they were gathered well above her waist. "*Stand up!*" she shouted. The hem of her skirt had caught in the crook of her elbow and her legs were exposed. "Hands up and get down to the road! Do anything stupid, Felix—there's another barrel here for you, *entienda?*"

Felix complied and half-walked, half-slid until his boots touched the road, aware that Adria was on a parallel course about twenty yards to his left. He stood and wiped at a bloody welt on his forehead.

In the woods above, Billy continued to scream and weep and while the sound made Adria feel sick, not once did she take her eyes off Felix. "Step back!" She noted again that his rifle was tied below the cantle of his saddle, above a rolled blanket, so she stepped forward and made him back away. With one hand, she untied the leather thongs around the blanket and threw it on the ground. She kept her eyes locked on his and groped for a knife she had seen tied to the horn. His horse pawed at the dirt and jostled her but she held the shotgun's stock steady in her armpit as she made a series of cuts in the blanket's edge. Finished, she threw the fabric on the ground at Felix's feet. "Carry that," she said.

"What for?"

She curled her lip and aimed the shotgun at his chest. "Take it."

"Worthless *bitch*," Felix seethed, but Adria marched him back up the ravine with the tattered blanket thrown over his shoulder. Billy had stopped screaming but he was babbling like someone who had no grasp of where they were or how they'd gotten there.

Adria untied Billy's mount and walked both it and Felix straight downhill until they drew near to her horse. At a point adjacent to where the Indian lay, they stopped again. "Tear that blanket into strips," she said. "Tie off his leg."

"He'll die, thanks to you."

"Or perhaps he'll live, thanks to *you*. Now, go get him!"

Felix scrambled up out of the ravine and traversed the ledge with Adria close behind. Her body ached in unfamiliar ways and she was exhausted from lack of sleep, but she remained powerfully focused. At one point, she saw Felix's hand had curl around a rock. Guessing what he meant to do, she warned him of the consequences and watched with satisfaction as he pushed ahead, unarmed. Billy got no better treatment on his descent, as Felix had to both skid him down the hillside on his back and lead Adria's old, brokedown mare by its reins. The Indian was pale and in shock, but the tourniquet had worked and he would live. Once Adria untied the panniers from her horse's saddle, she ordered Felix to lift Billy's limp form and throw it across the mare's back. Then Felix himself climbed on and felt the old horse sag under his weight.

With the shotgun still raised, Adria stared at him. The look he returned was so venomous that for a moment she thought to pull the trigger and be done with him. Then she felt an unaccountable pity for this husk of a man, so small and useless that he was beneath contempt. "I know what you're thinking," she said. "No need to tell me how much you hate me, how little you think of me—I don't care. I do not understand you, Felix, and will not try to now. Go back to Talpa—tell my father whatever you want. Tell him I know what you have done in his name. Go back and make of yourself what you will. For once in your life, go and be a man." She tapped the mare's rump with the muzzle and the animal started forward. Felix did not look back and within a hundred yards they disappeared behind a bend in the road.

Without delay, she tied Billy's horse behind Felix's and took everything useful she could find—weapons, food, and blankets. Aching and wary, her movements were brisk and businesslike. *Don't let your guard down—there is nothing to celebrate.* To paraphrase something Jacob had said on the night they'd met: unless this rebellion succeeds, none of the in-between will matter. Within ten minutes, she was riding south again, as fast as the horses would go.

The Canby Residence, Santa Fe, New Mexico Territory, April 10, 1862

A small Stars-and-Stripes stood out from its flagpole, held stiff by the furnace-like winds that had blown in from the western deserts. Even with the sun low on the western horizon, heat still clung to the soil and already, scant weeks into spring, Louisa Canby was sure that her newly planted garden would wither and die. *Onions and chilies alone can stand this weather.* She paused to mop her brow. She and her two hired girls had been working for hours, raking up debris left by the retreating Confederates. She was glad for the return to normalcy, certainly, though this did not mean that she wasn't worried—both for her husband, still in the field, and for those desperately unwell Texans who'd nevertheless risen from their cots and marched south with the others. She'd overheard a trader from El Paso insist that the Federals meant only to herd the Texans south, not to engage them in open warfare—but what did that mean? Wasn't there the possibility still—no, the *certainty*—of bloodshed? She thought it unlikely that some kind of gentlemen's agreement existed between belligerents but then again, being married to a solider did not mean she understood the rules, written or otherwise, that governed an ungovernable thing like war. She hummed softly to herself as she raked and noticed the bits of rag and rope littering her yard. The Texans had departed in a terrific hurry and there had been no chance to say goodbye to many, including Col. Green and Gen. Sibley. Of course, that was in keeping with the desultory nature of their whole venture—*Lo que volando viene, volando se va,* as her Mexican neighbors sometimes said.

That evening she meant to visit Governor Connolly before she delivered more bread to the Texans' hospital. She hoped the governor might have news about Edward, but she'd heard that Connolly, a Union firebrand who was calling for an attack on the retreating Texans, was displeased that she had come to their aid. Perhaps he would refuse to see her—an insult easily borne, and one that would free up her evening so that she might get to bed earlier than usual. Lost in thought, she did not hear the gravel crunching beneath the approaching buggy's wheels, nor did she hear Adria Carrizo calling her name. Not until one of the hired girls motioned did she look up and see her young neighbor.

"Mrs. Canby! Thank God you're here!"

"Goodness, Adria, hello!" Louisa set her rake against the porch rail and waved to this unexpected visitor. "I thought you'd gone north!" Adria practically fell out of the buggy in her effort to reach Louisa. She clasped her arms around the older woman and at first said nothing. Louisa thought the girl looked worn and tired, as if she'd ridden for days, even though the two mules hitched to the buggy looked fresh. "I'm glad you've come," Louisa said, somewhat baffled by the seriousness of the embrace. "I have a message for you."

"Mrs. Canby..." the girl began, but her tongue was dry and she choked on her words.

"Adria, what is it? What's the matter?" Louisa placed her hands on the young woman's shoulders and tried to look her in the eye. Then she noticed the scrapes and bruises, and her hand flew involuntarily to her mouth. "What did he do?"

"Mrs. Canby, I am in such trouble!"

Louisa clasped Adria's hands until the girl's breathing slowed. "No matter what it is, you are safe here," she said. "Let me get your things." She pulled a small valise from the buggy while the girl walked forward to loop the animals' reins around a porch rail. Both women took chairs in the shade. "You are safe here," Louisa repeated, but she noticed that her young friend continued to wring her hands.

"Mrs. Canby, I may never be safe again."

Louisa startled. "I can have soldiers here if necessary. Adria, tell me what happened!"

Adria gave a brief account of events over the previous ten days and concluded in tears. "I must leave New Mexico at once." She rose and began to pace.

"Stay here until your father calms down," Louisa said.

"He won't—not ever. And it doesn't matter now—"

"Of course it matters! What if the authorities come?"

"Who has authority now? I must leave, Mrs. Canby! I have to *leave!*"

Louisa stood, took the girl into her arms and held her tightly. "Darling, you will survive this. Somehow—we will find a way."

"What has become of Jacob? Wherever he is, that is where I must go!"

Louisa wrinkled her brow. "I told you I have a message for you— Jacob Stark brought a letter here before he left. He's fine, Adria—he rode away with the others."

"He's gone?" The girl's knees buckled and she sank into her chair.

For a long time Louisa tried to read the girl's expression. *So much fear, so much heartache, all on account of this wretched war.* While Adria rocked gently back and forth on the chair, Louisa motioned to one of the hired girls out in the yard. "Becky, go get the letter lying on top of my dresser."

The girl returned a minute later. "This one, Ma'am?"

"Yes, thank you. Adria, Jacob came here and asked that I give this to you."

Quickly Adria broke the wax seal and scanned the brief, undated note.

Dearest Adria, The Army of New Mexico is leaving, and so must I, but do not worry: somehow soon I will see you again. We are inextricably bound, you and I, and I believe that whatever happiness I am due in this life will come from time spent with you. You are perfection. Whatever the outcome in Albikirkie, I will wait for you in Peralta. If we are victorious, I will resign my commission; if not, I'll chance my parole. By whatever means, get to Peralta. If you cannot, send word of some other place and there I will go. If by June's end I have not heard from you, I will return to Santa Fe, no matter the result. Please do not stop looking for me and know that I will remain vigilant for any sign of your situation. You have completely absorbed me and with eager reluctance, I mark the hours until we are together again. I love you, now and forever. Jacob.

"Now and forever," Adria whispered. She clutched the paper to her chest, buoyed at finding her happier instincts confirmed. "When did he leave?"

"Two days ago." Louisa smiled at seeing her young friend brighten. "Word arrived yesterday that my husband has left Fort Craig with two-thousand men, which accounts for the Texan's flight."

"Will they stay in Albuquerque?"

Louisa shook her head. "They cannot stay in New Mexico."

"Then I must get to Peralta."

"Adria, no!" Louisa pursed her lips. "The army has closed all roads south and all travel save military concerns is prohibited."

Adria glanced south, as if she expected to see the rear of the Texans' column somewhere on the horizon. "I've come this far—"

"The army won't allow it," Louisa said. "Even with a pass, no one could protect you."

"I cannot go back," Adria whispered.

"Whoever he is, he isn't worth your life."

"Until I met Jacob, I didn't know what my life was worth. I *must* find him, Mrs. Canby."

Louisa looked at Adria, expecting her to grasp the futility of her desires; instead, the girl's eyes burned so brightly that Louisa herself was moved. Neither spoke; the only sound was the scritch-scritch-scritch of the hired girls' rakes in the dirt. Adria's gaze never left Louisa's face. Made uncomfortable by her own conscience—by her attempt at dissuading Adria from obeying hers—Louisa lowered her eyes. After a few moments, she looked up and laid a hand on the young woman's shoulder. "Stay here tonight—I will see what I can do."

Santa Fe, New Mexico Territory, April 11, 1862

Well before breakfast, unseen by anyone, Adria returned to her family's rancho west of Santa Fe, retrieved a few items, and left a note where only Benéfica would find it. Within an hour, she returned to the Canbys' and found Louisa drinking tea at her kitchen table. She thought Mrs. Canby looked exceedingly tense. Pangs of guilt made her stop in the doorway, sorry that she had requested such an extraordinary favor. "Ma'am, is everything well?"

Louisa's eyes flashed with uncharacteristic ire and she turned the empty cup in her hands. "Like a fool, I'd expected greater civility from our own—from *Americans!* My word, it's hot already!"

Adria hesitated, unsure how to react. "Mrs. Canby?"

"Officious wastrels," Louisa muttered, "scurrile idiots!" Louisa rose from her chair and crossed the room. She took Adria's travel bag and set it on a chair in the corner.

Worried that her father had somehow intervened, Adria's voice quavered: "Mrs. Canby, do you mean that I should stay in Santa Fe?"

"What? No, *no!* I'm sorry, dear." Aware that she'd upset her guest, Louisa softened the hard cast of her features. "We are delayed but a little."

"My father will be here tomorrow."

"I know. I'd hoped we would be able to travel with the army, but the commanding officer in Santa Fe is an unimaginative prig, a blockhead for rules, so it'll be a few hours more until we can leave."

"Is there anything I can do?"

"No, thank you—no one forges Col. Canby's signature better than I." She looked out on the yard, where swirling winds had raised small dust devils. "Actually, you can move my bag from the runabout into the larger buckboard that is parked inside the barn."

"The army rig?"

"I hope you can drive it—I can't."

"I think so."

"That one is better suited for desert travel, and I believe it will lend credibility to the story I am proposing to tell."

"'Story'?"

"Lie," Louisa said and smiled a little. "Seems I cannot leave Santa Fe with integrity, but leave it we will. No one can tell me otherwise."

Confederate Encampment, Isleta Pueblo, New Mexico Territory

---

13 April, 1862—Too tired to write much. Reports of a big battle in northwest Arkansas in early March, where it is said that Gen. Van Dorn won the field but lost the fight—sounds familiar. 2,600 dead between the two sides. Marched all day but covered only fourteen miles. Slow'd considerably by Col. Scurry's insistence that we drag the Yankee cannon captured at Valverde back to Texas as trophies. A more useless gesture I cannot imagine, though it is inexplicably popular. Our scouts bring conflicting reports: some have the Yanks up near Galisteo still; others say Canby's Yankees and the Coloradans have combined east of Albikirkie and may set upon us at any time. Once we reach Peralta, I will see if there isn't some place I can take cover. By to-morrow, certainly.

This was the only entry Jacob would make in his new journal. He spent the rest of the evening drafting a letter of resignation.

Village of San Antonito, New Mexico Territory, April 13, 1862

———•———

Mindful of the chaos (and spying) that had prevailed when civilians had been permitted to move freely on the Santa Fe Trail, following the battle at Glorieta, Col. Canby ordered roadblocks set on the major north-south routes until his forces could effect a juncture with Union troops under Gabriel Paul and John Chivington near the village of Tijeras. Travelers and traders without official passes were stranded in the capital.

While most every other corner of the territory roasted under cloudless skies, high on the Sandia Mountains' broad eastern slope, it was relatively cool and pleasant. There, pine forests swayed gently and aspen, newly leafed in ephemeral green, trembled in each passing breeze. Despite these pleasant conditions, Lt. James Hay found his roadblock duties terminally boring. His command, comprised of the Pinebark Independents plus an attached company of New Mexicans, took turns standing guard behind a freight wagon that they had parked across the track. In two days, those who weren't on watch had slept more than they had the entire two weeks prior. On the second evening, a few of the New Mexicans had even gone off to hunt and returned with a small buck deer, but otherwise the assignment had been uneventful.

On the afternoon of April 13, Hay and Douglas were standing in the shade and quizzing one of the interdicted teamsters about doings in St. Louis. Douglas had been sipping water from his canteen when he saw one of the New Mexicans waving for attention down at the block. He elbowed the lieutenant and pointed.

"What?" Hay shouted across the field.

"Wagon comin', Lieutenant."

"So what?" He faced Douglas. "What's his name again?"

"Juan Soler, I trou. S'what I've called him anyhow, and he don't object."

"No, Lieutenant," Soler called, "you'd better come see." Hay retrieved a Springfield from against a tree and waded downhill into the tall grass.

On the road, a green buckboard with orange wheels and black rims had pulled up to the block. In it were two dusty women—one white and middle-aged, the other Mexican and young. *Uncommon company,* Hay thought. As he drew close, he was struck by the younger woman's beauty—probably the prettiest girl he'd ever seen—and it was she who was driving the rig, four mules in-hand. No knowing whether to address her or the older woman, he tipped his cap to both. "Sorry, ladies—road's closed for the now."

"We have a pass." Louisa Canby proffered a folded sheet of paper.

"Aye?" Hay took the document. "Where to?"

"Atrisco, just across the river from Albuquerque."

Hay studied the papers intently and glanced a couple of times at each woman. "Ma'am, we've orders to turn aside all but them with Col. Paul's say-so, aye?" The New Mexican volunteers stood by impassively as Hay continued: "Ye can't continue us this road 'til the army moves. Should be done the night."

Adria chewed her lip nervously, but Louisa smiled, unfazed by the rejection. "We cannot wait that long."

This was the first challenge since the block had been set and Hay raised an eyebrow. "Ma'am, ye cannot continue."

Louisa glanced above Hay's head in the direction of Tijeras. "Your counterparts at the Cerillos block allowed us through."

"Is this a government wagon, Ma'am?" Something was amiss but exactly what Hay couldn't tell. He saw that the Mexican girl had removed her gloves, and with her delicate hands, he couldn't imagine that she could drive a mule in town, nonetheless across the desert and over a mountain.

"Yes—we use this wagon to carry my husband's effects between Santa Fe and the forts."

"Who's he?" Hay glanced again at Louisa's papers.

"The departmental commander," Louisa said. "Col. Paul's commanding officer, in fact."

Hay affixed his eyes to the names on the pass noting Col. Canby's signature, and his face turned so red that Adria had to raise her hand to stifle a laugh.

Hay fought to maintain his equilibrium. "Your driver, Ma'am— who's she?"

"My niece," Louisa said. "Do you need to see her papers, too?"

"They're right here," Adria said and reached for the strongbox behind her seat.

"No—hold by, please." Hay stepped away to speak with Douglas.

While Hay conferred with his sergeant, Louisa put her hand on Adria's. "Won't be long, now," she whispered.

Hay returned with Douglas in tow. Douglas, even more nonplussed to see Adria up close, didn't even try to maintain decorum: "Jaysus tonight," he whispered, loud enough that everyone there heard. Wide-eyed, he nodded along with everything Hay said, though in truth he didn't hear a word.

Hay waved his hand toward the south. "The roads aren't safe, Ma'am, but if your niece thinks she can manage—"

"I can," Adria said and donned her gloves.

"Steep grade ahead."

"I'll chain and skid the wheels if necessary."

"We appreciate your concern, Lieutenant," Louisa brightened, fanning herself.

Hay lifted his forage cap. "Ma'am, Sergeant Douglas here will accompany ye as far as Tijeras."

"Why, thank you!" Louisa said. "That's very kind. What is your name, Lieutenant? When next I see my husband I'll mention your thoughtfulness."

"James Hay, Ma'am." He shifted his weight from one foot to another, nervous at the prospect of official detection. "Pinebark Independents, First Colorado Regiment."

"Thank you, Lieutenant Hay." As soon as Douglas had untethered his horse and drawn alongside, Adria flicked the reins and the rig surged forward. When they rolled past Soler and the New Mexicans, Adria caught the sound of tongues clucked in mild disgust. Making sure Douglas did not see, she flashed a knowing grin at Louisa, who winked in return. "I've forgotten to ask," Louisa whispered, "where did you learn to handle a string such as this?"

Adria glanced at the reins in her hand. "I didn't want to be stranded like my mother, so I bribed one of my father's teamsters to teach me."

Louisa's eye traced the Sandias' broad, pine-covered slopes, slowly slipping past as the mules plodded south. Clouds of alkaline road-dust glittered white against the pale blue sky. "And how did you keep the don from finding out?"

"All those trips up to Talpa when I was younger, he rode with me only occasionally." Adria watched Douglas weave lazily in his saddle.

"Wasn't Benéfica with you?"

"Almost always."

Louisa watched as a grasshopper whirred over the wagon's tongue and lit in the blue-green sage growing alongside the track. "I wouldn't have thought that she'd permit such liberated adventures."

Adria smiled. "Honestly, it was her idea."

❧

Back across the meadow, Hay was greeted with loud complaints from the idled teamsters. "Shut up!" he snarled, "Their papers were in order." When the protests continued, Hay spat on the ground and set a harder edge to his voice: "Shut your goddamn holes or ye can rot here all summer!"

Village of Atrisco, New Mexico Territory, April 14, 1862

Louisa reached up and set a jar of water on the buckboard's seat. Her eyes were red—not from the bright mid-morning sun, but from crying—and her breath came in little gasps. "Now that we are here," she said, "I cannot believe that I ever agreed to such a reckless course. My heart flutters like a bird caught in a snare."

"Don't grieve, Mrs. Canby," Adria said, though her own face was tearstained. "I will be perfectly safe."

"Dearest girl," Louisa said, "I cry not only for your safety, but on the chance that you will succeed. If you do, I may never see you again!" She wiped at her eyes with a sleeve. "I did not bring you into this world, Adria, but I consider you my daughter—a sacred trust, and I fear your mother would not look kindly upon what I have done."

Adria turned her eyes east across the river. The broad *bajada* below Sandia Peak was stitched with crazy-quilt roads and dotted with greening vineyards, peach and poplar trees. Never before had she ventured so far south; never had she been untethered from her family. She inhaled deeply and brushed tears from her cheeks. "Mrs. Canby, I'm sure my mother is smiling. I am, too, though it may not look it."

Both women broke into gentle, rueful laughter. Adria leaned down from the seat, wrapped her arms around Louisa's shoulders, and held tightly. "These past few years, I've thought of you as my mother, too—words cannot convey the depth of my gratitude."

"They just did." Louisa returned the embrace and sobbed gently. "I'll pray for your safety, Adria, and expect that if the need arises you will send word."

"Yes." Adria squeezed her friend even tighter. "I will."

"Wherever you are, I will be there as swiftly as I can. Please be safe—*please!*"

"I appreciate everything you've done for me, Mrs. Canby. We will see each other again—I know it."

"Yes, of course," Louisa whispered and released her grip. She brushed a curl from Adria's face, before reaching into her own skirt pocket for an envelope. "Take this, Adria, won't you?"

The girl studied its blank cover. "What is it?"

"A letter for Col. Canby, should you chance to meet him. From here, I will watch the Army descend Carnuel Pass before it turns south. He will be somewhere in that procession."

"I hope you are reunited soon."

"As do I, dear. Now, you had best be going or they will slip ahead and all this will be for naught."

Adria pulled the reins taut. "Thank you, Mrs. Canby."

Louisa stepped away from the buckboard. She raised her right hand and clenched the other tightly. Adria waved in return as the mules pulled the wagon in a wide arc around the yard and turned onto the road. Within minutes, Adria was nearly beyond Louisa's sight, though at the crest of a small ridge she waved one last time. Again, Mrs. Canby raised her hand and watched the wagon vanish into the trees along the river—trees whose new leaves shimmered in the bright sunshine. Then she turned and walked back toward the porch, and once her feet touched the wooden planks, the owner of the home, who had observed Adria's departure from a polite distance, had to catch Louisa before she collapsed.

Village of Peralta, New Mexico Territory, April 14, 1862

With darkness, the crickets and cicadas began an insane musical racket, yet the Confederates' party at Henry Connolly's place was louder still. Having missed the pro-Union governor's house on their journey north, as Sibley's Brigade retreated southward, it had been sacked—stripped of anything useful, edible, or flammable. While the rank-and-file stomped through greening fields to throw furniture and fence rails into a constellation of bonfires, officers helped themselves to the contents of a well-stocked wine cellar. Many fell asleep, though others stayed drunk well into the early hours.

Jacob Stark, Briggs Hardy, and the other junior officers of the Fifth had each downed several bottles apiece, including—by Hardy alone—a rare and ancient seventeenth-century Madeira that he'd declared "damned peculiar" (but which he'd nevertheless finished). They toasted each of their dead comrades by name, which had taken some time. Jacob paced himself, but having gone without a drink for almost a year, eventually he fell victim to sheer numbers. "Shit," he whispered, "we really lose this many? Who'da known?"

"Me," Hardy raised a single index finger. "I'us kept score."

"Hush." Jacob pursed his lips and screwed up his features. "When'd y'all get so ob-servant?"

"Honest," Hardy protested. "Made'a lish the other day and it jes' grew and grew."

"'Lish'?"

"Lis-*tuh*. Y'all go t'hell." Then he fell silent and fearfully beheld the room as it began to spin.

391

Jacob turned to answer someone else's question and by the time he'd finished, Hardy was slumped over the table. "Hey, one'a you nasty cowpunchers come help me move this heavy bastard." They rolled him against the base of a wall with a coverless book for a pillow.

⁓

That afternoon a cold front had moved in and the temperature fell twenty degrees from what it had been just the night before. The sounds of barking dogs, glass breaking, and fiddles drifted over from the fields, and Jacob stumbled wildly as he walked. It was a struggle to find his borrowed horse, and his climb into the saddle was even worse. For good measure, he drove his face into an eave that overhung the porch roof and split his lip. He spat blood, reined the animal around, and tapped its sides with his bootheels. "Shit, go!"

Jacob rode slowly between bunkhouses until Pleasant Oakes lurched out of a doorway. The horse flinched and forced Jacob to grab its mane and hold on for dear life. Oakes stumbled badly and fell into a wall, but defied gravity long enough to find a handhold. "How's that?" he said, "what now?"

"Steady," Jacob whispered in the horse's ear.

"Someone stole m' rudder," Oakes declared. He squinted into the darkness. "Jake, ol' man—that you?"

"Spooked this horse, Pleasant."

Oakes leaned against the wall and relieved himself. "Damned hat's so fulla bricks, I can hardly walk right."

"Me, too, sure. Nice night for a piss."

"Underrated pleasure, certainly. Where y'all been?"

"That house," Jacob said and gave an underhanded wave.

"Well, come'n liquor with us. Giesecke and the other Prussians are telling stories, but damned if I can unnerstan 'em." Jacob did not reply but hoisted the bottle. "Oh, hey, don't drink alone," the lieutenant exhaled. "Come celebrate this joyous, wonnerful, goddamn occasion!"

"Which is?"

"Goin' home, man! Texas!"

"Got nowhere t'go," Jacob countered and threw the half-empty bottle into the weeds.

Confused, Oakes exhaled heavily before he brightened. "C'mon, pard—we're gonna dance. Local women."

"Thanks but I'ma go pass out—that's been my goal t'night and now I'm on the verge."

"Suit yourself." Oakes waved and disappeared back inside the door from which he'd emerged. "G'night."

"Yep," Jacob said. In the morning he planned to deliver his letter of resignation to Tom Green, look for a billet or work—hopefully both—and wait to see whether Adria had followed or not. As the horse cropped tufts of grass, Jacob swayed in the saddle and listened to the maddened sounds around him: two men arguing; a woman's laughter; some fiddler sawing out a wretched version of "Tenting Tonight on the Old Camp Ground." When he closed his eyes, he found that he could blot out the sounds of forced merriment and hear crickets and the wind in the trees. He opened his eyes again and looked across the fields toward the river. There, towering cottonwoods formed a black canopy that shrouded the lowest stars. Los Lunas Hill glowed pale in the moonlight, almost pretty despite its misshapen profile. None of these things stirred in him the bare joy of existence, but neither did it upset him to think that for a month, at least, Peralta would be his roost. "Only for now," he said, tapping the horse's sides with his spurs.

෴

A few hundred feet away, a pair of Federal scouts lay between the giant clumps of sagebrush that grew on the hillside above Connolly's home. As others from their company had already captured the Confederates' few pickets, it had been no great challenge to crawl well inside the Southerners' encampment. Neither was it a challenge to overhear Stark and Oakes's conversation. Lieutenant Hadrian Sill, the pair's leader, crawled backward until he was beside his comrade and settled onto his stomach in the dirt. "They're all of 'em loaded."

By the moon's waning light, Sill's partner had no trouble tracking Jacob's progress through the brass-tube scope on his rifle.

"This is shameful," Sill whispered. "They're in no shape to fight."

"So what do we do?" his partner, Private Davis Clark, whispered.

They watched as one Texan felt his way back inside the building and the other man slumped in his saddle. For a full minute, neither the Federals nor the mounted Texan moved. Private Clark—known throughout the regiment for his sharpshooting skills—looked up from his rifle. "He fall asleep?"

Sill squinted through the darkness. "Appears so."

Growing impatient, Clark reacquired Jacob's chest through his gunsight and eased the hammer back. "Gonna shoot someone tonight or what?"

"No." Sill leaned over, gripped the private's wrist, and forced him to lower the weapon. Scanning the field, the lieutenant tried to estimate the Confederates' total strength. "Canby wants to wait until our whole force is here," he whispered.

"Until broad daylight," Clark spat.

Finally, the mounted Texan stirred and spurred his horse forward. The Federals expected that the animal would veer, but to their growing consternation, it headed up a faint path, directly toward them.

"Split up," Sill whispered. "Don't do nothin' unless he trips over you! Quietly, if you must."

Clark clutched the rifle to his chest, rolled sideways, and unsheathed a knife. His heart pounded as the horse plodded uphill and the Texan began singing to himself. At first, the words were indistinct—half-spoken, half-sung and heavily accented with alcohol. As he drew nearer, they became clear:

"O! kiss me quick an' go my honeeeey-
Kiss me quick an' go!
T'cheat s'prise an' prying eyes,
Why, kiss me quick an' go!"

Sill's hands trembled as he thumbed back the hammer of his revolver. Jacob's horse was by then almost astride Clark, and it stamped its hooves and shied away, first left, then right, as it smelled living things lying in the weeds.

Jacob heard nothing but had to grip the horse's mane as it weaved from side to side. "Steady, y'old coot—steady." He stared into the darkness, figuring that the horse had seen a coyote in the sage or somesuch; whatever it was, he knew it was well beyond his impaired perception. As the animal settled, Jacob waved his hand dismissively. "Don't pay no mind." Clark gripped his knife and stared up at the Texan, studying how he might pull this fellow from the saddle if his horse strayed but two or three feet more. On his right, Sill wagged his head no, unsure whether or not Clark could even see him. Then the Texan slumped again and spoke in a voice that was barely above a whisper: "Hope you're okay. Oh, Lord, forgive me—I am a wretch." He exhaled heavily and then spoke to his horse: "C'mon, git!" Again, he tapped his heels on the horse's flanks and the animal stepped nimbly through the sagebrush, away from Clark.

As the Texan disappeared into an arroyo, Sill rose to a knee and exhaled. "I got a count—let's go."

From over the ridge, they could hear the Texan still mumbling and singing, this time a poor rendition of "The Bonnie Blue Flag":

We are a band'a brothers, natives of th' soil,
Fighting for our prop'ty we gained by honest toil;
But when our rights'uz threatened th' cry rose near an' far,
Hurrah for th' Bonnie Blue Flag tha' bears'a single star!"

Sill motioned for the private to follow and they returned to the trail, single-file and cautious lest they encounter others.

Clark sheathed his knife and glanced back at the field with its dozens of banked fires. "Bullshit," he whispered and nodded after the vanished Texan. "Tomorrow, I believe I'm gonna put you outta your misery."

South of Isleta Pueblo, New Mexico Territory, April 15, 1862

Men lunged from both sides of the narrow lane and grabbed the mules' halters. Others raised muskets and abruptly forced the vehicle halt. One bandit lit a dead-flame lantern and whistled before a half-dozen others emerged from the darkness. They converged on the buckboard from all sides, talking excitedly, their breath steaming in the cold night air. Another man lit a pitch-soaked torch and in the flickering half-light, the driver thought that a few of their faces looked vaguely familiar. They wore the gray uniforms of native militiamen, and their speech identified them as *Rio Arribeños*.

"*¡Alto!*" One man, somewhat shorter than all the others, rested a hand on the lead mule's halter. "*¡Alto! ¡No otro dedo!*"

To his complete surprise, the driver's voice was decidedly feminine: "I *have* stopped. *Mire*—take my money and let me pass."

"What the hell?" he said.

Another man, Itcaino, grinned at Adria, but the expression wasn't friendly. "Awfully late for a ride, Señorita. Roads aren't safe at this hour." He waved their leader over.

"Let me pass!" Adria shouted, but she felt panic rising in her stomach. Both shotguns—her father's and one she'd taken from Indian Billy's horse—were inside the strongbox, but she felt slowly, carefully and confirmed that a revolver was still under the blanket on the seat beside her.

"Wonder of wonders," Itcaino crowed, "a pretty little girl driving hardtails!"

Another man, Drusson—the estranged son of French immigrants—leaned in for a better view. "Look at all the traps in this wagon—two or three hundred dollars, if a cent!"

A fourth man with a dirty, matted beard, added up the four mules' value and whistled. The animals stamped nervously in their hitches. "We hit the jackpot, boys—real money at last."

Drusson stepped forward and took a lantern from its hook beside Adria's seat. "Where are you going? Home?"

"Please give that back—I must be going, *please!*"

The group's leader stepped into the circle of light cast by the lantern in Drusson's hand. Adria glimpsed Felix Ortiz's face and stifled a gasp. "She's a long way from home," Felix said. He walked the length of the wagon, glanced into its narrow bed, and saw the boxes of food, a barrel of water, oats for the mules.

"Felix," Adria whispered, frozen with fear.

"Knew I'd find you." His breath was sour with alcohol. "I *knew* it!"

"Felix, what are you doing?"

"Looking for troublemakers, traitors, liars. How do you answer these charges, Miss?" Adria said nothing as she tried to keep track of all the threatening forms that encircled the wagon. For an instant, she hoped Felix would tell the others to keep their distance and let her go, or at worst try and return her to Santa Fe. Then he spit on her.

The short bandit flinched. "You know her?"

"She's a whore."

"Take her money and go—too many Federals about."

"Go keep lookout if you don't want to see this."

The little man hesitated, and glanced between Adria and Felix. "I think—" he began, but Felix cut him short.

"*Pendejo*, your stomach is weak—get out of here!"

Unwilling to confront Felix, the man quickly turned and slipped into the *bosque's* secretive blackness.

‍❧

At the mention of soldiers, Adria glanced up the track. For hours, she had pushed her mules along the narrow, sandy lanes that dipped in and out of the *bosque,* finally crossing at the shallow ford east of Parea Mesa. Continuing down one-horse roads along the river's east bank, she had successfully evaded the Federal's scouts—though at that moment she could think of no one she'd rather see.

Itcaino drew up beside her, rapped the footrest, and jolted her from her delusion. "Girl, how'd you lay hold of a military rig?" Then, to Felix: "Can't do anything with it, can we? Have to leave it."

"I borrowed it," she said, which made the others snicker.

"We borrow things, too," the man with the filthy beard said.

Felix alone did not laugh. "She stole it so she could run away to Texas."

"Who *is* she?" the filthy man asked nervously, holding the lantern higher for a better view.

"Don Carrizo's daughter." At this, the others murmured loudly, but Felix continued: "Remember Bill Pelham and the other Southerners who fled with the *Tejanos?* Same with her—she thinks she's one of them."

"That true, Miss?"

"*¡Hostia puta!*" Felix raged, "Of course it's true! She is a traitor who fell in love with a *güero.*"

"I'm no traitor! And I haven't stolen anything!"

"Shut up!" Felix snapped. "Everything your family has is stolen!"

"Felix," she pleaded, "don't do this! Your parents—"

"I have no parents!" he thundered. "Because of you, I am disowned—hated by my own family." He reached into his haversack, pulled out a bottle of whiskey, and took an enormous drink. When he finished, he wiped his mouth and passed the bottle to another man. Adria trembled in silence as the bottle circled the wagon. When it came back to Felix, he drained it and hurled the empty against the wagon's side. Shards of glass sailed in and out of the lamplight like meteors. "*Puta,* you tried to leave me—tried to *leave!* With a *Texan,* moreover, and that, my dear, makes you a traitor."

"Felix! We grew up together—I, I was engaged to your brother!" Slowly, carefully, she wrapped her fingers around the revolver under the blanket on the seat beside her.

"You'd have killed me at Las Trampas," he said. He and the girl spent the next several moments trying to divine the others' next move until Felix broke the silence: "You had your chance."

The man with the tangled beard glanced nervously around the circle of faces. "You sure, Felix? She's Don Carrizo's *daughter.*"

"Shut up—I know what I'm doing!"

Itcaino rapped the footrest again. "What about this buckboard, *tipo?*"

Felix took the lantern from Drusson. "We're good citizens, loyal militiamen, so we'll return it to the army for a modest reward."

"And her?" Itcaino pointed at Adria.

"Don't care what you do to her," Felix said, "but once you're finished, I'm gonna knock the teeth clean out of her head."

Itcaino waved Drusson over. "That can wait."

Horror-stricken, Adria looked at Felix, whose cold eyes absorbed the enveloping darkness. "Any of you touches me, Don Carrizo will have you murdered!"

Leaning forward so she could see him, Felix enunciated every word: "Girl, your father said it's either you or me—"

"You're lying! When he hears—"

"You're going home in *pieces!*" Felix raged. "He doesn't care about you! No one cares about you—"

Adria's hand closed around the revolver's grip. In one swift motion, she lifted the weapon and pointed it squarely at Felix's chest. "Make them stop or I'll kill you."

Itcaino and Drusson trained their rifles on Adria but Felix was so drunk he merely grinned. "Oh, heavens! She's gonna shoot me!" He put a hand on the footrest.

Adria thumbed back the hammer on the revolver. "One..."

"Felix?" Drusson said, unsure how to react.

"Perra," Felix snapped, "You think this scares me? You think I'm scared?"

Knowing that she had nearly made it back to Jacob, tears of frustration spilled down Adria's cheeks. Sick of the anger that permeated her world, she knew that pulling the trigger would likely result in her death as well, yet even so she was satisfied knowing that Felix's dark light would be extinguished. "Two…"

"Do and you'll die with me," Felix seethed. "Conceited whore, I'll marry you in hell and then you'll *never* be rid of me!"

"Three." Adria choked back a sob, but even as she began to squeeze the trigger, a tremendous blow landed on her shoulder. She lurched forward in the seat and misfired; the bullet sailed harmlessly over Felix' head, though the muzzle-flash blinded them both.

Off-balance, she was unprepared as Itcaino grabbed her wrist and pulled her off the seat and onto the road. The revolver spun away into the weeds and with it went all hope of self-salvation. Sprawled in the dirt she saw Drusson, outlined by torchlight, holding his musket like a club. Then Felix kicked her ribcage with all his strength. Her breath went out, replaced by bolts of lightning that ricocheted inside her chest; thrumming across her back in white-hot jags, they found her spine and exploded into the space behind her eyes. She wanted to scream but her lungs were paralyzed. Writhing in agony, she felt rough hands pawing at her breasts and groping between her legs before they hurled her into the wagon's bed. Her head bounced against an iron fitting and lights danced before her eyes. Inhaling in one great gasp, she tried again to scream but the sound was cut short as Itcaino yanked her hair back and clamped his hand across her mouth. "Don't bother," he taunted, "no one can hear you."

Adria bit into his palm with all the strength she could summon; her teeth tore through skin, muscle, and nearly struck bone. When Itcaino bellowed in rage and pain, whoever was holding her feet twisted them until she cried out and released her bite. Leaping to his feet, Itcaino drove a knee into the side of her head and swiped at her face with his open, bloody hand. Drusson and the others laughed at the commotion but Adria would not look at anyone but Felix, leaning against the wagon's side and panting heavily. He drew a revolver from his belt, tapped the stock three times on a wheel rim, and thrust it toward the livid Itcaino. "Here," he said and Itcaino took the weapon.

Clutching the revolver in his uninjured hand, he clambered onto a wheel-hub and leaned over the bed. "Move," he barked at the others, and when they protested at having their sport prematurely spoiled, he shouted again, angrier still: "Bastards, *move!*"

Voices and footfalls began to carry from the *bosque;* panicked, the bandits stepped away from the wagon as Federal soldiers converged on them, seemingly from everywhere. Felix dropped his lantern, the filthy man his torch and a wild melee broke out in the gloom. Quickly gaining the upper hand, the Federals wrestled Felix and Drusson to the ground and shouted for the others to drop their weapons and lie down. All but Itcaino complied—driven to madness, he spun, fired at a soldier, and missed. Five muskets answered his outburst— burning lights that shattered his body and threw him backward from his perch upon the wheel.

South of Isleta Pueblo, New Mexico Territory, April 15, 1862

Accustomed to walking alone in front of his troops, Edward Canby paused to let several infantrymen dash past. The Federals' commander had only just ordered the column's foremost companies to un-shoulder their weapons when a New Mexican scout arrived with news that bandits were assaulting a traveler on the main road ahead. Then a gunshot sounded somewhere in the darkness on his right, nearer to the river. Leery of an ambush, Canby nevertheless detached the two companies and ordered them forward on the double.

His scouts had assured him that the Texans' camp in Peralta was poorly guarded and that all roads between there and Isleta Pueblo were clear. On this intelligence, he led his regulars toward a junction with Col. Paul and Col. Chivington's combined forces, which were approaching Peralta from the east. Of course, the darkness made certainty impossible and, having split his force, Canby was even more cautious than usual. Quite out of character, then, he asked the scout to guide him over to the fracas so that he might assess the situation there personally.

୭

Canby and his staff skirted a narrow *bosque* and continued toward a cluster of winking lights. The air grew colder as they neared the river; bats and nightjars wheeled overhead after the clouds of insects that were rising from the fields. Several muskets discharged and then voices carried across the sedge: one sounded an all clear, while others called for a surgeon. Alarmed, the normally imperturbable colonel began to run. Within minutes, he'd reached the upturn. To his dismay he discovered that in addition to holding several bandits at gunpoint, men under his command had taken turns beating one captive while their fellow soldiers cheered—one had even donned brass knuckles for the occasion. Followed closely by his adjutant, Canby hastened forward and grabbed the company's first sergeant. "Call him off!" he barked and the sergeant stopped a corporal before he could land another blow to Felix Ortiz's badly broken jaw.

"Keep him there!" the sergeant ordered before saluting the colonel.

"What in hell's name is going on?" Canby demanded. Before the sergeant could answer, a surgeon arrived and pushed through a cordon of soldiers around the buckboard.

The sergeant gestured at the kneeling captives. "Attacked a woman, meaning to rob and molest her, Sir. One resisted, so he's dead. The others say this one—," he pointed to Felix, "—is their leader."

"Who are they?"

"Can't say, Sir. Mexicans with militia-type kit and government weapons—likely deserters, Sir."

Canby gestured toward the man with the filthy beard. "You there—is this true?"

The man shrugged. *"No comprender."*

"Naturally," Canby shot a look of disgust at his adjutant, Gurden Chapin. Then he turned to Drusson. "What about you?"

"Militia, not bandits—Unionists."

"Which company?" Canby saw that the surgeon and others were helping the woman down from the wagon's bed.

"Hierro Company, Sir—First New Mexico Volunteers."

"The First is at Fort Craig."

Drusson ignored this contradiction and continued: "Texans are in Peralta. We believe she takes a message to them—we wanted only to prevent this."

"Pretty rough detention, don't you think?" Canby pointed at Ortiz, whose shirtfront was soaked with blood. "Can he speak?"

"Not now," the sergeant admitted.

Felix, who did not know Canby, glared through badly swollen eyes and nodded toward Drusson.

"You concur with what he said?" Felix nodded again, and the colonel turned back to Drusson. "I'll speak with her next. If your story holds up, you will be rendered to the nearest civil authority. If I find that you've lied, we'll bury you here in this field, understand?"

Drusson hung his head, but Felix merely continued to glare at Adria.

&

Canby addressed Chapin as they moved toward the buckboard: "Can't let this slow us down. Keep the column moving and I will follow as soon as I can. If you make it that far, stop at the Chical ditch."

Presuming that the entire valley floor was crisscrossed with canals and ditches, Chapin looked worried. "How will we know which one that is?"

"One of the Indians from Isleta will know."

"Yes, Sir. Any orders for Chivington and the Coloradans?"

"Tell Chivington not to move until I say so—not one bullet or shell. Man has been after me for days—'when, when, when will we attack?' Wants laurels and revenge, and all I want is for the Texans to leave. Damned nuisance, that one."

"Yes, Sir," Chapin agreed and turned to go find the other officers.

Canby greeted the surgeon and offered him a cigar. The doctor accepted and waited as the colonel struck a match. "Who's your patient?"

"Young Mexican woman." The doctor exhaled pungent smoke. "By her dress and manners, I'd guess she isn't from around here. High-born, driving a government wagon all by herself at night in this country—if you can believe that."

"She hurt?"

"Not too badly—she's lucky. Scrapes and bruises. May have a cracked rib, too, but she wouldn't let me examine it. Barely managed to clean her off and give her water. Insists she has to get going—I'm sure you'll hear it, too."

Canby thanked the surgeon, walked around the wagon, and threaded his way between the guards who were screening the girl from view. Seated on one blanket, she had another one draped across her shoulders. A canteen was in her lap. As he stood above her, even before she looked up, he experienced strange sensations of familiarity—her hair, her bearing—and fought against a tremor that tried to shake his frame. "Miss? My name is Edward Canby. I am the commanding officer here and I must...ask..." Faltering from shock, the last words stumbled out of his mouth. She looked a shambles, of course: scratched everywhere, a raised welt across her face, and—despite the doctor's attempts to clean her—splashes of Itcaino's blood on her chin and neck. But here was Adria Carrizo, unmistakably so, and her subsequent reaction confirmed it: as soon as she saw Canby, her eyes widened and she rose and hurled herself into his arms with such force that he had to wave for his bodyguards to let the outburst pass. "Adria, my God! What is this?"

She sobbed but did not speak and clung to him with all her strength. For several minutes, he let her be and motioned for a soldier to replace the blanket across her shoulders. That she had said nothing was just as well, for it had taken Canby several moments to recover. Sensing extraordinary circumstance, the guards moved away, glad to distance themselves from such an intimate scene.

ᥱᥱ

Canby held Adria tightly. He'd known the Carrizos for years, and to say that he was unprepared to find his neighbor's daughter so far from home and badly abused would be a gross understatement. Indeed, the Colonel had to quell an impulse to deal personally with her attackers. As her crying subsided, he placed his hands upon her shoulders. "Adria, what are you doing here?"

"Colonel Canby..." she faltered and closed her eyes. She struggled to speak, to breathe but finally managed a few words: "I have been so foolish!"

"This...the *strangeness* of it! Adria, I don't know what to say."

"There is too much to explain. Fate despises my errand, yet I mustn't stop. Please, I need your help!"

"I don't understand—"

"I must reach Peralta before...before—"

"Peralta? Good heavens, what for?"

"I am looking for someone. Mrs. Canby was helping me—"

"Louisa?"

"Yes, and my father tried to stop me—"

"Wait," he said, "none of this makes sense."

"Nor would it if I explained at length. Mrs. Canby told me that if I saw you, I was to give you a letter." She reached up, rifled through a small box beneath the wagon's seat—wincing from pain in her ribs as she did—and finally handed him a small envelope. "She said you'd understand."

"Highly unlikely," he said but he took the letter and began reading by torchlight. While the colonel squinted at his wife's familiar but loop-laden handwriting, Adria found it difficult to read the stoic man's expression. He paused and lowered the paper. "Your father will object to any action other than returning you home."

"The men over there were sent for exactly that purpose."

Even in the darkness, the shock on Canby's face was plain. "You cannot mean—"

"I am a liability."

Chapin approached and conversed briefly with Canby. The colonel glanced up, satisfied that the column was moving south in good time. Then he looked back at the wagon and became enraged all over again. He and Louisa had long adored Adria and, well aware that her situation was not ideal, always welcomed the lonely girl into their home. "Adria, what has driven you to take such risks? Who is in Peralta?"

Adria looked south, where distant lights beckoned between the trees. "A Texan," she fumbled.

"Adria!" he reproached.

"His name is Jacob Stark—he is one of their captains, but he means to resign his commission."

"You're certain that he's there?"

"I am."

"Have you any other motivation for coming here?"

"None," she said.

"No other communication?"

"Only Mrs. Canby's letter. I know they said I am a spy, but I am not—merely a lovelorn fool. You may search my effects as necessary to establish this fact."

He took her chin in his enormous hands and tilted it upward so she could see him better. "However resolved you may be, we are all of us at war—all of us. I cannot allow it, Adria." Inhaling sharply, the pain in her ribs flared and she took a backward step. Canby continued: "I'll have men to take you to back to Atrisco."

Adria glanced south, beckoned by the lights. She ached less from her injuries than from knowing that Jacob was so near.

"With each passing moment the road ahead is compressed," he said, "its hazards multiplied."

"Is there no other way?"

"None that I can see."

Across the road Adria saw her attackers kneeling in the dust, saw the thin soles of their boots. "I'll go back," she said, "but you must allow those men there to accompany me."

Canby, who had taken up Louisa's letter again, paused, baffled. "What's that?"

Slowly, for the pain in her ribs, she crossed her arms. "Perhaps they'll protect me from my father."

"Adria!"

"I knew the risk in coming here—do you really think me so impetuous? Colonel, I am despised in my own home—I cannot go back!"

Canby studied her face as though meeting her for the first time, which in a way he was. Although she looked older and wiser than she did in his memories of her, to him she would never be old or wise enough to turn loose into the world that he knew. Worried as if she were his own, his instinct was to protect her at all hazards. "Adria, you cannot go south. Neither Mrs. Canby nor I could live with ourselves...if anything happened."

Adria leaned against the wagon's side and took a shallow breath. "Whatever you can imagine, it will be worse if I am made to return to Santa Fe."

"Yes, I see." Canby's melancholy smile told Adria of his predicament. He bent once more to study the remainder of his wife's message.

Curious at the spectacle surrounding the wagon, rank upon rank of men continued past—New Mexicans and Federal regulars—quickening their pace like water accelerating in the channel before a fall. *So many,* Adria marveled, suddenly terrified for Jacob and his friends; so many that it would be hours before the freighters rumbled through—lumbering wagons loaded with staggering quantities of food, ammunition, and supplies; in short, everything that Sibley's Texans lacked.

Canby finished the letter and tucked it into a coat pocket. He smiled again, more placidly than before. "I am distressed to think that you may continue into my enemy's encampment. Do you understand why?"

"Yes."

"I cannot guarantee the safety of an innocent among them—"

"We will leave at once."

"Adria, even the best plans come undone," he said. "It's late—will you not wait in one of our wagons until daybreak?"

"If Jacob is hurt or killed, I'll have borne all this for nothing. No matter happens, I would rather find him first."

Canby leaned against the wagon and gently brushed the matted hair away from her face. "Officially, I am telling you to go back." She nodded. "But I will also tell you that your rig—"

"Your rig," she corrected.

"Thought so. Regardless, you must move it from this road so that my teamsters can get through. In doing so, you may discover that about one hundred yards back there is a fork. Anyone who turned onto that road would find that it takes a reasonably straight course into Peralta."

"Am I safe?"

"Decidedly not. There's scant time until daylight—you must find him and get away fast." He handed her his white handkerchief. "Take this."

"What, and wave it?"

"Your life may depend on it." He squeezed her shoulders. "Go down to Fort Craig—you'll be safe there, no matter who comes looking for you."

"Thank you, Colonel," she whispered. She leaned forward and held him tightly.

"Quickly, now. You have no more than three hours' head start and Peralta is still an hour away. Promise me that come daybreak you'll be gone—no flag will protect you then."

"I promise."

"The Texans may remove downriver or stand firm—you must be gone before they are forced to decide." He helped her climb into the driver's seat and handed her a tin canteen full of water. "Adria, I hate this—hate it intensely, but I also understand that this is where you have set your mind. I will pray to God, asking that He keeps you safe."

She leaned forward carefully and kissed his cheek before resettling on the bench. "Thank you, Sir," she said and flicked the reins. Canby watched the wagon's orange-painted wheels roll through the grass until the mules completed their turn and she disappeared in the gloom.

❧

Canby promptly sought another cigar and clamped it between his teeth. Halfway across the road Maj. Duncan, his head bandaged and his right arm in a sling (Duncan had been the sole casualty of the artillery duel at Albuquerque the week prior), met him. Limited to administrative duties, the major had become a quasi-adjutant to Canby, taking notes and assisting whenever possible, which wasn't often. "I take it that was unexpected."

Canby squinted into the darkness, no longer able to see Adria or the wagon. "Very much so—I shouldn't have let her go."

"Then why did you, Sir, if I may ask?" Duncan looked up as a gun carriage rolled past.

Canby exhaled heavily. "My wife wrote to remind me of a young man who took almighty risks to win a girl whose father did not approve."

"Someone you know?"

Canby quickened his pace. "Someone I used to be."

Duncan grinned at the thought, but by then Canby had reached the guard-detail that was watching over the bandits. "Sergeant, detach a provost to render these men to the authorities in Socorro."

The sergeant saluted and motioned the colonel aside so he could whisper, "Sir, the fellow who raised the alarm, that one there—," he pointed to a short man under guard away from the others, "—told me this weren't their first emprise. Says he knows of attacks up and down the valley."

Canby studied the bandits' profiles: all were staring sullenly into the distance. "All matters for the court. Protect that one with the conscience, but if any of the others act up or try to escape, shoot 'em. That is all." The sergeant saluted and turned away. Chapin and others fell in with the colonel in an effort to overtake the column's lead. "Let's pick it up, boys!" Canby shouted, "I want to be set before the rebels make coffee."

Village of Peralta, New Mexico Territory, April 15, 1862

Driven by a steady wind, airborne bits of sand and gravel stung Adria like unseen mosquitoes. She flicked the reins again, trying to make her jaded animals move faster. She was bleary-eyed and every bump, every rut in the road—even those she could anticipate—made her ribs ache and compounded her exhaustion. She knew that she was perilously late. The road onto which Col. Canby had directed her had indeed run straight to Peralta—except for one easily missed turn, and she had lost almost an hour tracking back. As she guided the wagon along a canal just north of the village, the grainy half-light began to give way and more and more buildings began to take shape. Farmers and their hands, already at work in the fields, paused to stare as she sped past.

"Only a half-mile more," she called to the mules, though she did not imagine that her apologetic tone made any difference. The wheel and lead animals on the right had gone balky and seemed liable to drop in their traces. *Mother Mary, ten more minutes.* She leaned into a gathering wind, farther and farther, until its force was the only thing keeping her firmly in the seat. The sky was quickly growing brighter and she could plainly see the village: whitewashed adobes that looked blue in the shadows; lime-colored bean fields, newly sprouted; and gray puffs of smoke that were promptly dispersed by the wind. A maze of low adobe fences ran between every building and around every field. It was a peaceful scene and her hopes began to rise.

Then in the far distance, a bugle sounded, shrill and frantic, and her heart froze.

ↄ

411

Above the town's eastern limits was a steep-sided gravel terrace, one hundred feet tall. Colonel Chivington's Federal troops were waiting on this wide landing, partially concealed by a riot of sagebrush. The wind continued to build, forcing these men to pull hat-brims and bandannas over their faces to keep from being sandblasted.

"Colonel, how much longer?" one of his captains shouted.

"Any minute now," Chivington roared, "keep a lookout!" A more cautious commander—Edward Canby, for one—might not have bawled from a concealed position, but Chivington was no such man. For weeks he had chafed at the stately pace of Canby's operation, enforced (he believed) to permit the unrepentant Confederates' escape. Now, having caught their adversary unawares and sodden with liquor, Canby's orders to forestall their attack had nearly driven Chivington insane with impatience. Since four a.m., the minutes had ticked by without instruction. Although he would abide by the letter of Canby's orders, he finally decided that he would "accidentally" stir the waters and see if he could rouse the slumbering Texans to fight before the weather turned. As the eastern sky lightened, Chivington ordered his soldiers forward on the terrace and to make no effort to conceal their actions.

Even then, the exhausted Texans not only failed to note the commotion above their encampment but also persisted in their slumber. It wasn't until a mess cook looked up from his fire and saw ranks of blue-coated men only a quarter mile away that an alarm was raised. Bugles blared and Texan artillery crews—some still in socks and long johns—raced to unlimber their guns.

A dark smile spread across Chivington's face. "First Colorado, arise and listen! As Gideon drove the Midianites from the valley and into the River Jordan, so shall we!" From its concealment behind a barn, the first Texan cannon threw a stand of grape shot into the hillside below. "Fight with malice in your hearts! Compassion for these wretches is reserved to the Lord! Hard now to that wall, and for God's sake, kill anything before you! Forward, lambs, *forward!*"

᜵

At the town's northern limit, Adria snapped the reins, no longer concerned for the animals' condition. "Faster, mules! *Faster!*" Like hornets spilling from a nest, the village suddenly swarmed with activity. Texans in every stage of dress—and most with aching heads—staggered out into the light, wild-eyed and fearful. As the sun's first rays lit the valley floor, the big Federal guns on the hillside roared in unison. On Adria's left, two heavy shells exploded, hurling iron shards and mud onto the road, and blowing out the windows in the nearest building. Then a third shell detonated, so near that the concussion sucked the air from her lungs, knocked her sideways on the seat, and reignited the pain in her ribs. As one building collapsed and another began to burn, she jerked hard on the reins and pulled on the hand brake, forcing the terrified mules to stop. Texans surged out of every doorway in no semblance of order. Some marched calmly to firing positions behind the walls while others dashed about without a thought in their throbbing heads. Beside Adria's wagon, several Confederates flung themselves into a ditch as more Federal shells sailed overhead. As the triple thunderclap faded, they rose and ran to fire in earnest at blue-clad forms pouring down from the hills.

⁊

In the village's southwestern corner, Jacob and his companions ran from their lodgings with nothing but the clothes on their backs, their weapons, and what ammunition they could carry. Reaching a lane, Lt. Col. O'Neill directed them to protect a wagon train left out overnight, stalled in deep sand along the river. From the road, Adria saw Jacob across a field. Almost delirious, she shouted his name, but her lungs would not fill and her voice was diminished by pain. No matter—Jacob could've heard nothing over the shrieking wind and thundering guns. She eased herself down from the wagon and began to run, but the ground was so soft that she slipped and slammed sidelong into an adobe wall. Lying within its cold shadow, she could do nothing more than gasp in agony. For several moments, no amount of will could move her, and by the time she recovered, Jacob was gone.

Shells continued to fall and the commotion was dreadful. Waves of civilians—Mexican and Anglo, Southerner and Unionist alike—flooded the fields and ran frantically for whatever protection they

413

could find. Texan sharpshooters climbed up onto the flat-roofed adobes to fire at the approaching Federal infantry, but Union artillerists began lobbing case shells over the buildings to drive them down. Fighting against a stream of panicked civilians, Adria made her way back to the buckboard, only to find one mule already dead and the others struggling frantically to escape their harnesses. Other refugees shoved her aside and tried to free the animals so that they might ride them to safety. When another shell detonated nearby, the crowd went mad with fear. Men and women fought one another in their panic to get away. Adria steadied herself against a low adobe wall but hands clutched at her elbows and pulled her into the frenzied current. "Leave me alone!" she cried, but other well-intentioned hands seized her anew.

"*Corra*, Señorita!" an elderly Mexican farmer shouted, "you must run!"

"*¡Mi dios, nos matarán todos!*" his wife sobbed: My God, they're killing everyone! Adria took the old woman's hand and pulled her onto the road.

ତ୬

Exiting a bank of cattails at the river's edge, Jacob's company immediately realized that the stranded wagons were beyond rescue: two full companies of Union infantry had already beaten them there and engaged the Texans' teamsters in a one-sided fight. Even as Jacob and the others were turning to run for cover, many of the drivers were raising their hands in surrender. Others were shot as they ran for the water.

ତ୬

The wind bent everything before it. Tongues of sand fifty feet high and ten feet wide lapped at the river's turbid surface. Like tornadoes set on edge, these sinuous fingers felt their way around the cotton-woods' massive trunks and bent or broke any lesser plants. The sky went dark red, as though a bloody drape had been pulled across the sun. Adria limped south alongside a mother and father with four small children, each of whom was leading a milking goat. On a bridge above a raised canal, the youngest boy tried to pull his billy to its feet, unaware that a shell fragment had slashed its throat. She made him drop its tether, dragged him toward another low wall, and—despite the pain in her side—handed him across to his mother. Though they were safely beyond the guns' range, concussions would continue to shake their bones for a good distance more.

⁓

Near the village's center, Col. Green's Texans took shelter within a long, dry canal. Here they formed a defensive line that finally checked the Federals' advance. Per Col. Canby's orders, Union forces on the other side of the fields took cover and waited. Returning from the river, Jacob's company found themselves in a no-man's-land between the ditch and the Federals east of the village. They made one ineffective volley and ran west toward shelter; crossing a wooden bridge, just twenty yards from cover, a Yankee bullet shattered Briggs Hardy's right kneecap and he fell. One of his companions stopped and tried to drag him to safety but took a bullet through both lungs and collapsed. Running to help, another ball grazed Jacob, though it merely singed his skin and tore the sleeve of his jacket. Grabbing Hardy by the arm, he dragged his friend behind an enormous cottonwood. There, others helped lift the injured man into the bed of a commandeered farm wagon and Jacob clambered up after.

Moments later, the Coloradans charged, dislodging every the last Texans east of the canal. Wary of being overtaken, the wagon's driver turned the vehicle and quickly started south. Jacob gripped Briggs's hand. The wagon-box's violent sway nearly tumbled him to the ground. "Hold on," he shouted, but Hardy's pain was such that he could not answer or even acknowledge that he'd heard; all he could manage was to clutch his friend's arm as the wagon sped south.

⁓

By the time Canby's reserves arrived, the Texans had formed a new defensive line and both sides settled in to exchange desultory rounds. Dozens of shells sailed back and forth but few inflicted casualties.

For Adria, the hours were nightmarish, if less hazardous. Dirty and exhausted, she watched from a hilltop southeast of town, crying softly and flinching at every bursting shell. Deadened to her core, she waited as the morning wore on, mechanically accepting blankets and food from kindhearted strangers. Still, no matter how she tried, she could not shake the fixation that Jacob had been killed.

∽

Around noon, Gen. Sibley emerged from his ambulance and ordered Texan reinforcements across the river to support Green's beleaguered Fifth, but troops under Col. Scurry's command mutinied. With but a few companies in tow, Sibley himself waded into the icy waters only to find that Union cavalry had effectively sealed off Peralta. Without firing a shot, these Texans returned to the river's western bank.

Only the sandstorm—by then grown to monstrous size—provided any cover. A mile wide and as black as muddy wool, at one-thirty the storm's hard edge roared across the river, blinding and choking anyone still outdoors. Ferocious, sand-laden winds stripped leaves from the trees and smothered every sprout in the fields; mere weeks after planting, that year's harvest was devastated.

Civilian refugees took what shelter they could and Green's entire force withdrew under the cover of daytime darkness. Fanned by cyclonic winds, fires ignited by exploding shells spread quickly. In some buildings the windows melted, while many stick-built structures simply collapsed. With the town's core smashed, it would be years before Peralta's population returned to pre-war levels.

Colonel Canby's Federal HQ, Peralta, New Mexico Territory, April 15, 1862

Around six o'clock that evening the sandstorm finally expired. Brief rain showers followed and a cool, blissful calm settled over the valley. Federal officers met at Governor Connolly's ranch—in the very chairs that the Confederates had occupied the night before. Most of the main house's windows were broken, which had a twofold effect: all heat had dissipated, which was pleasant, and swarms of flies flew unimpeded, which was not. Colonel Canby and Col. Paul were smoking; Gurden Chapin was scribbling in his notebook, and Maj. Duncan sat with his feet upon an ammunition crate, drinking in the smell of wet sage and greasewood. At issue was how to best deploy troops reportedly on the march from California.

Chapin looked away from his writing. "They'd best hurry before real heat comes up."

"No communications from Carleton?" Paul stubbed out his cigar.

"None." Canby exhaled. "Last I knew he was tamping down secessionist enthusiasms in southern California—the very existence of his column is anecdotal."

"Will you discharge the volunteers?"

"No."

Paul and Chapin exchanged looks. "Where can they be trusted?" Chapin said.

Canby stared out a window. "They know this territory best, so they will concentrate on Indian troubles up north. Then Carleton's brigade—if it exists—can address any sesech troubles as may arise. He'll certainly find no organized resistance between here and the coast—travelers say the Confederates' Tucson garrison has disappeared into Apache country."

"The miners in Piños Altos?"

"Too few and too busy holding off the Mimbreño Apaches to be a threat."

Duncan lowered his feet from the crate. "Suppose Sibley regroups in Franklin or northern Mexico—might they try again, perhaps along the Pecos?"

All eyes turned to Canby, who shook his head. "Unlikely, and even so, Governor Weld is sending another five hundred short-term enlistments from Colorado."

"Rather he sent five hundred sacks of corn," Duncan said.

"Right." Canby clicked his tongue against his teeth. "And General Hunter has written to say he's sending five thousand more from Fort Riley."

"We cannot feed a tenth of that number!" Col. Paul objected.

Canby stifled a yawn. "Gurd, draft a message for my signature—inform the General of conditions in this department and request that he scale accordingly."

"All this is talk out of school, isn't it?" Paul said. "The Texans are still across the river."

"On their way, though," Canby answered, "unless they turn and do something stupid."

"Such as launching an invasion without adequate supplies?"

An aide appeared at the door. "Colonel Canby? Sir, Col. Chivington has requested to see you—wants to speak in private, Sir."

Canby exhaled and gave Paul a subtle look of exasperation.

Chapin helped Duncan stand. "We'll go see how the boys are settled."

Canby motioned for Paul to remain. Moments later Chivington entered and saluted. "Permission to speak, Sir?"

"You may speak freely—Gabe here has my full confidence." Canby gestured toward Chapin's vacated seat.

The Coloradan sat on the chair's foremost edge and his agitation was clear. "Sir, I'd like to lead our cavalry across the river tonight. We can fall in behind and drive 'em until the main body fords at Sabinal."

Canby folded his hands beneath his chin. "To what end?"

"Their destruction, Sir."

Canby could feel hostility radiating from the enormous man's body, but recent outcomes had restored his confidence and he was surer of his own judgment. "Colonel, I know there's strong sentiment to punish the Texans, but that isn't my vantage. Already they're leaving—we needn't risk further losses."

"They are traitors, Sir!"

"Colonel, a hundred of them aren't worth one honest man's life."

Chivington looked incredulous. "We're letting them go?" Paul looked away and coughed.

Canby nodded. "We've plenty to do these next several months. We'll clear out the Mesilla Valley and seal the border, but for now our sole aim is to see that they leave."

Chivington knotted his hands and chewed at his lip. "They—," he wrung his hands, "—they rebelled against a government sanctioned by God Himself—this cannot go unpunished!"

Colonel Paul raised an eyebrow, but Canby remained impassive: "We don't use the Old Testament as a field manual, Colonel—the answer's no."

"Sir, this course is profane!"

"Practical considerations—"

"Sir, the Lord—" Chivington tried again, a little louder, but Canby cut him off.

"Colonel, I pray to God, too, and never has He commanded me to slaughter the weak—"

"And the wicked?" Chivington said, his voice still rising. "For them, God whets His sword and bends His bow. We are but instruments, instruments of retribution, and we mustn't rust for lack of use. Sir, I insist—"

"*No!*" Canby slammed his fist down on the tabletop. "I will *not* have this army co-opted to suit your aims!" Paul was astonished: having rarely heard Canby raise his voice in anger, he leaned forward in his seat.

"Suppose I allowed it?" Canby bristled. "Turned you and the First Colorado loose? Wouldn't take long to kill a few hundred and the rest would surrender. What then? Eighteen hundred Texans. The sick, the wounded—how would you care for them? Feed them, clothe them, shelter them? *Eighteen hundred!* Their clothes are tatters, their boots are destroyed. Men cannot be marched under those conditions—so would you *execute* them? Is that your solution? And those complicit in the fulfillment of such orders—how would they take it? Would they be right with God? *Would you?* Hear me, Colonel, and understand: we will follow the Confederates only until they quit this territory, and I will abide no further questions on the matter. Am I clear?"

In the silence that followed, all three men could hear soldiers out in the fields, talking and laughing. On the other side of the wall, cooks were banging about in an unfamiliar kitchen in pursuit of supper.

Chivington exhaled. "Yes, Sir."

"Very well—we'll pull up stakes at five o' clock tomorrow morning."

Chivington saluted and exited. Canby and Paul resumed smoking and swatting at flies. For several minutes, their conversation remained dormant, as each on his own wondered how Chivington's continued presence might affect operations, and whether an official reprimand was in order. At last, Canby exhaled and rested his pipe upon his knee. "Do all of them feel that way?"

Paul noted a new scuff on one of his boot-tips. "The Coloradans? No, Chivington's cut from different cloth."

"How'd he get that way?"

"Perfection is a lonesome business."

"Well, I wouldn't know."

Another moment passed in silence before Paul glanced at Canby. "They're saying that your ties to Henry Sibley are the reason we haven't pursued them with greater vigor."

Canby tapped out his pipe on his bootheel and tucked it into his coat. "I've heard that, but it's untrue—we simply cannot afford that many prisoners. If they mean that I want them gone, then indeed I do."

"Chivington reflects that sentiment, likely."

"My God, he's the angriest man I've ever seen."

Paul glanced through the open door and caught a glimpse of Chivington's back as he disappeared into his tent. "Who can say what shapes a fellow—what clings and what falls away—but I understand his time in Kansas Territory hardened him against slavery."

"Fair enough." Canby stretched his legs.

"And Sam Tappan told me that Chivington's brother was a rebel officer, killed in Missouri last year."

Canby stood. "This sordid mess."

"The well is poisoned," Paul concurred. "Someday the guns will fall silent, but I doubt it will matter—these wounds are too deep."

"Dismal thought, Gabe."

"You're welcome, Sir."

"Yes." Canby rose, brushed tobacco crumbs off his trousers, and started for the steps. "I have paperwork to finish. Let's talk again after supper."

⁓

For the next three days Canby's forces marched step-for-step with the Texans, albeit hundreds of yards apart on opposite banks of the river. At night each army's pickets would call to the other's, usually to trade insults but occasionally to inquire after friends or family in the other camp. For sixty miles, they continued this way, until one morning the Union forces awoke and found that the Texans had disappeared.

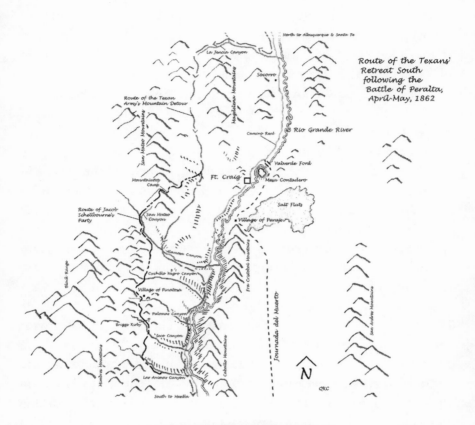

6-TEXAN RETREAT MAP

La Jencia Canyon, New Mexico Territory, April 18, 1862

Weeks before the debacle at Peralta, Bethel Coopwood had come north from Mesilla with a small grist of supplies, as well as dispatches from Austin and mail for the troops. In search of a safe route around Fort Craig, the captain hired New Mexicans familiar with the region's few springs to guide him through the Magdalena Mountains. Trapped between Fort Craig and Canby's brigade, Gen. Sibley decided that Coopwood's "mountain route" was the best alternative for retreat. Had he known that they were heading into a wilderness almost entirely without water, he might have thought otherwise.

೧

East of Ladron Peak, where the feeble Rio Salado empties into the Rio Grande, the Texans struck the river road, west and then southwest into dry, rugged hills above Socorro. For the able-bodied, this ascent was difficult; for the sick and wounded, it was perilous. After less than five miles of torture, the very worst-off simply sat down to either wait for death or rescue by the Union cavalry— whichever first arrived. By the first evening, all order had disintegrated; the brigade broke into dozens of camps strung out over ten miles. Some rode still: Gen. Sibley in his ambulance; the few remaining cavalry units; and numerous families—including Judge Spruce Baird's— who did not care to remain where their political views were no longer welcome. Most simply walked. In vain, Jacob tried to secure a berth for Briggs Hardy, whose pain was so awful that he could barely stand, nonetheless walk. Jake even appealed to a civilian family in an overloaded hack until he remembered that he'd left all his funds in Peralta. Seeing no alternative, he organized a remnant of his company to help carry Hardy across the steep hills and stubbled wastelands.

By noon of their third day off the river, they had crossed the dry plains west of the Magdalena Mountains. Exhausted, Jacob and his companions stopped in the warm shade beneath a solitary juniper. The only sounds were of hot wind whispering in the bleached grass and crows that called from high overhead. Taking inventory, they discovered that they were nearly out of food.

"Yucca's edible," Tom Birch offered and pointed to one of the spiny plants. "The roots."

"Won't never be that hungry," Charlie Spence said, though he was wrong.

Jacob eyed the hostile plant. "Rather feast on memories of breakfast. Let's save what we have for now." Everyone agreed that was best, though Jacob did slip Hardy a crust of bread on the sly.

They sat in silence, listening to the wind, until a strange droning sound caught Spence's ear. "The hell's that?" He stood, lifted his musket, and scanned the northern horizon. "Someone's comin'." The others rose for a better look.

Three men approached through the shimmering heat; like Jacob's group, they were helping an injured companion. They were moving quickly, though, and didn't notice Jacob's group until they had near to tripped over them.

"Jesus!" Jimmy Burdick yelped. "Y'all scared me like to death!"

Spence scowled in reply. "Lucky we ain't Indians, stupid."

"Gentlemen." Jacob touched the brim of his cap.

Tom Hegler's anguished moans accounted for the sound that Spence had heard. Arms outstretched, he slumped between his companions, delirious. "Down, down, down," he guttered, "no end, no end, never."

Wyatt Walker, also uninjured, wore an exasperated look; as soon as Burdick selected a place for them to rest, a little too quickly he let go of Hegler's arm and the injured man slumped and fell sideways into the brittle grass. "Goddamn, Jimbo—don't know how much longer I can take this."

Hegler's trouser-fronts were brown with dried blood, and he let out another low loan.

"How is he?" Jacob asked.

"Pitiful," Walker snarled, but Burdick silenced him with a look.

"Worse on account of this heat," Burdick began and mopped his brow. "Things were okay this morning, but they turned only this past hour." He explained how at Peralta, Hegler had taken a piece of shrapnel in his hip and how it had paralyzed his leg.

From his seat in the grass, Hegler gave a rueful laugh. "Sorry, boys—wish I was under my own power."

"Me, too," said Walker and cursed his luck.

Burdick, the oldest of the three, shot Jacob a pleading look. "Any water?" Jacob's party had refilled at a spring, so water was temporarily abundant and they gave the newcomers an extra canteen.

"Should've stopped there your own damn selves," Spence scolded.

"Missed the turn," Burdick said. "Couldn't go back."

Jacob pointed south. "Lieutenant Holden rode through about noon. Guessed it was nine miles on a southerly course between springs."

Spence cast a weary look at Burdick. "How'd y'all fall so far behind? Thought we were the very last." All day he'd been worried that they had lost contact with the brigade.

Burdick gazed sadly at a tiny speck of cloud. "Weighed our chances by the river and decided to wait 'til Yankees came along, but they never did. Seeing as two of our fellows were murdered by Mexicans at Los Padillas, though, we thought it best to hasten after."

"Spring ahead any good, Cap'n?" Walker said.

"No idea," Jacob answered truthfully. Hegler let out another long wail, so anguished that the others exchanged agitated looks. Walker turned away from his companions. Jacob stood and a hot gust of wind made his tattered shirttail flutter. "Have to keep up as best we can."

Burdick pulled one of Hegler's arms across his shoulder. "Could be worse—my cousin in Tennessee wrote that fourteen thousand are dead at Shiloh." He glanced over at Walker, who was facing away from the group. "How 'bout it, Wyatt? We'd best push on 'fore dark." Walker did not budge, though Jacob could see his shoulders heaving. "Walker!" Burdick snapped, "boy, get over here and help me lift him!"

"Easy," Jacob said, "we'll help."

"Sorry, Cap'n—Hegler here saved Walker's hide at Glorieta, so now he'd damn well better return the favor, hear?"

His face streaked with tears, Walker stood and did as he was told. "Gonna kill us, too."

"Come on," Burdick growled and pulled both Hegler and Walker to their feet.

For several minutes, none in Jacob's company said anything as the trio slipped slowly into the distance. Birch and Spence even nodded off, but Hardy, who was more alert than he'd been in days, refused to look away.

"Promise me, Jake," he said, "promise that if things get as bad as that, you'll leave me."

Jacob looked after Burdick and the others, but there was no evidence of their passing—merely an ocean of sunburnt grass hemmed by dark hills. "I will not." He shook the others awake and pulled them all back onto the trail.

❧

Near sunset, Jacob's party reached a steep and narrow canyon; mountain shadows had crawled east and filled this trough with darkness. Though it had taken a half-hour to carry Hardy down and across the jumbled rocks, on the opposite rim they found fallen timbers long and stout enough to build a makeshift travois. Hardy sat alone, looking back at the high, sloped prairie that they had just crossed, the heights of which were still golden beneath the day's last light. Wind stirred the grass so that it rippled and flowed like an unsettled sea.

While others lashed slender logs together with strips of cloth torn from a spare shirt, Jacob went to give his friend some water. "How do you feel?"

Hardy ignored the question. "Saw a picture once—man said there was a tiger hidden in the vines and shadows, but for the longest time my eye was confounded. Studied that damn thing until white went black and black went white. But don't you know, once I stopped lookin', it resolved, revealed as the artist intended—"

"Briggs?" Jacob said but Hardy continued as though he hadn't heard.

"—yet *because* I could see clearly, I was not satisfied. Couldn't *stop* seeing the tiger, understand? No matter how I squinted or blurred my vision, things never went back to the way they first appeared. Never went back. Stupid." He scratched at a raw patch of skin above the bandage on his knee. "Likewise, my situation is now clear to me—how foolish, how arrogant I have been—and though I want the world to go back to the way it was before we came here, it never will. Laws, I was spoilin' for a fight, remember? I was sure we would plant our flag in California. Now look at me—pathetic."

Jacob couldn't think of anything to say, but then the others dragged the travois over for inspection.

Spence cleared his throat. "Think we're ready, Cap'n."

Jacob tugged on the supports and nodded. "Much better."

Dan Goodman grinned at the praise. "Indians at Fort Bridger used to carry their traps on these things."

"Yeah, well," Spence complained, "you should've thought of it sooner."

"Kiss my ass, Charlie—there wasn't any timber before now."

Spence reared back, took a monstrous swing at Goodman's head, and barely missed. Quickly, Jacob grabbed the huge sergeant around his waist and pulled him away while others collared Goodman. Chests heaving, the two men continued to glare at each other, but as best he could, Jacob kept them separated.

Warily, they set off again.

છ૦

At first, the travois was a godsend and their pace improved. Then they started to climb: the ground became so rocky that the frame was broken repeatedly and each time, Hardy was thrown into the dirt. While the others tried to make repairs, Jacob helped his friend settle against a tree. Although his leg was no longer bleeding, the lieutenant's bandages were loose, dirty and, like the travois, in dire need of renovation.

Hardy tried to look his friend in the eye. "Jake, I'm sorry about this."

"About what?"

"About pryin' you away from Adria."

Jacob realized that over the past several days he'd hardly thought about her. Their time together seemed so distant, so ephemeral that it seemed unreal. *Running on like fools.* He pictured her clearly and he shook his head to clear the image. He picked up a twig and scratched a spiral in the dust. "Dan and Charlie are fighting; you're a mess; and Birch seems to have lost his mind. Someone has to look after y'all."

"Yeah, well, not much longer."

"Don't say that!" Jacob scolded, but Hardy couldn't see the harm.

"You're riskin' the others on my account."

"Shut up." Jacob unwrapped Hardy's bandages and winced. Not only had the bullet ripped away the kneecap and supporting tendons, but splintered the tibial plateau as well. Everything was decaying—no part of the joint looked solid. Swearing at the surgeon who had refused to treat Hardy because it would have delayed his flight from Peralta, Jacob began replacing the bandages.

Hardy refused to look at his leg, and instead watched the wind tossing branches against the stars. "Think you'll wait in Mesilla or go back to Brownsville?"

"Mesilla—I'm never going back to Texas." Jacob exhaled, drew the last length of fabric tight, and knotted it. "How's that?"

"Don't feel so good."

"Too tight?"

Hardy exhaled heavily and slumped against the juniper's trunk.

For a moment Jacob's heart froze and then he saw his friend's chest rise and fall. He seized the lapels of Hardy's coat and lifted him onto his one good leg. "Come on, Briggs—you can't die here."

"Neither of us has a say."

"Like hell," he said, rising unsteadily. "This place will not have you." Protesting weakly, Hardy tried to sit back down. "Remember how we wanted a fight worthy of our fire? *Stand up!*"

"No fire left, Jake."

Spence appeared out of the darkness with news that the travois was beyond repair. "Nothin' left to tie it with—no laces, no cords, no cloth—and we'll need our shirts once it gets cold."

Jacob fumed in silence. "Help me carry him, Charlie," he said at last.

The others went ahead, feeling for rocks and branches in the smothering blackness. It took them more than four hours to cover less than a mile.

Federal Encampment, Fort Craig, New Mexico Territory, April 21, 1862

As part of Col. Paul and Col. Chivington's combined forces, the Pinebark Independents had stalked the Texans as far south as the Rio Salado. Then, once the Texans disappeared into the mountains, they had continued downriver to Fort Craig. With Peter MacInnes still recovering from his wounds, James Hay had been appointed to lead their company. Their duties had been light: short patrols or formation and drills during the cool, early hours of the day, and afternoons they pulled guard duty as their New Mexican counterparts labored with pick and shovel to expand the fort's defensive perimeter.

On their third night at the fort, the Independents had drawn second watch along the western road. As midnight passed and the waxing gibbous moon sank, the Texans' fires—tiny points of light against the mountains' black hulk—began to gutter and fade.

Despite two shirts and a jacket on his back, plus close proximity to the fire, Bill Storey could not stop shivering. "Hate these long, cold nights."

"Cold like my stepmother's breath," Hay laughed, staring up at the starlit mountains. "How does a place so hot by day get so cold at night?"

"Nothing t'hold the heat," Storey said and yawned.

"Rocks hold heat—plenty of those around here."

Storey spat in mock disgust. "Don't ask questions ye don't want answered." He stared up at the mountains for a long while—so long that he did not see Peter MacInnes approach.

Peter clapped Storey on the shoulder. "Hello, noit. Weary hours here, but at least there is coffee."

"Pete, ol' son!" Storey embraced his friend before pulling a blanket tighter around his own shoulders. "Knew our captain was back, did ye, Jimmy?"

"He knew," Peter grinned. "I came down with the commissary train this afternoon, but Sam Tappan and the fort's surgeon wanted to make sure that I was up to snuff before they turned me loose."

"And are ye, Pete?" Storey put hands on his friend's shoulders and looked him over. "What about your eyes?"

"Eye," Peter corrected. "That is why God gave us pairs." After the battle on Glorieta Pass, Peter spent two weeks in Santa Fe recovering from his wounds; for the rest of his days he would wear a patch over the empty socket where his right eye had been. A dark red pucker of scar tissue ran between the socket and his ear, ruining what had formerly been a handsome face. The army surgeon had told Peter he could return to Colorado, but he wouldn't hear of it—not when his friends were still in the field.

"Very well," Storey said and clapped him on the shoulder. "I'm glad you're okay. Have ye heard what ye missed?"

"Only from everyone I've met. Ye want that coffee or no?"

"Sure, if it's hot."

A minute later Peter returned with three cups. He cradled his own with both hands in an effort to warm his fingers. All three men held silent as they stared into the darkness. An owl ghosted across the stars; Peter tried to follow its flight, but his remaining eye could not compensate. Hay glanced at Storey, who was staring intently at the firelights up in the mountains. "Same number as yesterday?"

"Essentially," Storey answered, "but now they sprawl. Last night they ran from here to there." He held up his hands, wrists together, and spread his fingers twelve inches apart. "Look, there's the main group still, but now there are gleeds way back there, there—even as far back as that first big peak." This time when spread his arms to point at the line's extremes, the distance between his left and right index fingers encompassed almost four feet of the horizon.

"Bet they are miserable."

"Hell, it's miserable down here awa," Storey said, "and we are well provisioned."

Peter scowled at his cup. "Sort of."

"Think they'll turn and fight us again?"

Peter glanced up and saw one of the points of light go out. "Maybe others will come," he said, "but not those ones—it is all they can manage just to run."

෴

Early the next morning Chivington led his brigade onto the river road, south toward Doña Ana. Around nine, Hay remarked on their stately pace, their frequent and prolonged stops for rest and water. It didn't seem to him that they were in any hurry whatsoever.

Peter adjusted his eye-patch and yawned again. "We aren't— Canby would have 'em know that we're here, but he don't want us to pull ahead." Over the next several nights, they saw fewer and fewer lights up in the mountains. By the fourth night out, they saw none.

San Mateo Canyon, New Mexico Territory, April 23, 1862

All that day they had made only eight steep up-and-down miles, and by four o'clock the exhausted Texans had to lie down and rest. Jacob startled awake and studied the sun's angle. Heavy clouds had built up in the west so that instead of long shadows, everything east of the mountains was dark and indistinct. Guessing that nightfall was less than an hour away, he scowled. Soon they would need to find shelter, for though they had roasted all along their march, once night fell the temperature would quickly follow. Pressing on even as the light failed, all they needed was to follow the trail of dead animals and detritus. Within a hundred yards of where they had napped, they discovered an old swayback mare, still cinched in its traces but half-eaten by wolves. Dan Goodman held his shirtsleeve over his nose. "Accounts for the smell."

Soon after they noted three fresh graves beside the trail, heaped with stones. A pick with a broken handle leaned against a nearby tree. Beyond this lay an old roan gelding—still alive but with one badly broken leg—and it whinnied mournfully as they passed. With a soft heart for animals, Goodman had wanted to put it out of its misery, except that Jacob insisted on conserving their scarce ammunition. Goodman obeyed, but as they passed, a sorrowful light in the creature's eyes made him weep. Counting to himself, he estimated that since noon they had spied no fewer than twenty dead animals. Even as he made his tally, they stumbled upon two more dead mules, both having walked until they collapsed, their bodies sprawled across the track. Coyotes slipped in and out of the trees on both sides of the trail.

The volume of cast-off personals was staggering—the way so littered that it looked as if dozens of traveling merchantmen had simply jettisoned their cargoes. A partial register included bootjacks; several sack coats; various bone and hard rubber combs; mechanical pencils; two inkpots; three snuffboxes; an enameled cooking pot; a pair of cotton underdrawers; matchboxes; saddle bags; a hammer; two meerschaum pipes; random playing cards and cribbage boards; belts—all torn; books, notebooks and diaries galore; a razor strop; numerous carpet bags; flasks; dozens of forage caps; sardine tins (empty); one Enfield carbine with a broken lockplate; three axes leaned against a single boulder; four shirts; a cornet; two nightshirts; torn and crumpled broadsides; various letters; mismatched boots; undarnable socks; two corkscrews; an artilleryman's red-trimmed shell jacket; ghastly surgeon's tools including catlins, bone saws, and bullet forceps; bayonet scabbards by the armful; pens; fuse pouches; more than fifteen knapsacks; cape pins; identification disks; curry combs; a brass candle holder; spurs; an oil painting of saint hovering above a New Mexican church; a saddle shield; a farrier's tool and more still—tons more. Regrettably, no one had cast off anything containing food or water in helpful quantities or condition. So plentiful were these things that after a while the boys walked past without noticing.

Night descended swiftly. As he had with increasing frequency since Hardy mentioned her, Jacob thought about Adria and wished he were by her side. Nearly tripping in the darkness, he cursed his own inattention and vowed to quit such fantasies. At the edge of a broad clearing, he tried to strike a positive tone: "Ten minutes and we'll stop, okay?" Spence, Goodman, and Birch all concurred, but Hardy stayed silent. His friend's head bobbed with each tortured step and Jacob wondered how much farther he could go. Falling back into despair, the next five minutes passed in silence.

Then Hardy looked up and around, from all appearances surprised by their surroundings. "Still? Colder now."

Jacob agreed that it was.

"We been walkin' this whole time?"

Jacob said that they had.

"I thought I had died—"

"Briggs, *stop*—"

"—but it was only a dream. The Most Reverend Bowe was there—how 'bout that?"

Jacob started at the mention of his stepfather's name. "Never met him, did you?"

"Nope."

"Wish I hadn't, neither."

Ten minutes later, they paused and Hardy sat on a tree that had fallen across the trail. Earlier that day wind had toppled this giant: its entire root wad, still loaded with dirt and rock, had been lifted nearly five feet into the air. Shallow notches on its trunk showed where feeble axe-strokes had fallen, yet the hill's steepness and jagged outcroppings had forced the abandonment of two badly damaged buckboards on its uphill side. Drivers had evidently cut their stock free and left behind several more boxes and bags of personal smalls— but again, no food or water.

"There's frustration," Goodman said, but Spence was unsympathetic.

"Quit worryin' about others," he said. "We got troubles of our own."

"Ain't worried about *you*, Charlie," Goodman spat, and again the others had to separate him and Spence before they came to blows.

Breathing heavily, Jacob handed a canteen to Hardy, who forced a few mouthfuls of water past his cracked lips. The others sat listlessly, panting and coughing from their exertions.

Jacob leaned in close to his friend. "Did he say anything?"

"Did who say anythin'?"

"My stepdad—your dream."

"Oh." Hardy's eyes fixed on the trees as a violent wind purled; it moaned across the hillside and he shuddered at the sound. "Light's going," he said, and held out his arms so that Jacob and Tom Birch could help him up. They slid their shoulders under his and returned to the trail. Within a few feet, Hardy tripped and his supporters had to lurch heavily to keep from falling. A few steps later, Hardy answered Jacob's question: "We were back in Texas. Looked it, anyhow—sea oats and lovegrass, cattle grazin' 'neath the scrub. Right about sunup and Reverend Bowe was wearin' a black suit—like an undertaker's."

"Strange," Jacob grunted.

"Well, he came straight toward me through the grass. From your accounts, I thought he would cuff me then—"

"Reckon that was reserved for me."

"—but he didn't. No, sir—he was as kind as could be. Wished us well and asked after you—how you were. Eli Fisher, George Orth, Bossard and Stanhope—all the others."

"They never met him, either," Jacob puzzled. "How'd you answer?"

"Told him the truth." The wind stilled. For several minutes they stumbled along in near silence, save for Hardy's raspy breath and the stones grinding beneath their boots. Indeed, the whole forest had gone silent, breathless as they staggered through its darkened galleries.

"He say anything more?" Jacob grunted.

"Said he'd pray for us." Hardy winced as the pain in his leg flared; even his good foot had begun to drag. He tried to make out individual trees within the darkness, but could not. "Pointed east and said that we where were goin' we would all be safe." Then he slumped again, tripped on a root, and nearly fell; it took all of Jacob and Birch's strength to keep him upright. They crossed a narrow ridge and descended. With only stars for light, there was nothing any of them could do but trust the trail or the next man ahead.

Birch spoke up: "Look."

Jacob craned his neck and saw an orange light between the trees. "Briggs?" he whispered in his friend's ear. "A few steps more—only a few."

Hardy lifted his chin from his chest and grunted that he'd heard. He moved his legs as best he could but even in his agony, he knew he'd become a terrible burden.

ᕫᔢ

Five minutes later, they reached a wide, sloped clearing between two sharp peaks. Within comfortable range of the fire, they lowered Hardy so that he could sit against a fallen ponderosa. Jacob glanced around and saw that Jimmy Burdick and Wyatt Walker—two of the men they had met the previous day—were seated there. Both were backed against a jumble of broken logs; neither said anything as Jacob's boys insinuated themselves into their camp. "Don't mind us," Jacob said.

Burdick startled a little. He scanned the newcomers' faces but did not smile. He turned again to stare at the fire. "Have any food, Cap'n?"

"Panda," Charlie Spence offered, pulling a tin box from his haversack. A food of last resort, panda was paste made from crackers and whiskey. Looking skeletal, Burdick took a pinch and choked it down.

Walker grunted. "Prefer water, if'n you have any."

Goodman pulled out his folding tin cup and poured a rationed serving, which Walker promptly swallowed. He repeated the process for Burdick, who thanked him.

Jacob looked rummaged in his haversack and winced. "Small bacon and hard tack. Anyone else?" Goodman had a quarter-pound of cornmeal and Spence some dry bread; the others shook their heads. "We'll share until we catch up, then." Jacob threw the bacon to Birch.

The corporal curled his lip at the sour meat but skewered it on green twigs. These he set near the coals while the others chewed on their allotted handful of meal. "Lord, what I wouldn't do for a boiled egg."

"Grits and scrapple," Spence said.

"Anything at all," Burdick whispered.

Jacob stared at Burdick and Walker. He thought back to their previous encounter and glanced around the meadow. "Where's your friend?"

Walker drew his knees into to his chest.

Burdick nodded at Hardy. "Beside the lieutenant."

Jacob stood, surprised to have missed someone else. Then at the firelight's farthest edge, he spied a low mound of dirt, outlined with stones.

Goodman removed his cap. "I am sorry, boys."

"Same here," said Birch. "Powerful sorry."

Jacob looked at Hardy and saw that he had fallen onto his side with his mouth open. He didn't appear to be breathing. "Briggs?" Jacob clenched his fingers into fists, but when Hardy made a weak gesture with his right hand, he went over and sat next to his friend.

"We are all dead now," Burdick whispered.

"How did he go?" Goodman glanced back and forth between Jacob, who was trying to give Hardy some water, and the dirt mound.

"Can't say." Burdick's eyes were as dull as his voice. "Sundown, we stopped to rest and Hegler never got up—he died right there. Not a word. Jesus, we carried him all this way..." his voice trailed off.

"For nothing," Walker whispered. "Nothing."

"Not for nothing!" Burdick shouted, but without energy.

"I'm sorry," Jacob said before wrapping his tattered blue coat around Hardy and standing. "Honestly."

"Thanks," Burdick said, sounding a little calmer.

"He's with Jesus now," Birch added.

Uncoiling, Walker took up his knapsack and empty canteen and shook his head. "The Son of Man don't have any use for us; we have not fulfilled His commands."

Birch looked at Jacob, but he did not move even as Walker shouldered his musket and slipped away into the blackness. Doubting his own eyes, Goodman stared at the place where Walker had been.

"Wait!" Jacob shouted, but there was no answer—only the sounds of the wind and their fire. Then the others stood, too, and called after Walker—all with the same result.

"He'll come back," Spence declared but Burdick, too, stood up and began to collect his meager kit.

"Wyatt's right—God's withdrawn his favor and now it don't matter what we do."

"Stay," Jacob said. "Don't go off alone."

Burdick paused to look at the shriveled bacon, sizzling as fat dripped into the fire; its smell was revolting. "Can't see that it matters."

"Come on," Goodman said and held up a shard of bacon for Burdick's inspection. "We don't know what's out there!"

Burdick gauged the void that had swallowed Walker. "Whatever it is, it cannot be worse than this. Good bye, boys." Then gaunt private paused beside Hegler's grave, whispered a prayer, and started after his companion.

"Wait!" Jacob tried again. "That's the wrong direction—we have to go southeast, downhill."

Hesitating, Burdick turned back, his face contorted with disgust. "Lord Almighty, no one will even own that we are *lost* up here! Everyone we meet tells us that food and water are just a ways ahead, but here we are, the same as you! No spring, no food—*nothing!* Nothing but death and darkness. Goddamn, it's so lonely now that I ain't gonna stay here and I will never follow no officer again." He spun away into the gloom.

"We're better off—"Jacob called, but Burdick would have none of it.

"Go to hell," he shouted, his voice already diminished by distance, "all y'all!"

Spence jumped up. "You damned son-of-a-bitch, get back here!" Burdick's hoarse laughter carried back through the darkness— evidence that he was already well down the hillside.

The wind gusted, scattering embers across the dirt. Spence took a step meaning to follow Burdick, but Jacob grabbed him by his sleeve. "Let him go."

"*Captain!*" Spence seethed but Jacob shook his head.

"Let him go."

"What is it, Charlie?" Hardy whispered, "What did he say?"Jacob saw that his friend had propped himself up on an elbow, though his eyes were hardly more than slits.

"He cursed us—told us to go hell!"

Hardy coughed. "Our good intentions have not keep us from it."

Too tired to care what anyone had to say, Birch and Goodman lay quickly down to sleep. Spence swore and tried to swallow but his throat was dry and the effort nearly made him choke. "Was that fellow right, Cap'n? Are we on a bad trail?"

"No." Jacob saw stars shimmering in and out of focus as the night air swirled over the mountaintop. "We ain't lost." Spence had his doubts, but Jacob shushed him and looked around to make sure the others were not listening. "Come daybreak, we'll be able to see forever and we'll take the shortest route down."

"No more mountains," Hardy said. "I'm done."

Staring into the fire, Spence agreed. "Can't any of us do this forever, Cap'n."

Jacob glanced at Birch and Goodman, both of whom were already asleep; neither had touched their meager shares of food. "Next canyon—downhill to the river."

For almost ten minutes, the three wakeful men watched the fire dance, each lost in thought.

Hardy shifted in a vain effort to get comfortable. "Should've stayed, Jake," he said, "should've stayed with her."

"Quit." Jacob put a hand on the back of his neck and looked up, where the Milky Way and quarter moon had turned the darkness into something beautiful. "I chose to be here."

"*None* of us should be here," Hardy retorted.

"For once—," Jacob held his hands toward the fire, "—this once I got it right."

Hardy closed his eyes and rolled onto his side. "Sometimes a fellow's just lost."

∼

The wind died away and bats began wheeling after the insects that darted in and out of the firelight.

Shivering, Spence stirred the coals with a branch. "Yanks'll have the river staked."

Jacob studied the dim eastern horizon and turned a few times before he found what he was seeking. He pointed to a distant cluster of lights: "There—that's Fort Craig. We sideslipped the Yanks, see?

Soon as we get off this mountain, we will find some water and make a run for Mesilla. We will get away yet—you'll see."

"Good fire," Hardy said, "but I'm still cold." Jacob tossed another log into the flames and helped his friend move closer. Hardy opened his eyes and looked at the stars. "Leg's rotten, Jake—hurts bad."

Jacob unrolled the bandage around Hardy's tattered pantleg and recoiled at the sight: red, swollen flesh, hot to the touch; blackened ulcerations around the wound—gangrene, clearly. It smelled like death. Without proper care, it was only a matter of time before Hardy's blood was fatally poisoned. Jacob cut off the dirtiest part of the bandage, scraped threads and putrefied flesh from the wound, and threw these things into the fire. Using the cleanest remainder of the fabric, he re-wrapped the knee as best he could.

"How bad?" Hardy asked.

"Seen worse," Jake lied.

"Nothin' to clean it with."

"We'll get away and find a doctor," Jacob said and placed his own tattered coat across Hardy's shoulders. "You'll make it."

More than anything—their fatigue or lack of food and water—seeing his friend's injured leg made Jacob feel small, useless, and unfit for such a desperate task. As the fire banked, Spence—eventually Hardy, too—drifted off to sleep but not Jacob; he couldn't keep from opening his eyes to count the hundreds of tiny fires burning around Fort Craig. *So many.* How many thousands of Yankees were down there? At last, he grew tired of wondering whether anyone at the fort had spotted their fire, guttering faintly on that cold, dry hilltop. Supposing that they had not, he finally fell asleep just before dawn.

Cuchillo Plain, New Mexico Territory, April 25, 1862

Farther south, the main body of the Confederate Army of New Mexico was faring only a little better. Heat rolled off the parched scrublands and dust devils spun across dun-colored flats. It was as if the air itself had caught fire, and as more and more of their draft animals collapsed, they had abandoned and burned dozens of broke-down wagons. Into these fires, the Texans threw empty knapsacks, empty cartridge boxes, and other paraphernalia so that each pyre continued to burn long after its initial fuel had turned to ash. By this time, few men carried more than basic weaponry, canteens, and the ratty clothes on their backs. Strung out under a pitiless sun, this motley gray pageant staggered southeast, desperate to strike the river before nightfall.

Around noon, a dust-caked cavalryman weaved in and out of the column, clearly searching for someone. "Sirs, have any of you seen General Sibley?"

Sibley, however, was long gone, having ridden ahead in an ambulance to "properly prepare Mesilla to receive his troops." In light of his absence, Lt. Col. Henry McNeill directed the cavalryman to Tom Green. Though many regarded Col. Green as Sibley's boon companion and believed that his tolerance of the general's weaknesses had doomed their entire campaign, he was still their commander.

"What's your message?" Green said.

"Sir," the rider began, "Col. Scurry sent me. That dust rising left of those hills. That's the Yankees, and they're closing fast."

"How many?" Green exhaled, adjusting his hat.

"Can't tell, Sir. Anywhere from one to five thousand."

"That's a broad range, son."

"Can't tell, Sir—sorry. Col. Scurry wanted you to know."

Green squinted through the glare to see what the messenger had meant. *Come to finish us off.* He could see that a column of beige dust had injured the cloudless sky—evidence that something huge was moving on the desert—and of course his Texans were in no shape to confront even an understrength foe. He nodded and removed his gloves. "Col. Scurry's back there?"

"Yessir—about four miles."

"Find him and tell him to hurry, thank you."

❦

On a loose, shaly slope above Cuchillo Canyon, the Texans' teamsters began lowering an ambulance packed with wounded men. Between the braying mules and their drivers' curses, these patients' moans and cries for water went unheard. The wheels with chains, and long ropes were tied to various points on the bed and axles. As they began to skid the wagon down the steep decline, halfway to the bottom a screech of metal announced that the wagon's rear springs had broken. More soldiers ran to help—moments too late, as the anchors that held the wagon's bed to its rear axle snapped, pitching the whole contraption sideways, downhill. For several moments, it threatened to break free and tumble three hundred feet to the floodplain below, likely finishing the work that Yankee bullets had started. The wagon's tongue rose and its traces pulled so that the mules began to scream. Swiftly, though, whole companies ran forward to help, and after a terrific struggle the broken vehicle was halted against a huge boulder and the mules cut free. Remarkably, none of those inside the wagon had their injuries worsened and only one man—with two broken fingers—had joined their ranks. A loud cheer went up and the soldiers set about transferring their comrades to other wagons.

The brigade's senior officers had watched this drama from the canyon's lip. Though most were still mounted, many others had been forced to walk. Wanting to conference without raising alarm, they stepped off the main track and formed a rough circle. Ill and barely

443

upright in his saddle, Tom Green raised a hand to shield his eyes. "Not too much farther—river's at the base of those hills."

Major Lazarus Smith, a lanky former schoolteacher, scratched his beard and glanced north. "No one's said it yet, but once we hit water, I reckon we should halt and wait for the Yanks."

"What?" someone unseen asked. "Why?"

"Need I say it?"

"Won't surrender, Major," the same voice protested.

Smith exploded: "For Christ's sake, my men can scarcely walk! They've no food and their tongues are so black and swollen from lack of water they can hardly breathe—this is suicide, Colonel!"

Conferees on both sides of the divide raised their voices until Green called for order. "*Stop!* Coopwood's Mexicans say there's a well between here and there—four, five miles at most."

Henry McNeill coughed harshly into a dirty handkerchief. "Sir, those Mexicans run off—no one's seen 'em since before noon."

Disheveled, with dust-reddened eyes, Smith stuck his thumbs in his coat pockets and scowled. "And even if we find that well, will Indians have filled it with dogshit and sheep carcasses like the last? Sir, the boys have had enough."

"Any reason to wait on a decision?" In vain, McNeill surveilled the track for answers. "Do we continue, or is this the end?"

Across the circle, Col. William Scurry pressed his horse's skeletal flanks with his bootheels. "*Goddamn* if I'll surrender!" he said and walked his animal through the group. "I *will* take Fourth Regiment through or die in the attempt! Y'all do what you will, but I'm taking mine back to Texas." He left to find and organize what was left of his command. Major Charles Pyron spat in the middle of the circle and followed, leaving the others to fume in silence. Burdened by the weight of their impending decision, none dared comment on Scurry's outburst for fear it would reveal his own misgivings.

Wordlessly, every man in the group started south again.

Less than a mile farther, Green glanced at the cloudless blue sky. "God forgive me. Boys, we are finished."

❧

The company officers went to find his individual units and deliver the news. While cautioned against striking off alone, he gave all men permission to proceed in whatever fashion they chose. Those that made it back to Mesilla would be organized for a return to Texas.

Over the next several hours the entire brigade disintegrated, its constituent members scattered across that hot desert plain. The silence was funereal, the sense of loss and futility almost palpable. Most continued on as before, though many left the track and started east, directly toward the river—a few even turned west. A drop of water on a hot steel plate couldn't have evaporated more completely than Sibley's forces did in that brief span.

Aware that the Army of New Mexico had dissolved on his watch, Green slumped in his saddle and sobbed, and neither he nor anyone else was much consoled when later that evening they finally reached the green banks of the Rio Grande.

Village of Placita, New Mexico Territory, April 25, 1862

On the morning after the sandstorm, Adria Carrizo had returned to the battlefield at Peralta to find that the buckboard she had abandoned was gone. By a stroke of extraordinary luck, however, she did find one of her bags—one containing some clothes and half her money—lying untouched where it had fallen. These funds allowed her to bargain for two reasonably sturdy mules and a small runabout and still have some left over. Into this carriage, she loaded a small stock of blankets, food, and water and joined a caravan of Southern-minded citizens headed for Texas. Following the main Union Army south from Peralta, they found themselves in the company of a great many ne'er-do-wells and unsavory characters, flushed from the lower valley in the way that scavenging creatures follow beasts of prey.

Among the refugees were Rafael and Manuel Armijo, who recognized Adria and permitted her to accompany them. This was fortunate not only because it made her journey more comfortable (in addition to their belongings, the Armijos had packed great quantities of goods and provender, necessitating a fleet of almost thirty wagons) but also because they were accompanied by heavily armed guards, which kept the criminal element at bay. On their third night, they passed Fort Craig, and while Union soldiers taunted them as they rolled past, none impeded their progress. At Paraje Fra Cristobal, however, the brothers' caravan left the river to cross the Journada del Muerto, leaving Adria to continue south by herself.

She carried a double-barreled shotgun ostentatiously across her lap and was thus able to travel as far as the village of Placita without incident. There she took refuge in the home of one her mother's cousins and waited. Each day she drove barrels of spring water up to the side canyons' rims as more and more of the Texan army filtered past. Though many she met knew Jacob Stark (a few of the Cameron Guards even recognized her) and had even seen him at various points since leaving Peralta, none could vouch for his whereabouts. One told her that Jacob, Charlie Spence, and others had started out from Rio Salado with the gravely injured Briggs Hardy, but could provide no other intelligence. Within days, the number of passing soldiers declined precipitously, and on the tenth day following the battle, when she counted only seven, she became overwrought with worry. By the eleventh day, when none at all appeared, she was seized, body and mind, with an unshakable dread. In haste, she left her relatives' village in the runabout, headed south.

Spring Canyon, New Mexico Territory, April 29, 1862

In eleven days, Jacob and the other able-bodied members of their group had carried Briggs Hardy more than one hundred and twenty miles from Peralta over some of the most rugged terrain on earth. On the twelfth day, they left their hilltop camp in the pre-dawn darkness, reached another saddle in the hills, and took a wrong turn. Jacob and Spence had both agreed that the dark, yawning valley before them simply *had* to join the Rio Grande, but in fact they were off the trail by only a few degrees and actually dropped southwest, down San Mateo Canyon toward Alamosa Creek. By a trick of geography, they had effectively crossed over the San Mateo Mountains. In itself, this error had not proved fatal, as a flowing spring in upper San Mateo Canyon had slaked their thirst. Alamosa Creek contained water, too, and when they found an isolated ranch house, they liberated a set-ting hen and its eggs. This detour had consumed two additional days, however, and set them on a course over far rougher terrain. Never did they find any evidence that Burdick, Walker, or any other Texan had preceded them.

Finally they turned east down Alamosa Canyon. Certain that they had cleared the mountains, they were elated to think that the only thing between them and the river was a long, sloping plain. Around six o'clock the next morning they emerged from a ravine and spotted a cavalry unit, riding fast. In fact, these were Confederates paroled at Fort Craig after swearing that they would return to Texas. Given food, water and five rounds of ammunition per man, these fifteen riders had learned of their comrades' detour and ridden west along Alamosa Creek to try and strike their trail. Emerging out of the low sun, however, Jacob's party had assumed they were Yankees and stayed hidden until well after they were gone. Warily doubling back, they lit south into a rising canyon and emerged among a warren of low hills with red-and-white striped soils. Following another sinuous and rocky ravine, they crossed a wide, grassy park from which several dry streams radiated. Desperate to find water, they followed the one with the greenest grass until it emptied into a wide canyon containing a small stream. At last, they had reached Cuchillo Negro Canyon, four days behind even the tardiest of their fellow Texans and still almost twenty miles west of where Col. Green had watched the Army of New Mexico crumble.

A little before noon, they stopped to rest. Within moments of lying down, Spence, Goodman and the others pulled their hats over their eyes and slept. Jacob returned from his lookout on a hilltop above their bivouac to find that only Hardy was awake. Briggs rolled onto his side to inspect his knee: the ulcerations were still spreading and he was running a constant fever. "See anythin'?" he said.

"More hills," Jacob answered. "Stormclouds in the west, though." He took a seat next to his friend. "You sound better today."

"I am not, though—won't ever be." Jacob objected, but Hardy waved him off. "I'm ready."

"We'll find a doctor."

"Won't let 'em amputate."

"Pard, there's no other option."

"I'll *die* before they take my leg!" Hardy bristled.

"That's forever, Briggs—*forever!* You ready for that?" Jacob's hand fell upon a small stone and he threw it as far as he could into the field. "What if forever ain't good? The things we done...what will happen?"

"After death?" Hardy asked, and Jacob nodded. Despite his friend's grim expression, Hardy couldn't help but grin. "Shoot, Jake, I don't know—no one does, and if they say they do, then they're lyin'. Honestly, pard—I didn't think you were that religious."

"I have moments."

Hardy shook his canteen, judged it about a quarter full, and took a small sip. "Nonsense—rules and superstition that your stepdad beat into you. Man's conscience is the only real religion."

"Well, mine gives me fits," Jacob countered. "Plenty I'd change if I had my time again—that's what worries me."

"What, you think you'll be punished after you die?"

"Perhaps."

"What would be the point? Torments in abundance right here."

"Briggs, every day," Jacob's voice cracked, "every day I regret the things I've done."

"See? That's your conscience—that's a hell you've made for yourself. What just god would send you down for another term after you die?"

Jacob shook his head. "Don't think I'll be let off so lightly."

"You done the best you could, Jake—ain't no fairness in this world. The strong abuse the weak, the weak abuse each other, and politicians and the clergy set themselves over everyone." Hardy set his canteen in the shade. "Don't take on troubles that ain't yours."

Jacob looked out over wind-bent grass and hurled another stone. "Just can't stand that she's gone."

"Jenny?"

"Her, too, but I meant Adria. We were right there—this close."

"Then go find her."

"I will."

"*Now*, pard! Leave me so you can get on with your life. Look, Jake, I'm sorry I—"

"You didn't. I know it was Fish who told Don Carrizo about Sarah."

"Shouldn't have encouraged him."

"No," Jacob said, "I understand why he did it—and you, too. I'm the one who's sorry." Off in the distance, a dust devil spun out against the bleached-blue sky. The seconds ticked away, each one insignificant in and of itself, but which taken together were the basis of life. As these moments receded into the past, their worth was multiplied—not only as a record of the events it contained, but because they were gone forever. Jacob folded his legs and stared out over a rugged plain until his vision blurred. There were trials ahead and hard miles to log, but Hardy was right: the only way out was forward. Getting on with his life meant leading his friends out of the desert—here was the only avenue by which he might redeem all the time he had wasted. Beyond their survival, all things—finding Adria, re-settling in California— were immaterial. Thinking of her, a lump formed in his throat, but he kept his eyes open, fixed on the shimmering horizon until every thought of her was gone. The past could not be re-made, but neither could he allow it to be the one thing that shaped the future. The clock would be re-set. "We are heading straight for the river," he declared."

Spence, whom both had assumed was asleep, rolled onto his side, and opened an eye. "Jacob's right, Briggs—the only thing now is to find a doctor. Yankee doctor, if'n it comes to it. No good draggin' you around this way."

"Won't surrender," Hardy swore. "Came here free, and that's how I'll leave."

Jacob stood and nodded to Spence. "Rouse the others. Big canyon across our way and we are gonna follow it. If we push, we might make the river by morning."

"Don't—" Hardy objected, but already Jacob and Spence had collected their meager kits and gone to wake the others.

～

They followed a faint trail eastward and just after sunset found themselves on a low hill above a tiny settlement. Jacob counted twenty-one adobe houses among numerous smaller sheds and barns, many surrounded by coyote fences. A donkey brayed on the village's far side. Corn and bean fields had been scratched into the pinkish soil, as well as what appeared to be squash or melon patches, though these were barely more than sprouts. No one was about and except for smoke rising from the chimneys, the place looked deserted. A herd of sheep was penned behind the nearest farmstead. A dog barked from somewhere in that direction, however, and since the pen was judged too near the house, the Texans decided to pilfer a chicken or grain from one of the outlying sheds instead. Volunteering, Spence and Goodman unshouldered their muskets and started down.

"Only enough for tonight," Jacob whispered. "Don't get greedy."

The others carried Hardy farther up the trail. A light appeared in one of the distant houses, and though Jacob and Birch held their breath, eventually they decided that there was no cause for alarm. Still, looking about, Jacob had an uneasy feeling that the darkness was no longer their friend.

෴

Spence pointed to a likely looking corncrib. Goodman tried the door, found it locked, and then reached between one of the slats to try and work it loose. Then he flinched and ground his molars together to keep from crying out. "Jesus, no," Goodman hissed, "I'm stuck!" Frustrated by a raccoon's persistent raids, the granary's owner had driven sharpened nails at forty-five degrees to the lath surrounding the latch: anyone or anything reaching quickly inside would have been caught. When he attempted to loosen the rigid wooden strips, it only made things worse and he stopped before the nails bit deeper into his hand. He motioned for help and Spence reluctantly abandoned his lookout.

"Be quiet," Spence growled, "let me see." He tried to lift the boards without piercing his own fingers, but the broken bone in his own hand had weakened him and the wood refused to give. First the dog in the sheep's' pen began to bark, and then others joined in.

"C'mon," Goodman pleaded, *"hurry!"*

"Tryin', goddammit—*shut up!"* Spence strained mightily, stabbing his own fingers in the process, but the harder he pulled the deeper the opposing nails dug into the back of Goodman's hand.

"God, you're killing me," Goodman moaned, but Spence kept at it until he managed to lift one nail free from his comrade's palm.

"Try and turn your hand now so it don't get stuck again," Spence whispered. "Think I can get others loose if those damned dogs don't wake the dead first." The barking grew louder, however, and the Texans' anxiety increased; both nearly shouted when Jacob suddenly appeared. Goodman's hand was re-impaled on the first nail and he bit his other knuckle to keep from screaming.

"What the hell?" Jacob swore and knelt alongside.

"Coon trap," Spence whispered. "Help me press down the bottom lath—it has more give." Jacob set his musket down and tried to help, but it was no use: Goodman's hand was hopelessly pinned. The more they pulled one direction, the tighter the nails bit from the other. "Not many get outta this one," Spence said, gesturing at numerous animal pelts tacked to the wall above Goodman's head.

"He will be the first," Jacob promised. Agonized and bleeding profusely, Goodman could only close his eyes and moan.

Spence looked helplessly at Jacob. "What now?"

"I see the nail heads," Jacob whispered. He peered into the gap and felt carefully along its length. "Think I can pry 'em loose from the other direction. Either of you have a knife?"

Spence said no, and Goodman shook his head.

"Then keep quiet—I'll be back in a moment."

Although the boys nodded, Goodman began to cry. "Sorry, man, I can't help it."

"Hold fast," Jacob said.

"Can't help it," Goodman repeated. "Can't believe I'm gonna die here—like *this*. Go on, boys—this is too much."

Spence leaned his musket against the shed, settled his back against its wall, and clasped Goodman's free hand. "Danny," he whispered, "Look at me—*look!* All we can do now is keep quiet, okay? No matter what happens, I will not leave you." Goodman nodded and then Spence closed his eyes and began to pray harder than he ever had before.

Jacob picked up his musket, briefly laid his hand on the top of each man's head, and then ran back uphill as quickly and quietly as he could. He slashed his shins on the sagebrush that overhung the trail—ran until he was breathless and sweat soaked his tattered shirt.

Behind him, the dogs' howls intensified and then he heard a shotgun's unmistakable boom. Someone shouted—Goodman, Jacob thought—and another weapon discharged. Goodman cried out again, but the sound was cut short and then an awful silence fell over the village.

Jacob's pulse thundered in his ears. He pivoted and flattened his body against the side of a sod-roofed shed beside the trail. Glancing uphill, he saw Birch descending cautiously and whispered his name.

"Captain?" Wide-eyed and trembling, Birch lifted his musket and continued downhill until he was standing within the shed's moonshadow. "What happened?" he whispered and the fear in his voice so plain that Jacob made an effort to mask his own.

"Get Briggs and head south, fast as you can!" From down in the village came the sound of slammed doors and footfalls. Several voices were shouting at once, angry, frightened, and indistinct. Jacob put a hand on Birch's shoulder and gripped it tightly. "Hide if you hear anyone coming. All night if you have to—"

"What about you?"

Jacob tamped a cartridge into his musket, tucked the stock beneath his armpit, and wrapped its shoulder strap around his forearm. "I'll catch up as soon as I can. Take my canteen."

"How long do I wait for y'all?"

"Don't," Jacob said. Across the field, more dogs began to bark and howl and someone shouted something that neither Texan understood. "Fast as you can, Tommy, get down to the river."

"What are you gonna do?"

"Gonna see if Spence and Goodman are still alive. Find Briggs, get down to the river road, and wave a white flag at anyone you see—Lord willing, they will be Yankees. Promise me you'll look after Briggs."

"Yes, certainly."

"Okay—," Jacob shook Birch's hand, "—good luck." Still crouched, Jacob turned and ran back toward the village. He moved hurriedly between the buildings and ducked around corners. Stopping to listen, he heard nothing, saw nothing. From the sound of it, he guessed that the dogs were moving away, up the creekbed. No voices, no footfalls—no crickets for that matter. Something felt off; the village had gone completely silent. He knelt and glanced quickly to his left. Still nothing. He pulled the musket's hammer back. A twig cracked on his left and he looked up. At the edge of his vision, a shadow shifted. There was a faint whoosh as though a bird had swooped past and then the night exploded.

Las Animas Canyon, New Mexico Territory, April 30, 1862

Away from the fire, it took a few minutes for Peter MacInnes's eye to adjust. Out on the desert, nights were cold, clear, and resplendent with millions upon millions of stars. One night during the crossing from Belfast there had been a fire in the ship's coal bunker; it had been the only time he'd been allowed up on the deck, and the sky that night had been similarly huge. Previously that memory had made him long to see Ireland again, but this time he was surprised to find that it triggered no emotion—if anything, he was struck by the realization that at long last he was home. *Here, of all places.*

He shook his head softly and whistled.

The Pinebark Independents had been among those units deployed to patrol the major side drainages west of the Rio Grande—according to Peter's map, they were in Las Animas Canyon. Sent to watch for Confederate stragglers they had seen no one at all, dead or alive. As evidence that anyone had *ever* been there, the Coloradans recovered only one worn-out boot, an arrowhead, an empty haversack, and a single broken spur. Even their footprints were quickly erased by the wind. Peter made a catalogue of the empty days and nights since they had left Fort Craig. With daytime temperatures near one hundred degrees, he'd limited their patrols from sunup until ten, and from five until sundown. In between, they had sought shade and rested. Not surprisingly, the company was growing restless. He saw a shooting star explode across the sky. Supposing it meant something, he thanked God, kissed his fingers, and tapped his chest three times—something he'd picked up from a cousin back in Ireland. *No need for old habits now—everything now is new.* Another meteor crossed the sky and this time he thanked God and kept his hands in his pockets. He adjusted his eye-patch, which tended to rub against the scar on his cheek.

James Hay approached and stood beside him. "See 'at, did ye?"

"The falling star? Aye, from here to there."

"Augur anything?"

"Beyond my ken. Probably hot again tomorrow."

"Every day the same." Hay glanced about for a landmark and finally settled on the silhouette of a rock shaped like a boot. "How's yer head?"

"One eye works."

"Now you're ugly like me—how does it feel?"

Peter laughed and turned toward the fire. "Take more than one lost eye to bring me down t'yer level. Boyo, tomorrow we will push further west, almost to the foothills—maybe see some Indians."

"No, thank ye." Hay scowled. "I've fought enough for one lifetime."

Peter clapped his friend on the shoulder. "We won't look very hard, then."

"I'd appreciate that."

Peter looked at the blazing stars. "Think we're almost done here—I really do." Their cook-fire had long since gone out, and except for the crickets, their camp was silent. Peter glanced up, hoping to see more fireworks.

Hay scratched at the back of his sunburned hands and yawned. "Soon as this is over, what then?"

"Weeks ago, I had thought I would go find Dan Conroy and be done with him, but now I think I'm done fighting. I only to go someplace quiet."

"That right?"

"Time we did something with ourselves."

"Believe this qualifies."

Peter nodded. "Montana, then. A homestead with cattle, chickens, hayfields."

"Think so?"

"Or Nevada. See if the women there don't like us any better."

"Ha, ha," Hay laughed. "Yer eye is gone, but yer delusions remain."

Town of Mesilla, New Mexico Territory, April 30, 1862

In Doña Ana, some thirty miles from Franklin, Texas, and fifty miles north of the Mexican border, Adria learned that Jacob Stark and a tenth of his company had failed to report. For three days, she haunted the disorganized Confederate camps that were scattered throughout the valley, and despite asking questions and demanding answers from every solider she'd met, she learned exactly nothing.

General Sibley corresponded with Jefferson Davis, Gen. Hamilton Bee, and others. At first, he minimized the extent of their troubles, but after learning that Robert E. Lee had authorized reinforcements (which would make it harder to forestall an unpalatable re-invasion), he came clean. To Davis he wrote that "...except for its political geographic position, the Territory of New Mexico...[was] not worth a quarter of the blood and treasure expended in its conquest." He admitted that supplies were too scarce to continue (which he blamed on the land's natural poverty, the failure of Confederate procurement agents in Mexico, and the government's failure to provide financial support) but insisted that his army remained undefeated on the field. To stage a return to San Antonio, Sibley proposed reconcentrating the brigade at Fort Bliss, immediately over the border in Texas. Limited reinforcements would remain in Mesilla to try and hold onto the Confederate Territory of Arizona and serve as a bulwark against any Federal advance. General Bee agreed with this plan, and very quickly, much of the army began to depart.

As various units assembled in the fields below Mesilla, Adria made one last effort to learn something—anything—about Jacob's situation. On the eve before his tattered company departed, someone directed her to Wyatt Walker, who described leaving Jacob's group on the mountaintop. She'd practically dragged him to a cartographer's tent and, as best he could, made him pinpoint the location on a map. Then she sketched a hasty copy for herself, traded her last gold coins and jewelry for new supplies, and set out again, upriver, into the gathering darkness.

Pinatosa Canyon, New Mexico Territory, April 30, 1862

The rancheros seized Jacob by his hands and feet and carried him to a shed near the village's center. One named Baca—short, solidly built, with broad, soft features reflecting his mestizo heritage—held Jacob's wrists and walked backward. "Let me change my grip."

Trujillo—younger, taller, and darker—grunted between breaths in mountain-Spanish: "Heavier than all but that big fellow—must be an officer."

"Skin-and-bones, all the same."

Reaching a cowshed, they set Jacob down near the other Texans' bodies. "Motherless *pendejos* got what they deserved," one said.

Trujillo pointed to Birch and whistled. "Another? Where'd you find *him?*"

A third man answered: "Tomas saw him running back uphill and shot him."

Moments later, other *rancheros* carried in Hardy on a makeshift litter and set him at the base of a wall. A dead-flame lamp was hung from a nail in one of the *vigas* and the *rabajeños* exited.

Baca paused in the doorway. "If he'll take it, give that one with the shitty knee some water."

Juan Lebrija, one of the men who'd helped carry Hardy, scratched his head. *"Porqué?"*

"Keep 'em alive for a little while longer. Need to know if they're stragglers or the first among other *Tejanos* coming down the canyon." The villagers went outside to smoke in the cool night air and to wait for one of the two surviving Texans to come around.

459

Lebrija gestured at Hardy, whose eyes fluttered open and shut and who appeared to be in great pain. "He's dying, sure."

"*Ya le tocaba.*" Trujillo stepped back into the shed, held Hardy's feverish head upright, and gave him sips of water from a clay jar.

Outside, Baca's younger brother, Tomas, threw a stick at a fence, irritated by a dog that would not stop barking. "Should've killed Trujillo's mutt instead."

"*Viva* Pico!" Trujillo beamed. "Who told us these whoreson bastards were here, huh?"

Lebrija emerged from the shed, stretched his arms, and took a drink of water from the jug. "Glad it was these ragged fuckers and not Apaches," he said, and with good cause: twice in the preceding decade, Apaches had attacked the village, burnt several buildings, and driven off livestock. Five settlers had lost their lives in these raids and only the year prior an old rancher, Blas Ruel, was caught all alone in the upper pastures and riddled with arrows. Tomas crossed himself and the others nodded.

"Hey, *tipo,* look—the one I hit on the head is coming around," Lebrija said. Baca jumped down from his seat on an adobe wall. He approached cautiously, unsure how quickly the *Tejano* soldier might regain his bearings.

He needn't have worried—Jacob moved with glacial slowness. Every heartbeat felt like a kick in the head, each pulse a jab in the eyes. The bones in his neck and skull ached, too, and he was beyond exhaustion, unable to do more than hold perfectly still and blink. Even sitting, he felt dizzy. He did not know the man standing above him and he worried that perhaps he *ought* to. "Who?" he asked, but received no answer. Baca offered him water and he took the jar, but he was too tired to raise it to his lips. The *ranchero* glanced over his shoulder at his comrades and raised his eyebrows.

Gradually Jacob's surroundings came into focus and he remembered what had happened: then the shed, the lamp overhead, the unfamiliar faces in the doorway began to make sense. On the right were his comrades' broken bodies and nearby, Hardy was propped haphazardly against a wall. He wanted to point, to speak, to ask questions, but all he could do was stare. He noticed that Hardy was still breathing. *Good.* "Briggs," he rasped in a voice like a crow's. He reached over, tapped the foot on Hardy's uninjured leg, and called his name again.

Hardy opened his eyes. "Jake."

"How..." Mere speech made his head pound worse but he forced himself to continue: "How you set?"

"Not well," Briggs whispered.

"Gonna ask them to get you a doctor."

"No—," Hardy exhaled, "—no more."

Jacob looked at the *ranchero* who had brought the water. *"Médico?"* he asked, pointing at Hardy. Around the room, his request was met with blank stares. Outside, thunder cracked and fat raindrops began to pelt the village. Many of the *rancheros* whooped for joy and scattered as they sought dry spaces beneath overhangs and eaves.

"Where is this?" Jacob asked.

"Todos Santos." Baca knelt so that he and Jacob were eye-to-eye. "Caught your friends stealing food."

Jacob saw no point in evasion. "Starving."

"Might've asked."

"Would you have said yes?"

Baca grinned unhappily. "Other *gringos* came through Sunday and took your share, see?"

The pain in Jacob's head was horrible, but he managed to gesture feebly toward Hardy. "Get my friend a doctor?"

Baca chuckled and translated for the others standing outside, and they laughed, too. "Nearest doctor's in Socorro—"

"Fort Craig," Trujillo corrected. "Why don't you try there first?"

"We did—in February." Jacob felt the bloody gash in his scalp. "They wouldn't have us."

Baca handed the jar to Jacob. "I get it, see? Man has to eat. But some of the boys out there *hate* Yankees—had family killed by *Tejanos*, see? Others have had cattle confiscated by soldiers from the fort. Me? I got no quarrel, *güero*, except that I have family to protect—that's all."

Jacob took the jar, pulled himself across the ground to where Hardy lay and held it to his friend's lips. "Will you turn us over to the Yankees?"

"No," Baca scoffed.

"Take him to the fort, at least."

"And say what?"

"That you found a wounded Texan—they'll take him in."

"And once he recovers? What will he say then? Sorry, but no *gente* in his right mind puts himself in a white jury's sights." Baca shrugged. "Your travels end here."

Jacob saw then that Baca held a revolver in his left hand. His pulse raced and the pain in his skull flared, but he became acutely aware of the sounds around him: the slackening rain, whispered Spanish out in the darkness, and moths battering themselves against the lamp-glass. Baca raised the weapon and pulled its hammer back. Jacob looked at Hardy, his mangled leg at a grotesque angle, septic. His face was a mask of pain. *Look how he suffers maybe death is preferred and please, Jesus, bear me over the river to see my dearest Jenny and I will live on in Adria's dreams and Lord, how the air is cool with rain and smells like wet earth and wool and how that lamp paints the air yellow like the last hour before a summer sunset when everything is still...* Fixated on a cobweb in the corner, Jacob waited, waited, waited for the jolt, but it never came.

"Don't move," he heard Baca say, and then he realized that he was still alive. The short Mexican stepped outside and Jacob never saw him again. He heard Baca's voice among others and then an older, harsher one, but after a brief exchange all talking ceased and there was only the sound of fat raindrops. For a full minute, Jacob listened, able to hear water rolling off the branches outside, dogs barking, and finally, the *rancheros'* voices again.

Briefly, Hardy emerged from his fog and glanced toward the door. "Jake, where are we?"

Jacob coughed to clear his throat and his head pounded from the effort. "Not sure."

"Don't care if they kill me now."

"Just hold on," Jacob rasped, but Hardy closed his eyes. Jacob studied the bodies of his companions: Spence and Birch had been shot, but even Goodman—stabbed repeatedly as he lay with his hand pinned inside the granary—looked peaceful. Jacob felt his heart ache and he wiped at his eyes.

Trujillo stepped through the doorway with a three-legged milking stool and set it before Jacob. As soon as he left, an old man walked in and sat down. Several moments of silence passed as he and Jacob studied one another. *"Tejano,"* the man said at last, "do you remember me?"

Jacob thought the man looked vaguely familiar but his thoughts were so turbid that he shook his head, causing fresh pain to overfill his skull. "No."

"My name is Don Sena. Two months ago, *güeros* killed my grandsons in a village across the river and you were there. Do you remember now?"

This news made Jacob's head hurt worse, but try as he might he could not fix the memory. He remembered the fight at Glorieta—most of it, anyway—fair bits from Santa Fe—especially Adria—but the rest was too scrambled, too fragmented to organize. "Sir," he began, "I'm sorry, but I *don't* remember. Your picture is familiar so I reckon that I *should,* but I do not. I am sorry about your boys. If I'd anything to do with their deaths, I am truly sorry." At this, Jacob expected the old man would leave and send in an executioner, but instead he merely stared. He stared so long that Jacob grew flustered. *What the hell do you want?*

The old man rose and motioned toward the darkness. Trujillo appeared, bowed, and took away the chair. He spoke to the don in Spanish: "Don Sena, what will we do with them?"

"Bury the dead in the *camposanto,"* Sena answered. "These two may go."

Trujillo looked stricken. "Don Sena—"

"Let them go!" Reverting to English, he pointed at Jacob: "I trust that you have told me the truth, so understand this—at least once in your life you acquitted yourself honorably. That alone has saved you tonight."

Jacob's head hurt from confusion as much as injury. "I'm not sure—"

Sena ignored his protest and pointed to Hardy. "Can he walk?"

"Him?" Jacob rose to a knee. "Four of us carried him this far."

"You'll have to manage."

"Can you spare a mule? Take the muskets or anything else we have."

"I don't want anything you have." Don Sena pointed outside. "I only want you gone." He stepped toward the door and nodded at Trujillo: "Give them some water and cornmeal. Then take them up to the high road and point them south."

Jacob stood—an act that unleashed torrents of pain and forced him to lean heavily against a wooden pillar. "Sir, I cannot carry him by myself."

Don Sena paused in the doorway. "Then leave him—it was your decision to come here." With that, he disappeared and Trujillo whistled for others to come and help. Tomas, Lebrija, and others entered the shed, lifted Hardy onto his sound leg, and motioned for Jacob to help. He slipped Hardy's arm over his shoulder and staggered outside. The tallest ranchero helped to steady the Texans until they reached the valley's rim, and then he started back toward the village.

Tomas handed Jacob a half-empty canteen and a small bag of cornmeal. He pointed south. "Two miles, this road, you find a watered canyon. Follow it east but not too far—it turns north again near the river. You'll see a cluster of low hills—head south for these. Beyond these is a big canyon—this is Seco and it runs dry all the way to the river. Cross it and continue south to the next one—it is Las Animas, and it usually has water. *¿Comprendé?*"

"No," Jacob protested. His head hurt so badly that just then even the simplest directions would've confused him.

"Good." Tomas handed him his empty Maynard rifle and started back.

Caballo Canyon, New Mexico Territory, May 1, 1862

———— ◆ ————

Jacob managed to drag Hardy nearly three miles before the skies opened again. Soaking wet, the muddy path grew slick and their footing grew treacherous. Every few minutes, lightning flashed and though the thunderclaps that followed tortured Jacob's head, he was glad for the light. On the rim of Caballo Canyon, he tried to build a fire but eventually gave up and helped Hardy into poor shelter beneath the porous canopy of a huge spreading cedar.

Then the sky cleared, the moon set, and in the darkness the stars emerged to throw soft light across a glittering landscape; every hillside looked as if it was covered with millions of diamonds. Teeth chattering, wracked with fever, Hardy whispered that he had never seen anything so beautiful. Exhausted, Jacob passed out almost the moment his head touched the ground, but he did remember that his friend clasped his hand and thanked him for staying with him for so long.

"Never would've seen this," Hardy exhaled. "Thanks, Jake." Then he, too, rolled onto his side and drifted off.

༄

When Jacob awoke the next morning, the sun was already up. For a while, he lay on his back and listened to the wind in the grass. The rain had all run off and left a top-dressing of mud underfoot, but the air was crisp and at once, he felt hopeful. From the cedar's highest branches, tiny songbirds called to one another. His head still ached, but less than before, and he thought that certainly they would reach the river by nightfall. Hard miles lay ahead but for the first time in days, he felt his confidence renewed. With luck, they might meet fellow stragglers or civilian refugees. They might even be able to trade the musket for Hardy's swift transport to Mesilla and a doctor's care.

He sat up and looked at his friend, lying on his side in the dirt. The wind tousled Briggs's hair and the collar of his shirt but otherwise he lay still. Jacob called his name, but there was no answer: released from pain, Briggs had died in his sleep just moments before sunrise.

Lower Las Animas Canyon, New Mexico Territory, May 1, 1862

By one-thirty that afternoon the temperature had reached one hundred degrees and every rock, every bush, every yellow blade of grass shimmered, hazy and indistinct. Adria turned the runabout uphill, away from the river. In the first two miles, she passed small, withered fields and tumbledown houses. The entire region seemed deserted and she despaired of finding anyone who could tell her anything about the Texans who might have passed this way. As much as she told herself to be patient—that this was but one of several canyons she would have to prospect—very quickly she was losing hope. In that heat-haunted land, each passing minute made it less and less likely that Jacob would be found alive—if, indeed, he could be found at all. Every cloud had been burned from the sky, and although it was cooler in the canyon's higher reaches, this was by scant degrees. Before long, Adria's lips were cracked and her eyes reddened. She rode past a grove of gnarled cottonwoods and made a mental note that upon returning, she would look there for water. The canopy she rigged from branches and a blanket afforded her a little shade, though it also limited her field of vision. For this reason, she had heard footsteps several moments before she saw soldiers scrambling out of the scrub on her right. A blue-coated rider ran directly into her path and lifted a rifle. Startled, she fumbled for the shotgun but suddenly they were everywhere, whooping and shouting like schoolboys.

"Hike, hike, *hike!*" they called to the mules.

She saw no means of escape and reined the animals to a halt. Her thoughts flashed back to her run-ins with Felix Ortega and fear wrung her vitals. Her heart beat wildly, even after the men removed their hats and drew closer.

࿂

None among the Pinebark Volunteers spoke Spanish. Peter MacInnes was steeling himself for a half-hour of hand gestures when the woman in the buggy spoke first: "Sir, please—I mustn't be delayed!"

Peter exchanged looks with Sammy Douglas and approached the rig. Incautiously, Peter kept his hands open at his sides, but Douglas set his musket's buttstock tight to his shoulder, its barrel a few degrees below level. "Jaysus, Miss, are ye lost?" Peter said.

Adria glanced around the circle of faces. "No—I've come here to look for someone."

"Hold by!" Douglas sputtered with astonishment. *"I know her!* I've seen at her afore!"

"Please," she said and looked over Peter's head to the rising canyon.

"Sammy?"

"At Tijeras—Hay had me ride with her and Col. Canby's wife. She's his niece, right? Find James—he'll tell ye the same!"

"He's in the lower camp." Peter gestured downhill and shouted: "Someone go get Hay!"

"Ain't that right, Miss—" Douglas started but Adria cut him off.

"Yes, but now I am looking for a Texan—one of their officers," she said. "Has anyone been down this way?"

"Not 'til now," Douglas said.

When he looked up, Peter had to shade his eye from the intense corona around her head. "Ain't safe here, Miss."

"Nor anywhere, truly."

Peter didn't know what to make her. "Are ye the Canbys' kin, true?"

She ignored the question. "No one's come this way? No one at all?" She turned head to scan the horizon and her hand fell across the shotgun's stock.

"Och, unhand that!" Douglas said and lifted his musket.

468

"Wait, Neil!" Peter said, raising his hand. "Wait."

"I didn't—" she hesitated, but for the kindness in Peter's smile she moved her hands to the edge of her seat. It took a moment for her heart to settle so that she could speak. She looked squarely into the Coloradan's uncovered eye. "Please, I need your help—you haven't seen anyone up here, have you?"

Squinting against the glare, he could see how dirty and ragged she was, how her fine clothes had frayed, yet she carried herself in such a way that he accorded her respect. "No one, Miss. There are farms near the riv—"

"No," she shook her head.

"There's no one up here," he said. "No one."

She inhaled sharply and felt the burning air hiss between her teeth. She closed her eyes and clenched her fists. "Are they all dead, then?"

Peter did not know how to answer. He had not personally seen the sad procession of *mujeres* who had gone south after Valverde in search of their missing husbands and sons, but he'd heard stories. His own family had been gone so long that took it some imagination to speculate on what might drive someone to face such risks. Then he thought of all he and his friends had been through together, and realized that he might very well have done the same thing. "Wait down at Hot Springs," he said. "Ye aren't safe up here."

She smiled sadly and shook her head. "I have to know."

Peter nodded as though he understood, even though he did not—not one bit. He leaned away from the carriage. "Is this fellow kin?"

"Yes," She said and wiped at her eyes.

He tried to sound hopeful, "Have ye been to Mesilla? It's said they're still—"

"He isn't," she said, "not him. He and others were last seen north of here. I'd hoped that they'd have made it this far, but it seems that my hopes are misplaced."

Peter could see no reason to detain her. Indeed, if she'd made it this far, he didn't want to be the thing that unmade her search. He lifted his cap. "Go," he said, "we won't stop ye."

"You're letting me go?"

He handed her his canteen. "Take this."

"Thank you," Adria whispered. She wanted to smile but her cracked lips hurt so much that nodded instead. "Truly, thank you."

He tipped his cap again and stepped away from the buggy. "We'll be here. Boys!" he shouted to the soldiers farther up the road, "let 'er by!"

"Bless you, soldier," she said and tugged on the wide brim of her hat. Then she flicked the reins and the mules went forward, westward into the desiccating wind.

∽

As the wagon lumbered slowly up the track, Douglas walked over and stood beside Peter. In silence they watched as heat waves rose, swiftly dissolving the vehicle and its driver.

Douglas shook his head. "We all go heels first, but she's downright anxious, ain't she?"

Peter lifted his cap to scratch his forehead. "Can't imagine the girl who'd brave the fiery huffles for me."

"No such a creature," said James Hay, only recently arrived from the company's camp.

Douglas turned at the sound of his voice. "Remember her? Rode with that other woman—said she was Canby's niece?"

"She lied."

"Sure," Douglas agreed. "Nothing is on the level down here. She's off her bap, though, travelling alone like that."

"She has her reasons," Peter said. "Now, let's everyone get back. Get your gear together—tomorrow we are going back to the river." As Hay and others turned and started down into the canyon, Peter stayed and watched the slow, black buggy labor higher and higher along the road. He tried to pull some of the dust off his teeth with his tongue, but his mouth was too dry. "Good luck," he whispered and turned to follow his friends.

Seco Canyon, New Mexico Territory, May 1, 1862

Jacob walked slowly and prayed that a wide cleft he'd spied earlier was just beyond the next rise. Indeed, within a tenth of a mile, he came to Seco Canyon, and it was as dry and barren as the Mexican had promised.

Directly ahead were the sun-scorched Caballo Mountains and he thought he recognized the pass through which he and Hardy had ridden back in January. *Briggs Willits Hardy, age twenty—goodbye, brother.* It wasn't until ten o' clock that he'd stacked the last rock on top of his friend's body, and already it had been blazingly hot. Feeling low, he'd started across another parched flat, hoping to find the river before he ran out of water. Despite ready landmarks, however, the ground was quite rough and the dry stream channels choked with brush, which made it necessary to backtrack repeatedly in search of easier routes. For two hours he threaded between red hills humped up above labyrinthine canyons, until he was no longer certain that he was headed the right direction. The sun was at its zenith and real heat—twenty degrees hotter than the air—began to radiate from the ground. His brain pounded so badly that the landscape—red rocks, yellow grass, blue sky—turned gray, washed out except for reddish auras around individual objects. He was consumed by the thought of water. When he passed a ledge that smelled strongly of animal urine, he realized that he had not pissed in two days.

Seco Canyon's steep walls were crenellated with hundreds of small side-canyons and Jacob found that he could walk for no more than ten minutes before he had to duck inside these folds and rest in their shade. He covered five miles this way—too slowly, he knew. His odds of surviving were negligible and falling.

⁓

At the top of a rocky cleft, he turned his ankle in a crevice between two volcanic boulders. He exhaled heavily. *Wait for dark? Dead by then—can't stop.* He spied a lone juniper on the canyon's rim, hobbled toward it and crawled beneath its lowest limbs. Its thorny dead-fall stabbed his hands and caught in his hair, but he hardly noticed. Taking a tiny swig of water, he vomited blood. Nauseated, he wiped at his mouth. *Don't know how much more of this I can take.* His memories and senses had begun to fuse, so that when he heard a familiar voice it seemed perfectly natural.

"Ain't this a wretched shape?" Jacob saw that Eli Fisher, too, had taken shelter beneath the tree, but his clothes were neat and his beard trimmed, as though he had just returned from church.

"Thanks." Jacob spat in an effort to clear his throat. "Won't tell me how good I look?"

Eli chuckled. "I am beyond lies."

"Lyin' was never your problem, pard." Jacob took another sip from the canteen. Mercifully, this time the water stayed put and he closed his eyes. "Lord, Fish, I'm sorry how things turned. Never meant for any of this—"

"No, things happen as they are meant to."

"Honest to God, I should've—"

"No, pard, I apologize for what I did—it wasn't but jealousy."

Glancing beyond the juniper's shade, Jacob saw one man walk past, then another—then hundreds. An entire army on the march, southward into the blistering heat. Men in uniform, others in homespun, and all drenched in sweat. He could taste the dust that they stirred. Low voices, shouted commands, and laughter—individual notes in a fading symphony—were indistinct beneath a drumbeat of worn-out boots. A bird warbled loudly from the juniper's highest branches and these figures faded from view—all except one.

Eli nodded. "See you down the road, Jake."

Jacob took another sip of water and guessed there was less than a cup left in the canteen. "Fish, do you think I'll make it?" he wondered, but already his friend was gone. Jacob crawled back into the sunlight. Feeling the heat upon his dirty hair, he put two fingers inside a bullet hole in his shirt, ripped away the lowest third, and tied this fabric across his sunburned scalp. White-hot, the sun refused to leave the cloudless sky.

෴

Gripping the musket, he took a ginger step on his bad ankle. It held. He took another, and another, and within twenty minutes, he had crossed a flat-topped ridge and reached the next gulch. There he found a faint deer path leading south. Then the trail vanished into a warren of low mud hills, overgrown with scrub oak and yucca, and with no obvious exit. "Shit," he said and leaned against a roasting boulder. His canteen barely sloshed but he drank anyway and held the vessel over his mouth until the last drop fell. He guessed it was around three in the afternoon, which meant at least three more hours of light and heat. A mile to the east, a lazy dust devil spun itself out. Then Jacob's thirst, already horrible, became a ravenous thing and he couldn't think of anything except water and what he wouldn't do for some. In the shade of another boulder, he heard birds warbling. For a moment, he thought about catching one of these creatures and drinking its blood, but quickly dismissed the idea as absurd. *Or a lizard.* "Shit." His mind went immediately back to his last drink. "I'll die out here."

"Jake." Hardy stood next to him and squinted into the distance. "You're on your way back. Does your head hurt?"

"Terribly."

His friend nodded sympathetically.

"How much farther?" Jacob shielded his eyes.

"Not much—don't stop now."

Jacob rose onto unsteady feet. Starting down the likeliest looking arroyo, each step was a labor unto itself. Branches slashed at his paper-thin skin and inflicted terrible cuts. "Sorry, Briggs—" He stopped and thought he might cry, except that he had no tears to give. With so much water lost without replacement, he had stopped producing sweat and his temperature continued to climb. "I'm sorry."

"Don't be—you stayed to the end." Hardy walked ahead, sometimes dissolving into shadow and at others, appearing so clearly that Jacob reached out to grasp his hand.

Vomiting another gout of dark, sticky blood, such pain flooded Jacob's head that he had to clutch at his temples with both hands. Rather than spit, though, he was so desperate for moisture that he swallowed everything he could, gagging at the coppery taste. "Wasn't enough."

"It was everythin' to me," Hardy said and faded from view.

Jacob set out again. Over the next hour, the rugged corrugations between Seco and Las Animas canyons slowed his progress. As he picked his way between greasewood and rocks, twice he mistook the wind's hiss for the sound of rushing water and his heart sank once he realized his mistake. His swollen tongue stuck to the roof and sides of his mouth; his lips were cracked and blackened. More and more often, he began to stumble, sometimes catching himself and at others pitching full into the rocks and sand. By the time he reached the rim of Las Animas Canyon, he guessed it was about four o'clock—still more than two hours from sundown.

Upper Las Animas Canyon, New Mexico Territory, May 1, 1862

Following her collision with the Yankee soldiers, Adria's situation grew steadily worse. Around four o' clock, she noticed that one of her two mules had begun to ignore its reins. She stopped and gave both animals more water, but it wasn't nearly enough to replace what they had lost. The balky creature looked shocked, barely able to continue; its mouth was tacky, gummed with dried spit, and its ears and lower limbs were cold. Feeling wretched, she stroked its mane and whispered apologies, but within minutes, it knelt in its traces and died. Its harness jerked taut, forcing the other animal to support its dead weight. The surviving creature whined and stamped nervously and Adria lost nearly twenty minutes as she struggled to work its cinches free.

All the while, the hot, dry wind continued unabated and blasted her with heated grit. She meant to tether the remaining mule in the shade of some trees along the creekbed and wait for nightfall, but once it was free of its harness the animal panicked, pulled loose, and ran. She gave chase for a few minutes but it evaded her every attempt to throw a rope around its neck and she could only watch as it fled back down the road. Within minutes, it had vanished from sight. Adria returned to the disabled rig and rummaged around it the box for the canteen the Yankee captain had given her. Mercifully, it was still full. She took a haversack with some bread and dried apples but left the shotgun lying across the seat.

A solitary bird trilled in one of the cottonwoods and Adria raised her eyes at the sound. As she did, she noticed a figure, very small, moving slowly along a distant ridge. Startled, she pushed away from the wagon and tripped over the dead mule's foreleg. She stumbled, fell, and gashed her hands on flinty shards in the soil. Still on all fours in the dust, not once did she take her eyes off the figure in the shimmering distance. She blinked and rose to her feet. "Is it you?" she whispered but the words caught in her mouth. After studying the land between her and this apparition, she fixed a path that would allow her to cross the canyon without having to scale its steepest walls or fall too far behind the moving figure. North and east were hills she was sure would still be visible from the canyon floor; committing these landmarks to memory, she set out.

၈

Jacob stood on the rim of Las Animas Canyon. Down below were cottonwoods and willows, as well as what he took to be pools of shimmering water. Here, though, the canyon walls were too sheer for him to scale—certainly in his weakened condition—so he turned east, downstream, to seek entry. *Cold fire, fallen star, death.* He no longer trusted anything his senses conveyed. As his skin dehydrated, the nerves in his back and arms began to fire erratically, making him itch. In frustration, he ripped off the last tatters of his shirt and tried to scratch himself, but though he cut himself, it did not help. With every limitation dissolved by heat, dreams overtook reality and he found himself among hundreds of other soldiers. "This is my fault—led y'all into a void."

"Someone had to." Eli Fisher moved aside as Jacob stumbled east along the canyon's rim. "Rain don't blame the river for leading down to the sea—that's just the order of things." He appeared again, a little lower on the trail. "Doesn't' matter if at some point we believed we'd be somewheres other than here—that wasn't meant to be."

"Failed," Jacob croaked.

"No," Eli whispered, sounding like the wind in the grass. "I see now what I could not then."

Looking ahead, Jacob spotted Hardy standing at the head of a small, sinuous defile that led down into the larger canyon. Standing beside him, George Orth pointed. Jacob started down.

❧

His heart was full of joy. *He held little Jenny on his arm beneath a flowering tree and she reached out to touch the white blossoms. Sunlight filtered through the green leaves and the white blossoms and he could smell the flowers and his sweet little girl's hair. He reckoned he was in heaven. I was so lonely before—would that I had held on with all my strength. Adria reached out and took his hand and together they walked out of the desert. Hundreds more were there with them: fathers, sons, brothers, husbands, each beloved of someone weeping sad and lonely at home. Shropshire, Adair, Buckholts, Lockridge, Raguet, Metzger, Hardy, Spence, Orth, Goodman, Birch, Garza, Miller, and others—so many others—all marching forever. Bloody footprints in sand and snow.*

The light was turning, the day's heat diminished, but Jacob did not notice. When he looked west, a blast of hot air punched him in the face and he trembled in fear. *Light played across her face as she turned toward me and smiled. I stood before her, even closer, and smelled her hair, her skin, and I would not close my eyes for fear the moment might vanish. With tender haste, I leaned in to kiss her and her lips were even softer and sweeter than I had imagined.* "God save me," he whispered, pushed away from one boulder, and reached out to steady himself on another.

❧

The canyon's floor was green, but there was no water there. He tripped over a root and cut his hand, but his blood was so thick that it wouldn't flow. He crawled toward green shocks of grass, crushed to find that the plants had taken up all the moisture there. He scratched weakly in the sand, and though it was damp beneath the surface there was no sustenance in it.

With all his will, he kept his aching head out of the dirt; with his elbows, he pulled himself across the dry bed until he reached the trunk of a giant cottonwood. Gripping its rough bark, he steadied himself in a seated position; with his sunburned back against the trunk, his chin fell onto his chest. His breathing was slow and heavy. Hearing no footsteps, he nevertheless sensed that someone was kneeling beside him. Lifting his head, he opened one eye and beheld the huge tree's limbs against a turquoise sky.

"Hold on," Briggs Hardy said. "Not the last." His voice was quiet and sounded almost like wind stirring the leaves, but it was him—unmistakably so.

In excruciating pain, Jacob let his eye close and listened to the leaves rustling overhead. His hand fell upon a stone: he tried to curl his fingers around it but could not. "Again?" he choked.

Hardy leaned closer, but now his voice was even less distinct: "Everythin' leads here."

"Can't..." Jacob's tongue caught in his mouth and he couldn't finish. He leaned to forward but his arms were too weak to support his weight and fell forward and rolled onto his side. Shadow pooled on the canyon floor; sunlight glinted off the leaves, yellow against blue. "Sorry," he whispered.

Beside him, Hardy shielded his eyes against the dying light and glanced toward the road. "Not yet." He rose and blocked the light. Jacob opened one eye wide enough to see lengthened shadows wavering overhead. Hardy raised his hand. "Only family I ever had, Jake—only one who ever stayed. So long, brother."

Then Jacob closed his eyes and the shadow was gone, replaced by orange light on pale green leaves.

Lower Las Animas Canyon, New Mexico Territory, May 1, 1862

The sun was a half-hour off the horizon when Peter heard the sentinels' shouts. Indeed, heard their voices long before he saw them come down from the road and into the draw where their company had taken shelter. He listened for a moment and then ran uphill until he could see the whole broad plain that rolled down from the mountains toward the river. To the west was nothing—merely an empty road, its highest reaches vanished within the sun's glare.

Then one of the sentries pointed east and Peter turned and saw it—a solitary animal running downhill. Already it was barely more than a black speck, and soon it descended into a broad swale and disappeared.

"Jimmy, are ye sure?"

"Aye," O'Dowd answered. "Certain."

Again, Peter glanced up and down the road but saw nothing. The mule did not reappear. Then he thought of the girl in the wagon and shouted for the rest of his company to bring up weapons and water and follow him west into the dying light.

Las Animas Canyon, New Mexico Territory, May 1, 1862

He opened his eyes, unsure of what he saw. Overhead, a watery blue dome, crazed with jagged cracks, spanned his limited horizon. His pain was no longer excruciating, but every part of him still ached. When he tried to move, his heart raced, but for once the pounding inside his skull did not worsen. Understanding nothing, he stopped struggling and closed his eyes. Pale red radiance surrounded him. When he awoke, she was cradling his head in her lap and her tears were falling upon his face—these he felt and he opened his eyes. She removed the cap from a tin canteen and poured water over his bruised lips, but his tongue was too swollen and it ran off his face and dripped from the backs of his ears. "Drink, Jacob," she whispered, but words were painful in her mouth. "Stay with me."

He recognized the voice and tried to focus. "Adria," he whispered, so softly that she had to lean closer to hear. "You are..."

"Jacob, what? Please don't leave me!" She looked around the grove, wishing for help, for hope, but they were alone.

He felt hot everywhere, except for his hands and feet—these were deathly cold. "Thank you," he whispered, and this time she heard. He closed his eyes again. His head settled into her hands and she tried to keep him from sinking further into the dust.

"Jacob?" she pleaded, "don't go! Stay with me, please!" She whispered his name again and for a moment, his mind was clear. He thought about how much he loved the sound of her voice, how content he had been in the hours that they had spent together. He could tell that she'd been weeping. The shattered sky faded and he exhaled. In the welter of voices that followed, hers was lost. These were strange voices, confusing, and he supposed they were simply a trick played by his ruined senses. Other sounds followed as whirling shadows flittered across the reddish light. Before it was too late, he wanted to say something more to her, but for the wind, he did not think that she would hear.

"Jacob," she said, and this time her voice carried clear. He felt light, as if gravity had released its hold, though his aching head seemed to want badly to return to earth. Shadows fluttered across the light like the passing of days and nights. Again, Adria cradled his head and her pleading voice came to him as if across a great distance: "Jacob, don't give up—*please!*"

"Forever," he whispered and he knew that she'd heard because he felt her hand on his, and he held onto hers with what strength that he had left. He looked where the light had been, but it was no longer there—it was everywhere and nowhere all at once. Light and shadow became one, so that neither had dominion, and his fevered brow began to cool. He heard the voices again. The earth rumbled and swayed as though it had shaken loose from its axis, and still she stayed with him. Indeed, she had found him and at last, he understood that he would never again know loneliness. Then the hot wind stilled and he opened his eyes, wider this time, and saw a sky the color of sapphires, ringed with orange. A girl with a smile like sunshine was there, waiting. He closed his eyes and rested.

༄

Though Jacob's eyes remained closed, that magnificent blue sky stayed within him until at last it grew dark; and when in the darkness he opened them, at last he beheld field upon field of stars.

Back east—in meadows and woods, upon oceans of water and grass—rivers of blood continued to flow, but there on New Mexico's sere wastes the war was nearly finished. Holdouts would fight to control the Mesilla Valley and Kit Carson would lead scores of companies against the Navajo, culminating in the infamous "Long Walk," but the Confederates' dreams of a Western empire were dead. New Mexico remained with the Union.

THE END

1195424R00283

Made in the USA
San Bernardino, CA
30 November 2012